Pam Steiner has written a pathbreaking study of collective trauma, providing a compelling analysis of a concept that scholars and practitioners often invoke but until now have not fully understood. By using extensive data from the Armenia-Turkey-Azerbaijan case, Dr. Steiner demonstrates how crucial it is for effective policy prescription to be based on conflict analysis with deep historical and psychological elements. This book will revolutionize how conflict analysis is done, as it gives both urgency and guidance for why and how a 'walk through history' must be conducted.

Eileen Babbitt, PhD, Professor of Conflict Resolution Practice, The Fletcher School of Law and Diplomacy, Tufts University

A powerful and deeply moving contribution to the field of conflict resolution. Using her unique collective trauma lens, Steiner, while probing deeply into the traumatic underbelly of the tormented relationship between Armenia and Turkey, provides a powerful framework for understanding and diagnosing the nature of all intractable conflict. In a world becoming increasingly polarized, this compelling book offers a much-needed vision for how human beings might begin to heal the deep, historic wounds that keep so many communities divided and imprisoned.

Hugh O'Doherty, Adjunct Faculty, John F. Kennedy School of Government, Harvard University

In this unique, groundbreakingly multidisciplinary, and exceptionally valuable book, Dr Pamela Steiner provides a lucid history of the long, complex, murderously intractable antagonism between Armenians and Turks and Azerbaijanis. More ambitiously, she also integrates recent international research on individual psychology, collective trauma, reconciliation and peace building as foundations for a comprehensive understanding of the underlying dynamics of other intergenerational cycles of atrocity, trauma, humiliation, denial and revenge, which remain so depressingly prominent in global politics. And all of this is combined with vivid, often sobering, illustrations from her own professional experience as a psychologist and psychotherapist with regional peace activists.

Paul Schulte, Institute for Conflict, Cooperation, and Security, University of Birmingham
**Founding Head of the UK's interdepartmental Post Conflict Reconstruction (now Stabilisation) Unit*
**Former Honorary Consultant Group Psychotherapist, York Clinic, Guys Hospital, London*

A deep, insightful exploration of the psychological dimensions of one of the pivotal events in the history of the 20th-century and its relevance to us today.

Steven Pinker, Professor of Psychology, Harvard University

The author's statement that 'I decided to write this book when I believed I had a fresh and useful perspective to share,' perfectly encapsulates the importance and value of the book you are holding in your hands. Steiner examines, perhaps for the first time, the role collective trauma played among three peoples – Armenians, Azerbaijanis and Turks – and in their mutual relations. She shows how this collective trauma and those that followed are not only the product of their yet unresolved conflicts, but also serve as major stumbling blocks for a better future in the region. For them, the Armenian genocide is like an inescapable psychic maze, one in which they are trapped and unable to see beyond. If there is indeed a way out of this labyrinth, Steiner's work will serve as a torch, lighting the way.

Taner Akcam, Professor of History, Clark University

Pam Steiner offers a fresh and enlightening perspective on otherwise well-known events and conflicts. *Collective Trauma and the Armenian Genocide* constitutes an important contribution to the understanding of conflicts and the difficulties in resolving them. Steiner has painstakingly researched a wide array of sources and professionally analyzed the role of collective trauma in the apparent intractability of two conflicts, Turkish/Armenian and Armenian/Azeri. Rather than attempting to seek a reconciliation of two seemingly irreconcilable positions in each by trying to find a middle point, Steiner has used the concept of collective trauma to humanize and integrate the problems of both sides. She has done so by manifesting much empathy and genuine concern for the human experience of everyone concerned. Steiner has also provided a most useful list of steps that can be taken to overcome the impact of the traumas that have compromised the judgment of the traumatized groups.

Gerard Libaridian, Historian and diplomat, University of Michigan

A close Arab Israeli friend once told me: 'the Middle East has always devoured its children'. In this thoroughly researched and deeply engaging book, *Collective Trauma and the Armenian Genocide*, Pam Steiner, an experienced psychotherapist and peace negotiator, illustrates the truth of this statement in her history of Armenian-Turkish-Azerbaijani relationships over the past 180 years. Tragically, it shows how not only individuals, but whole ethnic groups derive a deep sense of collective meaning from past injury, and that a quest for justice (or revenge) can sustain, and even nurture, national identities from generation to generation. This book can make a significant contribution to any discussion about how collective historical trauma can be laid to rest, so that communities can re-focus their energies on building a better future for themselves and their children.

Bessel van der Kolk, Psychiatrist, Boston University School of Medicine
** President, Trauma Research Foundation*
** #1 NYT Bestseller: the Body keeps the Score: brain, mind and body in the healing of trauma*

Collective trauma displays a compounding character that multiplies the impacts of its many dimensions and confounds the work of post-conflict healing. Pamela Steiner guides her readers through a trauma-informed understanding of what she calls the "frozen ethno-national conflicts" that haunt modern Armenian, Turkish, and Azerbaijani relations. As the Great Granddaughter of Henry Morgenthau and an experienced facilitator of conflict resolution, Steiner adds personal and professional linkages to the case studies she addresses and the insights she offers regarding the complicating power that collective trauma adds to this complex history and situation.

Henry F. Knight, Professor Emeritus of Holocaust and Genocide Studies, Keene State College

COLLECTIVE TRAUMA AND THE ARMENIAN GENOCIDE

This book re-examines more than 100 years of destructive ethno-religious relations among Armenians, Turks and Azerbaijanis through the novel lens of collective trauma.

The author argues that a focus on embedded, transgenerational collective trauma is essential to achieving more trusting, productive and stable relationships in this and similar contexts. The book takes a deep dive into history – analysing the traumatic events, examining and positing how they motivated the actions of key players (both victims and perpetrators), and revealing how profoundly these traumas continue to manifest today among the three peoples, stymying healing and inhibiting achievement of a basis for sustainable, civil relations.

The author then proposes a bold new approach to 'conflict resolution' as a complement to other perspectives, such as power-based analyses and international human rights. Addressing the psychological core of the conflict, the author argues that a focus on embedded collective trauma is essential in this and similar arenas.

Volume 26: Human Rights Law in Perspective

Human Rights Law in Perspective

General Editor: Colin Harvey
Professor of Human Rights Law
School of Law
Queen's University Belfast

The language of human rights figures prominently in legal and political debates at the national, regional and international levels. In the UK the Human Rights Act 1998 has generated considerable interest in the law of human rights. It will continue to provoke much debate in the legal community and the search for original insights and new materials will intensify.

The aim of this series is to provide a forum for scholarly reflection on all aspects of the law of human rights. The series will encourage work which engages with the theoretical, comparative and international dimensions of human rights law. The primary aim is to publish over time books which offer an insight into human rights law in its contextual setting. The objective is to promote an understanding of the nature and impact of human rights law. The series is inclusive, in the sense that all perspectives in legal scholarship are welcome. It will incorporate the work of new and established scholars.

Human Rights Law in Perspective is not confined to consideration of the UK. It will strive to reflect comparative, regional and international perspectives. Work which focuses on human rights law in other states will therefore be included in this series. The intention is to offer an inclusive intellectual home for significant scholarly contributions to human rights law.

Recent titles in this series

Governing (Through) Rights
Bal Sokhi-Bulley

Gender Equality in Law: Uncovering the Legacies of Czech State Socialism
Barbara Havelkova

Investment and Human Rights in Armed Conflict: Charting an Elusive Intersection
Daria Davitti

Specifying and Securing a Social Minimum in the Battle Against Poverty
Toomas Kotkas, Ingrid Leijten and Frans Pennings

Protecting Human Rights and Building Peace in Post-Violence Societies
Nasia Hadjigeorgiou

Collective Trauma and the Armenian Genocide: Armenian, Turkish, and Azerbaijani Relations since 1839
Pamela Steiner

For the complete list of titles in this series, see 'Human Rights Law in Perspective' link at www.bloomsburyprofessional.com/uk/series/human-rights-law-in-perspective/

Collective Trauma and the Armenian Genocide

Armenian, Turkish, and Azerbaijani Relations since 1839

Pamela Steiner

OXFORD • LONDON • NEW YORK • NEW DELHI • SYDNEY

HART PUBLISHING

Bloomsbury Publishing Plc

Kemp House, Chawley Park, Cumnor Hill, Oxford, OX2 9PH, UK

1385 Broadway, New York, NY 10018, USA

29 Earlsfort Terrace, Dublin 2, Ireland

First published in Great Britain 2021

A catalogue record for this book is available from the British Library.

Library of Congress Cataloging-in-Publication data

Names: Steiner, Pamela, author.

Title: Collective trauma and the Armenian genocide : Armenian, Turkish, and Azerbaijani relations since 1839 / Pamela Steiner.

Description: Oxford, UK ; New York, NY : Hart Publishing, an imprint of Bloomsbury Publishing, 2021. | Series: Human rights law in perspective ; volume 26 | Includes bibliographical references and index.

Identifiers: LCCN 2020042215 (print) | LCCN 2020042216 (ebook) | ISBN 9781509934836 (hardback) | ISBN 9781509943135 (paperback) | ISBN 9781509934850 (pdf) | ISBN 9781509934843 (Epub)

Subjects: LCSH: Ethnic conflict—Turkey—History—20th century. | Collective memory—Turkey—History—20th century. | Human rights—Turkey—History—20th century. | Armenian massacres, 1915–1923. | Genocide—Turkey—History—20th century. | Armenians—Turkey—History—20th century. | Turkey—Ethnic relations—History—20th century. | Azerbaijan—Ethnic relations—History—20th century. | Genocide (International law)

Classification: LCC HM1121 .S7674 2021 (print) | LCC HM1121 (ebook) | DDC 956.6/20154—dc23

LC record available at https://lccn.loc.gov/2020042215

LC ebook record available at https://lccn.loc.gov/2020042216

ISBN: HB: 978-1-50993-483-6
ePDF: 978-1-50993-485-0
ePub: 978-1-50993-484-3

Typeset by Compuscript Ltd, Shannon

To Henry for his Essential Support
and
To the Essential Workers of the Conflict Resolution Field

Foreword

THIS IS A monumentally important book that I thought could not be written. I have known Pam Steiner for many years. Dr Steiner is an accomplished trauma psychologist. She has also over the years become an authority on Turkish-Armenian history and its group pathologies resulting from murder and genocide dating back over a century. She is also deeply steeped in issues relating to the divisions that plague Israel-Palestine. A key factor in these entrenched crises is how perceived threats to land and concepts of a homeland culture of religion and language sustain denials regarding what may have gone wrong in the past and resistance to suggestions about what might be done in the present.

I have participated in her workshops and met many trauma authorities through her good offices. She supported me as I tried to engage people from Sri Lanka (Tamils and Sinhalese) in a discussion of their history – only to be overwhelmed by the insistence of the Sinhalese participants that that they originally came from a divine community. With colleagues I have worked on resolving conflicts between Serbian and Kosovar physicians after the war, to minimal avail. And as a medical doctor also trained in public health, I am deeply aware of the responsibilities that such training has instilled – to ease injustice as well as respond to individual harm. Beneficence is a major feature in medical ethics. Yet in clinical practice it rarely expands beyond supporting and sustaining good public health law. I have worked as a human rights investigator in conflict and post conflict settings and seen how our reports and advocacy create small and evanescent ripples, provide history with more data, but rarely change situations. In my view, only when large numbers of people call collectively for policy change, as with Darfur, perhaps Kosovo, has there been much movement – and this delayed – in the international or national stance on what is to be done.

From these experiences, I came to believe that changing a society first required oversight through law and justice mechanisms. And through these years of conversation and occasional teamwork, Dr Steiner, as a good friend and mentor, knows full well my ambivalence about addressing collective injustice and collective trauma through the lens of trauma psychology. I have preferred testimony, the rule of law, punishment of individual perpetrators as the only way forward. Yet I have in the past years also become deeply involved in communities and official circles intent on genocide prevention – and much of the bedrock reasoning is that societies must learn how to investigate their own collective trauma and perceive how these traumas, pitting one kind of people against another, occurs in cycles and must always be guarded against. Vigilance, kindness, and steady awareness of triggering events are essential to genocide prevention.

Traveling different routes, I have come to appreciate the power of Dr Steiner's insights into both individual and collective trauma. Hatred and fear are mixed; unpacking the fear may lessen the feelings of hate; learning that the 'other' is actually a distorted or different mirror of yourself may rearrange understanding and expand compassion as well as regret, regarding one's own complicity. But I continue to be concerned that the leap from fruitful discussions among three or 20 participants is too great to affect the mindset of millions. The book's final chapter addresses this key matter.

Yet in this gloriously detailed and painful book on Turkish, Armenian and Azerbaijan relations, Dr Steiner has managed to encompass her deep understanding of individual trauma to shed light on what motivates leaders and populations, playing off collectively-based apprehensions and hatred to sustain decades if not centuries of stubborn communal antagonisms. Most impressively, in my view, is the way she creates a balanced historical fact picture, a meticulous analysis of political, legal, and normative shifts in the body politic, to help us understand not just how Turkey, Armenia, and Azerbaijan have become locked in stereotyped narratives of what 'their people' and the 'others' have done to create the reality they believe they face.

What is highly unusual is that Dr Steiner moves easily from political shifts in the country to penetrating analysis of the motivations of pivotal leaders, based on a wide range of historical documents and memoirs. The quotations are devastating in their revelatory power to bring us into the fears, suspicions, and reactive aggressions of consequential players. She manages to sustain this difficult balance throughout her account of how Turkey evolved from the Ottoman Empire. There is an apparent inevitability about the atrocities laced into this evolution. Yet Dr Steiner manages to show that none of these were necessary, despite the fact that they did happen. Traumatized leaders, seeing threats to land and language, reacted aggressively and fed fear to the population, enabling them over time to complete cycles of local and then national ethnic cleansing, at least one of them a universally acknowledged genocide.

This is a cross-disciplinary work of exemplary merit that is dangerous to write. All the experts who study this region or other areas of entrenched conflict or absolutism come from their own disciplines – history, politics, economics, sociology – none of which embrace a psycho-social approach as deeply as does Dr Steiner. Yet the many contemporary biographies of prominent leaders all give respect to the psychological dynamics affecting their subject. I believe this book will receive appreciative recognition, granting permission to those from other disciplines to pay serious attention to the psychological trauma affecting leaders in all contexts – especially where the trauma is also collectively based and is in reciprocity with the leader's own background.

Many people from different disciplines involved in atrocity prevention or in trying to help societies recover from atrocity are aware of the notion of collective trauma. Certainly those in the potentially victimized groups are very alert to signs of impending atrocity and are aware of the deep-seated psychological roots of what may overwhelm them. They may not be clear-sighted about their own participation in the escalations surrounding them, but they are able to describe the attackers in starkly psychological terms of resentment, fear, revenge, and focused antagonism toward members of specific groups.

The good news is that one does not have to embrace the complex clinical intricacies of collective trauma to become adept at recognizing the strength of psychological insights in assessing or understanding the roots of mass atrocity. Once described and presented, in any conflict situation, the notion of collective trauma has application with fascinating implications for what might come next, what should be done. And what is characteristic of Dr Steiner, who listens and learns as the years go on – her years of effort in small group or Track 2 diplomacy – is that her views shift as the data and information accumulate. She recounts with great frankness and helpful detail the journey she has made from these strenuous smaller group efforts to the realization that her insights are fundamental but the fulcrum of change has to rest on a very large, population-based process of reconsidering their past and re-ordering their views and feelings about the present and the future. This process will require inspired leaders and brave followers. It will also require time and resources.

This book will come out in the United States as we are uncomfortably enmeshed in the struggle to understand the valence of 1619, our institution of slavery, on current American politics and society. Structural racism has supported the economic development of this country through vicious mobilization of slave and contract labor and extraction of the wealth they have produced, while it has alienated whites from blacks in profound ways that many white Americans have never been asked to understand. For the US, to mobilize understanding and commitment to redress and repair is going to be much of the work of this century. And that work will require facing our collective trauma.

In this sense, I would suggest that this book will be valuable reading even for people not deeply interested in these particular nations. It is a great account of the grandeur of the collapse of empire, the frenzied machinations to hold on to power and assets, the pernicious interplay between aspirations in peace and aggression in war, and the persistence of the trauma narrative. This account of unjust loss and need to protect through all means any future loss – this account maps to many histories of nations from the past and to the ones we are creating now.

Jennifer Leaning MD SMH
Professor of the Practice of Health and Human Rights
Harvard School of Public Health
Associate Professor of Emergency Medicine
Harvard Medical School
Former director and Senior Fellow
FXB Center for Health and Human Rights
Harvard University

Preface

How Can We Liberate the Present from Being Captive to the Past and Learn from It?

HALIL BERKTAY IS a rare, prominent Turkish historian who acknowledges that a genocide of the Armenian people was carried out by the Ottoman government beginning in 1915. In 2005 he identified the main problem in Armenian-Turkish relations: 'How can we liberate the present from being captive, in bondage, to the ghosts of 1915? How can we liberate the present from being captive to the past and learn from it?'[1] My book as a whole seeks to address this problem, while this Preface lays out what led me to undertake the project. The book as a whole gives an account of my experiences, failures, and successes as I gained an awareness of the nature of collective trauma, became knowledgeable about the history, including the genocide, its background, and what flowed from it, and pursued answers. My journey may be meaningful to others also dealing with the most critical, sensitive, and difficult matters tormenting traumatised peoples and groups – be they defined by their political leanings, the religion they belong to, the language they speak, or the values and culture they share.[2]

The term 'genocide' was coined during World War II to describe not only the fate of the Jews in the Holocaust but equally that of the Armenians in the *Meds Yeghern* ('Great Crime') carried out by the Ottoman Turks. (Official) Turkey has adamantly denied that characterisation ever since. In an interview published in the Armenian media in late 2005, Berktay noted a phenomenon that often plays out in meetings in which the collective trauma of the genocide is discussed:

> [I]f you say yes it was genocide, the Armenians cheer you and the Turks boo you, and everybody stops listening, because they heard what they came to hear. And if you say no, it was not genocide, exactly the reverse happens: the Armenians boo, the Turks cheer, and, again, everybody stops … listen[ing].[3]

[1] 'The Specter of the Armenian Genocide: An Interview with Halil Berktay', *Aztag Daily* (Lebanon), 12 November 2005, available at https://hyetert.org/2005/11/15/the-specter-of-the-armenian-genocide-an-interview-with-halil-berktay/ (accessed 29 July 2020).

[2] This is without putting too fine a point on it. I recognise that none of these are necessarily closely bound terms and there is considerable overlap between them. For two important studies on the subject, see R Brubaker, *Ethnicity without Groups* (Cambridge, MA, Harvard University Press, 2004) and EJ Hobsbawm, *Nations and Nationalism since 1780*, 2nd edn (Cambridge, Cambridge University Press, 1992).

[3] Interview with Halil Berktay, *Aztag Daily*.

Berktay was in effect describing the manifestations of hypervigilance, a common trauma symptom. The ghosts, or memories, are transmitted to later generations and displayed in the overall negative relationship between Armenians and Turks today. But they surface not only in that relationship. Toward the end of World War I the Ottomans extended their hostility to Armenians living in neighbouring Transcaucasia, prolonging the misery of the people for many more months to come. In today's troubled relationship between both the Armenians of Armenia proper and Artsakh (also known as Nagorno-Karabakh or simply Karabakh) and the Azerbaijanis, who often refer to themselves as the 'brothers' of the Turks, the hostility is palpably present.

The starkly defined situation Berktay describes is typical of other so-called 'frozen,' or static and repetitive, ethnic conflicts in which collectively traumatising events occurred. As both a clinician and a practitioner of conflict resolution work,[4] I arrived at the same question Berktay did. I decided to write this book when I believed I had a fresh and useful perspective to share.

I. TRAUMATIC EXPERIENCES, SYSTEMATIC TRAINING, AND FAMILY HISTORY IN THE PRELUDE TO THIS BOOK

No psychotherapist or historian can convincingly claim that they are free from personal motivations for their chosen vocation. The motivations often arise out of powerful emotional experiences. In late childhood and early adolescence in the 1950s, I first became aware of a huge collective trauma in the making. I watched in disbelief, horror, helplessness, and anger as countryside, farmland, and townscapes – much of my town, a wealthy suburb of New York City, my local homeland, which I loved, identified with, and held as sacred – was torn up by ever-expanding, land-wasting housing lots, and ever-expanding provision for motor vehicles in the forms of parking lots, shopping malls, one-way streets, and commercial strips. I became deeply concerned about the disappearance of the land, my land, my place. For many years thereafter I was an activist for land conservation and improved public transportation. I suspect that the trauma which I experienced then is becoming increasingly widespread and intense throughout the world and will blend with justified fears over climate change.

My personal history then took me through a traumatic experience of divorce. I entered individual psychotherapy and group psychotherapy and I began years of processing the patterns from traumas incurred in my own upbringing and adult

[4] When it was conceived after World War II, the term 'conflict resolution' denoted a new theory and method for bringing about constructive relations between decision-makers and civil societies of long-conflicted parties. This non-official work, also called 'Track 2 diplomacy' ('Track 1' being official diplomacy), now has a substantial literature. It aims to build better relationships based on an understanding and acceptance of the parties' basic needs. These needs are, above all, for security and respectful recognition of collective identity. Conflict-resolution work is not negotiation but supports the negotiation of settlements by helping develop constructive, understanding, and tolerant relationships pre-, during, and post-negotiation. Conflict resolution has not achieved its aims in the Israeli–Palestinian situation, to which a great deal of its effort has been directed. The Oslo Accord and the other Track 2 efforts leading up to and following it were very successful in the short term but didn't hold together in the long term. Today much Track 1.5 (semi-official) and Track 2 diplomacy is underway in Libya to prevent internal conflict from escalating. In Tunisia, labour unions spearheaded useful Track 1.5 work after the Arab Spring. Track 2 has also been helpful, if not crucial, in Northern Ireland and Colombia. Track 2 efforts have been underway for some time between Nagorno-Karabakh and Azerbaijan. The conclusion expands discussion of this work.

emotional life, as well as from my concern about the continuing devastation of land and nature. I explored different psychotherapeutic schools, and underwent various types of training, to become a therapist myself. In midlife, the personal internal transformative change I gained led me to speculate that aspects of that process could be adapted to resolve protracted, unyielding collective problems.

I decided to pursue this idea with different frameworks. As a doctoral student, I specialised in the interdisciplinary intersections of the psychology of the mind's evolution, leadership, and conflict resolution. At the same time, I trained as a psychotherapist for individuals and practised conflict resolution in different situations. In writing this book I have been able to reflect extensively on the differences and overlaps between my individual life experiences and the painful events of entire societies, with their lasting consequences.

I believe that the hurts I processed, and from which I gratefully received 'good enough' healing (see Introduction), have enabled me to empathise with those damaged by the very different historical traumas this book covers. That mix of painful experiences and systematic reflection on them also established within me what I regard as a strong enough centre to be explicit about the moral dimensions of traumatic events, which I am convinced are always present.

I am aware that declaring this personal background might attract accusations that I am motivated by elements of a Saviour Syndrome. Readers have the right to be wary about that. But my motivation emerges from a family history, about which I am as open and fully mindful as I can be. I have always felt a duty to engage my intense interests in the wider world with knowledge and concern, to give back as well as to take from society. Awareness of being the great-granddaughter of Henry Morgenthau, American ambassador to the Ottoman Empire during the main phase of the Armenian genocide, and knowledge that others will be interested in what I say because of that, has indeed in recent years fostered a continual fire within me to create as careful, accurate, critical and inspiring a book as I am able to. In sum I have no reason to believe that I remain at risk of unrecognised distortions in what I present. The groups, one-to-one dialogues, and scholarly contacts in which I have participated for decades have provided continual reality checks. I enjoy life and do not feel grandiose responsibility for the tragic histories and destinies which I try conscientiously to understand, though I am only too aware of the immense sensitivity of so many to so much of what I write about. While I do not claim authoritative perfection, I consequently see no grounds to fear that my work has been deformed or distorted by my personal history and circumstances. And my arguments have been carefully developed and researched over the years, fully referenced and openly presented here for examination, proof, or refutation. You can judge them in the book that follows.

At the time that I trained as a clinical psychotherapist for individuals and groups and entered clinical practice in the late 1980s, I also attempted to understand, from a psychological perspective, the evil of the massive collective trauma of Nazism. Because one side of my Jewish family of origin had been in the United States since the mid-nineteenth century and the other side since the beginning of the twentieth, we experienced no personal losses under Nazism. But my great uncle, Henry Morgenthau Jr, the only Jew in the cabinet of President Franklin Delano Roosevelt, had tried with little success to alert his colleagues to the dangers of Nazism well before the US entered the war. For years after the war, the occasional anti-German comments of my father, who had served in the US Army during the war, stayed with me. I have never ceased to be shocked when exposing myself to accounts of Nazi crimes, and the impunity so many Nazis then enjoyed. Yet, as an adult, when I came across the frequently expressed view that the evil of the Holocaust was so great as to be incomprehensible, though I could understand why people might think that, I could not accept that view. As I saw and see it, the perpetrators, and those who were bystanders, were people, other humans, and so must be understandable. In fact, I wondered how I would have acted had I been a young Christian German woman in Nazi Germany.

When I met Germans, I became aware of how self-conscious, ashamed, and embarrassed I would have been were I German myself. This was because at those times my mind automatically, silently, accusingly, and self-righteously, asked them, 'What did you or your parents do during the war?' Internally I felt morally superior and triumphant. I wanted to show that the Nazis hadn't succeeded in killing all Jews – here I was! – or in making all Jews grovel – I wasn't. In a mild revenge fantasy, I imagined throwing them off guard by asking, 'How does it feel to be talking to a Jew?'

I assumed that they must have felt what I projected onto them. I assumed that when a German and a Jew met, there was this elephant in the room. But I kept these musings and imaginings to myself. Today I remain curious about conversations that do or do not take place about the Holocaust within German families. Over time the intensity of my feelings has lessened with my exposure to many Germans who can speak of their shame and apologise, work to improve their country and the world, and knowing what Germany as a country has done collectively in changing, memorialising, and making reparations.

In the 1990s I joined a German-Jewish dialogue group in Boston. It was sponsored by the German consulate and the American Jewish Committee. Group members did not know what they might be getting into, but they were willing to find out. Most of the Jewish members were survivors or children of survivors and group discussions turned out to be mostly about Jewish fate and suffering. After participating for two years, I decided that I wanted to hear more about how the German group members felt about their country's Nazi past and about themselves as Germans.

I wanted to know if, as I imagined, these particular Germans felt shame, guilt, and little pride in being German, although they surely knew that, after being forced by the Allies to face the Nazis' crimes, their country had taken major and unprecedented steps to acknowledge them – apologise, pay certain reparations, memorialise, and educate Germans from a very young age about the facts. What would happen if they talked together about how it was for them personally to be German? Would they start to feel self-respect as Germans, if they had not? I felt sure that their recovery of self-respect, which would include appropriate guilt, was important to the maintenance of their country's commitment to responsible policy-making in general. I was convinced that it was important that Germans should have their own space to talk about the meaning of the Holocaust to them personally and collectively. However, as I saw it, the culture of the existing dialogue group did not offer that opportunity, and the time did not feel right to me to try to introduce such a change with the limited understanding and skills I then possessed.

Thus, outside that group, I asked several of the German members if they would participate in a separate group for Germans only, which I would facilitate and where they could explore what it meant to them to be German. About eight members from the dialogue group decided to participate in as many monthly meetings for this purpose. The meetings were powerful. Their traumatising experiences from decades earlier dramatically entered our confidential working space. Older members relived memories of being disoriented and frightened when, as young children, they were hurried into underground bomb shelters. Younger members spoke of the effects that their parents' wartime experiences had had on them and their children. Some of their parents' or grandparents' families had been Nazis. Many had endured great losses. They wanted to talk about it all and at the same time found it anguishing. All expressed long-standing shame and guilt after learning about the horrors of Nazism. Some spoke about the impact it had on whether they felt they had a right to hold up their heads. Although one member left after a few sessions, the remaining participants worked through some of their own pain and were re-evaluating their German identity.

II. WORKING WITH ISRAELIS AND PALESTINIANS

The concept of the group with the Germans grew out of my two professional commitments. One was clinical work with traumatised individuals in small psychotherapy groups (as well as in individual psychotherapy). The other was facilitating encounters in non-official conflict-resolution workshops, as 'Track 2 diplomacy'. The aims of the workshops were to contribute to the end of long-standing, intractable, and destructive conflicts. Most which I cofacilitated (we usually worked in teams) were off the record and convened for Israeli Jews and Palestinians who were influential in their communities. The workshop methodology and agenda had been designed by Herbert C Kelman, the renowned professor of Social Ethics (emeritus) at Harvard University, himself a survivor of *Kristallnacht*, and a 50-year veteran of non-official Israeli-Palestinian peace-making efforts. I was lucky to have him as a mentor.

My initiation into Israeli–Palestinian work began at about the same time as my involvement in the German–Jewish dialogue group. At the time, Palestinians were widely referred to as 'terrorists'. The first time I was ever in a room with Palestinians or with 'terrorists,' it was with those individuals who had come to participate in a Kelman workshop. I, partly thrillingly and partly ever-so slightly anxiously, observed myself thinking that I was with 'terrorists', feelings which evaporated as soon as discussion began. As I listened to the Palestinians' stories, I came to appreciate that by 1948, having emerged from Ottoman and then British rule, they faced the establishment of the state of Israel on their homeland. They went to war to prevent this and lost. Hundreds of thousands of them were then driven from their homeland. Some were massacred,[5] while those who remained in the state of Israel became enemies and second-class citizens.[6] The enmity smouldered. After Israel prevailed in the 1967 war, all Palestinians living in the West Bank and Gaza were placed under Israeli military occupation. Since then they have protested peacefully and not so peacefully to demand to return to their homelands and homes, obtain justice, and redress for violated human rights.[7]

[5] One such massacre occurred in the village of Deir Yassin.

[6] See, for example and for more information, N Rouhana (ed), *Israel and Its Palestinian Citizens: Ethnic Privileges in the Jewish State* (Cambridge, MA, Cambridge University Press, 2017).

[7] Y Berda, *Living Emergency: Israel's Permit Regime in the Occupied West Bank* (Stanford, CA, Stanford University Press, 2018).

Seeing all this as I did, did not prevent me from also putting myself in the Israelis' shoes. I found it entirely understandable that the Israelis would feel impelled to act as they did. They faced Palestinians who resisted the establishment of the fledgling state and continued to do so. They faced a war in 1948, a mere three years after the end of a world war. That was the war that forced the Jews who had survived the Holocaust and then made it to Israel to join the few Jews already there to fight all over again for their lives and a place to live in their ancient homeland. I was among Jews everywhere who, after 1948, held their breath for many years for the survival of the Jews securing this new state in the Middle East.

I remained involved from the late 1980s for close to 30 years in Israeli–Palestinian conflict-resolution efforts. I have heard possible solutions weighed up, discussed, and debated over and over again and witnessed Israel taking more and more land in the West Bank and exercising more and more control over Palestinians. The enormous efforts and little success at resolving this conflict are as heartbreaking as disturbing. I kept asking myself what it is that has kept these parties so destructively captive to the past?

III. ENTRY INTO THE ARMENIAN–TURKISH RELATIONSHIP

I first met Roger Hagopian in 2005 when he came to clean rugs in my home in Cambridge, Massachusetts. I learned he was an Armenian American and that outside of work, he made films memorialising Armenian family life from 100 years ago. From childhood I was aware that Armenians treasured the support Morgenthau had offered during the genocide.

Ambassador Henry Morgenthau, Professor Samuel Dutton, and Cleveland H Dodge in New York City, 1916

Source: Library of Congress, LC-B2-3758-10.

I showed Hagopian a photo taken in 1946 of the extended Morgenthau family surrounding my great-grandfather on his 90th birthday. We talked about how he had gone outside the usual ambassadorial role to let the world know of the crimes being committed against Armenians when he pressed the Ottoman government to stop the slaughter. We talked about how the death marches, which the Ottomans had forced Armenian women, children, and the elderly to take, and suffering they endured had given rise to the popular phrase, 'the poor, starving Armenians.'

Hagopian suggested that I visit the National Association for Armenian Studies and Research (NAASR) in Belmont, Massachusetts and attend its lectures and conferences. He urged me to speak to them about my conflict-resolution work. I agreed, and began to learn about Armenian–Turkish relations. That led me, under the auspices of the Harvard Humanitarian Initiative and the FXB Center for Health and Human Rights at the Harvard TH Chan School of Public Health, where I was a senior fellow, to form a facilitation team to conduct Track 2 workshops with Armenians and Turks.

In these workshops, I knew I needed to maintain an even-handed stance as a facilitator, although, at the start, my feelings were entirely pro-Armenian and what may be termed anti-Turk. I had internalised what I understood as a child of my great-grandfather's legacy and felt loyal to it – that is, to his loyalties. I yearned to make a difference through use of the Kelman process, which, at that point, I believed was sufficient to accomplish that. In preparing for these meetings, my team, which included an Armenian and a Turk, enabled me to begin to take in the depth of difficulty in the relationship.

IV. MEETING HASAN CEMAL

Engaging in Armenian–Turkish relationship work (as I call it now) meant becoming familiar with some of the splits between them regarding their joint history. I came to feel aligned with those in both communities who sought understanding and acknowledgment of the historical realities, including genocide. I hoped to help create a common understanding of the past to provide the basis for a productive and civil relationship going forward. I hoped that the Turks who would attend the workshops would come to understand that genocide had occurred and want Turkey to make appropriate changes. I learned quickly how difficult it was going to be to reach this goal.

Nonetheless, in 2008, en route to Istanbul, I stopped in Brussels to meet with a Turk and an Armenian from whose organisations I hoped to raise support for more workshops. The fund-raising failed but my Turkish interlocutor informed me that a leading liberal Turkish journalist, Hasan Cemal, had just made two extraordinary gestures of understanding and reconciliation toward Armenians. Cemal is the grandson of Djemal Pasha, the erstwhile Ottoman minister of the navy and an important figure in the last Ottoman government. He bore significant responsibility for the genocide. In the aftermath of World War I, he was especially reviled among the Arabs, who called him 'the butcher'.[8] My informant told me that Cemal had just been

[8] E Thompson, *Colonial Citizens: Republican Rights, Paternal Privilege, and Gender in French Syria and Lebanon* (New York, Columbia University Press, 2000) 23.

in Yerevan, the capital of Armenia, where he covered the Turkish president's historic visit to participate in 'football diplomacy' – 'historic' because it was a rare move by officials of both countries towards resolution of the past.

It was while in Yerevan that Cemal went entirely beyond his work remit to make the two significant, unexpected gestures. The first was to place flowers on the steps of the Armenian genocide memorial. The second was to meet with Armen Gevorkyan. Cemal's grandfather, Djemal, was shot in cold blood after the end of World War I. Gevorkyan is the grandson of one of Djemal's assassins.

My informant had given me Cemal's contact information. Once in Istanbul I contacted him. He suggested we meet for tea. I was immediately impressed by his sincerity. On the spot, he accepted my invitation to speak at Harvard about the inner journey that led him to make these gestures. I then took great trouble to plan the meeting to avoid the course of meetings Berktay described.

Late in 2009, Cemal spoke at Harvard to a standing-room crowd composed mostly of Armenians and Turks in about equal numbers. The audience expressed strong emotions and manifested great curiosity. They and Cemal listened carefully and interacted respectfully. Cemal did not use the term 'genocide', and no one commented on that. By the end of the event, it seemed clear to me that the audience had felt Cemal's genuineness. Robert J Lifton, the psychiatrist and scholar who has written about Nazi doctors, Turkish denial, and the human impact of the atomic bomb on Hiroshima, was present. Afterward Lifton commented to me, 'The event succeeded because it pleased no one completely'. Some of these Armenians and Turks who had attended appeared to have loosened stereotypes about each other enough to consider each other, psychologically, as who they were at the occasion – cautiously open and genuinely curious. In the conclusion to this book, I draw on my learning from this event, as well as my Track 2 work and the event described below, to offer some answer to Berktay's question, 'How can we liberate the present from being captive, in bondage, to the ghosts of 1915?'

V. ANOTHER MEETING, ANOTHER INSPIRATION

A year and a half after Cemal's talk at Harvard, I was part of a dramatic meeting at UCLA. Cemal was the main speaker. The distinguished Armenian–American historian Professor Richard Hovannisian and I were also on the platform. It, too, was perhaps an historic event because of Cemal's and Hovannisian's joint presence, along with myself, a descendant of Ambassador Morgenthau.

Cemal was well received. While his actions in Yerevan were no substitute for the Turkish government's obligation to recognise, apologise, reassure, and make official reparations for the genocide, his actions and willingness to speak publicly to a largely Armenian audience surely added to understanding of possibilities for change, as it had at Harvard just a year and a half before. Hovannisian is most deservedly a celebrity historian, predictably interesting, thoughtful, and knowledgeable.

In preparing my remarks, I bore in mind that Los Angeles was the home of the largest Armenian diasporic community in the US and that I would be speaking publicly for the first time about my conflict-resolution work with Armenians and Turks.

I thought my remarks would challenge Armenians and Turks to think more about each other. I anticipated strong reactions and assumed that they would stimulate an instructive dialogue between the audience and me.

Such hopes were misplaced. When the event opened up for interaction between the speakers and the audience, the journalist Harut Sassounian spoke up first. A passionate advocate for official genocide recognition from Turkey, he pointed out what I didn't say: 'Hasan Cemal used "genocide" – Morgenthau's great-granddaughter did not'. Exactly as Berktay predicted, much of the audience then seemed to lose any interest in what I had said, even though I didn't think anyone else had noticed that I had not used the word.

It took me a while to realise if and how I had erred. Finally I realised I had failed to explain my facilitator role as I then conceived it, which was to be 'even-handed'. But I was not far enough along in my consciousness to do that. At the time, I accepted what I had understood I had been taught as a conflict-resolution facilitator – that each side's narrative was valid *for them*, whatever it was, and that facilitators must accept their narratives as such. I think this is true, although a more complex matter than I then comprehended. My failure to talk about the dilemma that the word 'genocide' posed for a facilitator meant I was stuck, as Bertktay said. I was damned with one group if I used the word and damned with another if I did not. As a result, my message of contextualising some of the history and suggesting a new angle to it was not considered.

The audience in Los Angeles had been informed that I was Morgenthau's great-granddaughter. Because of that, and since I had never deviated from what he stood for, I assumed that Armenians would take it for granted that I shared his views about the crimes that had been committed against their ancestors. (Writing before the term 'genocide' was coined, Morgenthau had described the orders of the Ottoman government as 'the death warrant to a whole race'.[9]) But afterward I realised that, even if true, Armenians would expect that, of all people, the great-granddaughter of Ambassador Morgenthau would, and *had to*, use the actual word.

Thus, I was unprepared for the reaction after Sassounian spoke. Suddenly it felt that I were being perceived with mistrust, and viewed as disloyal, an enemy, a betrayer. There was also a small vocal group within the 500 who made it clear that they were so not perceiving me. I learned later that this group had been participating in an Armenian–Turkish dialogue group.

VI. HARD, NECESSARY LEARNING

For quite some time after the event, I felt somewhat traumatised – shocked, unheard, angry, humiliated – but finally accepting. My distress and anger were reignited, as my words and overall perspective were completely distorted in the Armenian press and gloated over in the Turkish media. One lengthy, thoughtful, and very critical article was written by a well-respected scholar, but I later learned that he had not attended

[9] H Morgenthau, *Ambassador Morgenthau's Story* (Garden City, NY, Doubleday, Page, & Company, 1919) 309.

the event and had not read my talk, yet critiqued me for not adhering to ideas that in fact I had more than embraced for years.

I decided to take some time off. During those months, I was honoured when an Armenian associate and friend, the statesman, diplomat, and historian Gerard Libaridian, encouraged me not to give up. Were it not for his words, I probably would have. It was during this time off that I gained perspective and began to think of writing about my experience.

I had lost some innocence around my own inadequate understanding and good intention. I needed to. I finally concluded that the audience had had an open mind before Sassounian's comment, and perhaps had not noticed that I had not used the word 'genocide.' But Berktay's point is that at such an event, someone is always going to listen for the word and point out if 'genocide' was used or not. I reflected that the reaction to what I had – and hadn't – said, in part reflected the collective trauma in the audience transmitted by their ancestors' suffering. That would have been triggering and interfered with the ability of many in the audience to ask why I had not used the word or to consider something new on this topic that I did say, even as they might criticise how I said it.

Not long afterwards, I learned something in a confidential meeting with a highly placed Turkish official who of course publicly denied that a genocide had been committed. In private, he told me, 'We know it was genocide, but we do not want to pay reparations'. This was another turning point for me. I became impatient with the indecency of Turkey's refusal to undertake good-faith measures to improve relations with Armenians as well as the country's denial of genocide.[10]

After the event in Los Angeles, my facilitation team and I produced a substantial proposal for conflict-resolution work in anticipation of the 100th anniversary of the Armenian genocide. I submitted it to a suitable foundation, which expressed serious interest but asked me to explain more. To do so, I soon realised, after conversations with my long-time friend and colleague, Professor Eileen Babbitt, that I had to write this book. With encouragement and help from my team and others, including some of his admirers, I have taken up Henry Morgenthau's labour in the cause of truth and conciliation.

By the time this book went to press, war had come again to the South Caucasus, triggering past traumas, creating new but familiar ones and predictably eliciting interventions from the usual two regional powers. This war was fought over Nagorno-Karabakh in autumn 2020. Within two months Azerbaijan, with the active military support of Turkey, inflicted a catastrophic defeat on the Armenian side. Before it could press its gains, however, Russia stepped in to broker a new peace agreement. These events only underscore my analysis and recommendations.

[10] U Kurt et al, 'At Best, the Endless Arc of International Justice: Reparations after the Armenian Genocide' in J Bhabha et al (eds), *Time for Reparation? Addressing State Responsibility for Collective Injustice* (Philadelphia, University of Pennsylvania Press, forthcoming).

Acknowledgements

THIS BOOK WAS put together with wonderful help, professional and personal. Parts II and III could not have been written without the great assistance of Armen Manuk-Khaloyan, an Armenian American doctoral student in history at Georgetown University with command of Armenian, French, German, Russian, and Turkish. His extensive knowledge of much of the history I was writing about, his great disciplined, persistent, and endless curiosity about the rest, and his strong memory are all reflected in general and in particular in erudite footnotes and little-known sources as well as some well-known ones that I just could not get to. A tireless and meticulous researcher and editing assistant for the last four years of working on this ten-year project, he enabled me to pull an extraordinary volume of material together and thus fulfil my aim, which turned out to be far more ambitious than I had any idea of when I began. I cannot thank him enough.

For the last more than two years, the immediate comprehension of the book's aims by editor and researcher, Kate Rouhana, has been invaluable. Her own knowledge and concern about the Israeli-Palestinian situation made her excited about the book's purposes, reinforcing my faith in the project when it waned. She found much material for and acutely edited Chapters 1–3 and edited other chapters in their early stages. She was able to take the needed long perspective on the conclusion and offer precious guidance on how I might re-organise three quite different drafts.

Fletcher School graduate student Marina Vanya Lazetic, an American of Serbian origin, edited, helped with research, and offered valuable criticisms of most parts of the book. Her personal experience and processing of transmitted collective trauma enabled her to understand the importance of the effects of the phenomenon this book discusses.

Before she returned to Turkey to complete her dissertation, I was assisted by Eda Ozel, a Turkish doctoral student in history at Harvard. Her suggestions and corrections were thoughtful and lastingly useful.

Throughout my many years of engagement with this project, I have worked on and off with editor Matt Seccombe. He has elegantly clarified and edited a number of chapters. At the earliest stages of this project, Daniel Orth and Nic Jofre were helpful for short periods – Daniel helped me make sense of some dense historical texts, while Nic helped organise my files and folders.

I am very grateful to the FXB Center for Health and Human Rights at the Harvard TH Chan School of Public Health where I have presented my developing ideas for the book in useful and lively discussions over the years. Jennifer Leaning's patient belief in the project has been sustaining.

Debi Dulberg and Joanne Lipner, colleague clinicians and friends for three decades, all offered essential comments to the chapters on trauma. Stephanie Beukema, also a clinical psychologist, offered vital comments on the chapter on meaning making. She and I were graduate students together under the guidance of Robert Kegan, now professor emeritus of human development at the Harvard Graduate School of Education, who also generously offered clarifying and insightful suggestions for Chapter 16.

My treasured friend, psychiatrist and now emeritus law professor Alan Stone, MD, and I had many provocative and informative discussions over the years, particularly regarding the broadest issues at the intersections of trauma, mind, and brain, as well as the intersections of trauma, meaning making, and moral responsibility. Alan, along with Kenneth Blum, director of the Center for Brain Science at Harvard, and Professor Fred Stoddard, MD, helped me to understand how much is still to be learned about the brain and trauma.

Marc Mamigonian, director of Academic Affairs at the National Association for Armenian Studies and Research, and a colleague for more than 10 years, commented on Chapters 9, 16, and 17. I will always be grateful to Marc for sharing his extraordinary knowledge and excellent judgement, and for being willing to debate, always enjoyably, controversial and consequential matters.

Paul Schulte teaches and consults worldwide on defense and security, and peace and reconciliation. Also a group psychotherapist, I am happily indebted to him for our many talks on the relationship between change and peace-building. They led to his unstinting, informed comments in a number of chapters and added greater depth, precision, and clarity.

Ara Sanjian, professor of history at the University of Michigan, most helpfully offered many useful suggestions and specialised information when he reviewed the first chapters of Part II.

Asbed Kotchikian teaches international relations at Bentley University and specialises in the Caucasus. He offered corrections and asked important questions about the chapters in Part III at different moments in the course of work on this project.

Zulfiyya Abdurahimova, a doctoral student in political science at Harvard, provided extremely helpful and generous comments on three chapters.

I acknowledge a debt of gratitude to Professor Taner Akçam for our profound discussions about important issues concerning Turkey. For years his linking of the goal of furthering human rights in Turkey with genocide recognition has been inspiring.

I am grateful to Sinead Moloney and Sasha Jawed at my publisher, Hart, for their understanding, help, friendly support, and good cheer. Copy-editor Maria Skrzypiec has been thorough, acute, responsive, and a pleasure to work with.

This book has benefited from my friendly connections with many others in different ways. They include Tuncay Babali, John Berger, Jeff Dean, Maureen Freely, Müge Gocek, Ayşe Gözen, Dalita Roger-Hacyan, Maria Hadjipavlou, Donna Hicks, Gerald Holton, Herbert Kelman, Ümit Kurt, Kelly Messier, Hugh O'Doherty, Anna Ornstein, Paula Parnagian, David Phillips, Brady Polka, Lew Sargentich, the late Yona Shamir, Lori Shridhare, Margaret Smith, Gonca Sonmez-Poole, Ronald Suny, and Steve Wagner.

I acknowledge the special contributions of Eileen Babbitt and Gerard Libaridian in the preface, essential to my effort from the get-go to completion. Eileen and Gerard were generous in discussing and correcting parts of chapters, and also served as wise, encouraging friends to the project at any moment. I am very grateful to them.

On the personal side, above all has been my husband Henry, to whom the book is dedicated, for his unwavering patience, emotional support, acute editing, and good discussions. Talks with and short bits of editing by one of my brothers, Steve Pomerance; my son, Duff Johnson; my daughter, Jacoba Johnson Zaring; and my sister-in-law, Prudence Steiner, mattered and helped. The enthusiasm of another sister-in-law, Lenore Pomerance, who read the preface, came at a needed moment. Close friends' support, discussions, and comments also mattered, especially those of Rose Marie Grgic Morse, John Low-Beer, and my late and much beloved friend, Patricia Gercik Haseltine. I also had informative talks with two cousins, Lucy Tuchman Eisenberg and the late Henry Morgenthau III.

I don't know who among those acknowledged will agree or disagree with the understandings I came to. But I do know that some anticipate with me that this book may evoke strong reactions from those individuals who still helped and allowed me to mention them here, for which I am grateful.

Errors of fact or judgement are my responsibility as well as a potential source of my future learning.

A Note on Dates and Names of People and Places

THE OTTOMAN EMPIRE employed three different dating systems at the turn of the twentieth century, including the Julian Calendar (Old Style), which was also used in the Russian Empire. After 1900 it ran 13 days behind the Gregorian Calendar (New Style), by then in use by much of the rest of the world. Events exclusively focusing on the Ottoman Empire are given according to the Gregorian dating system. In line with imperial Russian historiographic practice, dates pertaining to events and happenings in the empire prior to 31 January 1918, when the Bolsheviks switched over to the Gregorian system and the following day became 14 February, are given according to the Julian Calendar. Where confusion might arise or where international events are concerned, the Gregorian system has been used and further clarification provided in parentheses.

Over the long history covered in this book names of many people and places acquired different spellings. I have tried to be consistent by using a simplified version of the Library of Congress' system of transliteration; diacritical marks in Armenian and Russian names, for example, are not used. Towns and cities in the Ottoman and Russian empires are given in their contemporary official forms rather than the name the native population might have used. Thus, Istanbul rather than Constantinople, Erzincan rather than the Armenian Erznka, Tiflis rather than the Georgian Tbilisi, and Elisavetpol instead of today's Ganja in Azerbaijan.

Where a certain name has acquired familiar usage in English, I use that form. So, for example, I refer to Sarikamish and to Djemal Pasha rather than Cemal Pasha. In one case only I separated the Armenian name for the town Shushi/Shusha from the Azerbaijani name for it.

Contents

Introduction

Much of history is about how groups of people, sharing an identity as tribes, castes, races, faiths, or nations, caused collective traumas through wars, genocides, massacres, rape, anarchy, enslavement, starvation, super-exploitation, expulsion and resource control, often in conditions of frigid cold, burning heat, or outbreaks of infectious disease. These traumas are human affairs, not the outcomes of natural calamities like droughts or earthquakes (as understood before climate change). In addition to the toll in human lives, collective trauma is associated with destruction of ancestral and arable lands and other resources, communities, cultures, institutions, and symbols of civilisation. For peoples so affected, when many lives are lost and worlds destroyed, so is the prior understanding of a life's meaning or even meaning itself.

As will be discussed in Part I, the term 'collective trauma' frustratingly refers at times both to people who have been traumatised – that is, to members of large groups of traumatised individuals – and to the events that caused their traumatisation. The Dalai Lama speaks particularly clearly of his own feelings as inseparable from those of his people regarding the traumatic events they collectively underwent. Threatened by the Chinese government in the mid-twentieth century with destruction in their ancestral land, Tibet, they fled to northern India. He recalled, 'Everywhere … were reminders that this was a community that had been traumatised by oppression and exile'. He spoke of the hurt of banishment: 'Nothing can be more devastating than being exiled from your home, from the things that are precious to you'.[1] In 1909, six years before the Armenian genocide began, the intrepid Armenian journalist Zabel Yesayan described what was left in the place where Muslim Turks massacred thousands of Armenians in what is now southeastern Turkey, exemplifying, too, that 'collective trauma' refers to both traumatised individuals and traumatic events:

> Under a superb, dazzling sun, the devastated city stretches outward like a boundless cemetery. Ruins everywhere … Nothing has been spared; all the churches, schools, and homes have been reduced to formless piles and charred stone … From east to west, from north to south, all the way to the distant limits of the Turkish quarters, an implacable, ferocious hatred has burned and destroyed everything. Over this deathly wasteland and these vast piles of ash, two minarets, unscathed, rise up arrogantly.
>
> Dressed in bloody, tear-stained rags, a crowd of widows, orphans, and old people presents itself to us. This is all that is left of Adana's Armenian population … [I]ts pain and inconsolable sorrow are hidden in its depths and sometimes rise to the surface. The hope of living, of being reborn, has been snuffed out in them … They remain silent for a long time,

[1] His Holiness the Dalai Lama, Archbishop Desmond Tutu, with Douglas Abrams, *The Book of Joy: Lasting Happiness in a Changing World* (New York, Penguin Random House, 2016) 22, 23, 32.

> as if following the thread of their memories, involuntarily carried along by the ghastly succession of them and breathing heartfelt sighs that seem to rip through their breasts: 'Aman …' Sometimes they break out in sobs. In a moment's time, their faces are flooded with such an abundance of gushing tears that their words of complaint and lamentation are drowned out. Then … the whole crowd, seized by a fit of inconsolable grief, writhes in despair. It is impossible to imagine what portion of that crowd's sorrow each particular individual represents.[2]

Zabel Yesayan
Source: Wikimedia Commons.

For well over a century, the relations among Armenians, Turks, and Azerbaijanis have been filled with collective traumas and collective transmitted traumas. This book applies understandings from today's trauma psychology to that history. These understandings build on early-twentieth-century developments that generated new theories and findings in individual and group psychologies and also build on eastern traditions. Powerful new possibilities for healing and improving functioning and relationships, both personal and professional, have emerged. But trauma psychology is painfully neglected at the collective level. This book aims to inspire people who work in different roles and fields with or in relation to collective traumas to engage with this perspective.

[2] Z Yesayan, *In the Ruins: The 1909 Massacres of Armenians in Adana, Turkey*, trans GM Goshgarian (Boston, Armenian International Women's Association, 2016) 11–12.

The recovery at both individual and collective levels offered by trauma psychology relies in important part on grasping the meanings that individuals and peoples make of traumatic experience. Hence, this book stresses the meanings made of traumas. What was it was like for these three peoples to live in fear of one another for long periods? The book also asks readers to comprehend when the fears of these peoples involved third parties altogether (ie not just the fears between Armenians, Turks and Azerbaijanis as they related to each other).

The book also brings attention to a number of important individual historical actors who contributed significantly to shaping their collectivity's psyche. They speak eloquently for many more people than themselves, and their views presented opportunities that might have changed the history of relations among these three different ethnic groups. Remembering them in the context of the history of generations and decades of collective trauma might inspire the conflicting parties today to reconsider what remains relevant in these individuals' messages.

I want to stress that while this book looks at the psychological effects collective trauma and collectively transmitted traumas on relations among three peoples, I am well aware that this history is more usually understood in terms of political and economic factors that predisposed actors to create disputes and keep them going. This book in effect proposes that troubled histories might be productively understood through the psychological trauma lens, too, to see if that can contribute to better relations. It does not propose that it be a substitute for the usual lenses, but an addition to them.

I. MY VALUES

This book's purpose emanates from and rests on my moral values, and I believe I should make the source explicit. While, for many people, religious revelation reveals such values, for others, including myself, Charles Darwin's account of the development of social instincts provides their basis: humans are relational beings who evolve and develop rules of what is valued and devalued, of what is right and wrong, in order to survive and thrive with one another.

I view morality as a part of human biology and relational and collective psychology, although science cannot yet tell us how all this works and may never be able to. I hold the infliction of the collective traumas to be discussed as immoral because those actions destroyed achievements of hard- and soft-wired human evolution and possibilities for all to survive and thrive. I hold that we should live lives in which it is possible for all to survive and thrive, sustainably. Often vexingly and discouragingly complex when principles conflict, the exercise of conscience is essential. As one of the novelist Martin Amis's characters put it:

> That's that other feature of national life: permanent desperation. We will never have the 'luxury' of confession and remorse. But what if it isn't a luxury? What if it's a necessity … ? The conscience, I suspect, is a vital organ. And when it goes, you go.[3]

[3] M Amis, *The House of Meetings* (New York, Knopf, 2006) 211–19. 'I' is the protagonist, who spent 15 years in a Soviet work camp in Siberia.

This statement about my moral values is the most extensive in this book, although moral judgments are made evident in places, especially in the stress laid on the UN Convention on the Prevention and Punishment of the Crime of Genocide, which makes clear its absolute illegitimacy. No moral question is more complex for anyone other than pacifists than that of morality in war. The Armenian genocide was carried on during war, and Turkey has officially and often argued that the Armenian deaths and losses took place during the fog of war and hence the government of the Ottoman Empire bears no responsibility for them. But international relations specialist Paul Schulte's careful discussion of morality and war does not even bring genocide into it, writing that warfare is seen as 'the most ruthlessly amoral of all human activities' but one that we also accept as 'legitimate' and 'honourable' because otherwise 'military organisations and soldiers themselves could not … be respected as potential heroes rather than murderers'.[4] Genocide, however, is about murder.

II. THE BOOK'S ARGUMENT

The collective traumas described in this book have both shaped the relationships among these peoples and help to explain their perennial destructiveness. Just as individual trauma affects the meaning making of individual victims – the sense they make of their individual experience – collective trauma affects the meaning making of collectivities – the sense the relevant group makes of its common experience. Victimised collectivities, like individuals, are always subject to painful memories about what they have lost. Like individuals, peoples often react to reminders of past trauma so emotionally and automatically that perceptions about the past are not distinguished from those of the present. This central phenomenon can lead to impaired judgement and decision-making.

It is indisputable that the education about trauma and healing from trauma for individuals has led to life-changing improvements and breakthroughs. This book proposes that greater awareness of the existence of collective trauma and its impact may lead to the same. But to achieve such progress, collective trauma and collective transmitted trauma must be taken seriously as factors, and hence conditions, to be addressed. Thus, it is not my primary purpose to lay out steps as to how collective trauma can be healed to a 'good enough' extent. I and many others have spoken about certain steps for years, which, in the words I use to name them, are for parties, as appropriate, to acknowledge what they did, to apologise, to express regret, to give assurance not to repeat, to pay reparations, memorialise, and rewrite textbooks. I will refer to some of these steps in the last chapter, which discusses collective trauma healing with regard to the dispute between Armenians and Azerbaijanis over Karabakh. But this book's emphasis is on what I understand as the heart of the problem: the recognition of the existence and impact of collective trauma and collective transmitted trauma, and of the need for parties to process and heal in situations of protracted, frozen conflict. That is the very first step on which other steps need to be based.

[4] P Schulte, 'Morality and War' in J Lindley-French and Y Boyer (eds), *The Oxford Handbook of War* (New York, Oxford University Press, 2012).

If Armenians, Turks, and Azerbaijanis were to open themselves to understanding their relations emotionally and intellectually with regard to collective trauma, that understanding could give them a new perspective on their meaning making about the trauma, themselves and each other, and thus play a valuable role in mitigating destructive patterns (see the Conclusion, but also Chapters 17 and 18). However, complete, full or unconditional recovery from collective trauma, if that means forgetting, forgiving, or fully trusting, is probably an impossibility. Those wholly reconciled mental states are also unnecessary. 'Good enough' healing or recovery can be achieved without those mental states,[5] meaning that these three peoples became capable of pursuing non-violent, productive, and responsible relationships. This book aims to contribute to the achievement of step-by-step recovery that would permit and encourage such relationships to develop, out of which parties would seek good-enough justice, settlement of some of the concrete issues, and a process in which to plan next steps. Gradually the kind of trust necessary for sustained improvement could emerge and build. Taking account of collective trauma is not a one-time effort. As will be discussed in different places throughout this book, because we humans do not forget, we remain potentially subject to our memories of violations and losses. Thus, going forward means trust but verify: recovery may well require renewed attention to the memories with each step of improving relations.

III. THE IMPORTANCE OF COLLECTIVE IDENTITY

We are born with some elements of our identities and grow into others. As we experience these identities in life, we may shape them in different ways. The elements of our identities are important to us. We care about them. We have feelings or emotions about them. Feelings or emotions tell us that, and how, we value them or care about them. As psychiatrist Bessel van der Kolk writes, it is '[o]ur emotions [that] assign value to experiences'.[6] Thus, historian and sociologist Taner Akçam writes, 'One of the most important characteristics of national identity is the emotional connection'.[7] If our emotions tell us what matters to us, such as strong, positive feelings about our large-group identities, and what we experience in relation to those identities, then understanding emotions is essential to understanding traumatised peoples. The social psychologist Eran Halperin and colleagues hypothesise about how the emotional connection between an individual and a collective works: individual members of a collectivity engage in a mental process in which they identify themselves as part

[5] The idea of 'good enough' originated in 1953, when Donald Winnicott, a paediatrician and psychoanalyst, proposed that mothers did not need to be perfect to be 'good enough': being a good-enough mother was sufficient to raise psychologically healthy children (DW Winnicott, *The Child, the Family, and the Outside World* (Harmondsworth, Penguin, 1973)).

[6] B van der Kolk, *The Body Keeps the Score: Brain, Mind, and Body in the Healing of Trauma* (New York, Viking, 2014) 64.

[7] T Akçam, *From Empire to Republic: Turkish Nationalism and the Armenian Genocide* (London, Zed Books, 2004) 41.

of a collectivity 'rather than as unique individuals … and, via this psychological mechanism, experience emotions on behalf of the group'.[8] Many such individual experiences add up to collective emotions, ones 'that are shared by large numbers of individuals in a certain society'.[9]

In turn, understanding emotions in this way contextualises reason. Van der Kolk thus relates reason to emotion: 'Emotion is not opposed to reason: Our emotions assign value to experiences and thus are the foundation of reason'.[10] The two parts of our brains interact: the right brain produces the emotions that assign value to our thoughts and experiences. The left brain constructs our reasoning.

Acceptance of the subordinate role of reason relative to that of emotions is no longer confined to the field of psychology. Economist Richard Thaler, for example, explores 'the consequences of limited rationality, social preferences, and lack of self-control', showing 'how these human traits systematically affect individual decisions as well as market outcomes'.[11] Thaler demonstrates that, although we offer reasons, presumed to be rational, for our spending decisions, these decisions are ultimately neither rational nor reason-based but rather emotionally motivated.[12] In other words, reasons are frequently 'rationalisations', or rational explanatory cover stories for what motivates our actions. We may think our rational minds are in charge, but they are not. Psychologist and cognitive scientist Paul Bloom describes it like this: 'We are wrong to see rationality as the dog – it's actually the tail'.[13] That is true, until we become conscious of that dynamic, at which point we can alter it. Today, while it may be theoretically accepted that feelings matter in decision-making in many realms, that acceptance of a range of emotions as a reality to be analysed and worked with is regrettably mostly absent in interstate and intercommunal relations.[14] This book aims to add to other voices about the need to address this omission.

IV. WHY THIS BOOK FALLS WITHIN A SERIES ON HUMAN RIGHTS LAW IN PERSPECTIVE

This book can primarily be described as offering a perspective on conflict-resolution theory and practice, aiming as it does to show that the phenomenon of collective trauma has been left out of the work of conflict resolution and needs to be included. The book also offers an indirect perspective on human rights law. Had there been acceptance and enforcement of today's basic human rights norms, the history of well

[8] E Halperin, *Emotions in Conflict: Inhibitors and Facilitators of Peace Making* (New York, Routledge, 2015) 167.

[9] Halperin, 167.

[10] B van der Kolk, *The Body Keeps the Score: Brain, Mind, and Body in the Healing of Trauma* (New York, Viking, 2014) 64.

[11] *Royal Swedish Academy of Sciences*, 'The Prize in Economic Sciences 2017' (press release), 9 October 2017.

[12] The Nobel Prize in Economic Sciences 2017 was awarded to Richard Thaler.

[13] P Bloom, *Against Empathy* (New York, Harper Collins, 2017) 223, citing J Haidt, 'The Emotional Dog and Its Rational Tail: A Social Intuitionist Approach to Moral Judgment' (2001) 108 *Psychological Review* 814.

[14] Bloom, *Against Empathy*, 53.

over 100 years of almost continuous violations in the relationships of Armenians, Turks, and Azerbaijanis covered in this book would, of course, have been very different. But that is not the book's primary perspective on human rights law. If this book is about the period that brought on what we today call violations of human rights and their recurrence, it is about dealing with them in such a way that prevents more violations in the future. Thus, in this book's perspective, bringing violators of human rights to justice is essential, yet insufficient. This is because it would mitigate only some of the effects of victims' and survivors' trauma.[15] Deep effects of trauma would remain. This book is about the effects that achieving justice does not bring, although justice would surely facilitate successful processing of those effects. This is the perspective the book offers on human rights law.

V. THE BOOK'S ORGANISATION

The introductory section of the book leads into the three chapters of Part I, which presents an overview of psychological trauma, trauma symptoms, and collective trauma. The impact of trauma on meaning making is given particular attention because of its important, usually negative, effect on peoples' ability to resolve persisting conflicts.

In Part II, Chapters 4–9 narrate a history of the relationship between Ottoman Christian Armenians and Muslim Turks from the mid-1800s to the build-up to World War I and the genocide. It identifies the opportunities for reform, beginning in 1839, for an equal playing field, and other important changes for renewal that the ruling but weakening Ottomans needed and at first seemed to embrace, but that they then experienced as traumatic threats to their social status and imperial survival. The Armenians of the Ottoman Empire, too, counted on and felt entitled to the opportunities embodied in the promised reforms. The more threatened the more powerful Ottoman elites felt, the more they scapegoated the less powerful Armenians. In 1915, when the genocide began, those Armenians who could do so fled to neighbouring Transcaucasia (today the South Caucasus), then ruled by the Russian Empire under the banner of Orthodoxy. There they joined their ethnic kinsmen, who formed an equally important community in the region.

Part III's focus shifts to Transcaucasia, where some of the same kinds of ethnic tensions witnessed in the Ottoman Empire were present among its different ethno-religious groups. But in Transcaucasia the Muslims bore the brunt of official discrimination, although the Armenians were also subject to St Petersburg's threatening assertions of dominance. During World War I, the dynamics between Armenians and Turks intensified in the borderlands region between the two empires, engulfing the region in anarchy and violence, traumatising all, and mixing with pre-existing Armenian-Muslim issues in Transcaucasia as a whole. Close to the war's end the Russian Empire collapsed and the far more ruthless Bolsheviks took over Russia, but not yet Transcaucasia. In the few years before the Bolsheviks did take over

[15] P Akhavan, *Reducing Genocide to Law: Definition, Meaning, and the Ultimate Crime* (Cambridge, Cambridge University Press, 2012).

Transcaucasia, the Ottoman army marched into the region, resulting in a perfect, tragic storm, and helping account for the still unresolved conflict today over the Transcaucasian territory of Nagorno-Karabakh (also Karabakh or Artsakh). These events are related in Chapters 10–15 of Part III.

Part IV's Chapters 16–18 identify and analyse the symptoms or marks of collective trauma and collective transmitted trauma evident today but coming out of the complex and problematic historic relations of the three peoples. Chapter 16 analyses two contemporary memoirs, one by an Armenian and the other by a Turk. It shows the role of transmitted trauma on the two individuals' meaning making about the historical trauma transmitted to them. Chapter 17 explores how the symptoms of collective trauma, transmitted from the past and occurring in the present, shape the meaning making of Armenians today. It brings focus to what I regard as the major symptom of that transmitted collective trauma: the conflict between Armenians and Azerbaijanis in the South Caucasus over Karabakh. Chapter 18 explores how Turks have made meaning of the same historical events.

The conclusion takes up the current gloomy status of the Karabakh conflict, understood in terms of all three nations' unprocessed trauma. Much of the conclusion's discussion, however, is composed of a number of specific suggested additions to conflict-resolution processes for working with collective trauma in general, applicable to the Karabakh situation, but also more widely.

VI. SOURCES AND METHOD IN PARTS II AND III

Parts II and III are history and I am not a historian. Yet I allowed myself to write history. My aunt, historian Barbara W Tuchman, was untrained as an historian but nonetheless wrote history. My memory includes her as an inspirational source. And like her, I found the research, as she said in her inimitable style, 'endlessly seductive [... but one] must stop before one has finished'.[16] 'Otherwise', she notes, 'one will never stop and never finish'.[17] After about ten years, though I certainly could have done more research, it was time to finish. Yet I wish this book included all that I have learned of importance to my narrative, not to mention the wealth of material I wished I could have read but could not get to. The unattributed paragraph shown at the very beginning of the film *Gandhi*, here slightly paraphrased, profoundly expresses my aspiration:

> No history such as this can possibly be encompassed in a single telling. There is no way to include each event, each person who helped to shape it. What can be done is to have identified the dominant spirit that ran through this long period and to find the words to express its heart.[18]

[16] B Tuchman, *Practicing History – Selected Essays* (New York, Knopf, 1981) 21.

[17] Tuchman, *Practicing History*, 20.

[18] This comment is partly cribbed from the unattributed sentences in the opening of Richard Attenborough's film *Gandhi*: 'No man's life can be encompassed in one telling. There is no way to give each year its allotted weight, to include each event, each person who helped to shape a lifetime. What can be done is to be faithful in spirit to the record and to try to find one's way to the heart of the man'.

The historical narratives in Parts II and III are informed both by the works of well-known, widely-respected historians and by others less known; by talks and conferences attended; discussions with various specialists; and interactions with American Armenians and Armenians from the Republic of Armenia, Turks, Azerbaijanis, and others. Works of literature and films have also been helpful. As historian Tadeusz Swietochowski wrote about his use of the literary work *Ali and Nino*, on which I also draw, 'A literary vignette offers a plausible insight into the way of thinking of some of the native elite'.[19] My trips to Armenia, Turkey, and Nagorno-Karabakh were important introductions to the distinct history and relationships covered in the book.[20]

During the years of working on this project, colleagues, friends, and family asked how it was going, and I'd say 'slowly'. Early on two successive research assistants asked, 'Where is the trauma?' Since I had thought it was obvious, thereafter, as I wrote and rewrote the chapters in Parts II and III, I kept asking myself, What is the essential collective psychological trauma or traumatising issue in this chapter? Slowly the traumatic essence of each chapter became clearer.

VII. 'OBJECTIVITY' IN PARTS II AND III

When I first became involved with Armenian-Turkish issues, I was aware that a genocide of the Armenian people had occurred. But it was only once involved that I learned that there were the so-called two sides regarding the veracity of its occurrence. So I read not only works that describe the genocidal events but also some works of the 'denialist school'. I came to agree with historian Mark Baker's observation, that today persistent Turkish denial of having committed the Armenian genocide is the single most conspicuous fact about it: 'The Armenian Genocide stands out, perhaps, not so much for its scale or particular brutality – though these were certainly sizable – but for the Turkish republic's long-standing denial of its occurrence, or scale, or the intentions behind it'.[21]

VIII. MULTIDISCIPLINARY APPROACHES AND SOCIAL CONCEPTS

What disciplines should be brought to bear on this study, aiming as it does to address the history of collective trauma among these three peoples over this long period? Kelman sensitively answers the question in general:

> [E]thnic struggles … become … an inescapable part of daily life … The conflict pervades the whole society … not only when it takes the form of explicit violence, but even when violence is muted. Thus, analysis of the conflict requires attention not only to its strategic,

[19] T Swietochowski, *Russian Azerbaijan, 1905–1920, The Shaping of a National Identity in a Muslim Community* (Cambridge, Cambridge University Press, 1995) 83.

[20] I had hoped to visit Azerbaijan, but my visa application was rejected because I would not admit to my 'error' in having visited Nagorno-Karabakh, express regret, and commit to not doing so again.

[21] MR Baker, 'The Armenian Genocide and Its Denial: A Review of Recent Scholarship' (2015) 53 *New Perspectives in Turkey* 197.

> military, and diplomatic dimensions, but also to its economic, psychological, cultural, and social-structural dimensions.[22]

For clinical psychologist and traumatologist Yael Danieli, too, '[m]assive trauma causes such diverse and complex destruction that only a multidimensional, multidisciplinary integrative framework can adequately describe it'.[23]

Among the book's relevant social concepts from different disciplines are those of the 'individual' and the 'collective'. For example, that multiple forces shape the psyches of both individuals and collectives validates the observation that '[t]he hermit in a desert … cannot be understood unless one knows the group from which he has separated himself geographically'.[24] That statement demonstrates the inter-penetrable, inter-dependent nature of individual and collective systems and ways of understanding them.

Another example of the inter-dependent nature of systems at different levels arose in writing about some of the conflicts in Transcaucasia involving 'Tatars'. Should 'Tatars' be qualified by 'ethnic' or 'national' or 'Muslim'? During the relevant period, nation-states were coming to be seen as forming the natural order of political organisation in the world. The so-called Tatars, who had been labelled as such by other regional powers at the time, coalesced to form such a modern nation and nation-state. After 1918 'Tatar' referred to a national group – the Azerbaijanis. Azerbaijanis, strictly speaking, refers to citizens of Azerbaijan, which did not quite come into common usage until after the declaration of the first republic in May 1918. Before that, one usually encounters Tatars and Azeris or some variation of the two and sometimes simply Muslims in the historical record.

'National' is another complex and relevant social concept. Historian Bedross Der Matossian observed, '"National" is a byproduct of modernity, but "ethnic" entails a sense of longer historical existence'.[25] Each of these words, then, describes different periods in the development of group identity. 'National' then spawned 'nationalism', another relevant complex term, referring to the political principle that would organise a theoretically homogenous society over a certain territory.[26] Der Matossian quotes the social anthropologist Fredrik Barth to remind us that such concepts do not exist in reality other than as products of the human mind: 'Ethnic boundaries … are best understood as cognitive or mental boundaries situated in the minds of people and are the result of collective efforts of construction and maintenance'.[27]

[22] HC Kelman, 'Social Psychological Dimensions of International Conflict' in IW Zartman (ed), *Peacemaking in International Conflict: Methods and Techniques*, revised edn (Washington, DC, US Institute of Peace, 2007) 61, 69.

[23] Y Danieli et al, 'Multigenerational Legacies of Trauma: Modeling the What and How of Transmission' (2016) 86(6) *American Journal of Orthopsychiatry* 639.

[24] M Rioch, 'The Work of Wilfred Bion on Groups' in AD Colman and WH Bexton (eds), *Group Relations Reader* (Washington, DC, AK Rice Institute, 1975) 22.

[25] Private correspondence, 2017.

[26] 'Nation', people', 'community', 'ethnic groups', and so forth are used throughout the text. There are overlaps among their meanings and, as suggested, serious writing about the differences. I attempt to use them as appropriate, context by context.

[27] B Der Matossian, *Shattered Dreams of Revolution: From Liberty to Violence in the Late Ottoman Empire* (Stanford, CA, Stanford University Press, 2014) 4, citing BD Jørgenson, 'Ethnic Boundaries and the Margins of the Margin in a Post-colonial and Conflict Resolution Perspective' (1997) *Peace and Conflict Studies* 4.

A question I often thought about in writing this book was how to make delineations among the social concepts just discussed and others used throughout this book – that is, until I read and embraced with a smile economist and philosopher Amartya Sen's memorable remedy:

> [T]he capacious content of a social concept or its diverse manifestations may often be lost or diminished through the maneuver of trying to define it in sharply delineated terms. A rich phenomenon with inherent ambiguities calls for characterization that preserves those shady edges rather than being drowned in the pretense that there is a formulaic and sharp delineation waiting to be unearthed that will exactly separate out all the sheep from all the goats.[28]

IX. WHEN LACKING DOCUMENTED EMOTIONS AND UNCONSCIOUS OR INADMISSIBLE MOTIVATIONS

Accurate assessments of collective trauma's emotional meaning and significance ideally require knowing the core emotions and motives of actors. But in many instances when I cannot document them, I posit what protagonists 'must' or 'probably' or 'likely' felt. I base my suppositions on many factors: other information about those individuals and the groups of which they were members; the conditions in which they were living; the events they were experiencing; my knowledge from being a sentient being who has deeply probed her own psyche and those of others; and from facilitating individuals' collectively contextualised emotions. When I offer such opinions, I beg the reader's indulgence in the words of Simon Sebag-Montefiore:

> If I covered myself comprehensively in every case, the most common words in this book would be 'maybe', 'probably', 'might', and 'could'. I have therefore not included them on every appropriate occasion, but I ask the reader to understand that behind every sentence is a colossal, ever-changing literature.[29]

*

I sometimes speak of Armenians as a whole although I am well aware that not all Armenians are alike and that Armenians make up a heterogeneous whole – in the diaspora, in Armenia, in Turkey, and so on. When at times I aim to speak of a general phenomenon that applies to Armenians collectively, I do not mean that what I say applies to every Armenian or to every subgroup of Armenians. The same applies to references to Turks and Azerbaijanis. Nonetheless, I wish I were sure that I have not overgeneralised.

[28] Amartya Sen, foreword to P Farmer, *Pathologies of Power: Health, Human Rights, and the New War on the Poor*, California Series in Public Anthropology (Berkeley, University of California Press, 2003) xiii.
[29] S Sebag-Montefiore, *Jerusalem: The Biography* (New York, Random House, 2012) xxviii.

In these privileged years of working on this book, I am saddened to admit that my hopes for positive change in the painfully protracted kinds of conflicts described here have greatly diminished. But, if we would heal our collective traumas, the process would entail our evolving into tolerance and responsibility, neither of which can be learned overnight, and could lead to the needed reevaluation of values and principles. The need for such evolution has never been greater.

Part I

Collective Trauma: An Introduction

1

Introduction to Trauma, a Capacious Social Concept

THE WORD 'TRAUMA' originates from the Greek *trauma*, meaning 'wound'. It first appeared in English in the 1690s as a medical term denoting a physical wound. It was not until the late nineteenth century that 'trauma' came to connote a 'psychic wound, [an] unpleasant experience which causes abnormal stress'.[1] Today's expanded meaning still rests on 'wound'.

The experience of serious trauma impacts and often shatters our understandings and assumptions about the world and our place in it. Some trauma survivors experience lasting, if not permanent, psychological and physiological distress, influencing behaviour, feelings, and functioning. For most of human history, people who sought to understand and heal from such traumas looked to religious or spiritual practices or supportive connections with others. But by the late nineteenth century, the work of the French doctor Pierre Janet conceptualised much about psychological trauma as it is understood today, viewing 'the trauma response basically as a disorder of memory which interfered with effective action', and making 'the first attempt to create a systematic, phase-oriented treatment of post-traumatic stress'.[2] Freud, according to psychoanalyst Peter Loewenberg, was soon to define 'trauma' as 'an experience that, within a short period of time, presents the mind with an increase of stimulus too powerful to be dealt with or worked off in the normal way'.[3]

Trauma first became a major psychiatric concern during World War I.[4] Troops on all sides of the conflict experienced wide-ranging neuropsychiatric symptoms, termed 'shell shock', even those without any physical injuries.[5] Psychological wounds were linked to physical wounds.[6] After World War I it was generally

[1] 'Trauma', *Online Etymology Dictionary*, at www.etymonline.com/word/trauma (accessed 17 July 2020).

[2] O van der Hart et al, 'Pierre Janet's Treatment of Post-traumatic Stress' in JM Lating and GS Everly Jr (eds), *Psychotraumatology: Key Papers and Core Concepts in Post-traumatic Stress* (New York, Spring, 1995) 1.

[3] Ibid.

[4] M Suárez-Orozco and ACGM Robben, 'Interdisciplinary Perspectives on Violence and Trauma' in ACGM Robben and MM Suárez-Orozco (eds), *Cultures under Siege: Collective Violence and Trauma* (Cambridge, Cambridge University Press, 2000) 13.

[5] Suárez-Orozco and Robben, 'Interdisciplinary Perspectives on Violence and Trauma', 13.

[6] P Loewenberg, 'Clinical and Intergenerational Perspectives on the Intergenerational Transmission of Trauma' in G Fromm (ed), *Lost in Transmission: Studies of Trauma across Generations* (London, Karnac Books, 2012) 74.

understood that traumatised individuals required psychiatric or medical intervention.[7] Nonetheless, in spite of so many sufferers, for a time scientific study of psychological trauma and development of healing or recovery methods was intermittent at best. World War II and the Korean War brought another wave of the study of trauma when soldiers returned home with now-familiar symptoms.[8] By the 1960s and 1970s different survivor populations were raising awareness of psychological trauma. The feminist movement led to the identification of the 'syndromes' of rape trauma and battered women. Toward the end of the Vietnam War in 1975, a 'post-Vietnam syndrome' was proposed, referring primarily to soldiers' trauma symptoms.

Finally, in 1980, the clinical diagnosis, post-traumatic stress disorder (PTSD), was formally acknowledged by inclusion in the American Psychiatric Association's *Diagnostic and Statistical Manual of Mental Disorders* (known as the *DSM*). Acceptance of the concept promised momentous change in the understanding of much human suffering. As the National Center for PTSD's website puts it, 'the significant change ushered in by the PTSD concept was … that the etiological agent was outside the individual (i.e., a traumatic event) rather than an inherent individual weakness (i.e., a traumatic neurosis)'.[9]

Overall, thereafter, the existence of PTSD and the understanding that its cause was outside the individual came to be recognised in the United States and internationally. Psychiatrist Judith Herman's classic work, *Trauma and Recovery*, published in 1992, became the first to link two populations of individuals, soldiers returning from Vietnam and sexually abused women, each with a high percentage of trauma. She found that the existence of trauma or traumatic events and the internal state of being traumatised in both groups was more widespread than had previously been acknowledged. As mental health professionals absorbed her message, advances in understanding psychological trauma and processes for recovery followed. Soon afterwards, the idea took hold that whole societies or groups could be similarly affected.

*

This chapter and the next respectively emphasise individual trauma, the third collective trauma. The three chapters provide the foundation of the trauma-informed perspective that shapes the historical narratives and analyses in the rest of the book. But although this book's focus is more on peoples than on individuals, it also offers brief portrayals of a number of individuals who are emblematic of their entire people or a significant segment among them as they cope with traumatic challenges in their societies. Some captured and influenced the public mood, if not their people's collective psyche and actions.

[7] G Reyes et al (eds), 'History of Psychological Trauma' in *The Encyclopedia of Psychological Trauma* (John Wiley & Sons, 2008) 317.

[8] Ibid.

[9] MJ Friedman, 'PTSD History and Overview', National Center for PTSD, US Department of Veterans Affairs, www.ptsd.va.gov/professional/treat/essentials/history_ptsd.asp (accessed 17 July 2020).

I. PTSD AND TRAUMA: CLINICAL AND POPULAR USES

Today both 'trauma' and 'PTSD' are capacious social concepts in common use with somewhat varying but overlapping meanings. Strictly speaking, PTSD denotes a clinical diagnosis. The American Psychiatric Association specifies PTSD's meaning and application through a periodic process in which a group of experts reexamines, and sometimes redefines, mental disorders and publishes them in the *DSM*. (The 2013 fifth edition of this volume, commonly referred to as the *DSM*-5a, remains current,[10] but at the time of writing, a cohort of international mental health clinicians is at work redefining PTSD.)

PTSD is the best-known trauma-specific diagnosis in the current *DSM* and is applied when a person manifests one or another specified set of reactions or symptoms. Thus, having some of the symptoms of PTSD does not mean a person has PTSD. Indeed, many individuals who experience traumatic events and have symptoms may not be clinically diagnosable with PTSD because their symptoms fail to meet one or another set of DSM symptoms for assignment of the diagnosis. Nonetheless, most who go through terrible events are traumatised to some degree. On the other hand, researchers estimate that many more individuals would be diagnosed with PTSD or trauma, but never seek treatment and thus never receive this diagnosis.[11]

Since 'PTSD' is widely if loosely used outside clinical contexts as well, PTSD, the clinical diagnosis, cannot be fully conflated with the popular use of PTSD – or with trauma. All in all psychological trauma is a much broader category than clinical PTSD.

II. TRAUMA

Trauma refers to events or ongoing conditions that 'create harm or threat of harm'[12] and cause intense physical and psychological stress reactions or symptoms. Trauma disrupts individuals' major biological systems for coping with stress,[13] overwhelming the ability to manage or make sense of the experience. Thus, in their foundational handbook on trauma therapy, psychiatrists John Briere and Catherine Scott wrote that 'an event is traumatic if it is extremely upsetting, at least temporarily overwhelms the individual's internal resources, and produces lasting psychological symptoms'.[14]

[10] American Psychiatric Association, *Diagnostic and Statistical Manual of Mental Disorders*, 5th edn (Arlington, VA, American Psychiatric Publishing, 2013).

[11] Eg BD Grinage, 'Diagnosis and Management of Post-traumatic Stress Disorder' (2003) 68(12) *American Family Physician* 2401.

[12] M Cloître et al, 'A Developmental Approach to Complex PTSD: Childhood and Adult Cumulative Trauma as Predictors of Symptom Complexity' (2009) 22(5) *Journal of Traumatic Stress* 1.

[13] See, eg, K Kozlowska et al, 'Fear and the Defense Cascade: Clinical Implications and Management' (2014) 23(4) *Harvard Review of Psychiatry* 263; K Roelefs, 'Freeze for Action: Neurobiological Mechanisms in Animal and Human Freezing' (2017) 372(1718) *Philosophical Transactions of the Royal Society B* 20160206; K Zilberstein, 'Trauma's Neurobiological Toll – Implications for Clinical Work with Children' (2014) 84 *Smith College Studies in Social Work* 292.

[14] JN Briere and C Scott, *Principles of Trauma Therapy: A Guide to Symptoms, Evaluation, and Treatment (DSM-5 Update)*, 2nd edn (Thousand Oaks, CA, Sage Publications, 2015) 10.

Similarly, Loewenberg distinguishes the core objective from the subjective elements of traumatic experience: 'The external stimulus is too powerful to be mediated by the normal adaptive coping mechanisms; the person is overwhelmed and helpless'.[15]

At the same time, the word 'trauma' and its offshoots such as 'traumatic' elude precise distinction between objective events and subjective experience. Does 'trauma' refer to the objective stressor event, the victim's subjective experience of the stressor, and/or the victim's subjective symptoms that arise in response to the stressor? It is used for them all. As noted, when I began writing this book, I thought I could use 'trauma' and its related terms to refer to either subjective or objective experience, not to both. I attempted to use 'traumatic event' to refer to the objective event and 'traumatised' or 'being traumatised' to refer to the condition of having one or more of many possible symptoms after the event. But I found that the distinctions among the family of words just didn't hold consistently.

Clarification is complicated because individuals exposed to the same traumatic events often respond differently. Some people are little traumatised by events that seriously traumatise others. All manifest a wide range of reactions or symptoms. And assessing whether or how much an individual or group is traumatised depends on the criteria used. In this book, 'trauma' refers to both objectively and subjectively known experience, and at times to both simultaneously.

III. TYPES OF TRAUMATIC EVENTS

Because traumatic events and traumatic situations come about by accident, nature, or are inflicted by humans, deliberately or not, a very wide range of types of events and situations may be so identified. They include physical and verbal abuse, aeroplane/train/automobile accidents, death, discrimination, fires, life-threatening or debilitating illness, isolation, losses of many kinds, material and psychological, including of reputation, status, or regard, mugging, rape and sexual assault, starvation, and torture. This book is centrally about humanly caused events and situations imposed without concern for those affected or with deliberate malintent – discrimination, massacres, genocide, ethnic cleansing, enslavement, and starvation – that often led to complex if not traumatising situations. Traumas are also 'acts of omission … (such as neglect or abandonment) where the absence or withdrawal of certain resources may create a threat to [human] survival or well-being'.[16] Witnessing others experiencing trauma or discovering a victim is another category of events that are often traumatic.[17]

Much trauma literature conveys the impression that all traumatic experiences are events in the sense that there is a clear beginning and end, and that survivors cope with their aftermath. Increasingly, however, awareness is growing that there are situations

[15] Loewenberg, 'Clinical and Intergenerational Perspectives', 73.

[16] Cloître et al, 'A Developmental Approach', 7.

[17] See, eg, K Weingarten, *Common Shock: Witnessing Violence Every Day – How We Are Harmed, How We Can Heal* (New York, New American Library, 2003).

of protracted wounding and of continuous, ever-present facts of life.[18] Thus, ethnic cleansing, large fires and floods, genocide, terrorist attacks, and war, all entailing vast collective hurts and losses, are generally understood as traumatic collective events. In contrast, conditions of ongoing discrimination, impoverishment and environmental degradation make for collectively traumatic situations.

In writing about trauma, neuroscientists Joseph LeDoux and Daniel Pine refer to 'threats', not 'events'.[19] Are threats of trauma 'events'? 'Threats' ordinarily denotes not the possibility, but the occurrence, of events. But even if what is threatened does not materialise, being threatened may nonetheless be traumatising. Receiving threatening phone calls from dangerous persons or living under constant threat of arbitrary arrest, torture, or death are likely to be traumatising. Another example is that of the threat of a whole social class's loss of superior status. In 2018 a study found that Trump voters were 'motivated by … fears of waning power and status in a changing country'.[20] The recent book by political scientists Steven Levitsky and Daniel Ziblatt, *How Democracies Die*, recognises that white Republican men's fears are leading them to do anything to keep their social status and possession of society's powerful positions.[21] These powerful men in high positions fear losing both when others may exercise one or another form of overwhelming power against them.

IV. OTHER FEELINGS GENERATED BY TRAUMA, WHO GETS TRAUMATISED, AND HOW SEVERELY?

When trauma is inflicted through the systematic and deliberate imposition of power, verbal or physical, aiming to destroy (something in) the individuals and/or their community, dismantling (some aspect of) their identity, and/or removing (some aspect of) their freedom, it means victims are unable to protect themselves and have been forced to surrender. For most, being forced to surrender is humiliating, shaking their trust in the world, their intrinsic sense of day-to-day invulnerability in it, and their worthiness. Life may feel alien and meaningless, according to trauma expert Michelle Sotero and many others.[22]

Such traumatic experience can affect any human being regardless of age, gender, race, nationality, class, powerful position, or other defining characteristic. It can affect any grouping from couples, families, groups, and work colleagues, to communities.[23]

[18] G Eagle and D Kaminer, 'Continuous Traumatic Stress: Expanding the Lexicon of Traumatic Stress' (2013) 19(2) *Journal of Peace and Conflict: Journal of Peace Psychology* 85.

[19] JE Ledoux and DS Pine, 'Using Neuroscience to Help Understand Fear and Anxiety: A Two-System Framework' (2016) 173(11) *American Journal of Psychiatry* 1083.

[20] DC Mutz, 'Status Threat, Not Economic Hardship, Explains the 2016 Presidential Vote' (2018) 155(19) *Proceedings of the National Academy of Sciences* E4330, available at www.pnas.org/content/115/19/E4330.short?rss=1.

[21] S Levitsky and D Ziblatt, *How Democracies Die* (New York, Crown/Penguin, 2018).

[22] MM Sotero, 'A Conceptual Model of Historical Trauma: Implications for Public Health Practice and Research' (2006) 1(1) *Journal of Health Disparities Research and Practice* 95.

[23] Substance Abuse and Mental Health Services Administration, *Trauma-Informed Care in Behavioral Health Services*, Treatment Improvement Protocol (TIP) Series 57, HHS Publication No (SMA) 13–4801 (Rockville, MD, 2014) 7.

Reactions or responses to traumatic events are mediated through a mix of factors unique in each person. Prior individual experience and family history, including mental health disorders, cognitive outlook, coping style, personality disorder, or genetic predisposition, matter and may indicate greater or lesser vulnerability.[24] Age matters, too. The younger the exposure, the more severe the effect.[25] Members of groups marginalised by race, gender, or class also tend to be more vulnerable.[26]

Those who experience multiple traumatic events or who are exposed to a traumatic situation over time usually have more serious and chronic symptoms than those who experience a single trauma.[27] Victims of interpersonal traumas are statistically at a greater risk of experiencing additional interpersonal traumas.[28] Earlier traumas, especially when unaddressed, can set the stage for a downward spiral of events likely resulting in multiple traumas and multiple symptomatic responses. They can make the adult response to retraumatisation especially severe.[29] The nature of the prior relationship between the victim and perpetrator matters with deliberately imposed trauma. If a parent molests or verbally abuses a child, the effect is likely to be more serious than if a stranger does. The more the victim trusted the perpetrator, the greater the psychological trauma.[30] With collective traumas, caused by nature, accident, or humans, the relationship between the victim and the uninvolved outside world also matters. For example, humanitarian response to natural disasters is not controversial, whereas in situations caused by humans it can be highly contentious.

V. TRAUMA'S EFFECT ON INTERNAL INTEGRATION

Building on Janet's work, on work by others since, and on their own research, psychiatrists Onno van der Hart, Paul Brown, and van der Kolk write that traumatic memories are set apart from 'the totality of people's identities' and as such constitute 'the core issue in post-traumatic syndromes'.[31] They, Loewenberg, Sotero, and many others agree that traumatic experience commonly alters how we think about and cope with life afterwards. The experience may stand outside our overall understanding, which otherwise remains intact, un-integrated into that understanding. At the other extreme the traumatic experience may have been so great that it upends victims' entire previous understanding or worldview. I characterise this range of possibilities as the effect of trauma on meaning making.

The effect of trauma on meaning making is central throughout this book, but it differs in individuals even if they have experienced the same or a very similar

[24] Briere and Scott, *Principles of Trauma Therapy*, 26–27.
[25] Zilberstein, 'Trauma's Neurobiological Toll', 294.
[26] Briere and Scott, *Principles of Trauma Therapy*, 26.
[27] SAMHSA, *Trauma-Informed Care*, xviii.
[28] Briere and Scott, *Principles of Trauma Therapy*, 21.
[29] Ibid, 21–22.
[30] Eg, W Middleton et al, 'The Abused and the Abuser: Victim–Perpetrator Dynamics' (2017) 18(3) *Journal of Trauma and Dissociation* 249, https://doi.org/10.1080/15299732.2017.1295373 (accessed 17 July 2020).
[31] van der Hart et al, 'Pierre Janet's Treatment of Post-traumatic Stress', 1.

traumatic event. Some demonstrate compartmentalisation of the experience, and others that they have been affected in all realms of their lives. The psychiatrist and psychoanalyst Anna Ornstein analysed this kind of difference in trauma's effect on meaning making in Holocaust survivors. She considered the claim for the existence of a universal 'survivor syndrome' in those who experienced the Holocaust. Ornstein knew Holocaust experience from the inside and outside. She was in her mid-teens when the Nazis deported her and her mother from their village in Hungary to Auschwitz towards the end of World War II. Both survived. Ornstein married a survivor, also a psychiatrist and psychoanalyst, whom she had known before deportation. In her decades of professional work and teaching, she treated and interacted with many Holocaust survivors.

Ornstein's own experiences and work led her to disagree with many mental health professionals that everyone who went through the Holocaust had a 'survivor syndrome', one in which the symptoms acquired as a result of Holocaust experiences affect all aspects of their lives similarly.[32] She agrees that the experience of the Holocaust probably left survivors with one or another symptom or symptoms, but she did not find that the overall common experience typically shaped or explained other parts of these individuals' personal lives. She hypothesises that those who proposed a 'survivor syndrome' failed to factor in their own strong reactions to the horrors their patients endured and were therefore unaware that their conclusions were based on their assumptions about the effects of those horrors.

In addition, Ornstein found that these clinicians' studies had not taken into account their patients' histories prior to the Holocaust, specifically and significantly, the factor of their degree of internal organisation, cohesion, or integration.[33] She concluded that those who had been children at the time they experienced the Holocaust did not have what she calls the 'intrapsychic cohesion' or ego development that would have enabled them to avoid the global impact of the traumatic Holocaust experience on their later lives. Those who were adults during the Holocaust, whose internal coherence had also not greatly matured, would also have been similarly affected. Ornstein contrasted these two categories of survivors with a third group, survivors who had developed an integrated self before the Holocaust. She found that they 'were able to retain their values and ideals [and that] … [a]mbitions, values, and ideals, the constituents of a cohesive nuclear self, became the psychological foundations for the survivors' post-Holocaust recovery'.[34]

Individuals who demonstrate cohesiveness and integration and have developed and retained 'ambitions, values, and ideals', are likely to have evolved a capacity – or the basis for one – for more complex meaning-making (see Chapter 16). Ornstein proposes that such adults have the foundation for recovery from trauma

[32] A Ornstein et al, 'Survival, Recovery, Mourning, and Intergenerational Transmission of Experience: A Discussion of Gomolin's Paper' (2019) 88(3) *Psychoanalytic Quarterly* 541, doi.org/10.1080/00332828.2019.1630190.

[33] A Ornstein, 'Survival and Recovery: Psychoanalytic Reflections' (2001) 9(1) *Harvard Review of Psychiatry* 15.

[34] Ornstein, 'Survival and Recovery', 15. See Ornstein's memoir of her experience as a deported Hungarian Jew and life afterwards in *My Mother's Eyes* (Cincinnati, OH, Emmis Books, 2004), a worthy accompaniment to Anne Frank's *Diary of a Young Girl*.

that those without such inner evolution lacked. This group is probably composed of a limited number of individuals. The majority of human beings, not assessed for trauma, are not so integrated,[35] a fact that helps underscore my assumption and accounting that a whole people, or significant parts of one, manifest common reactions to the collective traumas they went through (for a fuller discussion, see Chapter 16).

VI. TRAUMA AND FUNCTIONALITY

Many traumatised individuals cannot function well, but many can. I offer an anecdotal example. Five friends, including Ornstein and her late husband, survived the Holocaust into their 90s. Four are still alive. Two were separated from their parents at age seven, one survived the horrors of two concentration camps, one regained full health and capacity to work and love after time spent in a series of forced-labor camps, and the fifth endured the Anschluss. Each of these individuals is or was accomplished, responsible, and enjoyed deep, lasting personal and work relationships. Yet one of them told me that he has had repetitive nightmares, a trauma symptom, every night since the separation from his parents, even into his late 80s. You would never guess that from meeting him.[36]

VII. FACTORS IN HEALING INDIVIDUAL AND COLLECTIVE TRAUMA

The premise of this book is that peoples who experience humanly caused traumatic events suffer from long-lasting, often unconscious, psychological wounds from which full recovery is impossible. Neither the memory of fear, pain, and anger, nor the vulnerability to reminders thereof, disappear. If repressed and ignored, trauma may significantly unconsciously shape that peoples' lived experience or aspects of it, often negatively. Healing, understood as retrieving and integrating traumatic memories in order to live lives more in the present than in past traumas, is possible. For many people the experience of 'good enough' recovery is very positive.

Perpetrator accountability may play an important role in healing and recovery. Individuals and collectivities who undergo deliberately-imposed harm, are owed understanding, acknowledgment, apology, reassurance not to repeat, and reparations

[35] Psychologist Robert Kegan's concept of the evolution of a high degree of consciousness in individuals is of those with integrated 'ambitions, values, … ideals', as well as high functioning in relationships, work, and in the world. Extensive studies of the concept find that this category makes up considerably less than half the population (Kegan's work provides the basis of the understandings in Chapter 16).

[36] How best to refer to people who have been traumatised? Some resent being referred to as a 'victim', as they survived. They prefer 'survivor' because it implies that they have overcome their traumas and are not defined by the events. Others believe that post-trauma, evolution takes place from 'victim', in the immediate aftermath of the experience, to 'survivor' and then even to 'thriver' once recovery has been achieved. In this book, the use of the different terms, including 'victim/survivor', is intended to be sensitive to context.

or restitution from perpetrators. Perpetrators should be brought to justice. With individual trauma, if perpetrators take such steps, or are brought to justice, it usually remains a relatively private matter. But with collective trauma those steps need to occur in interactive public processes of different kinds. Further, in view of what we have learned from interactive public processes, healing collective trauma may entail attitudinal and structural change reflected in official policies and practices in the provision of education, public health and safety, and justice (see Conclusion).

Acceptance of responsibility by perpetrators requires, then, that they execute great steps. Yet this does not accomplish a crucial part of the healing that victims need, which is the healing that results from retrieving and integrating traumatic memories. This is because the effects of trauma tend to persist, with or without perpetrator accountability, in individuals or a whole people. Throughout this book, reference will be made to 'processing' traumatic experience. Processing, even without perpetrator responsibility-taking, can go far in healing trauma. Processing entails work by the victim party, and may also – but not necessarily – entail work by both the victim party and perpetrator party (for discussion see Preface and Chapters 17 and 18). Healing processes can lead to integration of experience and open up the victim to conscious and deep understanding. Processing is hard but rewarding – and far easier and infinitely less costly than the alternative of conflict and war, as this book aims to demonstrate.

However, I wish to stress that only the victim or survivor can take responsibility for retrieving and integrating traumatic memories. In a way it is fortunate that victims of individual trauma can do this for themselves, even if they may need support from others in so doing, because it is more common than not that individuals must live without any perpetrator accountability. Individuals and people who are victims of collective trauma probably receive justice even less frequently than individual victims of personal traumatic wounds. Further, they may continue to live under ongoing traumatising collective situations and structures. However, though rare, 'good enough' recovery for traumatised peoples seems to exist. This book searches for what 'good enough' recovery in such instances might be, and offers a possible, and surely only partial, answer.

VIII. THE DAUNTING SCOPE OF COLLECTIVE TRAUMA

Both PTSD and trauma are very large social constructs referring to individuals generally. Social psychologist and psychotherapist Marcus Brunner puts these concepts so used in perspective. He notes how PTSD is yet narrowly focused on the individual while ignoring the wider societal impact of trauma on collectivities. 'We need', he says, 'a concept of trauma that can handle the complex relationships between the traumatising event, the psychosocial framing, the subjective experience, and the later processing within a social context'.[37] I do not know that we need another concept but rather

[37] M Brunner, 'A Plea for a Fundamental Social Psychological Reflection of Traumatization Processes' in C Barrette et al (eds), *Traumatic Imprints: Performance, Art, Literature and Theoretical Practice* (Oxford, Inter-Disciplinary Press, 2012) 204.

greater consideration of collective trauma in and across the disciplines of anthropology, peace and conflict studies, history, philosophy, politics, psychology, public health, religion and sociology. Collective trauma's many names include 'cultural memory';[38] 'repeated and prolonged mass disasters';[39] and social, mass, cultural,[40] chosen,[41] and historical[42] traumas. As psychologist John Ehrenreich correctly says, to date, no name captures 'all aspects of it'.[43] Perhaps no one name can.

[38] J Assmann and J Czalpicka, 'Collective Memory and Cultural Identity' (1995) 65 *New German Critique* 125.

[39] JH Ehrenreich, 'Understanding PTSD, Forgetting "Trauma"' (2003) 3(1) *Journal of Social Issues* 19.

[40] Alexander et al, *Cultural Trauma and Collective Identity.*

[41] V Volkan, 'Transgenerational Transmissions and Chosen Traumas: An Aspect of Large-Group Identity' (2001) 34(79) *Group Analysis* 79.

[42] Sotero, 'A Conceptual Model of Historical Trauma'.

[43] Ehrenreich, 'Understanding PTSD, Forgetting "Trauma"', 19.

2

Impaired Meaning Making, Trauma's Meta-Effect

THOSE WORKING CLINICALLY with psychological trauma know that trauma influences our bodies, brains, minds, emotions, health, behaviour, and relationships.[1] Yet they also know that much remains to be learned about the ways in which these factors interact, especially the brain and mind. Some psychologists and neuroscientists at work on unsettled questions regarding that relationship hypothesise that our conscious and unconscious minds continually interact with our brains, organising and assigning meaning to all our raw experience, thereby creating personal narratives. This is my understanding.

The proposition that the brain and mind work together to produce the meaning humans make of their experiences suggests that making meaning is our core psychological process and our mind's meta-process, and that is how I conceptualise it. Van der Kolk explains how traumatic experience interferes with the meaning-making process: 'Traumatic experiences are initially imprinted sensations and feeling states and are not collated and transcribed into personal narratives … *Traumatic memories come back as emotional and sensory states with little capacity for verbal representation*' (emphasis added). This means that the capacity to process information, which 'is essential for proper categorization and integration with other experiences',[2] ie meaning making, is compromised by trauma.

Traumatic experience assumes core importance to victims. Their 'personal meanings and images of the [traumatic] event, extend … to the deepest parts of [their] inner experience of self and world'.[3] The narratives of peoples, similarly to those of individuals, emerge over time out of meaning made and continuously being made from the wealth of the experiences of its individual members, leading figures, and subgroups. A collective's experiences and meanings also extend to its members' deepest parts. This chapter goes into what happens to individuals during traumatic experiences and some of the symptoms or after-effects of trauma, especially regarding meaning making.

[1] Eg Substance Abuse and Mental Health Services Administration, *Trauma-Informed Care in Behavioral Health Services*, Treatment Improvement Protocol (TIP) Series 57, HHS Publication No (SMA) 13–4801 (Rockville, MD, 2014) 61.

[2] BA van der Kolk et al, *Traumatic Stress: The Effects of Overwhelming Experience on Mind, Body, and Society* (New York, Guilford Press, 1996) 296, 282.

[3] L McCann and LA Pearlman, *Psychological Trauma and the Adult Survivor: Theory, Therapy, and Transformation*, Brunner/Mazel Psychosocial Stress Series no 21 (Abingdon, Routledge Taylor and Francis Group, 1990) 6.

As with individuals, collective trauma significantly defines and redefines peoples' meaning making, identities, and narratives.

I. THE BODY'S REACTIONS TO TRAUMA

That psychological trauma reverberates not only in the brain and mind but also in the rest of the body is aptly captured in the title of van der Kolk's recent book, *The Body Keeps the Score*.[4] To understand trauma's effect on meaning making, it helps to understand it from the perspective of the series of sequential, involuntary, hardwired physiological reactions that are activated in the brains of all individuals confronted with acute threat. The rapidly occurring reactions have been characterised as the human body's 'defence cascade'.[5] Once the body enters a high state of anxiety (hyperarousal or hypervigilance), each reaction is mediated by a specific neuron circuit extending from the brain into the body. These reactions enable optimal response, that is, the channelling of resources away from less necessary responses and focusing them where most needed for self-defence. At a certain point, individuals' remarkable sensory processing may also briefly numb pain so as not to detract from their defences mobilising for survival.

A. Arousal: A State of Alert

The defence cascade is activated by a perceived threat. A signal goes to the brain, which interprets it and sends a distress signal to the brain's command centre. There, the brain communicates through the two branches of the autonomic nervous system (sympathetic and parasympathetic). These two branches generally counteract each other: the sympathetic stimulates the body, revving it up and preparing it for action, while the parasympathetic slows down the body, calming it after danger has passed.

The sympathetic nervous system signals the release of adrenaline, generating a response that not only increases alertness but entails physiological changes that shift the body away from its normal equilibrium or homeostasis. Blood rushes to the brain and heart, heart rate and breathing accelerate, body temperature rises, digestive activity ceases, the mouth goes dry, the voice becomes high-pitched, muscles tone up, posture stabilises, and the body sweats. The body is preparing to act.[6]

B. Freeze – Then Fight or Flight or Freeze

In a split second, while the brain assesses whether fight or flight is possible, the body freezes, diminishing the likelihood of detection while scanning the environment.

[4] B van der Kolk, *The Body Keeps the Score* (New York, Viking, 2014).

[5] K Kozlowska et al, 'Fear and the Defense Cascade: Clinical Implications and Management' (2014) 23(4) *Harvard Review of Psychiatry* 263, 264.

[6] Harvard Health Publishing, 'Understanding the Stress Response' (March 2011), www.health.harvard.edu/staying-healthy/understanding-the-stress-response (accessed 18 August 2020); and Kozlowska et al, 'Fear and the Defense Cascade', 267.

If neither fight nor flight is possible, the brain instinctively keeps the body in 'freeze' (see 'Immobility' below) until the danger passes or an active response becomes possible.[7]

C. Fight or Flight

If in the initial moment of decision-making in 'freeze,' the brain 'authorises' the person either to confront the attacker in fight or run away in flight, another split second later the body prepares for a particular response. Although a person who has been previously traumatised may go straight into arousal for fight or flight without going through freeze, in both cases, the sympathetic nervous system revs up the heart, muscles, and brain and the parasympathetic blocks pain. The brain facilitates the expression of the 'fight' emotions that are normally tamped down. Rage appears, and focus tunnels in on the threat.

D. Immobility

If in imminent danger but unable to fight or flee, individuals stay in 'freeze' and become, involuntarily, partially or altogether, immobilised. The body cools but the person is unable to call out. According to psychologist Kasia Kozlowska, '[V]ictims describe subjective experiences of fear, immobility, coldness, numbness and analgesia, uncontrollable shaking, eye closure, and dissociation … as well as a sense of entrapment, inescapability, futility, or hopelessness'.[8]

In this state, the brain may remove an individual's awareness as an embodied presence such that, for example, they do not feel pain during traumatising moments, although those who become immobile generally have vivid, if incomplete, recall.[9] The person may experience watching the event unfolding as if from a distance, and not being part of or feeling it. Being thus traumatised is the classic state of dissociation, the out-of-body experience. While frozen yet focused on the threat, some people collapse and some feel terror, panic, and extreme anxiety. Partial or full loss of consciousness is possible.[10]

E. Quiescent Immobility

When individuals sense safety, a state of quiescence occurs, promoting rest and recovery. It usually lasts as long as needed for physical healing from the trauma and is accompanied by social reengagement.[11]

[7] Kozlowska et al, 'Fear and the Defense Cascade', 270.
[8] Ibid, 273.
[9] MA Hagenaars, 'Tonic Immobility and PTSD in a Large Community Sample' (2006) 7(2) *Journal of Experimental Psychopathology* 246.
[10] Ibid, 274.
[11] Kozlowska et al, 'Fear and the Defense Cascade', 275.

II. POST-TRAUMA SYMPTOMS

Post-trauma individuals are sensitive to reminders of the trauma event or situation. Reminders 'trigger' reactions or responses. 'Being triggered' does not mean that survivors are reacting to all the concrete details of the event, but to more general representations. Triggers can thus be of any kind or degree, no matter how apparently remotely connected or seemingly trivial[12] – a particular sound, smell, kind of weather, visual scene; holidays, anniversary dates; a child reaching the age or stage of life when a trauma had affected a parent, and so on.

Triggers involuntarily flood brain structures with the emotions experienced during the original trauma, such as fear, anger, shame, humiliation, and also numbness. Simultaneously survivors may re-experience body sensations such as rapid breathing, a racing heart, or sweaty palms. Thinking and meaning making may revert, momentarily or longer, to the most basic needs, survival and safety. To different degrees and lengths of time (reactions to triggers vary in intensity), triggers make an individual feel as if they are again in the threatening situation. Thus, for a longer or shorter time, individuals may be convinced that what they are experiencing is occurring in the present, unconsciously projecting past experience onto their experience of the present.

Trauma symptoms occur along a continuum of severity from mild, specific, time-limited, and isolated from the rest of life to wide-ranging, entrenched, and enduring.[13] The hardwired reactions that occurred during the event may gradually die down in intensity, sometimes altogether, or they may remain as intense as originally. They may be present continuously, causing a permanently triggered state, or they may occur only when a survivor is specifically reminded of the trauma.

A. Flooding

In experiencing trauma or triggering, strong emotions take over or 'flood' the mind.

B. Dissociation and Flashbacks

When reminders of traumatic events trigger persons to feeling and believing that they are literally reliving the event, completely without awareness that they are not, they are understood to be dissociated. Flashbacks are another extreme, post-trauma, form of dissociation. In contrast, when a person spaces out and is not fully present, this may (or may not) be a trauma symptom; if due to trauma, they are dissociated, such as when individuals do not have detailed or accurate perceptions of their immediate situation and lack a sense of being embodied in the present. If they feel under

[12] SAMHSA, *Trauma-Informed Care*, 118–19.

[13] Briere and Scott, *Principles of Trauma Therapy: A Guide to Symptoms, Evaluation, and Treatment (DSM-5 Update)*, 2nd edn (Thousand Oaks, CA, Sage Publications, 2015) 25.

continual threat, as, for example, do many children growing up in dysfunctional families, dissociation can become a ubiquitous defence mechanism. My reasonably well-functioning adult client, N, had been severely traumatised by verbal abuse and neglect by his divorced mother and his mostly absent alcoholic father. In therapy, he was triggered immediately by being in my presence, a parental figure, and it took him many months to trust me sufficiently to say that he was terrified being in the therapy room. Cognitively aware of being in the room, he did not feel that his body was there. He was partially dissociated.

C. Somatisation

Studies have found lasting biological changes leading to diagnosable medical conditions in trauma survivors.[14] Somatisation, however, refers to psychological stress that produces physical complaints with no plausible medical explanation but rather serve to block conscious remembrance of the trauma.[15] The state commonly manifests as physical symptoms like headaches, chronic pain, and chronic fatigue.[16]

D. Intrusive Thoughts, Images, and Repetitive Nightmares

Traumatised persons may relive the experience repetitively when the same thoughts, images, and nightmares invade the mind (see 'Emotional Dysregulation' below).

E. Silence

Those who have experienced or witnessed extreme traumas like rape, genocide, war, and torture may always remain shut down, not speaking about these events, or not speaking at all. Silence about traumatic experiences frequently signifies the loss of meaning-making capacity and the presence of fear of conscious remembering. Such fears may well be correct to different degrees, depending on context. But remembering them in the presence of understanding human support can help healing.

Some who eventually reveal their fears report that various concerns prevented them from talking about the experience. One common fear is that consciously remembering what happened by speaking of it will mean reliving the event, and thus again being overwhelmed with the terror, horror, grief, humiliation, or shame. Another fear is that speaking endangers the victim, especially with perpetrators who do not want their deeds known and would punish them.[17] Some do not speak because they feel

[14] SAMHSA, *Trauma-Informed Care*, 64.

[15] P Tucker and EA Foote, 'Trauma and the Mind-Body Connection' (2007) *Psychiatric Times*, 1 June, www.psychiatrictimes.com/somatoform-disorder/trauma-and-mind-body-connection (accessed 18 August 2020).

[16] SAMHSA, *Trauma-Informed Care*, 7.

[17] CE Ahrens, 'Being Silenced: The Impact of Negative Social Reactions on the Disclosure of Rape' (2006) 38(3–4) *American Journal of Community Psychology* 263.

guilty, responsible, ashamed, or embarrassed about their own role in the event. Others fear being condemned or punished or marginalized for having survived or for taking advantage of the situation. Some individuals who know but deny a reality yet lack other signs of psychosis may not speak about the event to avoid being known to be aware of it (or them).

Many persons do not speak because they are afraid of not being understood. In a 1996 study of Armenian Americans who survived the Armenian genocide, psychotherapist Dr Anie S Kalayjian and her peers report that 75 per cent had not spoken to anyone about their experiences. They remained silent and isolated, initially out of fear, and then because they felt that talking about their experience created an unbridgeable rift of understanding. 'The ones who witnessed [the Genocide] know about it; the others don't want to know'. The few who did share did so only with others of Armenian descent.[18]

F. Denial

Most silence can be understood as motivated by the conscious or unconscious desire to deny all or part of reality. Elisabeth Kübler-Ross, in *On Death and Dying*,[19] normalised such denial. Denial, she wrote, was the first and usually short-lived reaction to a death, as in 'Oh, no! This can't be true. It cannot be'. Van der Kolk refines this understanding in observing that denial is likely to be only a mental rejection of reality since people's 'bodies register the threat' while 'their conscious minds go on as if nothing has happened'. In this situation, 'even though the mind may learn to ignore the messages from the emotional brain, the alarm signals [involuntary body sensations that] don't stop'.[20]

G. Chronic Despair and Sorrow

Depression and despair are common after trauma. In the following poem, Radmila Lazić, a Serbian survivor of the horrors of the Balkan wars of the 1990s, exemplifies 'chronic sorrow', a concept applied to parents of children with severe, permanent illness or impairment, but also regarding unbearable burdens of permanently and massively tragic situations.[21] She writes of having lost everything and of the multigenerational transmission of the experience (see 'transmitted trauma' below). Her entire physical environment and its spirit have been destroyed. Her losses and injustices are overwhelming. She acknowledges all this in words and thus accepts the reality as such.

[18] AS Kalayjian et al, 'Coping with Ottoman Turkish Genocide: An Exploration of the Experience of Armenian Survivors' (1996) 9(1) *Journal of Traumatic Stress* 93.

[19] E Kübler-Ross, *On Death and Dying: What the Dying Have to Teach Doctors, Nurses, Clergy and Their Own Families* (New York, Simon and Schuster, 1969).

[20] van der Kolk, *The Body Keeps the Score*, 46.

[21] CL Lindgren et al, 'Chronic Sorrow: A Lifespan Concept' (1992) 6(1) *Scholarly Inquiry for Nursing Practice* 27.

Psalm of Despair

I dwell in a land of despair
In the city of despair
Among desperate people
Myself desperate
I embrace my desperate lover
With desperate hands
Whispering desperate words
Kissing him with desperate lips.
In despair we make children
In despair we strangle them
And feed our desperate offspring
With our own despair
So that they may multiply
By giving birth to ever more desperate children
And so on.
For the God of Despair is our Lord
And his envoys of despair
That coat our homes with despair
Drape our windows with despair
And board up our doors with it
As despair rises around us like walls.
Preaching the religion of despair
For gain and wealth
Instructing us in Holy Despair
For which we are to earn life eternal
So our dead will rise again
In despair.
The wandering lamb
That found no path or shelter
No dawn and no mourning
Forever and ever—
Damn you wicked hand
That wrote this in the year of our Lord.[22]

Lazić has integrated her realities into this psalm or narrative of despair, but facing her reality written down brings her pain. Her acceptance suggests she is mourning and making meaning. But she seems to be both struggling to heal and fighting it at

[22] R Lazic, 'Psalm of Despair' in *New York Review of Books* trans C Simic (19 December 2013).

the same time. The latter is implied by the curse she utters against her own voice and pen at the very end. At this point in her life, Lazić remains both in complete despair and acceptance, an uncomfortable place she must stay in and with, if and until that acceptance brings her some moments when she is not in despair.

H. Guilt, Remorse, and Shame

Guilt, remorse, and shame are feelings about something individuals desired to do, or did, but know they should not have done, or about something they failed to do, but know they should have done, or wish they had done. In 'survivor guilt', for example, survivors may feel less worthy than those who died and that they should have been the ones who died. Often they feel responsible for the outcome, even if rationally they know they are not. Similarly, with remorse, survivors believe they could have done something different and wish they had.

A large literature exists about how guilt, remorse, and shame lead to maladaptive attitudes and behaviours. Depression, hopelessness, and bitterness often accompany these emotions and may lead to suicide. Physician and academic George M Weisz studied distinguished Jewish writers who had survived the Holocaust but later committed suicide. He found that they 'suffered from self-incrimination and [felt guilty about] … their inability to communicate the horrors of what had been experienced in the camps, and … prevent the atrocities they had witnessed and their reoccurrence'.[23]

I. Moral Injury

A foundation of all human communities is its code of right and wrong. All children are taught concrete rules of right and wrong and later they probably learn what is considered moral and immoral and perhaps as adults even struggle with conflicts between moral principles (see Chapter 16). Even if the majority of people believe in and conform to basic rules of moral codes, a large percentage deviate, often violating their moral code by engaging in nontrivial immoral behaviours that hurt others.

After observing a particular mental state in soldiers, psychiatrist Jonathan Shay proposed the concept of moral injury, also referred to as 'perpetration-induced trauma, meaning that people experience trauma as a consequence of committing violent acts against others. According to the *Encyclopedia of Psychological Trauma*, ordinary soldiers who follow orders from superiors and kill others universally experience trauma symptoms,[24] including 'unwanted recollections or flashbacks, hyperarousal, nightmares, depression, or "psychic numbing'.[25]

[23] GM Weisz, 'Secondary Guilt Syndrome May Have Led Nazi-Persecuted Jewish Writers to Suicide' (2015) 6(4) *Rambam Maimonides Medical Journal* e0040.
[24] G Reyes et al, *Encyclopedia of Psychological Trauma* (Hoboken, NJ, Wiley, 2008) 467.
[25] Ibid.

Presuming one has developed a conscience, acting against one's moral code leads to bad conscience, admitted or not. Clinical psychologists Shura Maguen and Brett T Litz provide an expanded definition of the term:

> Like psychological trauma, moral injury is a construct that describes extreme and unprecedented life experience including the harmful aftermath of exposure to such events. Events are considered morally injurious if they 'transgress deeply held moral beliefs and expectations'. Thus, the key precondition for moral injury is an act of transgression, which shatters moral and ethical expectations that are rooted in religious or spiritual beliefs, or culture-based, organizational, and group-based rules about fairness, the value of life, and so forth.[26]

Maguen and Litz's expanded definition of moral injury finds that behaving, with or without legitimate instruction, or what is taken as legitimate authorisation, if in conflict with one's conscience, leads to 'moral injury'. Like other traumas, Maguen and Litz find that moral injury has lasting effects on emotions, behaviour, relationships, and meaning making.[27]

Post-trauma the injury can be intensified by having enjoyed imposing it. Sebastian Junger writes about the excitement of war and its later psychological cost:

> War is about a lot of things and it's useless to pretend that exciting isn't one of them. It's insanely exciting … In some ways twenty minutes of combat is more life than you could scrape together in a lifetime of doing something else … The core psychological experiences of war are so primal and unadulterated, however, that they eclipse subtler feelings, like sorrow or remorse, that can gut you quietly for years.[28]

Elspeth Ritchie, a long-time army psychiatrist, similarly observes:

> Especially troubling to the psyche is when the service member enjoyed the act of killing. Commonly secrecy and shame accompany an internal conflict. War crimes may also give rise to a corrosive seepage into the soul.[29]

Moral injury demands more study.

J. Feeling Sanctified and Entitled by Traumatisation

Some trauma survivors believe that their suffering indebts others to them, makes them closer to God, and entitles them to act without accountability.

K. Impaired Memory

Trauma affects memory. Our minds are flooded with emotion, leaving little space for ordered or full detail. Thus, recall can be extraordinarily and verifiably crystal clear,

[26] S Maguen and B Litz, 'Moral Injury in Veterans of War' (2012) 23 *PTSD Research Quarterly* 1, https://pdfs.semanticscholar.org/38c5/d697a34d8e7da3dd82be5d919c45a12e63d8.pdf.

[27] BT Litz et al, 'Moral Injury and Moral Repair in War Veterans: A Preliminary Model and Intervention Strategy' (2009) 29(8) *Clinical Psychology Review* 695, doi.org/10.1016/j.cpr.2009.07.003.

[28] S Junger, *War* (New York, Twelve, 2010) 144, 145.

[29] E Cameron Ritchie, 'Moral Injury: "A Profound Sense of Alienation and Abject Shame"', *Time* (17 April 2013), https://nation.time.com/2013/04/17/moral-injury-a-profound-sense-of-alienation-and-abject-shame/ (accessed 18 July 2020).

but disordered, disjointed, and partial. Aleksandr Solzhenitsyn, chronicler of the Gulag, reports not only his memories but also his flooded mind and resulting memory losses associated with the ongoing torment he went through when imprisoned:

> Throughout the grinding of our souls in the gears of the great Nighttime Institution, when our souls are pulverized and our flesh hangs down in tatters like a beggar's rags, we suffer too much and are too immersed in our own pain to rivet with penetrating and far-seeing gaze those pale night executioners who torture us. A surfeit of inner grief floods our eyes. Otherwise what historians of torturers we would be! ... Every former prisoner remembers his own interrogation in detail, how they squeezed him, and what foulness they squeezed out of him – but often he does not remember their names, let alone think about them as human beings. So it is with me. I can recall much more – and more that's interesting – about any one of my cellmates than I can about Captain of State Security Yezepov, with whom I spent no little time face to face, the two of us alone in his office.[30]

L. Emotional Dysregulation

Subject to intrusive memories, thoughts, and nightmares, trauma survivors often have difficulty regulating their emotions. They may shift from being shut down to emotional expressiveness, from contracting, huddling, isolating, avoiding risks, staying close to what is familiar, to exhibiting emotions, possibly uncontrolled volubility, abruptly bursting out in rage, and then returning to shut down, possibly to abject retreat and whimpering.

This phenomenon in the extreme form was documented by Yesayan after visiting a building occupied by women survivors of the 1909 massacre of Armenians in Adana (see Introduction). She reported that these survivors had 'strangled their babies so that their hiding place would not be betrayed by their infant cries',[31] and later were subject to horrific intrusive thoughts, images, and dreams, and also to emotional dysregulation, taking first the form of numbness or entry into 'freeze', then the opposite:

> Sometimes they seem indifferent, as if the intensity of their grief had turned them to stone. With calm faces on which not a muscle stirs, they recount the dreadful events ... I saw women there who, paralyzed, their tongues lolling on their lips, were unable to cry out their heart's grief ... Then, suddenly, they pause, their eyes gleam with a crazy light – what image has flashed before their mind's eye? – and they shout, besides themselves, clutching at our emotion, imploring help from our tears, from our kindred feelings.[32]

M. Learned Helplessness

Experiencing powerlessness and fear is at the heart of traumatisation and remains present long afterwards. Under non-traumatic circumstances, non-traumatised

[30] A Solzhenitsyn, *The Gulag Archipelago 1918–56* (Boulder, CO, Westview Press, 2002) 144.

[31] Z Yesayan, *In the Ruins: The 1909 Massacres of Armenians in Adana, Turkey*, trans GM Goshgarian (Boston, Armenian International Women's Association, 2016). The tragedy of mothers destroying their children out of terror is also found in another woman's masterpiece, Toni Morrison's *Beloved*.

[32] Ibid, 13.

individuals assume and trust that most of the time they are safe and can protect themselves sufficiently to live their lives without continual anxiety or fear. But when trauma erodes or erases such trust, anxiety takes over. When someone imposes trauma on a defenceless target, the victim not only loses trust, but often feels humiliated, shamed, guilty, and inferior. Victims who do not become conscious of and process these feelings frequently act them out in different forms of aggression, or 'fight', against themselves, others, or both.

According to a now-famous behavioural (not attitudinal) study on 'learned helplessness', carried out on confined dogs but later investigated (differently) in humans, individuals who repeatedly endure inescapable, overpowering, painful, humiliating, and/or shaming situations come to believe that they are helpless and cannot alter their circumstances.[33] My client, E, was 'taught' learned helplessness as a child. She experienced continual abuse and neglect by her alcoholic, violent, single mother. Having lacked control over her life, she felt doomed to suffer and distrusted the world. She then married a man who threatened and abused her in every way while she embodied silent passivity, helplessness, humiliation, pessimism, and depression. She frequently left her husband but always returned, taking the abuse and suffering because he was the only person in her life. E said she loved him, even though he had tried to kill her more than once. She lacked all control over him, but also over herself, because she believed he controlled her very survival as her inadequate mother had. In lacking better experiences she also lacked confidence that she could have anything different. Like an individual, a people, too, can be beaten down and manifest helplessness, passivity, and dependency.

N. General Effects of the Trauma Symptoms on Meaning Making

Many of the symptoms discussed above are more about mental phenomena than actions, some about both. Flooding, nightmares, denial, and intrusive thoughts involve involuntary re-experiencing of the original trauma. However, some symptoms such as dissociation and somatisation represent unconscious ways of avoiding the re-experiencing. Emotional dysregulation involves a cycle of re-experiencing followed by a shutdown. Impaired memory can embrace any or all of these unconscious compulsions of focus on trauma. The various trauma symptoms can be understood as different ways in which the residue of traumatic experiences are cut off from, rather than integrated into, individuals' narratives.[34] Unconscious imposition of one's traumatic memories onto a difficult situation in the present can mislead and interfere with the assessment of the present situation. Gaining awareness of the emotions present in trauma symptoms is an early step in the often emotionally painful but relieving and freeing processing of trauma.

[33] MEP Seligman, 'Learned Helplessness' (1972) 23(1) *Annual Review of Medicine* 407.

[34] GG Noam, '"Normative Vulnerabilities" of Self and Their Transformation into Moral Action' in GG Noam and TE Wren (eds), *The Moral Self* (Cambridge, MA, MIT Press, 1993) 209; D Elsayed et al, 'Anger and Sadness Regulation in Refugee Children: The Roles of Pre- and Post-Migratory Factors' (2019) 50(5) *Child Psychiatry and Human Development*, doi.org/10.1007/s10578-019-00887-4.

III. ARE INDIVIDUALS WITH TRAUMA SYMPTOMS PATHOLOGICAL?

As recently as 2011, Shay still felt the need to write, 'For years I have agitated against the diagnostic jargon "post-traumatic stress disorder" because transparently we are dealing with an injury, not an illness, malady, disease, sickness, or disorder'.[35] Today most clinicians consider the effects of trauma to be normal, if sometimes maladaptive, responses to abnormal situations.[36] They correctly understand that individuals' symptoms are the result of very painful and challenging situations. At the same time, there is recognition that responses are also shaped by inner forces not necessarily related to a specific or repeated traumatic experience (see Chapter 1).

IV. COPING STRATEGIES: CONSCIOUS AND UNCONSCIOUS

After trauma, coping strategies help with functioning. These strategies are attitudinal and behavioural, like the symptoms with which they overlap.

A. Repetition Compulsion

Other things being equal, once victimised, individuals are more likely to be revictimised than non-victims are to be victimised.[37] Those children subjected to physical and sexual abuse, including rape and incest, are disproportionately made up of girls,[38] and are disproportionately likely to be victims of violence and abuse again as adults.[39]

Repetition compulsion is an involuntary, unconscious, or semi-conscious, compelled tragic coping strategy. Such individuals are primed to be reactive if presented with any type of reminder of the trauma, reliving it repetitively. As with E, for example, battered women manifest a pattern of undergoing abuse, leaving the abuser, returning, undergoing abuse, submitting, leaving, and so forth. Repetitive behaviour is also, of course, the rule in pleasure seeking. However, what demands explanation is repetition of what is painful, terrifying, destructive, and hurtful. Why would traumatised individuals repeat their traumatic experiences? Repetition of painful experience seems to occur for the same reason as repetitive nightmares – to change the past or correct our relationship to it.[40] Processing trauma unconsciously

[35] J Shay, 'Casualties' (2011) 140(3) *Daedalus* 179.

[36] SAMHSA, *Trauma-Informed Care*, 13.

[37] van der Kolk et al, *Traumatic Stress*, 199.

[38] 'Twice as many women with a history of incest as women without such a history reported physical violence in their marriages (27%), and more than twice as many (53%) reported unwanted sexual advances by an unrelated authority figure, such as a teacher, clergyman, or therapist. Victims of father-daughter incest were four times more likely than others to report being asked to pose for pornography … People who were abused as children (many of whom learned to blame themselves early for the violence around them) are particularly likely to become partners in abusive relationships later': BA van der Kolk, 'The Complexity of Adaptation to Trauma' in BA van der Kolk et al (eds), *Traumatic Stress* (New York, Guilford Press, 1996/2007) 199–200.

[39] See, eg, van der Kolk et al, *Traumatic Stress*.

[40] A Adams-Silvan and M Silvan, '"A Dream Is the Fulfillment of a Wish": Traumatic Dream, Repetition Compulsion, and the Pleasure Principle' (1990) 71(3) *International Journal of Psychoanalysis* 513.

in such repetition can be replaced by conscious processing – that is, gaining awareness of these matters, usually by putting the awareness into words, so that, in the face of the impulse or compulsion to repeat, we change our behaviour.

B. Revenge-Taking and Scapegoating

Desiring revenge is neurologically hardwired, a protective 'fight' response enabling the mobilisation of energy to defend and hit back after an offence. Experiencing traumatic threats and wounds leads to the desire, conscious or unconscious, for revenge even after insignificant infractions or rejections, which lead to a much modified revenge desire for getting back at someone or something. Nearly 4,000 years ago, justice was understood as 'an eye for an eye' and acquired the imprimatur of law in the Hammurabi legal code. Today many of us are taught to modulate the impulse for revenge. For many the result is that 'with sufficient self-control it's altogether possible to talk yourself down from reactive rage' and taking revenge.[41] Being able to do so indicates the existence of an imperfectly defined and understood but critical space between the brain's automatic demands during trauma (and afterwards) and the mind's freedom to decide whether and how to respond to the compulsions. Minor infractions may get their day outside court through, for example, sneaky little – and perfectly legal – paybacks.

If our minds remain in a strongly reactive mode, however, we may act out our vengefulness. If we judge that the object of our revenge is not within our reach, for whatever reason, we may take it out on an innocent – usually less powerful – party, a scapegoat. Scapegoating is often misplaced revenge. After a tough day with the boss at the office, the worker comes home and kicks the family dog. After a tough argument with a spouse at breakfast, the boss comes into the office and yells at the administrative assistant. It must be stressed that, while scapegoating exemplifies a situation in which emotions replace rationality, morally injuring the actor, as well as injuring the scapegoat, being 'rational' without an understanding of the role of emotions in our actions can be equally injurious in these situations. '[W]hat rationality actually involves is not letting emotions take over in place of reason'.[42] Reason should not repress emotions but enable us to evaluate them in a larger picture. It bears repeating that emotions indicate what matters to the *actor*, and may or may not have anything to do with the punished object.

C. Seeking Justice, Seeking Revenge

In general, seeking revenge is a destructive coping strategy and seeking justice is a constructive coping strategy. Psychologist Leon F Selzer finds that seeking justice

[41] LF Seltzer, 'Don't Confuse Revenge with Justice: Five Biggest Problems with Revenge and Their Best Remedies', *Psychology Today*, 22 January 2014.

[42] M Hurd, 'The Psychology of Anger and Revenge', *Capitalism Magazine*, 15 August 2002, www.capitalismmagazine.com/2002/08/the-psychology-of-anger-and-revenge/ (accessed 18 July 2020).

stems from the desire to right wrongs 'based on cultural or community standards of fairness and equity'. Rather than inflicting pain to equalise suffering, justice is about 'righting a wrong that most members of society (as opposed to simply the alleged victim) would agree is morally culpable'.[43] Thus, whether one is seeking revenge or justice, laws set common standards about what it is and is not permissible to do in many realms of life, and also lay out the consequences for infractions. Collectively, seeking justice is generally and widely assumed to be about improving societal structures, including the enactment of more just laws.

However, there are many kinds of situations when individuals seek justice and/or revenge outside the law. Sometimes those actions are accepted as legitimate and other times they are not. One such instance is when individuals are flooded with strong, fear-based emotions that compromise their ability to make careful assessments[44] – at such times what the law dictates may be overridden. Another kind of instance is when, in a de facto lawless, or relatively lawless, physical space, modulation is frequently overridden. Sometimes laws are simply unjust and not traceable to universal moral precepts like the golden rule; in such situations individuals, whether or not flooded with emotions, may override legal dictates in the name of those universal precepts. Thus, exacting revenge by taking the law into one's own hands is at times judged to be part of justice seeking.

The case of the Ottoman Armenian Soghomon Tehlirian can be seen as uniting the act of taking revenge and the act of obtaining justice into what might be called 'rough justice' or 'just revenge'. Tehlirian lost 85 family members in the genocide. After World War I, the Allies encouraged the establishment of a court in Istanbul to try those responsible for war crimes. To avoid trial, Mehmet Talât, the head of the Ottoman wartime cabinet and primary architect of the Armenian genocide, fled to Europe. Three years later in 1921 in Berlin, Tehlirian assassinated Talât in broad daylight. The German Foreign Office was not interested in seeing the case escalate into a 'political matter', and the Berlin jury, whether swayed by medical testimony attesting that Tehlirian was not in full possession of his mental faculties at the time of the murder, or sympathetic with the defendant's plight, or both, acquitted him of murder.[45]

V. PROCESSING TRAUMA

Unacknowledged, painful, buried past events are more likely to compel our actions and we become more likely to take revenge into our own hands. Individuals with a repressed history of painful rejection, for example, may live apart from others and eventually act out violently against innocent people, such as the perpetrator of the Sandy Hook school shooting in the US.[46] Repression, a form of denial, is not helpful

[43] Ibid.

[44] BA van der Kolk, 'The Compulsion to Repeat the Trauma: Re-enactment, Revictimization, and Masochism' (1989) 12(2) *Psychiatric Clinics of North America* 389.

[45] T Hofmann, 'New Aspects of the Talât Pasha Court Case: Unknown Archival Documents on the Background and Procedure of an Unintended Political Trial' (1989) 42 *Armenian Review* 41.

[46] 'Nation Reels After Gunman Massacres 20 Children at School in Connecticut,' *The New York Times*, 14 December 2012.

in controlling impulses for revenge. One kind of result may, instead, be displacement onto a weaker party, as apparently happened in Sandy Hook. On the other hand, if emotions have been processed and understood, use of lawful processes such as justice seeking, may serve as a helpful coping strategy in controlling impulses for revenge, if such control is a person or a people's aim. In recent years, advances in healing trauma have successfully combined those foci with that on body sensations to gain distance and perspective on ourselves and the events, enabling informed functioning.[47]

Recovery, to the extent possible, by whatever form achieved, requires processing the traumatic experience to achieve awareness and acceptance. Gaining awareness of symptoms is painful, but is very rewarding because it makes possible genuine, deep acceptance and relief. Acceptance has nothing to do with approving what happened, but is acknowledgment of fact. Together, awareness and acceptance facilitate the adoption of productive coping strategies, defined as bringing reasoning, emotions, and values together.

Thus, the healing that is possible is only accomplished by the exercise of human will, choosing to engage with and commit to uncomfortable work. Part of the processing of trauma, and recovery from it, also then takes place through choosing what to act on. Gaining such consciousness also gives us free rein to accept consciously and without guilt fantasies of taking revenge on a perpetrator. Such fantasies harm no one. Hiding the desires from ourselves in denial means having less control over their effects, especially when triggered.

In sum, when repressed memories contract our meaning making, the traumatic event, so important in our lives, remains outside of our awareness even to ourselves. But, if admitted to ourselves and processed internally or with others, we may then integrate it into our personal narrative about who we are and want to be.

VI. TRANSMITTED TRAUMA

Traumatised individuals frequently transmit their experience to others across space or time, often through silence. Trauma expert and clinical psychologist Yael Danieli writes about the combined effects of societal and individual silence:

> Because silence … most often follows the trauma, it is the most prevalent and effective mechanism for the transmission of trauma on all dimensions. Both intrapsychically and interpersonally protective, silence is profoundly destructive, for it attests to the person's, family's, society's, community's, and nation's inability to integrate the trauma. They can find no words to narrate the trauma story and create a meaningful dialogue around it.[48]

[47] There is now a body of literature and some controlled studies on this approach. See for example the recent work of van der Kolk, Peter Levine, Lawrence Heller, Gian Ross, and the backing in neuro-biology such as Danny Brom et al and DA Dana.

[48] Y Danieli, 'Assessing Trauma across Cultures from a Multigenerational Perspective' in JP Wilson and CS Tang (eds), *Cross-Cultural Assessment of Psychological Trauma and PTSD*, International and Cultural Psychology Series (Boston, Springer, 2007) 66.

Parent to child transmission can unconsciously assign others the task of making up for that person's own losses, and possibly taking vengeance on their behalf.[49] These assignments may create epigenetic changes that are 'not in the genes themselves but in the structure of the DNA and in the RNA'.[50] When trauma is thus transmitted, the child's development of a separate sense of self may be compromised.[51] Individuals or groups to whom the trauma is transmitted may also feel shame, humiliation, and helplessness.[52] They, too, may not process the trauma and will probably externalise it, passing it along to others.[53] According to psychologist and traumatologist Natan PF Kellermann, survivors may thus create ghettoised families:

> In such highly closed systems parents are fully committed to their children and children are overly concerned with their parents' welfare, each trying to shield the other from painful experiences ... Parents like this, who care too much and who become overly involved and intrusive, tend to enmesh their offspring in the crossfire of their own emotional problems and bind their children unto themselves in a manner that makes it difficult for the children to gain independence.[54]

Kalayjian and social worker Miriam Weisberg examined the generational impact of transmitted trauma on Armenian-American descendants of genocide survivors.[55] They found that the majority were

> saddled with a sense of forced responsibility for carrying the memories and helping their ancestors. [They expressed] deep and intense feelings of helplessness on many levels: personal, collective, and global. Much of this helplessness centered on the persistent Turkish denial of the Genocide'.[56]

The two also reported that participants were angry because they felt helpless and powerless, having been brought up not to trust anyone outside their own families.[57] Marian Mesrobian MacCurdy, the Armenian-American granddaughter of two sets of survivors, vividly recalls messages she received growing up:

> My father's parents ... survived the Hamidian massacres by fleeing – my grandfather into the woods and my grandmother with her infant daughter [Elizabeth] in her arms to the American mission. Years later she echoed for my father the high-pitched screams of the Turks as they charged through Kharpert, swords and scimitars raised. Elizabeth, my grandmother, died before I was born, but I can still hear those chilling sounds my father relayed to me.

[49] MG Fromm, 'Treatment Resistance and the Transmission of Trauma' in MG Fromm (ed), *Lost in Transmission: Studies of Trauma across the Generations* (London, Karnac Books, 2012) 113.

[50] J Gordon, *The Transformation* (New York, Harper and Collins, 2019) 235.

[51] I Kogan, 'The Second Generation in the Shadow of the Terror' in Fromm, *Lost in Transmission: Studies of Trauma across the Generations*, 15.

[52] V Volkan, 'Bosnia-Herzegovina: Ancient Fuel of a Modern Inferno' (1996) 7 *Mind and Human Interaction* 110.

[53] Ibid, 3.

[54] NPF Kellerman, 'Transmission of Holocaust Trauma – An Integrative View' (2001) 64(3) *Psychiatry* 262.

[55] A Kalayjian and M Weisberg, 'Generational Impact of Mass Trauma: The Post-Ottoman Turkish Genocide of the Armenians' in JS Piven et al (eds), *Jihad and Sacred Vengeance: Psychological Undercurrents of History*, vol 3 (Lincoln, NE, Writers Club Press, 2002) 254.

[56] Ibid, 269.

[57] Ibid.

> The family … [was] forced into the role of victim [and] became fearful and anxious. My father often said, 'There are only two things in life you have to do: die and pay your taxes'. Other than that one chilling Turkish yell Elizabeth mimicked for my father, she remained silent, her resistance evidenced only by her survival. They lived in fear of the streets of Detroit – not to mention the trauma they carried from the massacres – and their son inhaled this like tomato plants suck up water. When I as a teenager asked to use the family car, my sweet, fearful father's perennial response was, 'Why? Do you have to go out?'
>
> 'No, Dad, I don't have to. I want to'.
>
> 'Well, if you go out, something bad could happen to you. If you stay home, nothing bad will'.[58]

VII. MORAL INJURY AND REPETITION COMPULSION IN INDIVIDUAL OFFICIAL AND NON-OFFICIAL POLICY MAKERS

Why do individual policy makers in powerful states or organisations resort to one or another form of murderous power to settle things? Are they themselves thereby morally injured? Are they then part of an immoral, or morally injured societal structure? Processing traumatic threats, such as to assumed entitlements, must be incorporated into policy-making in order to replace exercise of the fight response with the arbitrary, if not murderous, exercise of power. To those with the impulse, murderousness generally means something deep and important, even if layered over by years of one or another pretense, and can and needs to be processed. Individuals with greater power in a situation can process their fears and wounds in consciously chosen contexts and rein them in and using their organisation's ability to act quickly and destructively as a way of protecting 'national security' or another often inchoate, catch-all rationale or excuse. Better instead engage in the slower and uncomfortable task of talking about the threats and fears involved with individuals who would provide new perspectives.

*

Some of the symptoms of trauma in individuals and some of the coping strategies presented in this chapter were illustrated in collective situations. In the next chapter, the focus is on those situations and the effect of collective traumas on whole peoples.

[58] M Mesrobian MacCurdy, 'Resistance and Resilience', *Armenian Weekly*, 22 June 2015, https://armenianweekly.com/2015/06/22/resistance-and-resilience/ (accessed 18 July 2020).

3

Some Distinctive Aspects of Collective Trauma

CHAPTERS 1 AND 2 explored psychological trauma primarily at the individual level. This chapter aims to present generalities about collective trauma. It begins with condensed, close to abstract illustrations of collective trauma in Rwanda, Hungary, Israel/Palestine, and Indonesia, places, peoples, and situations little addressed elsewhere in this book. In all these situations, at one or another time, one people or group imposed its will violently on another. The illustrations are as brief as possible in order to make certain patterns stand out and thus make similar patterns more recognisable in Parts II and III, where they are shown embedded and contextualised in the history of Armenian, Turkish, and Azerbaijani relations. This chapter then identifies general characteristics of collective traumas. It concludes by adding to the introduction's brief theoretical discussion of the relationship between the individual and collective.

I. COLLECTIVE TRAUMA ON FOUR CONTINENTS

A. Rwanda: When Victims/Survivors became Génocidaires (Genocidiers)

At the end of World War I, Belgian colonialists took over Rwanda and ruled its two main populations, the majority Hutus and the minority Tutsis. The Belgians favoured and elevated the Tutsis for their own reasons, a partiality that later helped account for the extreme enmity that opened up between the two indigenous groups. Meanwhile, the Tutsis joined the colonisers in oppressing and discriminating against the Hutus. But in the 1950s, Hutu nationalism gained strength, threatening the Tutsis who proved unwilling to share their power and privilege with the Hutus. The Hutus soon claimed exclusive entitlement to power. The Tutsis were now endangered and many were killed, while others fled to neighbouring countries. Independence from Belgium was achieved in 1962 in the midst of this turbulence, which continued until 1990 when Tutsi refugees returned and initiated civil strife in a country now under exclusive autocratic Hutu rule. Relations between the groups deteriorated. In 1994, the governing Hutus, fiercely determined not to give up or share power with Tutsis, carried out a genocide against them and moderate Hutus.

Mahmood Mamdani, a political scientist, anthropologist, and historian of the Rwandan genocide, regards the beginning of the Hutu violence as itself a 'counter' to violence, an empowering reaction, or coping strategy, to the traumatising policies imposed by the Belgians. 'Faced with the violent denial of his humanity by the settler, the native's violence began as a counter to violence … violence by yesterday's victims, resulting in the genocidiers' decision to empower themselves'.[1] Also, the Hutus feared, says Mamdani, being forced back into servitude under the Tutsis.[2] He argues that what distinguished native Hutu violence from the violence of the settler was that yesterday's victims decided to cast aside their victimhood and become masters of their own lives.[3] The situation remains unresolved today, seemingly immune to many efforts to improve relations.

B. Moral Injury at the End of World War II in Hungary

The film *1945* is a fictional portrait of a tiny Hungarian village inhabited by Christians and Jews at the moment of the arrival of Nazi troops. The Christians witness the soldiers forcibly sending the Jewish inhabitants to concentration camps, leaving behind their homes and possessions, a situation that was common as World War II was drawing to an end. Anna Ornstein and her mother might have been among them (see Chapter 1). The villagers realise that the Jews' property has been left unprotected. The head of the village is shown quietly scheming and taking what he wants for himself rather guiding the villagers about what not to do. Soon lawlessness prevails. Most of the villagers seize Jewish properties, and intently watch one another's moves. A few disapprove and a few others are ambivalent.

At the war's end, two Jews wearing distinctive Orthodox attire unexpectedly arrive at the train station located outside the village. Upon seeing them, the station attendant rushes to his bicycle and speeds off along the foot and bike path through the fields to the village to spread news of their arrival. Hearing this, the villagers panic, some reacting angrily, others 'freezing.' Some hide their looted goods. One commits suicide.

Meanwhile, the two Jews walk slowly to the village's main street along the same country path to the former Jewish quarter, never greeting anyone, never looking around, never speaking to each other. The villagers watch, but not a single villager shows recognition of them. When the two reach the empty Jewish quarter, they silently bury a few personal objects they had brought with them in the graveyard behind the deserted synagogue, thereby revealing why they returned. Still silent, they walk back to the train station.

When the villagers realise that the Jews had not come to reclaim their property, some indicate that they will keep what they have taken amd others that they are torn between guilt and desire to hold onto their takings. But those who instigated the

[1] M Mamdani, *When Victims Become Killers: Colonialism, Nativism, and the Genocide in Rwanda* (Princeton, NJ, Princeton University Press, 2001) 10.

[2] Mamdani, *When Victims Become Killers*, 233.

[3] Mamdani, *When Victims Become Killers*, 13.

looting in the first place suddenly lose all standing in the village. One villager, shown earlier to have been enraged by the looting, now sets fire to the largest and most public Jewish property, the village general store, seemingly compelled to express his strong feelings and impotence in his fight response. The fire spreads. All watch, transfixed in horror and helplessness. Some visibly fear being found out, punished, and losing what they have taken. In the end, not only is property destroyed, but so is the unwritten pact of trust that had bound the villagers together.

The traumatic removal of the Jews led most non-Jewish villagers, including its head, to reshape their 'mental organisation',[4] or understanding of acceptable behaviour. The removal of the Jews and the failure of village leadership gives the villagers licence to steal with impunity, and most do, destroying their prior understanding of right and wrong, shattering trusting communal bonds, and morally injuring them. Their relationships with each other are changed. They see each other differently. Sociologist Jeffrey C Alexander understands an event that so destabilises prior understandings, which he calls 'cultural trauma,' as putting 'the collective's identity at stake.'[5] Who are we? Can we look one another in the eye? If the Jews were to return to live in the village, could we live together again? How would we relate?

These questions ask what meaning those involved made of these collective traumas, which thereafter transforms, as social psychologist Gilad Hirschberger says, 'into a collective memory' and 'culminates in a system of meaning that allows groups to redefine who they are and where they are going'.[6] What today is Hungary's identity? Does its current right-wing autocratic and anti-Semitic government reflect its identity? Has its collective meaning making embraced the country's past collusion with Nazi Germany?

C. Transmitted Trauma and Scapegoating in Israel/Palestine

On the whole, Jews who survived the camps did not return to such villages. Large numbers migrated to Palestine, then formally 'Mandatory Palestine' under British control, others to elsewhere in Europe and the Americas. Having been engaged in their own national movement for independence for years, the Palestinians opposed the Jewish national movement. They had not invited the Jews to establish the state there, nor had they been consulted. During the 1947–1948 wars, David Ben-Gurion declared the birth of the state of Israel. The Jews soon prevailed over the Palestinians and their Arab allies. They drove some 800,000 Palestinians out and into neighbouring Arab states and territories. A sizeable minority remained in Israel and today constitute about 20 per cent of the state's citizens. Over the next two decades, Palestinian and other Arabs challenged the state of Israel's right to exist. Supported by American funding, Israel, today regarded as a settler colonialist

[4] R Scholz, 'Collective Trauma, Memories, and Identity' (lecture, International Association for Group Psychotherapy Trauma and Identity Workshop, Sarajevo, 10 May 2014) 2–3.

[5] JC Alexander et al, *Cultural Trauma and Collective Identity* (Berkeley, University of California, 2004) 10.

[6] G Hirschberger, 'Collective Trauma and the Social Construction of Meaning' (2018) 9 *Frontiers in Psychology* 1441, doi:10.3389/fpsyg.2018.01441.

state by Palestinians and others, maintained and expanded the state with military force that became more and more formidable. Today, Palestinians in the occupied West Bank as well as in Gaza live under military occupation, where they are denied fundamental human rights. The Palestinians of Gaza enjoy a very limited form of independence but are largely controlled by Israel.

Decades ago, Germany, after being forced to acknowledge some of its wartime crimes in the Nuremberg trials, began to come to terms with its past, officially acknowledging, in textbooks and memorials, and by paying reparations to the state of Israel, the crimes committed in the Holocaust. Because of the significant steps that the country took, which also included some collective processing of its past, Nazis no longer dominate Germany. The country is not so traumatised and shamed by its past as it once was when it denied or hid it and maintains amicable relations with Israel. However, today many Israeli Jews, and many Jews in the diaspora, still have not, as a community, processed the transmitted Holocaust trauma. The former speaker of the Knesset, Avraham Burg, writes that instead Israel adopted a 'legacy of insecurity characteristic of trauma victims. We have become a nation of victims, and our state religion is the worship and tending of traumas'.[7]

Disproportionate response to real threats and 'jumping the gun' can be trauma symptoms. When so, it indicates that people's brains and minds are triggered to overwhelming threats and destruction from the past, often leading to overreaction in the present. Under certain governments, Israel has exaggerated threats and then responded with excessive force, using the opportunity to destroy or seize Palestinian property with two assumed entitlements, one being the might to do it and the other being the immense past suffering, understood as justifying such measures. Having now awarded itself the power to act righteously with little restraint, Israel continues to act to seize much of what belonged to Palestinians and control the fate of their collective possibility. As Burg puts it:

> We live under constant pressure … unceasing armament to compensate and atone for built-in impotence and existential anxiety. A state that lives by the sword and worships its dead is bound to live in a constant state of emergency, because everyone is a Nazi, everyone is an Arab, everyone hates us, the entire world is against us.[8]

The state of Israel, founded for the long-suffering and traumatised Jewish people, has become a perpetrator of collective trauma against the Palestinians, thereby themselves incurring moral injury. Writer, politician, and peace-maker, Uri Avnery saw with great clarity and depth this tragic outcome of the Holocaust trauma:

> I will tell you something about the Holocaust … it would be nice to believe that people who have undergone suffering have been purified by suffering. But it's the opposite, it makes them worse. It corrupts. There is something in suffering that creates a kind of egoism. Herzog [the Israeli president] was speaking at the site of the concentration camp at Bergen-Belsen but he spoke only about the Jews. How could he not mention that others – many others – had suffered there? Sick people, when they are in pain, cannot speak about anyone but themselves. And when such monstrous things have happened to your people,

[7] A Burg, *The Holocaust Is Over: We Must Rise from Its Ashes* (New York, Palgrave Macmillan, 2008) 76.
[8] Burg, *The Holocaust Is Over*, 24.

> you feel nothing can be compared to it. You get a moral power-of-attorney, a permit to do anything you want – because nothing can compare with what has happened to us. This is a moral immunity which is very clearly felt in Israel.[9]

D. Indonesia: A Primary Perpetrator Begins to Come to Terms

In 1965–66, the government of Indonesia employed gangsters, hitmen, and paramilitaries to carry out a genocide against approximately one million suspected communists 'with the direct aid of Western governments'.[10] At first, Indonesia celebrated the crimes, but then came silence. Decades later, Joshua Oppenheimer travelled to Indonesia to make a distinctive film with some of the leading perpetrators as co-directors. Reenactments were staged and filmed.[11] *The Act of Killing* (2012) is a unique documentary about this dark chapter in Indonesia's history.

After the killings ended, Anwar, one of the leading mass murderers and the film's chief character, enjoyed living freely in Indonesia along with other perpetrators, as did many Nazis in Germany after the Holocaust, many leading perpetrators in Turkey after the Armenian genocide, and many leading American advocates and supporters of the Vietnam and Iraq wars. In the film Anwar plays himself, repeatedly and lightheartedly expressing pride and pleasure in his actions. Then, abruptly he turns to the camera and says, 'I try to forget these things. I dance, I drink, I take drugs, and I feel happy. I know my bad dreams came from killing people who didn't want to die'. Later, he decides to act the part of one of his victims as he kills him. As he does, he looks at the camera and remarks that, for the very first time, he feels their terror. Anwar seems to feel compassion and retrieves his conscience after having consciously revisited, through a staged reenactment, another's fatal trauma, but also his own – albeit not fatal – trauma.

The film led to acknowledgment of the atrocities and opened up a new space for conversation among Indonesians and a public demand for accountability. In a 2014 opinion piece for *The Guardian*, '*The Act of Killing* Has Helped Indonesia Reassess Its Past and Present', filmmaker Joshua Oppenheimer wrote:

> The film has had exactly the impact the survivors hoped for. It has been screened thousands of times in Indonesia, and is available for free online. The media and public alike are now able, for the first time without fear, to investigate the genocide as a genocide – and to debate the links between the moral catastrophe of the killings and the moral catastrophe of the present-day regime built, and still presided over, by the killers.[12]

[9] Quoted in R Fisk, *Pity the Nation: The Abduction of Lebanon* (New York, Nation Books, 2003) 394.

[10] I Buruma, 'The Violent Mysteries of Indonesia', *New York Review of Books*, 22 October 2015, www.nybooks.com/articles/2015/10/22/violent-mysteries-indonesia/ (accessed 20 July 2020).

[11] It is at least as close to reality as the two classic, shocking, famous experiments conducted by social science researchers Stanley Milgram (*Obedience to Authority* (New York, Harper and Row, 1974)) and Philip G Zimbardo (*Prison Experiment: A Simulation Study of the Psychology of Imprisonment* (Philip G Zimbardo, 1972)).

[12] J Oppenheimer, 'The Act of Killing Has Helped Indonesia Reassess Its Past and Present', *Guardian*, 25 February 2014, www.theguardian.com/commentisfree/2014/feb/25/the-act-of-killing-indonesia-past-present-1965-genocide (accessed 20 July 2020).

The screening was a breakthrough, but Oppenheimer's assessment may have been too optimistic, given recent developments. As yet the Indonesian government, an anonymous expert claims, has not apologised or investigated, actions now probably more unlikely with the rise of Salafi Islamism.

II. SOCIETY'S SHATTERED FABRIC

As with individual trauma, in collective trauma, as psychologist Marcelo M Suárez-Orozco and anthropologist Antonius CGM Robben put it, victims have had to 'surrender to helplessness' because they are overwhelmed by outside forces humiliating and destroying them.[13] Sociologist Kai Erikson, perhaps the first scholar to differentiate collective from individual trauma in 1976, saw collective trauma as the destruction of both the psychological bonds and material resources that unite a community, and enable it to function and function humanely, because 'the prevailing sense of communality' has been lost.[14] Not only might everything material that supported community or public life – farms, places of worship, homes, power generators, workplaces, roads, train tracks, airports, water resources, schools, hospitals, and government buildings – become untenable. Not only, apart from those who are dead, might many others who lived, worked in, and depended on these resources, if alive, be sick and disabled.[15] Not only may family units and women and children individually be disastrously damaged and whole communities destroyed by the weapon of rape. Psychologist John Ehrenrich conveys this immensity of disruption and destruction in traditional societies of 'hundreds of thousands, or even millions, of people … entire villages, and traditional ways of life … preexisting social structures, social roles, social arrangements and rituals', … [and] 'other massive upheavals in human relationships and activities and in culture itself'.[16] The total effect in any society, in Hirschberger's single word, is 'cataclysmic' because, he explains, collective trauma 'shatters the basic fabric of society'.[17]

If all this takes place as the original trauma unfolds, it could not end there. And it rarely does. Collective trauma is transmitted through time and space. In 2010, Hatsantour Karenian et al published a cross-sectional study of 689 residents of Greece and Cyprus who belonged to a community of about 20,000 descendants of refugee survivors of the Armenian genocide. The study assessed whether the descendants showed signs as individuals of trauma related to the Armenian genocide.[18]

[13] M Suárez-Orozco and ACGM Robben, 'Interdisciplinary Perspectives on Violence and Trauma' in ACGM Robben and MM Suárez-Orozco (eds), *Cultures under Siege: Collective Violence and Trauma* (Cambridge, Cambridge University Press, 2000) 15–18.

[14] K Erikson, *Destruction of Community in the Buffalo Creek Flood* (New York, Simon & Schuster, 1976) 153–54.

[15] Ehrenreich, 'Understanding PTSD, Forgetting "Trauma"', 19.

[16] Ehrenreich, 'Understanding PTSD, Forgetting "Trauma"', 19.

[17] Hirschberger, 'Collective Trauma and the Social Construction of Meaning', 1441.

[18] H Karenian et al, 'Collective Trauma Transmission and Traumatic Reactions among Descendants of Armenian Refugees' (2010) 57(4) *International Journal of Social Psychiatry* 327, doi:10.1177/0020764009354840.

The investigators found that more than one-third reported various trauma symptoms frequently present throughout their lives. Those with more intense symptoms reported a stronger connection to the Armenian community than others. The authors conclude that 'almost a century later, the negative consequences along with forms of positive elaboration of the same traumatic experience though fading from generation to generation are still present, active and widespread'.[19]

The four situations presented at the beginning of this chapter also made evident that the experience of collective trauma was transmitted to individuals and collectivities across space and/or time. Trauma victims'/survivors' children and others close to them take in the effects from those who were directly involved, internalising the emotions and attitudes in their narratives. When Danieli surveyed 32 populations around the world,[20] she learned that transgenerational trauma influences whole families in generations other than that of the original trauma victims, as well as whole nations worldwide, and 'shapes the collective experience of an entire generation, fundamentally altering the fabric of culture and society'.[21]

The dynamics of the situation to be described in this book have lasted for decades. They exist now. Israeli social psychologist Eran Halperin, surely speaking of living in Israel, describes what is it like to live under traumatic threat for a very long time, giving rise to the still entitled and immoral dynamic manifested today by, it appears, the majority of its people, and unquestionably by the Israeli state:

> ... this continuous and chronic feeling of personal and collective fear is difficult or even impossible for outsiders to understand. People who are not living in such contexts cannot really imagine how it feels to be concerned constantly about mere personal survival, that of your close ones, and sometimes even your entire society ... [T]ry to think of societies that experience these feelings continuously for dozens of years rather than just for a few weeks.[22]

III. ONE BASELINE FOR COLLECTIVE RECOVERY: SHORING UP COLLECTIVE IDENTITY

Under non-threatening circumstances, members of a people are generally aware of and enjoy the sense of protection accorded by their shared identity, however defined, but may pay it little attention. Under threat they pull together, enjoy shared patriotism

[19] Karenian et al, 'Collective Trauma Transmission and Traumatic Reactions among Descendants of Armenian Refugees', 1–2. A limitation of this study, which the authors acknowledge, was that it used a survey instrument designed to measure the direct impact of a personal trauma (experienced first-hand) rather than one transmitted over generations.

[20] Y Danieli, 'It Was Always There' in C Figley (ed), *Mapping Trauma and Its Wake: Autobiographic Essays by Pioneer Trauma Scholars*, Brunner-Rutledge Psychosocial Stress Book Series (New York, Routledge, 2006) 44, and in her edited *International Handbook of Multigenerational Legacies of Trauma* (New York, Springer Series on Stress and Coping, 1998).

[21] Danieli, 'It Was Always There', 44.

[22] E Halperin, *Emotions in Conflict: Inhibitors and Facilitators of Peace Making* (New York, Routledge, 2015).

and the empowering 'fight' response to having a common enemy. (The psychoanalyst and political psychologist Vamik Volkan finds a universal psychological need for a people to have an enemy in order to define and claim its distinctiveness.[23]) When violence comes, however, along with excitement for some (acknowledged by Sebastian Junger when speaking of the extreme excitement of the experience on the battlefield (Chapter 2)), there is also the realisation for most, as Hirschberger put it, that 'the value of human life is often reduced to nothing',[24] making the vulnerability of life very real to them. Afterwards, survivors focus on their individual survival but also on collective survival. 'It is at these times in particular', Hirschberger continues, 'that the collective self becomes invaluable; it substitutes the frustrated need for individual life with the promise that the collective will endure and survive over time'.[25] The heightened awareness of human vulnerability from trauma helps a group to regain a sense of community, says Hirschberger, leading 'to a re-evaluation of the resilience, durability, and importance of the collective'.[26]

Thus, a group's rituals and traditions become very significant as they are used to rebuild the broken bonds of the collective. After the Armenian genocide, family therapist Sarine Boyadjian observes how Armenians' rituals and traditions became central to community maintenance:

> [W]ith each event, we consciously or subconsciously pay tribute to the 1.5 million lives lost ... our beautiful and elaborate weddings become slightly more joyful when the unity is between two Armenians ... Each joyous ritual carries a significant subtext: keep the memory of your ancestors alive, ... perpetuate our people, remain Armenian for we are few ... but we sure are mighty.[27]

IV. COLLECTIVE AND INDIVIDUAL IDENTITY

Obviously, 'a collective and 'an individual' designate different hard realities, 'collective' designating 'many' persons and 'individual' just one. In that sense, collective trauma can be said to designate the state of traumatisation prevailing in its members individually. Although that is only a part of collective trauma, it is a very important part because the fact remains that much more is known psychologically about individual than collective trauma, as the political scientist Lucian Pye pointed out two decades ago.[28] But, as this chapter shows, collective trauma is much more than the manifestations of trauma in its members.

[23] V Volkan, *The Need for Enemies and Allies: From Clinical Practice to International Relations* (New Jersey, Jason Aronson, 1998).

[24] Hirschberger, 'Collective Trauma and the Social Construction of Meaning'.

[25] Hirschberger, 'Collective Trauma and the Social Construction of Meaning'.

[26] Hirschberger, 'Collective Trauma and the Social Construction of Meaning'.

[27] S Boyadjian, 'Haytoug Preview: The Psychological Impact of the Armenian Genocide,' Asbarez 13 October 2016. Accessed 20 December 2020. https://anca.org/haytoug-preview-the-psychological-impact-of-the-armenian-genocide/.

[28] L Pye, 'Traumatized Political Cultures: The After Effects of Totalitarianism in China and Russia' (2000) 1(1) *Japanese Journal of Political Science* 116.

However, sociologist Norbert Elias offered the insight that, just as an individual's identity is at one's core, ethnic/national identity lies at the core of a collective psyche. Since, on the whole, our identities are with us throughout our lives as individuals and as members of a collectivity, both identities, if not exactly indivisible, usually remain, in our eyes and in others', inclusive of the nationality or large group membership we were born with, even if we acquire a new citizenship, convert to a new religion, or reject much that that nation or collectivity does. If identity is 'the fact of being who or what a person or thing is'[29] and collective identity is the fact of being who or what a people is, individuals who share an identity, Elias argues, are united by it.

Elias further profoundly observes that this link is not, fundamentally, known intellectually, but emotionally. Commonly, the love for one's people or nation is the same as love for the self:

> [L]ove of nation is never something which one experiences toward a nation to which one refers as 'them'. This love is something we experience towards the group we refer to as 'we', [and is a form of] … self-love. This means national identity is an integral part of individual identity.[30]

Elias's understanding of the link between the individual and the collective is validated and expanded by van der Kolk's understanding of the brain: 'Our culture teaches us to focus on personal uniqueness, but at a deeper level we barely exist as individual organisms … Our brains are built to help us function as members of a tribe'.[31] Elias's understanding suggests why the brain evolved in this way: 'There is no "I" identity, and … no "we" identity, alone … [T]he image that one retains of one's nation [or left/right worldview] is at the same time a self-image'.[32]

Elias discerns that the love we have both for 'I', our own individual self, and for 'we', our people (or nation), leads conationals 'to identify with each other'.[33] This is love for what we share and is identified by historian Jan Gross, as well as Volkan, as being 'bonded together by authentic spiritual affinity … [and] national pride rooted in common historical experiences of many generations'.[34] Thus, self-love and love of conationals link individuals who may not know one another personally. When threatened, usually by outsiders, they become a source of assumed security for one another and will fight for one another's – that is, also for their own –survival. This amounts to a notion of one's nation that is admittedly so intangible and idealised that almost anything can be fitted into it; one that, however at odds we may be with what our nation or identity group is actually doing, we feel ourselves a part of it. Even Rioch's hermit (see Introduction) cannot be understood without knowing 'the group from

[29] 'Identity', *Lexico (Oxford) Dictionary*.

[30] N Elias, *The Germans: Power Struggles and the Development of Habitus in the Nineteenth and Twentieth Centuries* (New York, Columbia University Press, 1996) 151.

[31] B van der Kolk, *The Body Keeps the Score: Brain, Mind, and Body in the Healing of Trauma* (New York, Viking, 2014).

[32] Elias, *The Germans*, 151.

[33] N Elias, *Studien über die Deutschen* (Frankfurt, Suhrkamp, 1990) 196–97, cited in T Akçam, *From Empire to Republic: Turkish Nationalism and the Armenian Genocide* (London, Zed Books, 2004) 245.

[34] JT Gross, *Neighbors: The Destruction of the Jewish Community in Jedwabne, Poland* (London, Penguin Books, 2002) 89.

which he has separated himself geographically'.[35] (It is also possible that now, with polarisation intensifying along a left-right/cultural/worldview divide, those populating these two groups may be starting to outweigh identification with a country or ethnic group of origin.)

Political scientist Behlül Özkan calls attention to politician and author Michael Ignatieff's similar view: the threat of 'state collapse … creat[es] an unpredictable environment and "Hobbesian fear" [and] … is followed by nationalist paranoia' in which people stick together 'by the conviction that their security depends on it'.[36] If, at some level the core purpose of collectivities is – or even must be – survival, it explains why, as Volkan sees it, a people feel entitled to act to protect their collective identity and follow their leaders to destructive extremes:

> Under extreme and threatening conditions, they feel entitled to do anything, whether sadistic or masochistic, to protect their large-group identity, and will seek or rally around a leader who will help in this task, no matter what means he or she may use.[37]

From this statement it follows that a – if not *the* – problem of collective identity is when a people claim they must hold power over another people to express that identity, justifying it by claiming threat to an idealised identity.

V. THE NEED TO DE-IDEALISE COLLECTIVE IDENTITIES

Part II of this book shows how rage, fear, and frustration led the heads of the Ottoman state ('leaders') to do anything to protect themselves/ their collective identity, becoming paranoid and misperceiving reality as they did so, ultimately ending up, first, by committing genocide and then pursuing exclusivist, destructive nationalism. Although not describing the fear as traumatic, and building on his understanding of Elias, historian and sociologist Taner Akçam makes the observation that such fear leads to the cognitive inability to contextualise a situation and gain perspective on it. 'The mutual identification between self and collective makes it difficult to put distance between oneself and the crimes committed by one's nation, especially those against another nation'.[38]

Gaining perspective on the crimes of our own nation means seeing the hard facts about its crimes, just as we see, far more easily, its triumphs. And insofar as individuals identify with their nation, their collectivity, and their ethno-religious culture, criticism of their nation, collectivity, or culture is predictably and naturally taken personally by most, and admission of fault and its consequences, material and psychological, resisted. To choose blindness over seeing facts is to place our collectivity's actions beyond our own reflection and opportunity for learning. Our meaning making is thus limited, amounting to denial.

[35] M Rioch, 'The Work of Wilfred Bion on Groups' in AD Colman and WH Bexton (eds), *Group Relations Reader* (Washington, DC, AK Rice Institute, 1975) 22.

[36] B Özkan, 'Who Gains from the "No War No Peace" Situation? A Critical Analysis of the Nagorno-Karabakh Conflict' (2008) 13 *Geopolitics* 578.

[37] Volkan, 'Transgenerational Transmissions and Chosen Traumas', 84.

[38] Akçam, *From Empire to Republic*, 41–42.

As in the story of communal breakdown in the film *1945*, psychiatrist Anthony Charuvastra and psychologist Marylene Cloitre write that collective '[e]xposure to cruelty, perversion, or betrayal … represents not just the risk of physical injury but also the breakdown of social norms as well as the sense of safety associated with being a member of a rule-guided community'.[39] If social norms, particularly those of safety and accountability, are not reestablished after collective trauma, two reactions are likely: devotion to creating safety at all costs; and pursuing accountability through revenge.

The idealisation of collective identity is a psychological obstacle in unsticking profoundly stuck destructive relationships between collectivities. If our collectivity damages another, and these offences are either denied or ignored because inadmissible in our own people's idealised narrative of itself or themselves, a major component of our identity is left out. There may be countless collective traumas unrecorded in the annals of psychohistory and untriggered in our lifetimes. But the world has witnessed many cases that are revived when there is a trigger to unacknowledged hurts, moral injuries, and uncorrected wrongs. Those situations, rather than assuming inevitable violent escalation, may change course if collective trauma were processed and corrective steps taken.

[39] A Charuvastra and M Cloitre, 'Social Bonds and Posttraumatic Stress Disorder' (2008) 59 *Annual Review of Psychology* 4, www.ncbi.nlm.nih.gov/pmc/articles/PMC2722782/ (accessed 20 July 2020).

Part II

A Brief History of the Armenian-Turkish Relationship

4

The Tangled Roots of Homeland and Identity

[Heidegger] takes as his example a two-hundred-year-old farmhouse in the Black Forest. Such a place … combined religious belief, domestic life and local topography: Here the self-sufficiency of the power to let earth and heaven, divinities and mortals, enter in simple oneness into things, ordered the house. It placed the farm on the wind-sheltered mountain slope looking south, among the meadows close to the spring. 'Dwelling' … meant much more than just living in a house. It described a way of being in the world. In Old English and High German, he shows how the word 'baun' – meaning both 'building' and 'to dwell' – is linked to the verb 'to be' … So to be is 'to be in a place'.

Philip Marsden[1]

The sense of belonging to a land is a very personal and communal experience and cannot be reduced to statistical considerations.

Gerard Libaridian[2]

People's roots, the lands where they take root are very important … [T]earing people away from their language, their identity is a great crime against humanity. Tearing them away from their roots, their lands is as great a crime.

Hasan Cemal[3]

I. HOMELANDS

PARTICULAR LANDS UNDERLIE, support, and symbolise peoples, who relate to them as homelands. This chapter introduces the Armenians, Turks, and Azerbaijanis in the homelands where each dwelt for a very long time. Each people developed deep emotional connections with the earth that produced their food and with the forests and stones that enabled the construction of shelters and crafting of furnishings. They grew attached to the wonder and larger connectedness they experienced in particular places on these lands; to the religions practised in sacred edifices they built; to the languages spoken, livings made, traditions developed, and events shared. Their identities originated or developed in these homelands, in places,

[1] P Marsden, *Rising Ground* (London, Granta Books, 2014) 20.

[2] G Libaridian, 'Keynote Speech' (speech, The Clash of Empires: World War I and the Middle East, University of Cambridge, Cambridge, 14 June 2014) 3.

[3] H Cemal, *1915: The Armenian Genocide* (Istanbul, Hrant Dink Foundation, 2015) 141.

situations, and experiences predating the pull of modern nationalism. Although following different paths, all three ethnic groups ended up in nation states conceived as nationalist projects.

Homelands, as the roots of these peoples' identities, are seemingly absolute, not reconstructable. Their meaning is not easily transferable. Individuals and peoples may move from place to place, from homelands to new lands, but the loss, or threat of loss, of a homeland hurts. If the move is forced, it robs, wounds, and transgresses. Homelands cannot be removed from psyches or hearts. Whether the move is forced or voluntary, even if over generations subsequent knowledge of the exact locus of a homeland becomes less precise, homelands retain significance.

The formation of Armenian, Turkish, and Azerbaijani national identities was also entangled with the conflicts that took place in these homelands. This book shows how the three groups interacted with one another over time, how their relations unfolded across what were in great part shared homelands, and how nation states came to be established on these lands. It was a history studded with collective traumas.

II. THE ARMENIAN HOMELAND

A. Historic Armenia

In the Bible, the survivors of the Flood disembarked from Noah's Ark on Mount Ararat, located today in eastern Turkey. There, by at least the sixth century BCE, Armenians had formed a unique presence with their own language and customs in a region that came to be known as Armenia. Though its borders shrank or expanded over the centuries, Armenia was usually depicted in contemporary maps and travellers' accounts as bounded by the Euphrates river to the west and Mesopotamia to the south and east. Independent Armenian kingdoms of varying sizes came and went within the orbits of much larger powers from the Romans to the Persians. From the eleventh century CE, tribal forces from Central Asia began to overrun the small and by now weakened Armenian kingdoms. The newcomers, recently converted to Islam, conquered the kingdoms, and eventually settled and established their dominion over the Armenians. Ancient- and medieval-era maps show the territory of Armenia in varying guises, with early modern ones more accurately reflecting Armenia's division between large empires, yet overlaid as a unified area centered usually around Lake Van. Important Russian authors from Alexander Pushkin to Vasily Grossman travelled to this 'Armenia' and wrote about it.

Armenians were the first people to adopt Christianity as a state religion in the early fourth century CE. A distinct nation with its own customs, alphabet, language, traditions, and branch of Christianity, its members retained an abiding attachment to their historic homeland. Many Armenians also lived in areas outside the traditional borders of historic Armenia. Only periodic invasion, massacre, and social and political upheaval led some from both groups to abandon their homes and seek shelter elsewhere. The genocide of 1915 saw the complete uprooting of the Armenian people from both their homeland and other regions in the Ottoman Empire. Survivors made up another wave of Armenians, scattering worldwide.

Armenia in its Historical Setting

Source: Richard G Hovannisian (ed), *The Armenian People from Ancient to Modern Times: Volume I: The Dynastic Periods: From Antiquity to the Fourteenth Century* (New York, St Martin's Press, 1997) map 1.

B. Russian Armenia

Discussion to this point has been about only a part of historic Armenia – that lying in the eastern provinces of the Ottoman Empire and now modern Turkey. Armenians continue to refer to it as Western Armenia. Part of the border of this large territory is coterminous with that of its historic eastern half. Before World War I, 'Russian Armenia' typically referred to those parts of the Batum, Erevan, Elisavetpol, and Baku provinces that had substantial Armenian populations (these provinces together comprised Transcaucasia, now the South Caucasus). Turkish Armenia, as it was often referred to at the time, on the other hand, included the important Armenian centres of Van, Erzurum, Bitlis, Harput, and Sivas. Kars, Ardahan, and Batum were also important provincial towns along the Russo-Ottoman borderlands region, places known in Turkish as the Elviye-i Selase. The Ottomans lost these three provinces to Russia during the Russo-Ottoman War of 1877–78 and then briefly occupied them in 1918. This region will feature in Part III of this book.

At the turn of the twentieth century, the vast majority of the global Armenian population was thus split roughly between the adjacent Ottoman and Russian empires. Many of them lived in Transcaucasia's economic, cultural, and political centres, forming an influential, well-off group that rose to prominence in government and the economy. Many others lived in communities scattered throughout Russian Armenia, especially in Nagorno-Karabakh (also spelled Karabagh), Nakhichevan, southern Georgia, and also the northeastern region of Iran known as Azerbaijan, an area that, while adjacent to, was distinct from the country that would later adopt that name. Economic development in Russian Armenia was uneven. Erevan Province, now comprising the better part of today's Armenian republic, for instance, contained a substantially rural Armenian population, while Baku and Tiflis served as the home of the modern Russian-Armenian bourgeoise.[4]

By late 1917 the Russian Empire under the Romanov tsars was no more. In May 1918, within a few days of one another, three independent republics led respectively by Georgian, Azerbaijani, and Armenian leaders took shape in the Transcaucasus. With the consolidation of these nation states, the main Armenian economic, cultural, and political centres fell within the borders of Georgia and Azerbaijan, where suddenly the Armenians were no longer so welcome.[5] 'Ironically', writes Richard G Hovannisian, 'the very advantage that Armenians seemed to enjoy by their dispersal was to cripple them once Transcaucasia broke into separate states'.[6]

Each republic experienced just the briefest independent existence before being taken over in 1920–21 by a newly emergent Soviet Russia. The three remained a part of the USSR until 1991, when they once again became independent republics. The original Armenian homeland is thus split today between eastern Turkey, the third Republic of Armenia, and the unrecognised Nagorno-Karabakh or Artsakh Republic (see below).

III. THE OTTOMAN EMPIRE, TURKEY, AND TURKS

In the nineteenth century, the name 'Turkey' was still largely used interchangeably by both foreigners and native Ottomans to refer to the Ottoman Empire. For Ottomans, to speak of events taking place in Turkey could have referred to Jerusalem as readily as Anatolia or Salonika, in which case the former two would respectively be referred to as the Near East and Turkey-in-Asia and the latter as Turkey-in-Europe. Anatolia was likewise roughly coterminous with Asia Minor.

Claims to the ancient birthplace of the Turkic peoples in a place called Turan first emerged at the turn of the twentieth century. Turan does not appear on old maps. The history of the Turkic peoples in Anatolia and the South Caucasus usually begins in 1071, with the Seljuk defeat of the Byzantines at the Battle of Manzikert. In the period following, successive waves of Muslim-Turkic groups migrated to and settled in the new lands. In 1299, Osman, the leader of one Muslim-Turkic tribe of Central Asian origin, founded a small principality in Bithynia (in what is now northwestern Turkey), east of the Byzantine capital of Constantinople.

Within two centuries, in 1453, Osman's successors conquered Constantinople and its surrounding environs and then expanded eastwards, extending their hold over the lands inhabited by Armenians and Greeks. In 1517, they captured Egypt and assumed

[4] RG Suny, 'Eastern Armenians under Tsarist Rule' in RG Hovannisian (ed), *The Armenian People from Ancient to Modern Times*, vol 2 of *Foreign Dominion to Statehood: The Fifteenth Century to the Twentieth Century* (New York, St Martin's Press, 1997) 121–26, 133.

[5] RG Hovannisian, 'Armenia's Road to Independence' in Hovannisian (ed), *The Armenian People from Ancient to Modern Times*, 276.

[6] Hovannisian, 'Armenia's Road to Independence', 276.

authority over the Cairo caliphate (in later centuries, Osman's descendants would claim that the absorption of this defunct institution gave them claim to the mantle of the Prophet and the title of caliph). The vast imperial lands eventually came to encompass most parts of Albania, Algeria, the Gulf states, Bosnia and Herzegovina, Bulgaria, Croatia, Cyprus, Egypt, Greece, Hungary, parts of Iran, Iraq, Jordan, Kosovo, Lebanon, Libya, Macedonia, Montenegro, Palestine, Romania, Serbia, Slovenia, Syria, Tunisia, and, of course, Turkey. The Balkan Peninsula remained the empire's wealthiest and most populous territory until the Balkan Wars of the early twentieth century. Today, only a very small part of Turkey's territory extends across the western, or European, side of the Bosphorus Straits, its greater part lying on the Asian side.

IV. OTTOMAN ARMENIANS

In the Ottoman Empire, non-Muslims held special status as *dhimmis* ('protected peoples'). Dhimmis had fewer legal and social rights than Muslims.

Discrimination on the basis of religion was a common reality for non-Muslims. For example, they paid higher taxes and, as historian Ussama Makdisi notes, were subject to constraints ranging from 'how they dressed, to the prohibition on the construction of new churches or synagogues'.[7] Nor were non-Muslims permitted to serve in the Ottoman armed forces until the proclamation of the Imperial Rescript of 1856, which made them liable to conscription (an obligation most avoided by paying an exemption tax). Disputes between a Muslim and a non-Muslim were to be settled solely in Islamic courts. Despite all these limitations, so long as they fulfilled their role as loyal, tax-paying subjects, the empire's Christians and Jews were entitled to protection from the state and could reasonably expect to receive redress through different legal channels. Under what by the nineteenth century came to be referred to as the *millet* system,[8] the major non-Muslim ethno-confessional groups enjoyed autonomy in governing their internal affairs. They set their own laws and collected taxes on behalf of the state.

Until the early nineteenth century, the concerns of the empire's Armenian population came under the purview of the Armenian Patriarchate of Istanbul (most Armenians followed the Armenian Apostolic tradition in Christianity). Later, some Armenians embraced other Christian confessions, recognised by imperial authorities, such that by the mid-nineteenth century, Armenian Catholics and Evangelicals were able to secure their status as separate *millets*.

In line with the wide-ranging political and social programs implemented in the nineteenth century and known as the *Tanzimat*, in the 1860s, the Armenians, like the Orthodox Greek and Jewish *millets*, were permitted by the sultan to draft an

[7] U Makdisi, *Age of Coexistence: The Ecumenical Frame and the Making of the Modern Arab World* (Berkeley, University of California Press, 2019) 30.

[8] The term '*millet*', which originates from the Arabic *milla*, had three basic meanings in Ottoman Turkish: religion, religious community, and nation (MOH Ursinus, '*Millet*' in P Bearman et al (eds), *Encyclopaedia of Islam*, 2nd edn.

internal code of regulations and establish a national assembly on which representatives from all over the empire would serve and coordinate with Armenian clerical leaders. This was to be an important body as internal relations among Armenians and external relations with the Ottoman state developed.

V. THE END OF THE OTTOMAN EMPIRE AND EMERGENCE OF THE TURKISH REPUBLIC

After 400 years of expansion, in the eighteenth century the Ottoman Empire began to lose ground to its increasingly powerful European neighbours. The pace quickened from the 1820s to 1914 as nationalism became a force and large swathes of territories in Europe with significant Christian populations broke free from the empire. During the period of imperial expansion, ethnic Turks and other Muslims had moved to settle in its far-flung territories. As this haemorrhaging occurred, Muslims in the breakaway territories fled for safety to the empire's interior, escaping from vengeful local ethno-religious forces. During this same era, the Muslims of the newly-annexed Russian Crimea and North Caucasus fled violent state oppression and settled in the Ottoman Empire. Many of these refugees looked to Anatolia, in Hasan Cemal's words, as 'the ultimate homeland … not having anywhere else to go'.[9] This very large number of *muhacirs* (immigrant refugees), as they came to be known, came to resent the relatively better-off Ottoman Christian inhabitants, Armenian and Greek.

The Ottoman ruling class for centuries had been dominated by a Sunni Muslim Turkish-speaking elite. Beyond those markers, differences in culture, traditions, history, and notions of homeland among the general population were as diverse as the empire was wide. Historian Mark Mazower identifies the amorphous meaning that 'Turk' denoted in the Balkans even as late as the nineteenth century:

> Although Europeans had been talking about 'Turks' for centuries, it had not been a term much used within the empire. The ruling language was an amalgam of Turkish, Arabic, and Persian, with a smattering of Greek, Slavic, and Italian, and its ruling class … included individuals from an astonishing array of different backgrounds … If 'Turk' meant simply Muslim, then in the Balkans alone, there were Albanian, Cretan, Bosnian, Bulgarian, Jewish, and other Muslims in addition to a scattering of Sudanese slaves, Egyptian market gardeners, and the long-established peasant descendants of Nomadic Turcoman tribes.[10]

By the beginning of the twentieth century, however, 'the broad mass of Muslims in Turkey [are likely to have] understood themselves as Turks, or Kurds, rather than Muslims', writes Taner Akçam.[11] As the unity, and whatever safety the Ottoman imperial framework offered, disintegrated, nationalism elbowed its way in, offering a new vision of security, fairness, and belonging in a clearly defined territory. Once CUP leaders assumed complete political power, the next step, according to Akçam, lay in

[9] Cemal, *1915*, 76.

[10] M Mazower, *Salonica, City of Ghosts: Christians, Muslims, and Jews, 1430–1950* (New York, Vintage, 2006) 263.

[11] T Akçam, *A Shameful Act: The Armenian Genocide and the Question of Turkish Responsibility* (New York, Metropolitan Books, 2006) 15.

constructing 'a whole new political entity together with the Muslim-Turkic peoples of the Caucasus and Central Asia. The question – Where is the Turkish nation's homeland? – would have to be answered anew'.[12] The dénouement of the Ottoman Empire would come in 1922, when the Turkish nationalist forces, led by Mustafa Kemal, would dissolve the last government and found the Turkish Republic in the next year.

VI. THE KURDS

The Kurds form a sizeable minority in Turkey today. Like the Turks, they are largely adherents of Sunni Islam, though, unlike the Turks, they speak a separate language and belong to a different ethnic milieu. The Kurds also lived, and still live, throughout other parts of the Middle East. Within the Ottoman Empire they dwelled in the same provinces in eastern Anatolia as Turks and Armenians. Their way of life was semi-nomadic; their culture and language owed much to a shared Iranian heritage. While the Kurds play a small role in the account to follow, appearing primarily as mountain tribes inhabiting lands in Anatolia, it is worth noting nonetheless that, on the whole, they acted extremely brutally toward the Armenians before and during the genocide.[13] But since 1915, they, too, have been heavily discriminated against by successive Turkish governments. As they developed nationalist aims, leading to rebellion and protest, one million of them settled in or were relocated by the state to different parts of Turkey, which destroyed many of their villages. Their survival as a people in Turkey today remains extremely difficult, even questionable. In recent years, friendly and mutually supportive intercommunal relations, though not quite alliances, between groups of Kurds and Armenians have emerged.

VII. GEORGIA

Like Armenia and Azerbaijan, Georgia was briefly an independent republic from 1918 to 1921. It became a Soviet republic in 1921, regaining its independence only in 1991. As in the other large population centres of the South Caucasus, Armenians formed a large and powerful minority in Tiflis, the historic capital of Georgia under Russian imperial rule and the seat of Russian administration in Transcaucasia. Tiflis, now Tbilisi, remains the capital of Georgia.

VIII. AZERBAIJAN

From the early nineteenth century until 1917, all of Transcaucasia came under Russian imperial rule. Its boundaries extended downwards from the Caucasus Mountains in southwestern Russia to the eastern borders of modern-day Turkey, and widened out toward the Caspian Sea, to the east. Russian administrators and

[12] Akçam, *A Shameful Act*, 92.

[13] D McDowall, *A Modern History of the Kurds*, 3rd edn (New York, IB Tauris, 2004) 60–63, 97–98, 102–109.

travellers generally referred to the Muslims they encountered in Transcaucasia as 'Tatars'.[14] By the time the first republic of Azerbaijan was established in 1918, Muslim intellectuals in Transcaucasia saw themselves not as Tatars but as Azerbaijanis. The majority of the inhabitants of the land that became the Republic of Azerbaijan were of ethnic Turkic origin and had strong ties to the Ottoman Empire based on a shared religious (most Azerbaijanis are Shia Muslims) and linguistic heritage. Yet the Russian Empire left a major cultural imprint on Azerbaijanis, who formed the region's largest Muslim and Turkic-speaking population, as it did on the Christian ethnic groups. Azerbaijani identity remains a work in progress.[15]

Baku, the capital and largest city of Azerbaijan, dates back to antiquity but it only grew to become the second largest urban centre of Transcaucasia in the nineteenth century after the discovery of oil. Located on the Absheron Peninsula that juts into the Caspian Sea, it served as the seat of provincial government, where, aside from Azerbaijanis, Armenians and Georgians also lived in large numbers. In the late nineteenth century, many Armenians had moved to Baku, occupying important positions in the city's developing oil economy, and by the 1920s composed close to one-third of its total population.

Today's Republic of Azerbaijan borders Russia and Georgia in the north. Armenia lies to the west. To the south is Iran, whose borders abut the republic proper and the Nakhchivan (or Nakhchivan Autonomous Republic) exclave, a region that once contained a sizeable Armenian population and is now a site of occasional military flare-ups between Armenian and Azerbaijani forces.

IX. NAGORNO-KARABAKH

Nagorno-Karabakh is an enclave located in the South Caucasus (see Chapter 17) with a more complicated history than its relatively small size might suggest. The Nagorno-Karabakh Republic (or Artsakh Republic), which today governs the territory of Nagorno-Karabakh, borders Armenia to the west and Iran to the south. In 1923 this territory was assigned to Azerbaijan by the central Soviet government, but, in a nod toward the sensitivities of the population, permitted the creation of a local government, the Nagorno-Karabakh Autonomous Oblast (NKAO). Over the next seven decades, the NKAO's Armenian and Azerbaijani population lived under the full weight of Soviet power. Armenians had limited cultural rights in the NKAO and were discriminated against by Soviet Azerbaijani authorities. Nagorno-Karabakh was still part of Azerbaijan at the end of the Soviet era, when most of its majority Armenian inhabitants expressed, and not for the first time, a desire to unite with Armenia. As the Soviet Union collapsed, Armenia and Azerbaijan became embroiled in what proved to be a long and brutal war. The Armenians ultimately emerged on top as they extended their control over not only the former NKAO but five outlying districts around it.

[14] A Alstadt, *The Politics of Culture in Soviet Azerbaijan, 1920–40* (London, Routledge, 2016) 13.

[15] C Tokluoglu, 'Definitions of National Identity, Nationalism and Ethnicity in Post-Soviet Azerbaijan in the 1990s' (2005) 28(4) *Ethnic and Racial Studies* 724.

Though a cease-fire was signed in 1994, the conflict remains unsettled to this day. Azerbaijan considers Nagorno-Karabakh an integral part of the country and disputes its status as a self-proclaimed, de facto independent republic.

In 1923, the number of Azerbaijani Muslims living in the NKAO was fewer than that of Armenians. The 1926 Soviet census found that of the region's 125,159 inhabitants, Armenians constituted more than 90 per cent, while Azerbaijanis formed only 4 per cent of the population.[16] Today Stepanakert, with a total population of about 53,000, is the largest city and capital of the Artsakh Republic. Shushi (to Armenians; 'Shusha' to Azerbaijanis), the second largest town, had been rebuilt after the war in 1920, but it suffered further damage during the 1988–94 war. Since then, it has been under going reconstruction once more.

Relations among Armenia, Azerbaijan, and Artsakh are discouraging. The Azerbaijanis receive rhetorical and material support from their Turkish neighbours. Russia sells weapons to both sides, while Belarus, Israel, and Pakistan sell arms to Azerbaijan. Azerbaijan's government, bolstered by oil sales, is reportedly staggeringly corrupt, even according to the appalling standard established by the governments of other former member states of the USSR.[17]

For all the hostility and divergence of narrative, Azerbaijanis and Armenians agree on the important historical and cultural history of Karabakh and take great pride in what it has produced. The Nagorno-Karabakh horse, for example, is a magnificent and rare breed still valued by both peoples for its beauty and stamina. There are historical and cultural grounds for a more productive, friendly coexistence, though, as Part 3 shows, a history of mutually caused collective trauma accounts in part for prevention of its development.

2004 Armenian Stamp Showing the Nagorno-Karabakh Horse

Source: The collection of Hayk Demoyan.

[16] AN Yamskov, 'Ethnic Conflict in the Transcaucasus: The Case of Nagorno-Karabakh' (1991) 20 *Theory and Society* 644.

[17] See 'Overview of Corruption and Anti-Corruption in Azerbaijan', Transparency International, 7 September 2017.

1993 Azerbaijani Stamp Showing the Same Breed of Horse
Source: The collection of Hayk Demoyan.

These horses, like the lands of homelands, elicit pride and love.

X. A START OF AN ARGUMENT LINKING ATTACHMENT TO LAND/HOMELANDS WITH HUMAN RIGHTS LAW

Since time immemorial many peoples dwelt and worked, reproduced and worshipped according to their respective faiths and cultures in the Near East and the South Caucasus. The lands they inhabited became their homelands, valued as sacred, enabling survival, embodying their histories, grounding their cultures. All these people knew who they were partly because of where they lived. They felt attached emotionally to homelands and individual places they knew. At whatever stage of organisation as a group, a people's homelands became part of their collective identity. Threat of loss of homelands remained and remains today a very deep and unique collective fear analogous to bodily injury: 'dismemberment', for example, refers both to loss of the limbs of living beings and to loss of the territory of the homeland or part of a homeland belonging to a collectivity.

The idea of nationalism became significant in the Ottoman Empire and Russian Transcaucasia in the nineteenth century, especially to the downtrodden. As empires withered, many leaders of the post-World War I era came to accept the nation state model as the ideal form of political and social organisation. Groups sharing the elements of identity – territory, religion, language, history, and culture – became a 'nation' inhabiting a homeland. But Norbert Elias argued that the nature of attachments to homelands as 'sacred' would have changed in response to nationalism's rise:

> Nationalism … is … distinct from … group beliefs representing the attachment and solidarity of individuals in relation to collectivities such as villages, towns, principalities

> or kingdoms in earlier stages of social development. It is ... a belief of a characteristically secular kind ... sustained without justification through superhuman agencies.[18]

However, if nation states did not justify themselves in the eyes of God, that did not mean that peoples' religious or spiritual attachment to homelands simply vanished. These attachments to immediate land and places that were held as sacred, being very deeply meaningful gifts from God, remained, but as groups also recognised themselves as nations, Elias points to how an emotional attachment was generated not only about immediate locality but also about places not personally known and demanding of a people in new ways. The attachment was no longer solely or even at all experienced or known in the presence of the land and buildings all around one, but also in exposure to symbols of nation states that inspired a sense of solidarity and wholeness of communities, accompanied by development of obligation to them:

> A nationalist ethos implies a sense of solidarity and obligation ... with regard to a sovereign collectivity which ... is organized as a state ... and the attachment ... is mediated through special symbols, some of which can be persons. These symbols and the collectivity for which they stand attract to themselves strong positive emotions of the type usually called love.[19]

With the rise of nationalism, then, to different degrees, place by place, homelands may have declined in importance with certain segments of peoples. Whether or not that happened, Elias points out that nationalism evoked a new attachment, the love of nation, which is widespread across peoples. Our potentially boundless individual and collective psyches identified emotionally with and felt love for nation as well as attachment to the other elements composing national identities.

I posit, however, that whether or not homeland has declined in importance, recognition of this attachment as love of actual land, if not soil, may be mistakenly overlooked and inadequately respected by constructivists and internationalists. Land is central to collectivities' meaning, both as the source of survival and unconstructed locus of history. Nowhere can the importance of homelands be better gauged than in Israel/Palestine, where different subgroups of Israeli Jews, for example, focus on one or another element of their collective identity to claim exclusive rights to it.

Homeland remains a powerful element in the identities of Armenians, Turks, and Azerbaijanis. The long-standing conflicts among them have roots in what each people involved regards as the immutability, unreconstructability, and non-negotiability of its homeland, even if at times the relationships between these peoples and their lands evolved when others moved in and shared homelands.

Throughout the intractable conflicts that are the subject of this book, these questions beg addressing again and again: Can homelands be shared? Or should superior power establish whose categorical right it is to control a homeland to which

[18] N Elias, *The Germans: Power Struggles and the Development of Habitus in the Nineteenth and Twentieth Centuries* (New York, Columbia University Press, 1996) 151.

[19] Elias, *The Germans*, 151.

another people lays claim, also relating to those very lands as its homeland? Should and could resolving intractable, psychologically frozen ethnic conflicts include acceptance that a homeland must be shared because more than one people has historical roots and emotional relationships to it? Might sharing homelands, out of respect for each group's long-term existential, emotional, and sacred attachment to the same homeland, be a key requirement for securing peaceful, sustainable, productive coexistence? Might two or more peoples agree to the right of access to, if not necessarily governance of, the same land and the places of importance on it to the other peoples?[20]

[20] See HC Kelman, 'A One-Country/Two-State Solution to the Israeli-Palestinian Conflict' (2011) XVIII *Middle East Policy* 27.

5

The Riddle of Ottomanism

... Ottomanism entailed that all ethnic groups be brothers and equal citizens [and] also required [under the *Tanzimat*] that all the groups abandon their previously established privileges.

Bedross Der Matossian[1]

[F]ear seems to be the most significant political emotion ... [H]umans enter into a social contract to eliminate the state of fear they experience in nature, where they are without protection.

Fatma Müge Göçek[2]

We can compromise with the Christians only when they accept our position of dominance.

Young Ottoman leader Namık Kemal[3]

Over the span of six centuries, the Ottoman Empire ruled over different Muslim and non-Muslim ethnic groups across territories in Europe, the Middle East, and North Africa. Beginning in the 1770s, the balance of power that had held over the past century begin to shift in favour of the European states as they grew increasingly confident in challenging the Ottomans for control over their territories. The Great Powers of Europe exerted ever more pressure and influence in the region. By the early nineteenth century contemporaries could scarcely have imagined that in just over a hundred years this ancient and proud empire would collapse and dissolve into ruins. Decade by decade its territories were detached, and the state came under heavy financial strain as it accumulated enormous debts to service a persistently anemic economy.

[1] B Der Matossian, *Shattered Dreams of Revolution: From Liberty to Violence in the Ottoman Empire* (Stanford, CA, Stanford University Press, 2014) 70.

[2] F Müge Göçek, *Denial of Violence: Ottoman Past, Turkish Present, and Collective Violence Against the Armenians, 1789–2009* (New York, Oxford University Press, 2015) 33.

[3] MC Kuntay Namık Kemal, *Devrin İnsanları ve Olayları Arasında*, vol I (Ankara, 1949) 186, quoted in T Akçam, *A Shameful Act: The Armenian Genocide and the Question of Turkish Responsibility* (New York, Metropolitan Books, 2006) 49.

I. CONFRONTING MODERNISATION

To the Ottoman Empire's diplomatic and financial woes was added the challenge of new ideas revolving around political and social organisation originating from Europe and the New World. From 1821–1829, it was the Greeks, inspired by the revolutions in France and the United States, who first waged a war for independence from the Ottoman Empire. Throughout they were aided on the ground by a number of well-intentioned philhellenic young scions of highborn British, French, German, and American families, famously including Lord Byron, who idealised them as the descendants of Pericles and Solon.[4] When they appeared to be defeated, a combined Russian, British, and French fleet in Navarino Bay laid to waste the Ottoman navy and thereafter secured a negotiated settlement for an independent Greece.

The Greek War of Independence would go on to become an inspiration for other Ottoman Christians to follow in their own movements to break free from imperial rule. While the Greek war may be considered the earliest nationalist uprising in the Ottoman Empire, the international attention it garnered heralded the human rights movement as we have come to know it today, as well as the birth of American humanitarianism, described by historian William St Clair.[5]

In the late 1830s, a growing number of Ottoman statesmen became convinced that the empire's political and social misfortunes could be remedied by restructuring the imperial edifice. Part of this vision called for financial, judicial, and military reorganisation. Pressure mounted and the central government acted. Between 1839 and 1876, the state undertook a series of reforms, known as the *Tanzimat*, or reorganisation.

The Gülhane, or Rose Chamber, decree promulgated the first overhaul of the state administrative framework and structure in 1839. It promised to safeguard the 'life, honor, and property' of all the sultan's subjects.[6] The next decree, the Imperial Rescript of 1856, crafted by the British ambassador Strafford Canning, reaffirmed the traditional rights bestowed on the non-Muslim population; however, significantly, it went on to grant them equal status before the law irrespective of religion. The non-Muslim communities were asked to draw up communal regulations and create representative bodies. They were to enjoy loosened restrictions in the construction and repair of religious buildings, be permitted to serve in the military, receive equal treatment in matters of justice, taxation, admission to civil and military schools, and opportunities for public employment. They were permitted to create their own representative communal bodies with the primary task of seeing to the administration of their own internal affairs. Administrative centralisation meant constructing the rational state, with a modern bureaucracy with uniform laws and regulations that would replace informal arrangements agreed upon previously with local leaders.

[4] W St Clair, *That Greece Might Still Be Free: The Philhellenes in the War of Independence*, 2nd edn (Cambridge, Open Book Publishers, 2008).

[5] St Clair, *That Greece Might Still Be Free*.

[6] JL Gelvin, *The Modern Middle East: A History*, 4th edn (Oxford, Oxford University Press, 2016) 167–69.

The changes would bolster the empire's physical security and place its finances on an even footing, enabling it to better compete in the global market and fend off European encroachment, which increasingly manifested itself in the form of demands for better treatment of non-Muslim subjects. Thus were modernisation and what I call equalisation brought together in what, in time, would come to be called Ottomanism, the creation of a collective imperial identity inclusive of both Muslims and non-Muslims.[7]

While many elite Muslims in the empire showed themselves ready to adopt some Western ideas, manners, and institutions, most were not about to submit, as the Young Ottoman reformers (see below) saw it, to 'the annihilation of domestic culture'.[8] No more were they all 'ready to accept any absolute equality [and …] endorse the grant of particular privileges to Christians'.[9] The Ottoman Empire, which European leaders began to refer to as 'the sick man of Europe' in the 1850s, did not prepare imperial subjects for the sweeping changes envisioned in the *Tanzimat*.[10] Even apart from many subjects associating central control over the empire's far-flung civil service with increased 'despotism',[11] any preparation for equalisation would not have been at all easy. When Sultan Abdülmecid I (r 1839–61) proclaimed the enforcement of the principle that all non-Muslims be placed on equal footing with their Muslim peers, shocked Muslims in Jerusalem reacted violently against the Christians. Similar flare-ups took place in Ottoman Damascus, Aleppo, and elsewhere in the following years, leading to repeated European interventions.[12]

In 1865 a group among the reformist movement, known as the Young Ottomans, emerged on the scene of Ottoman politics. They aimed to limit the sultanate's absolutist tendencies through the establishment of constitutional government, while remaining strictly devoted to Islamic principles.[13] They favoured those elements of modernisation – military, judicial, educational, and economic reform – that would strengthen, not endanger, the empire's position and Islamic character. An 1872 article in the Young Ottoman journal, *İbret*, explained:

> In order to advance our civilization we shall try to obtain scientific and industrial progress from Europe. We do not want their street dances, amorality, and satanic afflictions, such as callousness toward people who are starving to death, or to view fairness and tenderness of heart as outlandish notions.[14]

While their calls for an Islamic constitutional system were not immediately heeded, their writings would hold sway in Ottoman intellectual circles for decades to come.

[7] I use the single word 'liberalisation' to sum up what the *Tanzimat* and its followers stood for. I use 'equalisation' to refer to that element of liberalisation that added equality before the law to all peoples of the Ottoman Empire.

[8] M Şükrü Hanioğlu, *The Young Turks in Opposition* (New York, Oxford University Press, 1995) 14.

[9] RH Davison, 'Turkish Attitudes Concerning Christian-Muslim Equality in the Nineteenth Century' (1954) 59 *American Historical Review* 864.

[10] For this phrase, see O Figes, *The Crimean War: A History* (New York, Metropolitan Books, 2010) 105.

[11] EJ Zürcher, *Turkey: A Modern History*, 3rd edn (London, IB Tauris, 2004) 68.

[12] Figes, *The Crimean War*, 428–32; E Rogan, 'Sectarianism and Social Conflict in Damascus: The 1860 Events Reconsidered' (2004) 51 *Arabica* 493.

[13] M Şükrü Hanioğlu, *A Brief History of the Late Ottoman Empire* (Princeton, NJ, Princeton University Press, 2008) 103–104.

[14] R Bey [Kayazade], 'Frenklerde bir telaş' (1872) 13 *İbret* 1, quoted in Hanioğlu, *The Young Turks in Opposition*, 14.

In December 1876 the *Tanzimat* era reached its culmination when the new sultan, Abdülhamid II, reluctantly consented to the creation of a parliament and a constitution. Despite their inherent limitations, these innovations inspired hope among those Ottomans and especially Armenians ready to break free from the constraints of the *millet* system. It was a momentous opportunity for the empire to adapt and progress. However, political liberalisation and equalisation threatened to destabilise the old order and do away with privileges and entitlements that the Muslim ruling class and other dominant elements in society had enjoyed for centuries.

II. OTTOMAN ARMENIANS

At the outset of the *Tanzimat* era, Armenians and other non-Muslims lived under the institutional framework for state and society provided by imperial Ottoman Islamic ideology. The political elite and Muslim clerical scholars (*ulema*) worked in tandem to devise the rules and regulations delineating the behaviour and public markers that set Muslims apart from Christians and Jews. Codes of conduct governed inter-communal relations that ranged from sartorial restrictions to barring non-Muslims from appearing in courts against Muslims in certain cases. The *millet* system kept non-believers (ie non-Muslims) separate from true believers (ie Muslims), permitting the former, however, to practise their respective religions without hindrance and to organise and see to the internal administration of their communities. Despite restrictions, in reality a small number of individual Armenians rose to hold important positions in politics and society in the pre-*Tanzimat* era, much of the system of governance being based on negotiation between state and communal leaders.[15] Following the uprisings in Greece and the Balkans, Armenians were so trusted by Ottoman authorities that they were called the 'loyal *millet*'.[16]

[15] K Barkey, *Empire of Difference: The Ottomans in Comparative Perspective* (Cambridge, Cambridge University Press, 2008); A Yaycioğlu, *Partners of the Empire: The Crisis of the Ottoman Order in the Age of Revolutions* (Stanford, Stanford University Press, 2016).

[16] For a somewhat dated but still useful study on the conditions of Ottomans Armenians in the nineteenth century, see H Barsoumian, 'The Eastern Question and the *Tanzimat* Era' in RH Hovannisian (ed), *The Armenian People from Ancient to Modern Times*, vol 2: *Foreign Dominion to Statehood: The Fifteenth Century to the Twentieth Century* (New York, Palgrave Macmillan, 1997) 175–202. The *millet* system, as it came to be known in the middle of the nineteenth century, was a complex process of the state both institutionalising and negotiating its relationship with the different ethno-religious communities of the empire. See B Masters, *The Encyclopedia of the Ottoman Empire*, sv '*Dhimmi*'; B Braude, 'Foundation Myths of the Millet System' in *Christians and Jews in the Ottoman Empire: The Functioning of a Plural Society*, vol 1: *The Central Lands* (New York, Holmes & Meier Publishers, 1982) 69. For a recent discussion study, see K Barkey, *Empire of Difference: The Ottomans in Comparative Perspective* (Cambridge, Cambridge University Press, 2008), 115–46. Until 1831, the Ottoman government had recognised only one Armenian *millet*, that of the Armenian Apostolic Church. In that year, following the signing of the Treaty of Adrianople, Roman Catholic Armenians received formal recognition of their own separate *millet*. This came after Sultan Mahmud II, in a fit of defiance, had issued in 1827 a decree banishing the Catholic Armenians from the empire, itself arising from more than a decade-long struggle with the Armenian Church. When Protestantism spread among Armenians in the early nineteenth century as a result of Western, mostly American, missionary activity, the Ottoman government recognised a Protestant (called Evangelical) *millet* for all the empire's Christians, including Protestant Armenians, in 1847.

The overwhelming majority (70 per cent) of the Armenian population consisted of peasants in the eastern provinces of the empire.[17] Most lived in the same *vilayets* (provinces) as the large Muslim Kurdish population. Though lagging far behind Istanbul, Izmir, and the other urban centers of the empire, the eastern provinces saw the beginnings of modernisation in the late nineteenth and early twentieth centuries. Armenians established a network of national schools, and founded industries, businesses, and other enterprises. The *Tanzimat* reforms may have partly been meant to ease religious tensions between Muslims and non-Muslims, but they did not easily translate into meaningful change everywhere. Despite their relatively elevated socioeconomic position, rural Armenians remained subject to the familiar predations by Kurds in a system often described as semi-feudal.[18] Well into the early twentieth century, the lands and crops belonging to Armenians continued to be usurped as they were forced to pay exorbitant taxes and extortion fees. They possessed little to defend themselves against the abduction of their women or against the impunity that the legal system gave to Kurds and Ottoman officials who robbed and murdered them.

The promise of administrative and legal reform gave Armenians in the provinces renewed hope for basic protection and fairness under the law. Yet the changes produced mixed benefits because the status quo was characterised by long-standing mutual dependencies that sustained regular if limited rewards for Armenians, which they were loath to surrender. The prospect of reform dramatically upset that balance and led to a further deterioration of relations between them and Kurds and Turks. If, Kévorkian writes, '[o]fficially, the *Tanzimat* had freed Armenians of their dependency on Kurdish begs [chieftains] … the result was to revive an ancient rivalry that had over the centuries yielded to a sort of "symbiosis", from which both parties benefited'.[19]

Thus, Armenian and other non-Muslim elites resisted forgoing certain privileges that they had enjoyed. Perhaps chief among them was exemption from military service.[20] It had bred resentment among the Muslims, who saw their Armenian neighbours avoiding the dangers and horrors of wartime service, while supposedly enjoying opportunities and more comfortable, prosperous lives at home at their expense.[21] The long-established heavy 'poll tax' had been paid only by non-Muslims and was justified as providing non-Muslim support for the (all-Muslim) military establishment – the non-Muslims' contribution to their own defence. But the Reform Edict of 1856 decreed that Christians would now be eligible – though not *required* – to serve in the military. Non-Muslims and Muslims who chose not to serve in the military would pay a new exemption tax, the *bedel*, levied at the same amount as the old poll tax. But by 1909, a year after the Young Turk Revolution, the new Ottoman parliament voted to abolish the exemption fee and made military service compulsory.

[17] Barsoumian, 'The Eastern Question and the *Tanzimat* Era', 192.

[18] See S Astourian, 'The Silence of the Land: Agrarian Relations, Ethnicity, and Power' in RG Suny et al (eds), *A Question of Genocide: Armenians and Turks at the End of the Ottoman Empire* (Oxford, Oxford University Press, 2011) 55.

[19] R Kévorkian, *The Armenian Genocide: A Complete History* (London, IB Tauris, 2011) 10–11.

[20] Akçam, *A Shameful Act*, 32.

[21] See the commentary of Bekir Sıtkı Baykal, *Şark Buhran ve Sabah Gazetesi* (Ankara, 1948) 148, cited in Akçam, *A Shameful Act*, 33.

Ottoman Armenian life in the cities and towns changed dramatically during the second half of the nineteenth century. In part due to the reforms, an increasingly well-to-do and educated class of Armenians, with access to a new mass-circulation press and civic associations, emerged to enjoy opportunities and prosperity on a level that contrasted with the older urban social classes of artisans and labourers, who often lived hand-to-mouth. But their situation worsened as they were forced to compete in the new global economy of which the empire was now a part.[22] The urban Armenian population still remained vulnerable to arbitrary dangers and predations, although, unlike Armenians in the countryside, their property and wealth were not expropriated and they were not evicted as wantonly as in eastern Anatolia.

III. REFORM WITHIN THE ARMENIAN COMMUNITY

If the *Tanzimat* era led to the rebalancing of relations between Muslims and Christians, it also restructured relations between rural and urban Armenians. Until the mid-nineteenth century, the wealthiest, and often most conservative Armenians, the *amira*, who were largely based in the urban centres, were accustomed to being regarded, along with Armenian clerics, as the natural leaders of the entire Armenian community. But now urban middle-class Armenians sought to play a larger role in community affairs and claimed to speak on behalf of all Armenians. They looked to relieve the plight of rural Armenians and for the same opportunities and the possibility of advancement in all spheres as Muslims. These Armenians had imbibed the new values promised in the *Tanzimat* as 'legitimiz[ing] the[ir] yearnings for freedom and equality … under Ottoman rule'.[23] They hoped to attain standing equal to Muslims in society, but also understood that reform was necessary within their own community, both to uproot the corruption and tyranny that had long plagued the clerical establishment and to introduce lay control in the administration of community affairs.

The Reform Edict of 1856 had required that each *millet* set up a commission to carry out the necessary reforms in their respective ethno-confessional communities. The Armenians drew up a constitution, or a code of regulations, that overhauled their community's structure and received approval for it from the Sublime Porte in 1863.[24] The constitution laid the groundwork for the creation of an Armenian National Assembly, whose delegates were to be made up of lay and ecclesiastical leadership. The document thus paved the way for a representative body comprised of elected officials from within the community 13 years before the Ottoman Empire adopted its own constitution.[25]

[22] Barsoumian, 'The Eastern Question and the *Tanzimat* Era', 192.

[23] GJ Libaridian, 'The History of Imperial Politics and the Politics of Imperial History', keynote speech delivered at the Centre for the Study of the International Relations of the Middle East and North Africa, University of Cambridge, Cambridge, UK, 13 June 2014. With the kind permission of the author.

[24] RE Antaramian, *Brokers of Faith, Brokers of Empire: Armenians and the Politics of Reform in the Ottoman Empire* (Stanford, Stanford University Press, 2020) 40–46. For an English translation of the constitution, see HFB Lynch, *Armenia: Travels and Studies*, vol 2: *The Turkish Provinces* (London, Longmans, 1901) Appendix 1.

[25] RG Suny, *'They Can Live in the Desert but Nowhere Else': A History of the Armenian Genocide* (Princeton, Princeton University Press, 2015) 59.

The reorganisation of the internal structure of the Armenian community did not necessarily alter Armenians' standing in relation to Muslims, but it did give them an important instrument to leverage demands on behalf of their compatriots across the empire. Patriarch Mkrtich Khrimian's activities in the 1870s reveal the sense of newfound hope he and others in the community placed in the *Tanzimat*. His office had long received grievances from the provinces asking for redress from the Sublime Porte. In 1870, the volume of these letters became so unmanageable that he tasked their compilation to the recently constituted Armenian National Assembly.[26] Two years later the patriarchate presented a detailed report to the sultan that spoke of 20 years of unresolved complaints and petitions.[27] These steps reflected new approaches to mediating state-society relations in the late Ottoman era as well as a growing sense that Armenians formed a part of a larger Ottoman nation.

All in all, the *Tanzimat* era ushered in a new wave of political and social development that spelled major changes for imperial subjects. Armenian intellectuals took to being more proactive in their community. Their efforts aligned with a general trend in Ottoman society in which educated, widely travelled individuals, well acquainted with the new ideas about civic responsibility and government accountability, increasingly participated.

IV. PARANOIA AND TRAUMA AT YILDIZ PALACE

Even with absolute power, a sovereign must trust some individuals who, in turn, must trust or learn to work with him.[28] Sultan Abdülhamid II, who reigned from 1876–1909, was a cautious monarch who relied on a small circle and trusted very few.[29] His mental state, observers reported at the time, bordered on paranoia. Abdülhamid had been brought to power by royal crises. As mentioned above, in 1876 a series of insurrections launched against Ottoman rule in the Balkans had been ruthlessly suppressed by imperial forces.[30] Soon afterwards the then Sultan Abdülaziz was deposed in a palace coup and later murdered or committed suicide. His successor, Sultan Murad V, ruled for a few brief months but was then deposed himself. The circumstances of his removal remain suspect, not least because Murad had signalled his support for constitutional governance. Yet court doctors found him mentally unfit to rule, opening the way for his dethronement.[31]

The traumatic fate of Abdülhamid II's immediate predecessors and the interest in the throne of others in line for it would have reinforced any paranoid suspicions of

[26] Antaramian, *Brokers of Faith, Brokers of Empire*, 135–40.

[27] Akçam, *A Shameful Act*, 36.

[28] The classic description of this was written by Eric Erikson in *Childhood and Society* (New York, WW Norton, 1950).

[29] BC Fortna, 'The Reign of Abdülhamid II' in R Kasaba (ed), *The Cambridge History of Turkey*, vol 4: *Turkey in the Modern World* (Cambridge, Cambridge University Press, 2008) 41.

[30] MS Anderson, *The Eastern Question, 1774–1923: A Study in International Relations* (London, Macmillan, 1966) 178–219.

[31] C Finkel, *Osman's Dream: The History of the Ottoman Empire* (New York, Basic Books, 2006) 482–83.

potential conspirators, a circle that included even his own uncle, a top-ranking army officer. The circumstances preceding his enthronement and the empire's brief experimentation with constitutional politics presumably helped push Abdülhamid towards the retrenchment of monarchical power. In 1878 he suspended the constitution and prorogued parliament by his own fiat, perhaps convincing himself that he was eliminating threats to his regime and his person, as well as retaining complete control over the conduct of international affairs. In so doing, the sultan foreclosed for the next three decades the profound possibilities for development the *Tanzimat* presented, abdicating the responsibility he might have taken for shepherding his people through the turn toward liberalism.

Despite his efforts to reassert the empire's international standing, train a loyal cadre of civil servants, and build popular legitimacy as the sultan-caliph, the situation worsened. Within years, Abdülhamid's policies and personality alienated him from many groups in society. His own subjects as well as the Great Powers increasingly worked to undermine his authority and sovereignty. Organisations formed in opposition to him, initially secretly and underground, and when driven into exile continued to operate against him by publishing articles, circulating pamphlets, and seeking support from European leaders. To them, one may also add disaffected elements among the empire's diverse ethno-confessional groups and the Great Powers. Numerous conspiratorial and assassination plots were hatched and discovered.

V. ANOTHER CRISIS IN THE BALKANS

The Balkans remained a sensitive region in the Ottoman periphery in the aftermath of the Greek War of Independence and 1853–56 Crimean War. In 1875, a new conflict rocked the region. It began as a series of peasant revolts directed against Ottoman Muslim landowners in Herzegovina but the discontent soon spread to neighbouring Bosnia and Bulgaria, where nationalist revolutionaries launched a full-scale rebellion against Ottoman rule. The Ottoman state immediately suppressed the uprisings with immense cruelty, earning it condemnation abroad, notably in Britain. Austria-Hungary and Russia tried to broker an international agreement in the shape of a reform package in Bosnia-Herzegovina. But months of back-and-forth diplomacy yielded no result and led only, on 24 April 1877, to a declaration of war by the Russian Empire. The Russians claimed to be intervening on behalf of the Christians while conveniently advancing their own territorial agenda and in the process waging a brutal campaign in the Balkans.

Within six months Russia had severed Serbia, Romania, and Bulgaria, comprising much of what remained of Ottoman Rumelia, from the empire. The Tsar's armies also opened up a second front in eastern Anatolia, capturing the formidable fortress-towns of Kars and Erzurum. In the midst of the fighting, Armenians living along the Russo-Ottoman border were massacred and their villages torched by retreating Ottoman forces, who held the Armenians responsible for the battlefield reverses.[32]

[32] See AO Sarkissian, *History of the Armenian Question to 1885* (Urbana, University of Illinois Press, 1938) 57–60.

Meanwhile, with their army firmly entrenched in the Balkans, Russian forces marched toward the Ottoman capital, halting on the outskirts of Istanbul at San Stefano (now Yeşilköy). The sultan sued for peace. Some 250,000–300,000 Muslim civilians living in the Balkans died in the fighting or from other causes related to the war, and approximately one million became refugees and fled to Anatolia.[33] Negotiations opened at San Stefano in January 1878. One month later, Abdülhamid would indefinitely suspend the empire's new constitution and prorogue the parliament.

Inspired by the victory of Russian arms, a delegation to the negotiations was led by the newly elected Armenian Patriarch Nerses Varzhapetian (Khrimian had stepped down in despair from his position in 1873). Varzhapetian asked the Russians to remain to ensure implementation of reforms for Armenians by retaining their forces in the occupied eastern provinces, appointing an Armenian general governor and other administrative officials, abolishing the privileges the Kurds claimed over Armenians, and imposing the fair collection of taxes. The Russians agreed to all these conditions and wrote them into Article 16 of the Treaty of San Stefano.

The Treaty of San Stefano brought a formal end to the war. But it awarded such vast swaths of Ottoman territory to the Russian Empire as to alarm Great Britain, France, and Austria-Hungary, and led them to call for an immediate revision of its terms to restore the balance of power. These states now convened, under German sponsorship, a new congress in Berlin. Just before it met, an Armenian delegation led by Khrimian visited the foreign capitals of Europe to press for autonomy for Armenians within the Ottoman Empire. Before departing, Khrimian reassured the sultan 'that they did not desire independence from Turkey but only an Armenian governor and a measure of autonomy in those areas where Armenians formed a majority'.[34]

The Armenian delegation to the Congress of Berlin, however, was not seated. What is more, the treaty concluded in Berlin not only pared down Russian territorial acquisitions in the Balkans and Anatolia but forced the Russians to withdraw. The new terms, embodied in Article 61, took the wind out of the sails of Article 16 of the San Stefano treaty by removing any reference to the continued presence of Russian forces in Anatolia. Rather, it simply obliged the empire to introduce reforms in the Armenian-inhabited provinces and report on their progress to the treaty's other signatories, who in the end did not seriously press the sultan on their implementation.[35] This allowed Abdülhamid to shirk responsibility by feigning compliance when he dispatched commissions to the provinces to 'study the issue'. The plight of the Armenians came to be referred to in international circles as the 'Armenian Question' and would remain a major issue in Ottoman-European relations over the next 40 years.

The Armenians were acutely aware of the sultan's failure to realise the reforms promised them in the wake of the Russian withdrawal. Returning empty-handed to Istanbul from the Berlin congress, a dispirited Khrimian told a gathering of

[33] B Pekesen, 'Expulsion and Emigration of the Muslims from the Balkans', European History Online (EGO) (Mainz, Leibniz Institute of European History, 7 March 2012), www.ieg-ego.eu/pekesenb-2011-en (accessed 20 July 2020); KH Karpat, *Ottoman Population, 1830–1914: Demographic and Social Characteristics* (Madison, University of Wisconsin Press, 1985) 75.

[34] Akçam, *A Shameful Act*, 38.

[35] Sarkissian, *History of the Armenian Question*, 92–105.

Armenians that the Great Powers had presented a 'dish of liberty' from which the other nations of the empire had drawn with their 'iron ladles'. But when it came to their turn, the Armenians only had a paper ladle, one that crumpled as it was dipped into the porridge. The idea implicit in Khrimian's speech, or at least how many Armenians interpreted it, was that only with an 'iron ladle' – that is, through arms – could Armenians finally see meaningful change.[36]

VI. MUSLIM-ARMENIAN RELATIONS IN THE RUSSO-OTTOMAN BORDERLANDS

In the years following the end of the 1877–78 Russo-Ottoman War, law and order in the eastern provinces, where Armenians and Muslims both lived in large numbers, broke down. Within the Ottoman imperial domains, the sultan adopted a policy to disempower Armenians by breaking up the areas where they had sought reform, gerrymandering boundaries to ensure that Armenians did not form a majority.[37] On the other side of the border, Russian rule in the recently acquired provinces in the Caucasus engendered uncertainty that was enough to convince many Muslims to leave, bringing about an unofficial population exchange between 1878 and 1881.[38] Approximately 83,000 Muslims immigrated to the Ottoman Empire. In the other direction, some 2,000 Ottoman Armenians applied to move into the Russian provinces of Kars and Ardahan. Although Russian authorities forbade Armenian emigration in any form, over 6,000 families still managed to cross the Ottoman border illegally.[39]

Abdülhamid II's suspension of the constitution gave him free rein to quash domestic opposition, chasing the original architects of the *Tanzimat* into exile or submission. But while the Young Ottomans and other reform-minded statesmen disappeared from the picture, a new circle of young, college-educated men found in each other the similar aim of opposing the sultan's arbitrary rule while striving to preserve and modernise the empire. Unlike the Young Ottomans, the Young Turks, as they were soon called, were not particularly religious. Comprised of a diverse set of actors, including intellectuals and writers, members of the ulema, and the junior officer corps of the Ottoman military, they would in time establish a base strong enough to challenge the autocratic regime.

[36] See R Panossian, *The Armenians: From Kings and Priests to Merchants and Commissars* (New York, Columbia University Press, 2006) 168–73.

[37] See F Dündar, *Crime of Numbers: The Role of Statistics in the Armenian Question (1878–1918)* (New Brunswick, NJ, Transactions Publishers, 2010) 36.

[38] C Badem, '"Forty Years of Black Days"?: The Russian Administration of Kars, Ardahan, and Batum, 1878–1918' in LJ Frary and M Kozelsky (eds), *Russian-Ottoman Borderlands: The Eastern Question Reconsidered* (Madison, University of Wisconsin Press, 2014) 221–22.

[39] AA Melkonyan, '"The Kars Oblast", 1878–1918' in RG Hovannisian (ed), *Armenian Kars and Ani* (Costa Mesa, CA, Mazda Publishers, 2011) 229.

VII. THE CALL TO ARMS

After the signing of the Treaty of Berlin, many Armenian community representatives gave up hope that the Great Powers would ever enforce Article 61. As Armenians in both the Ottoman and Russian empires learned more about the abject conditions under which so many Ottoman Armenians subsisted and understood the limits of negotiations and peaceful petitioning, they, too, abandoned hope for reform under the existing system of government. Oppression, fear, and hopelessness led most Armenians to turn inwards and restrict their relationships and activities to matters concerning their own communal affairs within the familiar, protective embrace of community and church.

However, a small segment of middle- and lower-class activists and members of the transnational Armenian intelligentsia now realised that they had to effect change themselves because others were not going to do it for them.[40] In Europe and the Russian Empire they formed two important revolutionary political parties: the Social Democratic Hnchakian Party (SDHP) in 1887, and the Armenian Revolutionary Federation (ARF) in 1890.[41]

Although the Hnchak and Dashnak parties differed in political philosophy and methods, both reflected a nationalist as well as revolutionary impulse. Historian Gerard Libaridian understands these 'agents of change' as aiming both for Armenians' emancipation in their homeland and liberation as a people:

> The ... revolutionary character [of the parties] was not defined solely by their willingness to resort to an armed struggle ... nor in their goal to achieve reforms [but in] ... their willingness to relate the crisis of the provinces to an oppressive social structure and regressive political-economic system; to understand that system in the context of the most progressive social thinking of the times ... and in their determination to transform the people from a subject of history into agents of change ... The revolutionary movement began when the political parties redefined the idea of liberation to include the emancipation of people and not just that of a territory.[42]

Both parties called for taking up arms, pointing out that the Balkan Christians had achieved their objectives only through such means. To be sure, from the beginning the ARF platform called for reform within the empire, not detachment from it. Its members regarded this goal as achievable.[43] The Hnchakians, on the other hand, believed that there could be no autonomy without territorial separation, and thus

[40] GJ Libaridian, *Modern Armenia: People, Nation, State* (New Brunswick, NJ, Transaction Publishers, 2004) 15.

[41] L Nalbandian, *The Armenian Revolutionary Movement: The Development of Armenian Political Parties through the Nineteenth Century* (Berkeley, University of California Press, 1963) 115, 151. According to Gerard Libaridian, the Armenakan Party, founded in Van in 1885, was not a revolutionary party in the true sense of the word nor a 'determinant of the character of the conflict'. See GJ Libaridian, 'What Was Revolutionary about Armenian Revolutionary Parties in the Ottoman Empire?' in RG Suny et al (eds), *A Question of Genocide: Armenian and Turks at the End of the Ottoman Empire* (Oxford, Oxford University Press, 2011) 339 fn 1.

[42] Libaridian, *Modern Armenia*, 105.

[43] See Libaridian, 'What Was Revolutionary about Armenian Revolutionary Parties in the Ottoman Empire?', 90–91.

that any change within the empire was pointless. They sought the creation of a socialist society in the independent Armenia they wished to establish.[44] To the Ottoman state, the revolutionary organisations were what it alternatively called *çete*s (bands) or *Komitaci*s (secret committee members). They viewed them as mortal threats to the empire.

In 1890, members of the Hnchakian Party applied its revolutionary stance to its people when they disrupted a mass led by the Armenian Patriarch in Istanbul to call attention to the failure of the Church and the Armenian National Assembly to support implementation of Article 61. They unsuccessfully attempted to persuade the patriarch to participate in a march to Yıldız Palace and engaged in a shoot-out with the police when the latter tried to intervene, leaving several policemen and demonstrators dead.[45]

Over the next few years, armed bands of Armenians known as *fedayees* would take the fight to the eastern provinces in skirmishes with the *Hamidiye*, the Ottomans' newly established irregular cavalry regiments, to put a stop to raids by Kurds, and other forms of oppression and threats.[46] While a full-scale rebellion never materialised in the provinces, an unlikely prospect even to the members of the independence-minded SDHP, the Armenian political committees soon developed a highly disciplined network throughout the empire, instilling fear in the sultan and other imperial officials.

VIII. EMERGENCE OF THE YOUNG TURKS

By far the most serious threat to the sultan's rule arose in conspiratorial circles formed in the empire's elite medical and military academies. In part, these opposition groups emerged in response to the empire's almost interminable domestic and foreign crises. In 1881, the imperial treasury was declared insolvent. By the end of the decade, the sultan had asserted his personal authority over the civil service and all other potential political and military challengers to his rule.[47]

Within a short time, the new block of opposition to the sultan coalesced out of these circles. The Young Turks were a mix of military officers, bureaucrats, members of the sultan's extended family, *ulema*, civil servants, and public intellectuals. Historian Şükrü Hanioğlu describes the group as broadly seeking to return to parliamentary government to preserve the empire through constitutionalism, even though 'under the strong influence of European elitist theories of the late nineteenth century … [they looked] down on a parliament as a heterogeneous crowd'.[48] Both aim

[44] Libaridian, *Modern Armenia*, 18.

[45] OR Miller, '"Back to the Homeland" (*Tebi Yergir*): Or, how Peasants became Revolutionaries in Muş' (2017) 4 *Journal of Ottoman and Turkish Studies* 305.

[46] On the Hamidiye, see J Klein, *The Margins of Empire: Kurdish Militias in the Ottoman Tribal Zone* (Stanford, Stanford University Press, 2011).

[47] See Fortna, 'The Reign of Abdülhamid II'.

[48] M Şükrü Hanioğlu, *Preparation for a Revolution: The Young Turks: 1902–1908* (Oxford, Oxford University Press, 2001) 3.

and method were embraced by the newly formed (Ottoman Muslim) political parties (called committees), including that of one stratum of Young Turks, the Committee of Union and Progress or CUP (*Ittihad ve Terakki Cemiyeti*). The CUP would assume complete control of the Ottoman government in 1913.

IX. THE HAMIDIAN MASSACRES

Sultan Abdülhamid II laid claim to absolute power that rested upon tradition and was legally unconstrained. He perceived his empire's troubles as entirely caused by others. He believed that the Armenians' demands for outside assistance, rather than putting up with the state-sponsored discrimination and oppression, were by and large responsible for the interference of the Great Powers, that they claimed rights to which they were not entitled, while at the same time endangering and betraying imperial principles.[49] To be fair, the Great Powers had pushed him for their own ends and he was powerless to resist. With good reason to fear for the survival of his office, his empire, and his person, feelings of helplessness and impotent rage overcame Abdülhamid, limiting his ability to distinguish real from imagined threats, leaving his thinking distorted, defensive, and unreliable. His rambling diatribes would not move the Great Powers, yet his frustration and anger could be channelled in the direction of punishing the Armenians for what he and others regarded as their impudence.

Matters came to a head against the backdrop of worsening relations between Armenians and Kurds in the east. In the early 1890s, more acts of violence were visited upon Armenian villagers. The inhabitants of the mountainous Sasun district in south-eastern Anatolia, long a bastion of Armenian self-rule, rebelled against rampant over-taxation and oppressive tax collection abuse in the late summer of 1894; they were consequently subject to a series of massacres.[50] By then the Armenians in the eastern provinces had made great strides in education and advanced further socioeconomically. Due to the teaching of Protestant missionaries, many converted to Protestantism, attaining greater freedom than that offered by the Armenian Church. In these ways, the Armenians' lives, despite persecution and hardship, were distinguished from the Muslims', breeding fierce envy and hatred.

The wave of indiscriminate killings, pillaging, and rape seen in Sasun swept across Armenian-populated villages and towns in Anatolia from 1894 to 1895.[51] In southeastern Anatolia in Aintab the massacres began on 15 November 1895, writes historian and genocide scholar Ümit Kurt:

> The doors of Armenian homes in the Muslim quarter were marked .... [L]large crowds of villagers poured into the town .... That evening the *mufti* (religious official of the state) and *kadi* (a Muslim judge) issued a *fatwa* stating the 'the lives and property of Christians

[49] See S Astourian, 'On the Genealogy of the Armenian-Turkish Conflict, Sultan Abdülhamid, and the Armenian Massacres' (2012) 21 *Journal of the Society for Armenian Studies* 184–85, 195.

[50] See OR Miller, 'Sasun 1894: Mountains, Missionaries, and Massacres at the End of the Ottoman Empire' (PhD thesis, Columbia University, 2015).

[51] For the most recent appraisal, see Suny, '*They Can Live in the Desert but Nowhere Else*', 104–13. See also Astourian, 'On the Genealogy of the Armenian-Turkish Conflict', 199.

> were lawful prey for Muslims.' … A mob of Turks and Kurds began the slaughter … where Armenian shops and businesses were located. The mob butchered shopkeepers and pillaged stores, killing all Armenians in sight. Attackers used stones, clubs, and axes. … The violence then spread to the Armenian residential neighborhoods that were least defensible. Dr Shepard, the missionary in charge of the hospital, heard 'the terrible [cries] of Kurdish and Turkish women cheering on their men,' and saw 'a crowd of Kurds armed with guns, axes, clubs, and butcher knives … swarming out of their quarter … to attack their Armenian neighbors'.[52]

Despite the carnage, a number of conscientious Muslims intervened to prevent further violence from being carried out against their neighbours. They are credited with having saved the lives of as many as 2,000 Armenians.[53]

While most acts of violence took place in the eastern provinces, Istanbul was also rocked by the onslaught. In August 1896, about 20 ARF operatives launched a daring operation to seize the European-run Ottoman Bank to draw the Great Powers' attention to the Armenians' plight. The plan went completely awry. Government forces quickly showed up and killed many of the conspirators in a day's standoff. European diplomats eventually helped broker a deal to grant the plotters safe passage to Marseilles, but not before massacres broke out against the city's Armenians, leaving perhaps as many as 6,000 dead.[54] The local press and the regime attempted to shift the blame to the Armenians by highlighting the deaths of ten Ottoman soldiers killed during the siege, framing it as an outrageous, unforgiveable affront.

There is no direct evidence that the sultan ordered this massacre or the others, but he undoubtedly allowed, if not encouraged, an unrestrained atmosphere that unleashed his subjects to attack with impunity, discharging their resentments and frustrations over what he and they viewed as the Armenians' outrageous, presumptuous activism.[55] Gustave Le Bon's groundbreaking 1886 study, *The Crowd: A Study of the Popular Mind*, on the psychology of crowd behaviour, illustrated the kind of implicit understanding that existed between the sultan and the crowds, such that the crowd's hateful emotions were stimulated and acted on without a direct order.[56] Thus, an effort was made to create the impression that the massacres broke out 'spontaneously' in different places, especially where the state had abetted Kurdish chieftains in levelling greater demands on Armenians.

Tellingly, the Young Turk members of the recently formed Committee of Union and Progress showed little sympathy toward the Armenians during this crisis, despite their own avowed commitment to constitutionalism and opposition to despotism.[57]

[52] Ü Kurt, 'Reform and Violence in the Hamidian Era: The Political Context of the 1895 Armenian Massacres in Aintab' (2018) 32(3) *Holocaust and Genocide Studies* 411.

[53] Barnham to Currie, November 1895, FO 195/1883, cited in Kurt, 'Reform and Violence in the Hamidian Era', 413.

[54] See F Riedler, 'The City as a Stage for a Violent Spectacle: The Massacres of Armenians in Istanbul in 1895–96' in U Freitag et al (eds), *Urban Violence in the Middle East: Changing Cityscapes in the Transition from Empire to Nation State* (New York, Berghahn Books, 2015) 164.

[55] See Suny, *'They Can Live in the Desert but Nowhere Else'*, 130–31.

[56] Göçek, *Denial of Violence*, 33.

[57] The mantle of the Young Ottomans had by now passed to the Young Turks. An elite group of them formed the Committee of Union and Progress (CUP) or in Turkish, *İttihad ve Terakki Cemiyeti*. Its members were also known as Unionists and İttihadists. Historians differ about the date of the formation of the CUP but agree that it was sometime in the 1890s or early 1900s.

An article by a leading Young Turk, Ahmed Rıza, in *Mechveret*, at the time the CUP's unofficial journal, argued that the raid on the Ottoman Bank had 'sacrificed Turkish-Armenian relations'.[58] The CUP sympathised with the sultan and called for a halt to 'Armenian impudence'. They posted flyers around Istanbul declaring, 'Muslims and our most beloved Turkish compatriots! The Armenians have become so bold as to assault the Sublime Porte ... They have shaken the very foundations of our capital'.[59]

European investigations into the 1894–96 massacres led to condemnation of the state's manipulation of the facts and the creation of a diplomatic crisis, though all they got out of the sultan was another fruitless promise of reform.[60] These 'Hamidian massacres' were headlined in the major newspapers of Europe and the US, earning Abdülhamid II the title of 'the Bloody Sultan'.[61] All told, the killings resulted in perhaps 90,000 Armenian deaths and left some 50,000 Armenian children orphaned and destitute.[62] Thousands of other Christians were also massacred. But the Great Powers imposed no serious consequences on the Ottomans, setting an apparently acceptable precedent for further massacres of Armenians a well as other Christians. If the incident in Istanbul marked the last large massacre of Armenians in that decade, acts of violence on a much smaller scale in the east continued right up until the start of the genocide in 1915. The exception was the large province-wide massacre in Adana in 1909 (Chapter 7).

Ottoman antipathy and contempt for collective Armenian 'impudence' at times assumed the language of insulted honour and threatened entitlement to imperial territories. At least one sizable segment of the population found it difficult to reconcile the new ideas embodied in the *Tanzimat* with the traditional understandings of Muslim superiority over Christians.

X. ARMENIAN–TURKISH RELATIONS AT THE END OF THE NINETEENTH CENTURY

The violence that broke out in 1894–96 was all-encompassing. Armenian neighbourhoods, villages, and towns were looted, confiscated and torched.[63] Vast tracts

[58] Mardin, *Jön Türklerin siyasi fikirleri*, 150, cited in Akçam, *A Shameful Act*, 61.

[59] Akçam, *A Shameful Act*, 60.

[60] Suny, *'They Can Live in the Desert but Nowhere Else'*, 130.

[61] This section relies in part on recent research presented by E Gölbaşı, 'The Anti-Armenian Riots of 1895–1896: The "Climate of Violence" and Intercommunal Strife in the Ottoman Eastern Province', and by Ü Kurt, 'The Breakdown of Previously Peaceful Coexistence: The Aintab Armenian Massacres of 1895', papers presented on a panel titled 'Reform, Violence and Revolutionary Organizations in the late nineteenth-century Ottoman East', at the Middle East Scholars' Association (MESA) annual meeting held in Boston on 19 November 2016.

[62] N Maksudyan, *Orphans and Destitute Children in the Late Ottoman Empire* (Syracuse, Syracuse University Press, 2014) 120. Johannes Lepsius, a German pastor and fervent supporter of Armenian rights, carried out a personal investigation into the aftermath of the massacres and came up with the following numbers: 85,000 dead; 2,500 towns and villages 'laid to waste'; 559 villages 'forced' to convert to Islam; 282 churches turned into mosques; and 500,000 left destitute. See J Lepsius, *Armenia and Europe: An Indictment* (London, Hodder and Stoughton, 1897) 1, at 18.

[63] RG Hovannisian, 'The Armenian Question in the Ottoman Empire, 1876–1914' in RG Hovannisian (ed), *The Armenian People from Ancient to Modern Times*, vol 2: *Foreign Domination to Statehood: The Fifteenth Century to the Twentieth Century* (New York, St Martin's Press, 2004) 222–26.

of Armenian agricultural land were expropriated. In addition to the deaths, the trauma of survivors, their impoverishment, and creation of thousands of orphans led tens of thousands to convert to Islam to save themselves, while many others fled to safety abroad to Russia.[64] Looking back in 1913, an official in the British embassy in Istanbul, Mr Marling, wrote to Foreign Secretary Edward Grey that he had discerned a clear pattern of removal of rural Armenians from their homeland by the Ottoman state since 1878:

> The Turkish Government, after the Treaty of Berlin, realising that a sense of nationality cannot easily live without a peasantry, and that if it succeeded in uprooting the Armenian peasantry from the soil and driving them into the towns or out of the country, it would in good part rid itself of the Armenians and the Armenian question, condoned and encouraged Kurdish usurpation of Armenian lands. This retail process was repeated on a wholesale scale after the big massacres of 1895–96.[65]

The logic of this attitude of the Ottoman state did not have to lead to genocide, but it is clearly evident that some contemporaries did not rule out the possibility that its leaders would be capable of pursing more radical and more devastating policies with the single aim of preserving geopolitical and domestic sovereignty.

*

The Ottoman social and political environment of the pre-*Tanzimat* era was rooted in a framework that set Muslims on a plane higher than Christians and Jews. These visible and invisible foundations of the social structure came under siege with the *Tanzimat*. The threat to the core of Ottoman Turkish Muslim identity made it, as Kévorkian writes empathically, 'difficult for people, set in their ways, to grasp in a short span of time the transformation that Ottoman society was now supposed to undergo'.[66] As a whole, the Young Turks and especially the CUP turned out to lack heartfelt commitment to that which, according to historian Taner Akçam, they had after the Greek War of Independence accepted as necessary to secure the empire – 'a new political and cultural identity'.[67] Instead, the grandeur of the Ottoman Empire was disappearing, both psychologically and territorially. The long-presumed superior status of Muslims was no longer assured.

[64] Hovannisian, 'The Armenian Question in the Ottoman Empire, 1876–1914', 218–26; S Deringil, '"The Armenian Question is Finally Closed": Mass Conversions of Armenians in Anatolia during the Hamidian Massacres of 1895–1897' (2009) 51 *Comparative Studies in Society and History* 344. Johannes Lepsius, a German pastor and fervent supporter of Armenian rights, carried out a personal investigation into the aftermath of the massacres and came up with the following numbers: 85,000 dead; 2,500 towns and villages 'laid to waste'; 559 villages 'forced' to convert to Islam; 282 churches turned into mosques; and 500,000 left destitute. See J Lepsius, *Armenia and Europe: An Indictment* (London, Hodder and Stoughton, 1897) 1–31, at 18.

[65] Memorandum by Gerald Fitzmaurice, enclosure in CM Marling (Istanbul) to E Grey (London), 27 August 1913, in GP Gooch and H Temperley (eds), *British Documents on the Origins of the War, 1898–1914*, vol 10, pt 1 (London, HMSO, 1936) no 567, 513.

[66] Kévorkian, *The Armenian Genocide*, 76.

[67] Akçam, *A Shameful Act*, 28.

Thus, among many Muslims, there was a growing perception that the existing and seemingly natural order of things, their once dominant position vis-à-vis their Christians neighbours, was changing. They increasingly felt threatened by and hostile toward Armenians. The *Tanzimat* made little difference to local Muslim stereotypes of Armenians. According to Kévorkian, Armenians were still seen as deceitful instead of trustworthy, entitled instead of grateful, traitorous instead of loyal, an enemy in their midst:

> [The Armenians'] status as gâvurs ('infidels') had improved somewhat since implementation of the *Tanzimat*, yet they continued to be perceived by the Turkish population as ungrateful, deceitful, and disloyal groups with a penchant for profiting from all the others .... The Muslim masses continued to regard the *millets* as foreign elements, almost as domestic foes.[68]

Akçam extends the impact of the loss of status by the Turkish population to its logical conclusion. The Ottomans' prior tolerance of Armenians, he argues, rested precisely on Armenians' inferior status. When that balance changed, so did Muslim tolerance: 'The loss of superior status had shaken the Muslims' confidence, which resulted in the loss of their tolerance'.[69]

People who have been pushed under and humiliated may overreact when released from the humiliating circumstance. Some Armenians adopted a cultural air of superiority as they experienced some release from centuries of discrimination. As Libaridian puts it:

> Educated and urban Armenians developed a sense of civilizational superiority over Muslims whom they associated with backwardness. It is possible that this was a countermeasure to the sense of superiority that even the humblest Muslim could have towards any Christian, a sense that was an integral element in the Ottoman system.[70]

In sum, over the course of the nineteenth century, the Ottoman state faced the increasingly potent political force of nationalism. For its ideologues, nationalism appeared as an instrument to mobilise popular support and construct political legitimacy. Nationalism's language and vision appealed to those who felt the heavy oppression of the state. Ottoman leaders would struggle with tempering its seductive message while maintaining imperial sovereignty right down until the Great War. For them the implementation of constitutional rule, in addition to fostering meaningful administrative, economic, and legal changes, was thought to be the best way to head off the challenge of nationalism.[71]

[68] Kévorkian, *The Armenian Genocide*, 10. For contemporary Ottoman Muslim attitudes toward Armenians and other non-Muslims, see also SH Astourian, 'Testing World-System Theory, Cilicia (1830s–1890s): Armenian-Turkish Polarization and the Ideology of Modern Ottoman Historiography' (PhD thesis, UCLA, 1996) 409–67.

[69] Akçam, *A Shameful Act*, 35.

[70] G Libaridian, 'The Clash of Empires: World War I and the Middle East', keynote speech, 13–14 June 2014, Cambridge University.

[71] CV Findley, 'The Tanzimat' in Kasaba (ed), *The Cambridge History of Turkey*, vol 4, 32; Zürcher, *Turkey: A Modern History*, 77.

Unsurprisingly, relations between Muslims and non-Muslims in the Balkans and Anatolia did not ease in the early twentieth century. If the *Tanzimat* heralded immense new changes in politics and society and represented a spirited endeavour by Ottoman elites to redefine and reinforce the meaning of imperial identity, it created new challenges for Ottoman rulers as both Muslims and non-Muslims adopted the new vocabulary of reform and progress.[72] The empire continued to suffer reversals. The Great Powers sensed weakness and sought to safeguard their strategic interests in the region by way of overt and much more subtle forms of intervention. The Ottoman state faced pressure from outside as well as from within. As its leaders saw it, the position of the Ottoman Empire was gradually evolving from one of a once-formidable imperial state to that of a helpless victim of the European powers, aided and abetted by its own suspect minorities.

[72] Findley, 'The Tanzimat', 37.

6

The Unlikely Alliance against the Sultan

> We were foes; from now on, we are friends. Yesterday, tyranny reigned; today, the Constitution does. 'I am convinced that we shall defend it together', declared the enemy of yesterday before the stunned Armenian leaders.
>
> Raymond Kévorkian (on the aim of the Armenians' unlikely allies)[1]

TOWARD THE END of the nineteenth century, the Ottoman Empire's problems, and by extension those of Sultan Abdülhamid II, mounted. The sultan was subjected to increasing pressure by the European powers to end the mistreatment that Christians in the Balkans and Anatolia suffered at the hands of Ottoman soldiers and officials. Failure to grant greater autonomy and rights, they warned, would result in dire consequences for the empire. Yet the sultan weathered the challenges posed by nationalism and threats of European intervention with varying degrees of success. It was the elite Ottoman Muslim opposition from within that now presented the most formidable challenge to the supremacy of his reign.

I. THE YOUNG TURKS AND FORMATION OF THE CUP

While the opposition that rose against Abdülhamid II was made up of individuals from disparate backgrounds, those who came to spearhead the movement had usually received some form of education at a higher institution of learning, particularly the imperial medical and military academies. Some had studied abroad in Paris and London and picked up ideas on modern administration, governance, and the emerging field of sociology. As a group, they became known as the Young Turks, a diverse movement of loosely affiliated factions sprawling throughout the empire, British-occupied Egypt, and Europe.[2] One faction, the Committee of Union and Progress (CUP), became convinced that only through restoration of the 1876 constitution could the poor governance under Sultan Abdülhamid II be remedied, his power

[1] R Kévorkian, *The Armenian Genocide: A Complete History* (London, IB Tauris, 2011) 59, paraphrasing Armenian records of speeches.

[2] M Şükrü Hanioğlu, *The Young Turks in Opposition* (New York, Oxford University Press, 1995) 213.

curbed and a more rational system of administration put in place. The first article in the CUP's regulations declared its aim of

> ... reforming the administrative system of the existing Ottoman government, which violates individual rights, such as justice, equality, freedom, stops all Ottomans from progress and precipitated the fall of the fatherland into the hands of foreign molestation and coercion.[3]

The CUP's membership grew in size and diversity. Significantly, its new adherents professed more traditional and conservative beliefs. The CUP disseminated propaganda across the empire, often through readings at coffee houses.[4] To the masses generally, the changes that modernisation and liberalisation would bring were still unfamiliar,[5] but the activities of the CUP raised expectations and ultimately won popular support.[6] But this never reached the level where Abdülhamid would willingly concede to the opposition's demands.

II. THE ISOLATED SULTAN-CALIPH

As part of his overall strategy to shore up the foundations of the state, Abdülhamid, following his accession in 1876, laid claim to the position of caliph, the supreme leader of the Muslim world. He sought to build up his primary base of support with the Muslim population at home and abroad, employing classic titles and symbols that promoted the position of the caliphate.[7] In both roles, he would have expected obedience, however arbitrary his demands.[8] His devotion to absolutism was evident in his conscious practice of 'always bas[ing] his decrees on "imperial will" (*arzu-yu şâhâne*) and [taking] special care never to refer to any particular law'.[9] He operated a wide spy network, and from 1888 employed censorship that prohibited 'any discussion of political matters, especially anything related to liberalism'.[10] He imposed restrictions even on the military, who he felt could be turned on him, in turn demoralising his own, the sultanate's, and the empire's, protectors.

The sultan's repressive regime won him few friends. Feelings against him ran high as the system he oversaw solidified over the 1880s and appeared unlikely to loosen its grip over civil society. Against his wishes, under his regime the empire witnessed the formation of embryonic political parties, called 'committees', against him. Abdülhamid even managed to alienate any support he may have had among members of the army officer corps, so great was the level of mistrust between the sultan

[3] Osmanlı İttihad ve Terakki Cemiyeti Nizamnâmesi (np, nd), cited in Hanioğlu, *The Young Turks in Opposition*, 76.

[4] M Şükrü Hanioğlu, *Preparation for a Revolution: The Young Turks: 1902–1908* (Oxford, Oxford University Press, 2001) 5.

[5] Hanioğlu, *Preparation for a Revolution*, 5.

[6] Hanioğlu, *The Young Turks in Opposition*, 77.

[7] The most authoritative study is S Deringil, *The Well-Protected Domains: Ideology and Legitimation of Power in the Ottoman Empire, 1876–1909* (London, IB Tauris, 1999).

[8] Hanioğlu, *The Young Turks in Opposition*, 23–24.

[9] Hanioğlu, *The Young Turks in Opposition*, 24.

[10] EJ Zürcher, *Turkey: A Modern History*, 3rd edn (London, IB Tauris, 2004) 78.

and the military.[11] A strongly worded manifesto issued against him by the CUP in 1896 encapsulated the grievances of many a pious Ottoman:

> Muslims!
>
> Abdülhamid is neither the sultan nor the caliph according to our religion. Those who doubt our words should look into the Holy Quran and Sunnah.
>
> Our committee revealed the orders of God and the Prophet to the government and the people ... Abdülhamid turned away from them and proved that he is a tyrant and does not hesitate to disobey God. Therefore, our people should have resorted to arms; sadly they have not done so and thus have proven that they were also unrighteous ... We silenced ourselves as if we believed the reform promises of Abdülhamid. However, he seized the opportunity and attained an apogee of inflicting suffering, destruction on our country and abasement of the state and caliphate ...
>
> Abdülhamid is annihilating the religion and the state. Please rise and slash this fake caliph and his accomplices to pieces. Give up your lives and kill.[12]

The imperial crisis required change and adaptation. But Abdülhamid refused to be challenged. His hold slipped, threats mounted, and, presumably traumatised with fear, he withdrew from others and resisted change. His paranoia – anxiety, fear, and impotent rage – would have been permanently aroused in this situation and stood in the way of his access to his own rational mind and others'. He would have distorted the very real dangers he and his empire faced much less had he sought counsel from others apart from palace favourites, yes-men, and sycophants. Instead, he went after individuals with different views, arresting those who did not exile themselves in time.

III. ADVICE NOT TAKEN

There were at least three able, prominent, and moderate members among the Young Turk elite from whom the sultan, had he not felt so threatened by hearing a point of view that, at first blush, he did not agree with, might have taken counsel. By the early 1900s, each of them was painfully aware of all of the markers of imperial collapse – the loss of territory, the treatment of non-Muslims, the insolvent treasury, maladministration of the empire, and the image abroad conveyed by the Armenian massacres. They favoured reinstatement of the constitution and convening of a national assembly, believing these measures were essential for fighting rampant corruption in the Ottoman bureaucracy and military and for ensuring that promotions in both institutions would be based on merit, not loyalty to the sultan. While convinced that advances in science and technology were also necessary to imperial survival, they realised that those alone would not solve the empire's problems.

[11] KH Karpat, *The Politicization of Islam: Reconstructing Identity, State, Faith, and Community in the Late Ottoman State* (Oxford, Oxford University Press, 2001) 171.

[12] A[rkivi] Q[endror] Sh[tetrëor] [Tirana], 19/60//25/1, as cited in Hanioğlu, *The Young Turks in Opposition*, 115–16.

Amid the Armenian crisis of 1895, the ambitious, articulate, and respected senior Ottoman bureaucrat Murad Bey had approached the sultan to see whether he could convince him to abandon his support of conservative groups.[13] The sultan had asked the independent-minded Murad to elaborate, but when his closest inside advisers, probably protective of their own positions with these groups, spoke poorly of Murad, the sultan did not follow up. Abdülhamid was unable to challenge these counsellors, allowing them to be his authority and reinforcing his and their mutual ignorance. Thereafter Murad worked openly against the sultan from abroad. In his writings, he called on Great Britain to persuade the sultan to improve the administration of the empire and advocated rapprochement with the Armenian political parties.[14] On his return to Istanbul, he continued to plot unsuccessful coup d'états and was eventually placed under house arrest.[15]

The CUP's Paris branch was led by the educational reformer Ahmed Rıza, an exceptionally articulate, complicated, and strong-minded activist who soon became

Murad Bey

Source: Wikimedia Commons.

[13] Hanioğlu, *The Young Turks in Opposition*, 76.
[14] Hanioğlu, *The Young Turks in Opposition*, 79–81.
[15] Hanioğlu, *The Young Turks in Opposition*, 171.

an outspoken Turkish nationalist.[16] Earlier in his life, the positivist Rıza had founded a public high school for girls in Istanbul that is still open today. In a letter to his sister, he expressed his views on women and aspects of Islam:

> Were I a woman, I would embrace atheism and never become a Muslim. Imagine a religion that imposes laws always beneficial to men but hazardous to women such as permitting my husband to have three additional wives and as many concubines as he wishes, *houris* awaiting him in heaven, while I cover my head and face as a miller's horse. Beside these I would not be allowed to divorce a husband who prevented me from having any kind of fun, but would be required to submit to his beatings. Keep this religion far away from me.[17]

Ahmed Rıza

Source: A Andonian, *Azatarar sharzhun banakin haghtakan mutkn i K. Polis* (Istanbul, Tparan ew Gratun HG Balakashian, 1909) 53.

In the midst of the Hamidian massacres, Rıza called for equal treatment for all ethno-confessional groups under the constitution. He criticised the sultan for the corrupting influence that his failure to uphold the constitution had brought on and for attempting

[16] Hanioğlu, *The Young Turks in Opposition*, 83.
[17] Hanioğlu, *The Young Turks in Opposition*, 115–16.

to win over others through out-and-out bribery. Rıza also called out those who allowed themselves to be corrupted, thus speaking truth to those currying power:

> The sultan does not take seriously those who request the reproclamation of the constitution, when he observes that he can silence those selfish profiteers who made publishing in Europe a capital of trade for themselves in exchange for an unimportant post, a small sum of money, or a concession.[18]

Rıza's understanding might have helped guide the sultan to defend the empire through more honourable means.

The third CUP member whose ideas could have made the greatest difference in the direction of progress for the empire and the Armenians was Prince Mehmet Sabahaddin, a member of the royal family. Having gone into exile in 1899 with his brother and father, the pro-British Damad Mahmud Celâleddîn Pasha and brother-in-law of the sultan, Sabahaddin was a conservative writer and sociologist.[19] Like Murad, Sabahaddin favoured foreign intervention to preserve the empire under a monarchy. He was, in historian Hans-Lukas Kieser's view, 'truly liberal' in his

Prince Mehmet Sabahaddin

Source: Wikimedia Commons.

[18] Hanioğlu, *The Young Turks in Opposition*, 113.
[19] Hanioğlu, *The Young Turks in Opposition*, 143–44.

belief in 'individual responsibility and private initiative regardless of religious or ethnic affiliation'.[20] In 1906, out on a limb and with a limited numbers of supporters, Sabahaddin founded the Society for Private Initiative and Decentralization on the basis of his belief that decentralisation of the imperial administration would hold the empire together. In 1908, Sabahaddin left the CUP to form and lead the second largest faction among the Young Turks, the Liberal Unionist Party. As he was in the line of succession to the throne, Sabahaddin posed a plausible threat to the sultan. Sabahaddin pursued his vision but with few supporters. His party won just one seat in the 1908 parliamentary elections.[21]

These three Ottoman intellectuals did not agree much among themselves on how to preserve the empire beyond ending monarchical absolutism and reinstating the constitution. Had the sultan considered seeking counsel from outside his immediate circle, and worked with and decided among them on various matters, things might have turned out differently. However, all three were anathema to the sultan on many counts and especially on the matter of personal religious belief. None was a devoted Islamist, agreeing that religion was an instrument that could at most be wielded to stir up Muslim enmity against Abdülhamid. The Young Turks generally abhorred the 'despicable' Muslim masses for their lack of political self-awareness and attachment to religion, reflecting a common Young Turks aphorism: 'Science is the religion of the elite, whereas religion is the science of the masses'.[22] They did not present this attitude publicly, not wanting to alienate their more devout allies.[23] But their form of secular modernism was known and pronounced enough that the sultan dismissed them as atheists.[24] What might have happened if the sultan and his close advisers had instead had serious discussions with these supposed enemies?

IV. THE AFTERMATH OF THE HAMIDIAN MASSACRES

The violence of 1894–96 set off a wave of immigration that saw thousands of Ottoman Armenians depart for safer shores. As they settled in their new homes in Europe and the United States, they also brought with them their religious and political traditions.[25] In 1900, the Hnchakian leader Stepan Sapah-Gulian wrote from exile

[20] H-L Kieser, *Talaat Pasha: Father of Modern Turkey, Architect of Genocide* (Princeton, NJ, Princeton University Press, 2018) 37, 60.

[21] Zürcher, *Turkey: A Modern History*, 95.

[22] Hanioğlu, *The Young Turks in Opposition*, 201, 206. When the leading Young Turks used Islam as a political tool, they presaged the dedicated Islamism of President Erdogan. For both sets of governors, Islam would become Islamism, a political ideology whose understandings dictated all behaviour, within the public as much as the private sphere. 'The word "Islamism" is appropriate, as it is an "-ism" like fascism and nationalism': S Cagaptay, *The New Sultan: Erdogan and the Crisis of Modern Turkey* (London, IB Tauris, 2017).

[23] Hanioğlu, *The Young Turks in Opposition*, 203.

[24] Hanioğlu, *The Young Turks in Opposition*, 21.

[25] D Gutman, *The Politics of Armenian Migration to North America, 1885–1915: Sojourners, Smugglers and Dubious Citizens* (Edinburgh, Edinburgh University Press, 2019).

about what had driven many like him from the empire and what he and others still sought, manifesting a belief in the empire's potential for all its citizens:

> ... What the Armenians are demanding today is not in any way intended to weaken or paralyze Turkey, to dismember and, ultimately, to destroy it, to pulverize the Turkish people and, on its ruins, re-establish the Home of the Armenians. The Armenian people's modest desire for reform and all the political, economic and social institutions to which it aspires contain, not the seeds of Turkey's destruction, but, abundantly, the seeds of its renewal.[26]

Stepan Sapah-Gulian
Source: Wikimedia Commons.

Years later, Sapah-Gulian would reflect that his and others' efforts had had no substantive effect on the Ottoman ruling elite. When the genocide began in 1915, he was travelling in the United States. He was condemned to death in absentia and never returned.

[26] S Sapah-Gulian, 'Երիտասարդ Թիւրքիա [Jeune Turquie]]' 11, quoted in Kévorkian, *The Armenian Genocide*, 18.

Many Armenians chose to emigrate to somewhere close, such as the Russian Empire. During the last quarter of the nineteenth century, Armenians from both the Ottoman and Russian empires had developed closer political and cultural ties with one another. Activist ARF members who did not emigrate organised to bring about change in the Ottoman Empire from within, with help from Armenians of the Russian Empire and elsewhere. Their efforts and influence became more pronounced as threats to Ottoman Armenians grew. Armenians had greatly benefited under Russian imperial rule. The Russian Empire had undertaken a series of reforms in the 1860s and 1870s that abolished serfdom and, like the *Tanzimat*, introduced judicial and provincial reforms while leaving the supreme authority of the Romanov dynasty undisturbed. The Holy See of the Armenian Church, which belonged to a different confessional line to Russian Orthodoxy, was located in Echmiadzin, in Russian Transcaucasia. Armenians in the region held disproportionately prominent positions in local government and business. The Russian Empire's Armenians were more widely accepted as a part of Russian society than were leading Ottoman Armenians by the Ottoman ruling elite, who never treated them as complete equals.

While official discrimination took on various forms in both empires, life in Russia proved relatively calm for Armenians. If in the Ottoman East, Armenians were endlessly subject to persecution, massacre, rape, and pillaging, in the Russian Empire, acts of state violence against them were rare. The only time in which a perceptible shift in Russian state policy toward Armenians came about was at the turn of the twentieth century, when Tsar Alexander III, and later his son and successor Tsar Nicholas II, clamped down so hard on Armenian political and cultural institutions that some Armenians began to question openly whether there was any difference between sultan and tsar.[27] From 1905 to 1907, conditions deteriorated so precipitously that Armenians and Azerbaijanis in Transcaucasia became embroiled in a bitter war, probably stirred up by the Russian administration (see Chapter 10).

The tsarist authorities later lifted the repressive measures and reconciled with the Armenians. But mutual suspicion did not disappear entirely. When ARF members from around the world met in annual congresses nearly every year during the first decade of the twentieth century to discuss common matters while embracing increasingly nationalist positions, the attentions of both the Ottoman sultan and the Russian tsar were aroused. They suspected disloyalty and trouble that would ensue should the Armenians agitate for reform or revolution in the Ottoman Empire.

V. THE ARF–CUP ALLIANCE

The mutual opposition to autocratic rule expressed both by Armenian organisations and the Young Turks was enough to convince their respective leaders to consider cooperation or even an alliance. The alliance was a roller-coaster ride. In 1897, the ARF party organ *Droshak* asked the Young Turks 'to join the Armenians and

[27] See RG Hovannisian, 'Russian Armenia: A Century of Tsarist Rule' (1971) 19 *Jahrbücher für Geschichte Osteuropas* 40–42.

by assassinating the sultan to overthrow the Hamidian tyranny'.[28] In 1900, Prince Sabahaddin's father, Damad Mahmud Pasha, issued a public letter from abroad urging the Armenians to join the CUP in common action.[29] In 1901, on the 25th anniversary of the accession of the sultan to the throne, the CUP published an article condemning the Great Powers' failure to take action against the sultan and accused them of bearing responsibility for the massacres:

> This blood-thirsty tyrant's countless victims caused the whole civilized world to weep. But unfortunately the Great Powers did nothing but give him some friendly advice … The civilized governments bear an enormous responsibility because of the tolerance they have shown for the crimes of the Red Sultan.[30]

In 1902, under CUP direction, the First Congress of Ottoman Opposition Parties was called to order in Paris by Damad's two sons. The congress was attended by CUP and ARF members, as well as representatives from the empire's other ethno-confessional groups, including Turks, Arabs, Greeks, Kurds, Albanians, Circassians, and Jews.[31] All were brought together by their mutual dissatisfaction with Sultan Abdülhamid II. Jointly convened with the ARF, it would testify to the limits of cooperation between the opposition groups. During the congress, the Armenian political committees demanded that its organisers recognise Article 61 of the Berlin Treaty, as well as other assurances made after the massacres by the Great Powers. Sabahaddin, in opening the event, optimistically declared that 'the Turks who constitute the greater majority … have no desire to interfere in the ethnic characteristics of other groups' in the empire. Armenians supported the CUP faction, pushing for constitutional central administration, but insisted that 'special reforms' be undertaken in the eastern provinces. The Young Turk faction under Sabahaddin, representing the majority at the congress, gave lukewarm backing to this position, arguing that the empire's survival rested on decentralisation that would allow for autonomy for the empire's different peoples.[32] Rıza's faction unsurprisingly argued against decentralisation as it would lead to the empire's partition. Sabahaddin's followers persisted, recognising the importance of homeland to peoples, and, as an Armenian delegate put it, desiring to 'preserv[e] their identity on their native soil'.[33]

At the start the informal alliance had not worked out a common purpose beyond removing the sultan from power. The principal reason the CUP allied with the Armenians was to improve its own image in Europe and thereby gain European support for whatever changes they would make, as admitted to by its central organ, *Osmanlı*, in 1902:

> The service that the Armenians are rendering to the Turks is that it would be easier to secure the moral support of the Western [Great] Powers should the Muslim and Christian

[28] *Droshak*, 20 January 1897, 9–10, as cited in JM Hagopian, 'Hyphenated Nationalism: The Spirit of the Revolutionary Movement in Asia Minor and the Caucasus, 1896–1910' (PhD thesis, Harvard University, 1942) 207.

[29] D Mahmoud Pacha, 'Lettre ouverte aux Arméniens' (1900) 2 *Pro Arménia* 3, as cited in Hanioğlu, *The Young Turks in Opposition*, 150.

[30] A[rkivi]Q[endror]Sh[tetrëor][Tirana], 19/60//639/18-4, as cited in Hanioğlu, *The Young Turks in Opposition*, 152.

[31] DM Kaligian, *Armenian Organization and Ideology under Ottoman Rule: 1908–1914* (Piscataway, NJ, Transaction Publishers, 2009) 1.

[32] Hanioğlu, *The Young Turks in Opposition*, 197.

[33] Kévorkian, *The Armenian Genocide*, 40.

elements [of our empire] demand the same reforms with one voice. The image of our compatriots working to secure reforms in Europe would be improved.[34]

The CUP were aware of the Armenians' situation. Even the CUP's Behaeddin Şakir and a colleague did acknowledge the Armenians' conditions as 'extremely bad':

On the one hand Russia, and on the other hand the government of Abdülhamid, were destroying this nation ... The Armenians who [had] been squeezed among these ... governments, [had] no other alternative but to ally themselves with us. They were shedding blood and getting killed for nothing.[35]

Disagreement among the parties led to operations that not all sides approved of, even if the opposite impression was conveyed. In 1904, the ARF took unilateral action against the sultan, secretly launching publications disguised so that they appeared to have been written by Turkish Muslims and calling for popular agitation. The regime was convinced that it was the opposition movement as a whole inspiring at least some of the revolts that were then taking place across the empire and against which the government reacted forcefully. And by now, some of the Young Turk opponents of the sultan regarded Armenian political parties as subversive organisations endangering the empire's security and territorial integrity. They accused Armenians, in effect, of sullying the Ottomans' honour by presenting a denigrating image of the empire in the West.[36] This is not to say the Young Turk groups themselves were not hatching all kinds of schemes for deposing the sultan, including assassinations and bombing of the palace – and coming close to carrying them out.[37]

The most spectacular effort to remove the sultan came in 1905, when ARF members planted a time bomb to assassinate him. It exploded, killing or injuring 78 people, but left the sultan unscathed. This highly visible attempt brought back fresh memories of the ARF-organised raid on the Ottoman Bank of 1896. The attempt led to accusations by some Turks who framed Armenians as outsiders unacceptably interfering in an imperial 'family affair' and assaulting Turkish honour.[38] But this view was not universally shared, and ARF-CUP collaboration, such as it was, continued.

At the turn of the century, the ARF had also explored the possibility of collaborating with other non-Muslim revolutionary organisations. It made common cause with groups in Bulgaria, linking their own struggle for long-delayed reform with that of Bulgarians and Macedonians. In 1906, with the former's support, they set up a secret

[34] Hanioğlu, *Preparation for a Revolution*, 14.

[35] Letter of H[üsrev] Sami and Dr Bahaeddin [Şakir] beginning 'Muhterem Arkadaşımız', dated [Paris], January [?], 1908/no 483, and sent to a Muslim in Caucasia, Kopye Defteri, 92–93, as cited in Hanioğlu, *Preparation for a Revolution*, 193.

[36] Kévorkian, *The Armenian Genocide*, 11. Sabahaddin's use of 'race' here denoted what we would understand today as at least 'ethnicity' in combination with what we mean by 'race'. Ambassador Morgenthau used 'race' similarly in his memoirs.

[37] Hanioğlu, *The Young Turks in Opposition*, 92.

[38] Kévorkian, *The Armenian Genocide*, 36. Kévorkian speculates that a more prolonged period of interethnic violence also occurred between Armenians and Muslims in Transcaucasia in 1905–1906, that 'eruption of violence ..., especially the Turkish-speaking population of Baku – probably had a greater impact on Young Turk circles than has previously been supposed. While this violence resulted, on the analysis of the Armenian Committees, from a policy orchestrated by agents of the Czar's regime, Turkish-speaking circles perceived it as a Turkish-Armenian conflict for control of the South Caucasus' (Kévorkian, *The Armenian Genocide*, 43–44).

military academy in Bulgaria to train their members in guerrilla warfare. In addition to holding workshops, the ARF and Bulgarians also collaborated in founding a factory to produce bombs and explosives. Although the academy shut its doors in 1907, just a year after its founding, some of the 50 graduates returned to their towns and villages in the Ottoman Empire, where they organised small armed groups and joined the ranks of the larger bands, the *fedayi*, who had already had years of fighting covert battles against the Hamidian regime.[39]

By 1908 representatives from the Armenian and Young Turks organisations and parties came to agree on a joint program for change: resisting the government by force, withholding payment of taxes, raising awareness within the army, fomenting rebellion and agitating for the sultan's abdication, and installing an administration that would restore and support the constitution.[40] The CUP directed Armenians to employ guerrilla bands and assassinations to defend themselves.[41] Their program even called for the autonomy of the Armenian-populated provinces within the Ottoman Empire, meaning formal equality for all minorities in the empire under the dominance of the Turks.[42] CUP members reiterated at the end of the congress that they 'regarded the agreement as a tactical alliance with a "deadly foe" restricted to "action"', not to permanent association.[43] The collaboration between the ARF and CUP stood on rocky ground from its inception.

VI. TENSION-PRODUCING DIFFERENCES BETWEEN OTTOMAN ARMENIANS AND MUSLIMS

The fragile state of the Ottoman economy and finances served only to compound its political and social ills, hindering its efforts at growth. International firms and enterprises did a brisk trade in the empire. A disproportionate share in this business was in the hands of Armenians, Greeks and Jews in Ottoman urban centres. The perception of prosperity bred envy and resentment. Even the sultan thought Armenians were too well-off, but the contrast in material well-being would have been stark, too, for lower-class Muslims.[44] The evident disparity and notion of Armenians as undeserving and having too much would later be used to justify the wholesale expropriation of their property during the genocide.[45]

[39] V Ketsemanian, 'Straddling Two Empires: Cross-Revolutionary Fertilization and the Armenian Revolutionary Federation's Military Academy in 1906–1907' (2017) 4 *Journal of the Ottoman and Turkish Studies Association* 339. On this relationship more generally, see GK Moumdjian, 'Rebels with a Cause: Armenian-Macedonian Relations and Their Bulgarian Connection, 1895–1913' in HM Yavuz and I Blumi (eds), *War and Nationalism: The Balkan Wars, 1912–1913, and the Sociopolitical Implications* (Salt Lake City, University of Utah Press, 2013) 132–75.

[40] Hanioğlu, *Preparation for a Revolution*, 205.

[41] See Hanioğlu, *Preparation for a Revolution*, 208.

[42] Hanioğlu, *Preparation for a Revolution*, 190.

[43] H[üsrev] Sami and Dr Bahaeddin [Şakir] to O[sman] Tevfik in Salonica, dated [Paris], 25 February [1]908/no 529, Kopye Defteri, 177, in Hanioğlu, *Preparation for a Revolution*.

[44] T Paşa, *Sultan Abdulhamid, Tahsin Paşa'nın Yıldız Hatıraları* (Istanbul, 1990) 182, as cited in T Akçam, *A Shameful Act: The Armenian Genocide and the Question of Turkish Responsibility* (New York, Metropolitan Books, 2006) 43.

[45] B Morris and D Ze'evi, *The Thirty-Year Genocide: Turkey's Destruction of its Christian Minorities, 1894–1924* (Cambridge, MA, Harvard University Press, 2019) 497.

Anger and resentment were surely also felt about the non-material advantages Armenians were perceived to possess, like their affinity for enterprise and industry; modern education; and community cohesion, organisation, and development. Turkish Muslims and Armenians typically attended separate, and quite different, schools. Armenians emphasised a secular as well as religious curriculum, preparing to continue their education abroad, establish ties with foreign firms and businesses, and allow for the emergence of an affluent bourgeois class.[46] Historian Michael Reynolds has noted the massive social and economic disparities between Armenians and Kurds, contrasting the former's 'expanding petty merchant, banking, and quasi-industrial classes' with good outside contacts with the latter's semifeudal practices, abject poverty, and mistreatment of Armenian tenant farmers and peasantry.[47]

Muslims who attended the Ottoman state schools established in the late nineteenth century generally received a well-rounded education in Ottoman Turkish, arithmetic, history, geography and moral instruction, or learned a particular trade. Toward the turn of the century, the Hamidian regime sought to strengthen the Islamic content of the curriculum in an effort to produce a loyal and dedicated cadre of students. That many of these same students joined the imperial civil service and bureaucracy rather than enter into agriculture or trade was at the same time a source of deep concern for Ottoman educators and led to a push for the opening of more schools in commerce and industry.[48]

After the sultanate, the military was the pre-eminent institution in the empire and believed to be the strongest guarantor of its security. It was the principal recipient of the state's largesse.[49] Yet this attention showered upon the military paradoxically generated great anxiety in the sultan. He feared that academy graduates too readily accepted reformist ideas, and resented those who were better-informed; he trusted the less educated officers who had risen gradually through the ranks.

VII. THE OTTOMANS' IMAGE PROBLEM

The Ottomans' image problem in Europe predated the Armenian massacres of the 1890s. The 'Terrible Turk' label may have originated as early as 1453, after the fall of Constantinople, whereas the metaphor of the 'sick man' had been first articulated in the 1850s. While 'Terrible Turk' had been widely internalised, the 'sick man' was recognised as fact by contemporaries. As dissatisfaction with the sultan gained wider currency, Ottomans searched for some evidence that would counter this humiliating image. Some drew inspiration from the military victory of the 'yellow' Japanese

[46] PJ Young, 'Knowledge, Nation, and the Curriculum: Ottoman Armenian Education (1853–1915)' (PhD thesis, University of Michigan, Ann Arbor, 2001).

[47] MA Reynolds, *Shattering Empires: The Clash and Collapse of the Ottoman and Russian Empires 1908–1918* (Cambridge, Cambridge University Press, 2011) 51.

[48] S Akşin Somel, *The Modernization of Public Education in the Ottoman Empire, 1839–1908: Islamization, Autocracy, and Discipline* (Leiden, Brill, 2001); and BC Fortna, *Imperial Classroom: Islam, the State, and Education in the Late Ottoman Empire* (Oxford, Oxford University Press, 2002).

[49] HN Akmeşe, *The Birth of Modern Turkey: The Ottoman Military and the March to World War I* (London, IB Tauris, 2005) 7.

in 1904–05 over the Russian Empire, the Ottomans' perennial enemy.[50] An article published in the Young Turk organ *Şura-yı Ümmet* pointed to that victory to refute the stereotype:

> Some Europeans and some Ottomans, who imitate whatever they see without understanding, regard us as a race in the lower part of the racial hierarchy. Let's say it in plain Turkish: They [Europeans] view Turks as second-class human beings. Japanese people, being from the stock of the yellow race, are obliterating this slander against nature with the progress in their country, and with their cannons and rifles in Manchuria.[51]

This victory validated a collective wish that Ottoman Muslims could rise through the 'racial hierarchy' and regenerate.

VIII. THE YOUNG TURK REVOLUTION OF 1908

At the turn of the twentieth century, the CUP's centre of gravity moved from Paris to the Balkans' center, Salonika. The leading members of the Salonika CUP branch included Ismail Enver and Mehmet Talât. From Salonika, the CUP's large membership disseminated anti-Hamidian propaganda and distributed pamphlets criticising the sultan and advocating his assassination.

Sensing the danger brewing in the region, Abdülhamid deployed troops to Macedonia to prevent it. But the Salonika CUP harassed the imperial military garrison as well as Ottoman administrative officials. They established Muslim bands and freed criminals from jail to join their volunteer military force.[52] (The release of criminals set a dangerous precedent, for in several years it would lead to the formation of the Special Organization [*Teşkilat-ı Mahsusa*] overseen by Dr Şakir – see Chapter 9.) International tensions exacerbated the situation in the Balkans. At a Baltic port in the summer of 1908, the British monarch and the tsar met to decide on the question of the creation of an autonomous Macedonia. The royal summit cemented a new anti-German alliance, which, with Russia, would compose the Triple Entente. The sultan interpreted this entire set of moves at the hands of his greatest enemies as presaging the partition of the empire.[53]

The Salonika CUP shared the sultan's fear that rewarding Macedonia with autonomy would spell another disastrous loss for the Ottoman Empire, but they believed that they, not the sultan, were in the best position to avert it. By July, the CUP branch of Salonika had decided that this was their moment to act. They persuaded the imperial troops stationed nearby to join them and march on the capital. The sultan's military support thus crumbled. İsmail Enver, one of the chief military commanders then stationed in Macedonia, who would in a few years become the military chief

[50] R Worringer, *Ottomans Imagining Japan: East, Middle East, and Non-Western Modernity at the Turn of the Twentieth Century* (New York, Palgrave Macmillan, 2014).

[51] 'Me'yus'Me'yus Olmalı Mıyız[?]' (1904) 62 *Şura-yı Ümmet* 1, as cited in Hanioğlu, *The Young Turks in Opposition*, 210.

[52] Hanioğlu, *The Young Turks in Opposition*, 226.

[53] Hanioğlu, *Preparation for a Revolution*, 236.

of the wartime government, led his men 'to the hills demanding restoration of the constitution'[54] 'under the banner of "Liberty, Equality, Fraternity, and Justice"'.[55]

In Istanbul, the sultan quickly acquiesced, reinstating the constitution and parliament he had suspended in 1876. Shortly before the event, the Salonika CUP had not only organised guerilla forces, but murdered representatives of the sultan's administration, including a high-ranking officer, and attempted to murder another high-ranking Ottoman official in his home. Most significant, the sultan now would not have to deal with what must have been his worst-case scenario – Major Enver marching his troops the 350 miles to Istanbul and confronting and humiliating him personally.

Publicly, Abdülhamid II capitulated with grace, if not gratitude, to the revolutionaries, claiming that he was the victim, the wronged, the benevolent monarch led astray by bad counsel, and it was 'his constitution' he was restoring 'after solemnly declaring that times were ripe to do so'.[56] This constituted the Young Turk Revolution, carried out in the name of Ottomanism and in which all citizens would not only have equal rights but also, according to historian Erik-Jan Zürcher, thereby become 'loyal citizens'.[57] There followed a period in which, for a brief couple of years, the future of the empire suddenly did not seem so dim.

Armenian, Greek, and Muslim Religious Leaders Seen Sitting at the Voting Table during the 1908 Parliamentary Elections

Source: Charles Roden Buxton, *Turkey in Revolution* (London, T Fisher Unwin, 1909) 173.

[54] BC Fortna, "The Reign of Abdülhamid II" in R Kasaba (ed), *The Cambridge History of Turkey*, vol 4: *Turkey in the Modern World* (Cambridge, Cambridge University Press, 2008) 60.

[55] Zürcher, *Turkey: A Modern History*, 90.

[56] Kieser, *Talaat Pasha*, 65.

[57] Zürcher, *Turkey*, 128.

IX. REACTIONS TO THE YOUNG TURK REVOLUTION

In Istanbul and throughout the empire, the revolution elicited wild street celebrations, public gatherings, and overall great rejoicing that stimulated hope for the betterment of conditions among Christians, Jews, and Muslims alike. Censorship was lifted, and freedom of association was granted to Ottomans. 'Generally', writes Der Matossian, 'the speeches ended with hand shaking and hugging between spiritual leaders of different ethnic groups'.[58] The euphoria, however, was short-lived. The revolution did not cause high levels of inflation that the empire had recently seen to disappear. Disappointed workers soon went on strike, exercising their freedom and demanding satisfaction of basic needs.[59] The new government, elected after the revolution, along with its CUP supporters, no longer had the right to repress the strikers but did so anyway. Since the 1876 constitution did not include the right to organise for political purposes, the newly elected deputies to the national assembly took their seats as individuals, not as members of a party. CUP members won the majority of seats, demonstrating the popularity the party enjoyed in the wake of the revolution. Now firmly ensconced in the capital, the CUP comfortably espoused democratic ideals and faith that parliamentary government and constitutional rule would be enough to keep European intervention out of Ottoman affairs.[60]

X. ARMENIANS AFTER THE 1908 REVOLUTION

Following the revolution, Armenians were eager to embrace the political and social changes made possible by the restoration of the constitution and parliament. After more than 30 years of disappointment and dashed hopes, Armenians felt a sincere sense of optimism and hope.[61] In the empire-wide elections held in autumn 1908, they won 10 of 323 seats in the Chamber of Deputies, the lower house of parliament. For a short time thereafter, Armenian national assembly members, journalists, and bankers seemed to be accepted and trusted by the government's leadership. They seemed to trust in return. At the national level, members of the Ottoman and Armenian elite(s) even found the notable and important common ground to work together to frustrate the schemes of the empire's geopolitical rivals, including Russia.[62]

Armenians had briefly been enjoying self-governance through community institutions like the Armenian National Assembly. They probably were better prepared for working under parliamentary rules than CUP members, whose experience in politics had largely played out in the shadows and had shown a penchant for terror and revolutionary plots. The most notable Armenian parliamentarian, Krikor Zohrab, demonstrated an ideal mind for serving in office.

[58] B Der Matossian, *Shattered Dreams of Revolution: From Liberty to Violence in the Late Ottoman Empire* (Stanford, CA, Stanford University Press, 2014) 47.

[59] D Quataert, *Social Disintegration and Popular Resistance in the Ottoman Empire, 1881–1908: Reactions to European Economic Penetration* (New York, New York University Press, 1983) 64–66.

[60] Akçam, *A Shameful Act*, 79.

[61] Der Matossian, *Shattered Dreams of Revolution.*

[62] See Reynolds, *Shattering Empires*.

Krikor Zohrab

Source: A Andonian, *Azatarar sharzhun banakin haghtakan mutkn i K. Polis* (Istanbul, Tparan ew Gratun HG Balakashian, 1909) 60.

On return from exile in Paris, Zohrab immediately became the Armenians' supremely articulate and progressive spokesman. He was widely recognised as a principled lawyer, writer, and law professor. He spoke Ottoman Turkish as fluently as Armenian and was popular even with the other Muslim deputies with legal backgrounds – mainly because he had trained them. He promoted tolerance and cooperation between Muslims and Christians. Not a member of any Armenian political party, he nonetheless became a leader in the Chamber of Deputies. He manifested a sensitivity to where politics should go in a modern democratic world and courageously confronted the government on a host of issues, from officially sanctioned torture to corruption, speaking truth to power much like Rıza. 'Our common religion,' this Hrant Dink-like figure proclaimed memorably at one public meeting, 'is freedom'.[63]

In a dangerous moment presaging violent confrontation after the counter-revolution of 1909 (see Chapter 7), Zohrab even led a delegation from Istanbul to meet with the leaders of the approaching Action Army in an effort to head off a 'bloodbath' between them and rebel troops and 'prepare a negotiated solution'.[64]

[63] Kévorkian, *The Armenian Genocide*, 55.
[64] Kieser, *Talaat Pasha*, 73.

Three years later, he attempted to intervene in the ongoing Macedonian crisis that had led to the first Balkan War,[65] indicating in an interview that

> … he deplored the lack of organized political groups into which 'the nationalities could melt' instead of working in the form of antagonistic national blocs. The Armenian deputies … [wanted] above all, to work toward the general welfare of the Empire. The particular interests of the Armenian nation came afterwards.[66]

Zohrab was still a duly elected member of the Ottoman Chamber of Deputies when he and fellow deputy Vartkes Serengiulian were tortured and murdered at the start of the genocide in 1915.[67]

XI. EVALUATING THE YOUNG TURKS

In 1918, when Ambassador Morgenthau published his book on his tenure as ambassador to the Sublime Porte, he was well aware of the difficulties of saving the empire and was convinced that the effective implementation of constitutional rule could have helped accomplish this. Yet he reflected, 'Let us not criticize too harshly the Young Turks, for there is no question that, at the beginning, they were sincere'.[68] Perhaps Morgenthau had not perceived how superficial their sincerity was. The Young Turks had not themselves seen the depth of the conflict between the ideals of Ottomanism and the ceding of autonomy to other groups, which might lead to the further fracturing of the empire. Constitutional restoration appears initially to have been understood as an obviously impressive set of ideals, adherence to which would impress Europeans. At some point the CUP's demonstration of support for the constitution became primarily a means to preserve the empire's geopolitical and domestic sovereignty. Armenians wanted a constitutional monarchy to gain equality to protect their communities in their homeland.[69]

XII. A WORD ON THE ROLE OF HONOUR

In 1906, in a letter to 'our Muslim brothers in the Transcaucasus [where the civil war between Armenian and Muslim was winding down]', high-ranking CUP member Şakir proposed 'putting an end to Armenian wealth and influence … only in order to defend their [the Muslims'] property and honor'.[70] He then directed his Caucasian

[65] Kieser, *Talaat Pasha*, 127.

[66] Kévorkian, *The Armenian Genocide*, 68.

[67] RH Kévorkian, 'Zohrab and Vartkes: Ottoman Deputies and Armenian Reforms' in H-L Kieser et al (eds), *The End of the Ottomans: The Genocide of 1915 and the Politics of Turkish Nationalism* (London, IB Tauris, 2019) 169–92.

[68] H Morgenthau, *Ambassador Morgenthau's Story* (Garden City, NY, Doubleday, Page, 1919) 12.

[69] GJ Libaridian, 'The History of Imperial Politics and the Politics of Imperial History', keynote speech delivered at the Centre for the Study of the International Relations of the Middle East and North Africa, University of Cambridge, Cambridge, UK, 13 June 2014. With the kind permission of the author.

[70] Letter sent from Paris to the Turkish-speaking correspondents of the Caucasus, of 23 November 1906, as cited by Hanioğlu, *Preparation for a Revolution*, 160.

Muslim 'brothers' to 'weaken the Armenians, who are, above all, one of the obstacles to freeing ourselves from Russia's stranglehold; with this in mind, we must also destroy their wealth, which is their greatest strength'.[71]

Throughout the Near East, the honour of oneself or one's group's was determined by the regard of others, and was greatly valued. If someone showed lack of respect, honour was insulted and had to be avenged. Many Ottoman Muslims envied Armenians, particularly for their wealth. But to admit envy consciously meant that Armenians were superior, which was not admissable. Instead, an unconscious process validated treatment of Armenians. Armenians would have been inchoately understood as insulting their, Muslims', honour. Being dishonoured meant that revenge had to be taken. Armenians must be punished for making Muslims envious. Reducing Armenians to something unthreatening, unenviable and inferior validated Muslim-Turkish superiority. The culture of honour thus provided a familiar, conventional, and above all automatic unthinking response for dealing with inadmissible feelings of envy, resentment, and inferiority.[72]

[71] YH Bayur, *Türk Inkilabı Tarihi*, vol 1, 343, as cited in Akçam, *A Shameful Act*, 65.

[72] AK Uskul et al, 'Honor Bound: The Cultural Construction of Honor in Turkey and the Northern United States' (2012) 43 *Journal of Cross-Cultural Psychology* 1131, 1133.

7

The Final Path to Imperial Ruin

> [I]mperial generations began to be socialized with fear and anxiety when the empire started to physically shrink ... as it fought wars for eleven years straight ... but [these generations] became even more agitated by the worry of racial extinction.
>
> Fatma Müge Göçek[1]

THE JULY 1908 military coup orchestrated by the Committee of Union and Progress (CUP) against Sultan Abdülhamid II led to the restoration of the 1876 constitution and parliament. The sultan then appointed the grand vizier and cabinet, which included CUP members, but none who had led the revolution. In the parliamentary elections that autumn, CUP members won the most seats of all the committees, a cohort that included the revolution's leaders. Thirty-seven Armenian and Greek deputies were elected into office out of a total of 323 members in the Chamber of Deputies, the lower house of parliament.[2] The new government and deputies rapidly encountered major challenges that ranged from following proper constitutional procedure, political reform in the eastern Anatolian and Arab provinces, to matters of secession in the Balkans.

As noted, Armenian lawyer and writer Krikor Zohrab proved to be one of the earliest and most fervent supporters of the new constitutional order. Returning from self-exile in Paris in July 1908, Zohrab embraced his duties as a responsible national and local politician with a zeal unmatched by his peers. He was also elected to the newly reopened Armenian National Assembly, where he soon tackled the issues then afflicting the wider Armenian community. During one session convened in late 1908,

[1] FM Göçek, *Denial of Violence: Ottoman Past, Turkish Present, and Collective Violence against the Armenians, 1789–2009* (New York, Oxford University Press, 2015) 36–37. Historian Michael Hawkins writes 'During the nineteenth century there was a marked tendency to equate race with an ethnic group which could be distinguished by certain hereditary physical and psychological traits' and 'race remained an imprecise concept and was often conflated with nation or applied to ethnic aggregates, e.g., the 'European race'': M Hawkins, 'Social Darwinism and Race' in S Berger (ed), *A Companion to Nineteenth-Century Europe: 1789–1914* (Chichester, Wiley-Blackwell, 2009) 227, 228. In recent correspondence, Göçek adds to her observation, 'The imperial generations refer to Ottomans who at this particular time first started to perceive themselves as Turks. So their identity as Ottomans started to be fractured at this particular juncture into ethnic and racial identities, this time as Turks'.

[2] See B Der Matossian, *Shattered Dreams of Revolution: From Liberty to Violence in the Ottoman Empire* (Stanford, CA, Stanford University Press, 2014) 120. The first parliamentary election had been held in 1877. The parliament or General Assembly was composed of two houses. Members of the Senate, the upper house, were appointees of the government, while the members of the lower house, the Chamber of Deputies, were elected.

he presented a report on the conditions of the Armenians in the eastern provinces, as a way of highlighting the community's need to mobilise resources and seek recourse to action. The report itself identified problems that had long tormented the beleaguered Armenian peasantry: unfair judicial practices, expropriation of farmland, and Muslim landowners' refusal to renew tenancies held by Armenian peasants.[3] Zohrab proposed the establishment of a Turkish and Armenian commission of inquiry with executive authority to ensure that any officials and military officers found responsible for committing abuses were dismissed, that looters and murderers be tried in an Istanbul court, that confiscated land be returned to their owners, that populations facing famine be provided with wheat and seed, and that the commission's decisions be carried out in the field by the military.[4] Zohrab's approach to politics was representative of all Armenians' hopes tied to the 1908 Revolution.

The constitutional process unfolded in fits and starts over the course of the next few months. The new government lifted censorship, disbanded Abdülhamid's reviled spy network, sacked or pensioned off bureaucratic and military officials associated with the old regime, and allowed for a public sphere to open up greater participation among the populace. Ottomans debated the meaning of imperial citizenship, what sort of society they sought to build, and whether the many peoples that made up the empire were to maintain that diversity or assimilate under the banner of a narrower, namely, Turkish, cultural fold. The CUP in effect ceded the governance of empire over to ministers and the legislature, but it continued to pull the political strings in the background and resorted to extra-constitutional means to prevent the return of the old order.[5] Unsurprisingly, the CUP's heavy-handed measures antagonised many in the empire, including a new political opposition composed of followers of Prince Sabahaddin and the more conservative elements in the Islamic leadership, thereby paving the way for the events of April 1909.

I. THE COUNTER-REVOLUTION AND THE TRAGEDY IN ADANA

The changes resulting from the revolution came about rapidly and decisively and were enough to alert members of the old political elite to the potential loss of both office and the privileges they had once enjoyed. When the CUP began a purge of officers in the Ottoman military, this set off the disaffected elements of the *ancien régime* to launch their own counter-coup in April 1909. An Ottoman military unit stationed in Istanbul took the lead by mutinying. Their demands included the resignation of key government officials, the expulsion of CUP members from the capital, and the reintroduction of Islamic law. The government capitulated to their demands, which then emboldened some of the soldiers and students in the medreses to hunt down military officers and CUP officials on Istanbul's streets. One parliamentary deputy and the minister of

[3] R Kévorkian, *The Armenian Genocide: A Complete History* (London, IB Tauris, 2011) 65–66.

[4] Kévorkian, *The Armenian Genocide*, 66.

[5] The CUP's interference in constitutional politics during the first months after the 1908 Revolution is discussed in N Sohrabi, *Revolution and Constitutionalism in the Ottoman Empire and Iran* (Cambridge, Cambridge University Press, 2011).

justice (Muslims) were murdered. One soldier forced his way into the parliament building and aimed a bayonet at Bedros Halajian, an Armenian deputy. Standing his ground, Halajian reminded him of the legitimacy of his parliamentary seat:

> We have come here upon the will of all peoples of the Ottoman nation. The representative of the people has no right and cannot submit his conscience or his beliefs for bargaining under the threat of bayonets … We cannot allow for this abasement … Look outside these windows – the innumerable rabble is out there and they are pointing determinedly and menacingly at our breasts.[6]

Bedros Halajian

Source: A Andonian, *Azatarar sharzhun banakin haghtakan mutkn i K. Polis* (Istanbul, Tparan ew Gratun HG Balakashian, 1909) 40.

Halajian dared his assailant, 'Go ahead, kill me, I'm on my feet'.[7] Halajian survived this moment, but would later perish in the genocide.

Amid the chaos on the streets, disaffected citizens joined the soldiers in their pursuit of important CUP deputies. A number of prominent Armenians, at great risk to themselves, provided protection by sheltering the hunted in their homes. Some of those who received shelter were the very men who would go on to become among the

[6] V Papazian, *Im hushere*, vol 2 (Beirut, Hamazkayin Unkerutiwn, 1952) 107–108.
[7] (1909) 66 *Azadamard* 1, as cited in Kévorkian, *The Armenian Genocide*, 73.

main proponents of the genocide. The ARF leader Khachatur Malumian (Aknuni) hid Mehmet Talât, the deputy from Edirne.[8] Zohrab took in the prominent CUP politician Halil Bey (Menteşe),[9] and ARF militant Azarig provided refuge to Dr Mehmed Nâzım.[10]

While most of the counter-revolutionary violence was limited to Istanbul and its environs, its effects would be felt most acutely in far-flung Adana Province. Located along the northeastern littoral of the Mediterranean, political, social, and economic developments in Adana in the months prior to the counter-revolution had created an environment that would make possible the devastation that unfolded there. This agriculturally rich region attracted a high level of seasonal labour migration every year. Its more enterprising merchants maintained close relations with foreign firms and imported Western machinery for the production of the province's chief commodity, cotton. Critically, as Bedross Der Matossian writes, Adana's Armenian population had welcomed the restoration of the constitution with street processions, the staging of theatrical plays, and the importing of weapons.[11] This alarmed provincial Muslim notables and elites, many of whom had lost their power after the revolution, as well as the Muslim population at large, paving the way for the events of 14 April.

On that day, a large mob made up of armed Turks, Kurds, Circassians, and others formed to go on a rampage in the eponymous provincial capital, attacking Armenians wherever they encountered them.[12] Policemen who had been deployed to restore order unconscionably joined the mobs; over the next few days they murdered Armenians and plundered the property of those who already lived there.[13] Those Armenians who could, fought back, but the Armenian quarter of Adana was turned to ruins. Kévorkian describes how:

> … the first day of violence … was mainly devoted to destroying Armenian shops at the market – signs had been carefully nailed up on those belonging to Muslims – and to massacring the Armenians who had lived dispersed … on the outskirts of the city or in inns …, which were visited one by one by the mob. Around 300 people were killed in these [inns], mostly seasonal workers or mule-drivers … the mob consisted, at this time, of between 20,000 and 30,000 people made up of some five to ten groups … Turks, Kurds, Fellahs, Çerkez, Avshars, nomads, and Muslims from Crete … led by local notables.[14]

Adana's Muslim clergy played a role in the slaughter as well, most notably when the *hocas* at the Sultane-Valide Mosque exhorted the mob to 'promise not to leave a single

[8] H-L Kieser, *Talaat Pasha: Father of Modern Turkey, Architect of Genocide* (Princeton, NJ, Princeton University Press, 2018), 70–72.

[9] R Kévorkian, 'Zohrab and Vartkes: Ottoman Deputies and Armenian Reforms' in H-L Kieser et al (eds), *The End of the Ottomans: The Genocide of 1915 and the Politics of Turkish Nationalism* (London, IB Tauris, 2019) 180.

[10] GF Minassian, 'Les relations entre le Comité Union et Progrès et la Fédération Révolutionnaire Arménienne à la veille de la Premiere Guerre mondiale d'après les sources arméniennes' (1995) 1 *Revue d'histoire arménienne contemporaine* 62–63, cited in Kévorkian, *The Armenian Genocide*.

[11] See B Der Matossian, 'From Bloodless Revolution to Bloody Counterrevolution: The Adana Massacres of 1909' (2011) 6 *Genocide Studies and Prevention* 152.

[12] Kévorkian, *The Armenian Genocide*, 69. What follows about the Adana massacres and the Young Turk government is derived from the section Kévorkian, 'Young Turks and Armenians Facing the Test of "the March 31 Incident" and the Massacres in Cilicia', 71 ff. This may have been the moment of creation of the 'deep state'. For another recent analysis on the massacres in Adana, see Der Matossian, *Shattered Dreams of Revolution*, 163–70 and his article 'From Bloodless Revolution to Bloody Counterrevolution', 152–73.

[13] Der Matossian, *Shattered Dreams of Revolution*, 167.

[14] Kévorkian, *The Armenian Genocide*, 84, 85.

Armenian alive'.[15] The members of the old guard must have felt that the state would allow them to act with the same impunity as the perpetrators of the 1890s massacres.

Local officials thus failed utterly to protect the Armenians, whose safety they had sworn to uphold. When an Ottoman notable living in Adana's Armenian quarter appealed to the authorities to stop the killing, they agreed. But the Armenians, they said, would first have to surrender their arms. They did so after the Armenian Patriarchate in Istanbul urged them to cooperate and local British diplomats assured them of protection. The authorities then ordered their troops to end the violence, but atrocities resumed a day later and did not relent. The French clergyman Father Rigal witnessed the result:

> One of the first buildings to go up in flames was the Armenian school … where a large number of refugees had found shelter … When groups of them made their way into the street, the soldiers fired at them point-blank … The next day and the following night … the fire continued to rage. It devoured … seventy-five percent of the big Armenian quarter … The crackling of gunfire mixed with the crackling of the fire, incessantly, for days and nights on end, and the hell of a city in flames, the thunder of the crumbling walls, heaving clouds of fire heavenward: the piercing cries of the unfortunate felled by the bullets and still louder, the savage cries of the men busy slitting people's throats; the wrenching appeals of … people in a circle of flames, as their tormentors prepare to burn them alive; this frenzied, despairing population that stretches its arms out toward you and begs to be saved; the emotion that chokes you the more powerfully the closer the fire comes and the more helpless you feel, delivered up to a pack of arsonists and throat cutters; the sinister gangs running past, laden down with booty; … the unfortunate daubed with oil and transformed into living torches; a mother whose belly has been cut open and made over into a cradle for her new-born baby …[16]

It is estimated that some 20,000 Armenians were murdered and 90,000 made homeless during the two waves of violence. Armenians who fought back killed several hundred Muslims.[17]

A few months after the slaughter, Zabel Yesayan visited Adana on a relief mission (see Introduction) and recorded what she witnessed:

> Even those who experienced that reality cannot describe it as a whole. All … stammer, sigh, weep, and relate only to disjointed events. The despair and terror had been so great that mothers had failed to recognize their children … Listening to a savage, bloodthirsty mob's diabolical cawing laughter, people went mad before dying. Mangled limbs and children's bodies still throbbing with life and pain were crushed underfoot. Trapped between rifles on one side and flames on the other, women, children and the wounded who had taken refuge in churches and schools had wrapped their arms around each other, crazy with fear, as they were burned black … Some … seemed as empty as bottomless chasms. Others looked at you without seeing, because one image had been indelibly impressed on their field of vision …[18]

[15] Terzian, *The Catastrophe of Cilicia*, 37, as cited in Kévorkian, *The Armenian Genocide*, 85.

[16] P Rigal, 'Adana. Les Massacres d'Adana', Lettres d'Ore, relations d'Orient [Confidential Review of the Jesuit Missions Edited in the Order in Lyons and Published in Brusells (sic)], November 1909, quoted and cited in Kévorkian, *The Armenian Genocide*, 91–92.

[17] According to an authoritative report published in the aftermath of the massacres, 620 Muslims died during the turmoil in April. See R Kévorkian, 'The Cilician Massacres, April 1909' in RG Hovannisian and S Payaslian (eds), *Armenian Cilicia* (Costa Mesa, CA, Mazda, 2008) 352–54.

[18] Z Yessayan, *In the Ruins: The 1909 Massacres of Armenians in Adana, Turkey*, trans GM Goshgarian (Boston, Armenian International Women's Association, 2016) 11–12.

The counter-revolution and the killing frenzy in Adana were brought to an end only by an armed volunteer force of CUP-loyal soldiers, hastily organised in Salonika, still the committee's headquarters. This newly formed Army of Action, which included Mustafa Kemal, entrained to the outskirts of Istanbul and restored order in the capital. Elements of the same army were dispatched to the city of Adana, where they finally brought the violence to an end.[19] The entire event, later referred to collectively as the 'March 31 incident', interrupted the first year of governance under the restored constitution. The CUP was determined not to risk a second coup.[20] The country was placed under martial law and the army given a preeminent position that placed it 'above the law'.[21]

II. THE NEW CUP GOVERNMENT

After the counter-revolution was halted, a new government was formed. Deputy of parliament Talât Bey took his first cabinet portfolio as minister of the interior. Although little prepared for this position, he would occupy it, with the exception of a brief stint as minister of post and telegraph, for the next eight years, until he assumed the post of grand vizier in 1917. In the first months at his new post, Talât's biographer writes, he 'staggered and failed to maintain constitutional principles of equality, freedom of the press, and justice in the provincial administrations'.[22] Rather, he and the CUP government remained steadfast in their commitment to the continued existence of the empire 'dominated by Muslim Turks in the Ottoman tradition'.[23]

The new CUP government strengthened central control while severely limiting individual and civic rights.[24] It implemented measures and resumed the work of state-building. It did enact some policies that saw an improvement in conditions in places in the eastern provinces, sacking former elites and replacing them with more competent administrative and judicial officials who immediately took steps to return land taken from Armenians, curtail depredations by Kurds, and restore some semblance of security of life and property.[25] The CUP also benefited from these measures, as many of the former officials were old adherents of the Hamidian regime and thus potential impediments to their policies.[26]

However, in most of the east, little changed. CUP authorities were willing to overlook the usual abuses of Armenians by Kurds and Turks as they centralised

[19] M Bardakçı, 'Askerin siyasete yerleşmesi 31 Mart isyanıyla başladı', *Sabah*, 16 April 2007; and VD Volkan and N Itzkowitz, *The Immortal Ataturk: A Psychobiography* (Chicago, University of Chicago Press, 1984) 65.

[20] EJ Zürcher, *Turkey: A Modern History*, 3rd edn (London, IB Tauris, 2004) 99.

[21] Zürcher, *Turkey*, 100.

[22] Kieser, *Talaat Pasha*, 63.

[23] Kieser, *Talaat Pasha*, 64.

[24] Zürcher, *Turkey*, 100.

[25] MA Reynolds, *Shattering Empires: The Clash and Collapse of the Ottoman and Russian Empires 1908–1918* (Cambridge, Cambridge University Press, 2011) 56.

[26] D Mesrob Kaligian, *Armenian Organization and Ideology under Ottoman Rule: 1908–1914* (Piscataway, NJ, Transaction Publishers, 2009) 43.

administration of these provinces, in part by insisting that powerful Kurdish chieftains forgo some of their control and yield it to government bureaucrats. This did not prevent a sense of alienation and bewilderment from spreading among the Kurds, who felt betrayed by the state and its gestures of support for the Armenian population, even though state officials assured the Kurds that they would not be required to return land to Armenians.[27]

Parliament voted to depose the sultan, sending him packing to Salonika to spend the remainder of his life under house arrest. The new sultan, his half-brother, assumed the throne as Mehmed V Reşad. He was content to rule in name only, 'simply a quiet, easy-going gentlemanly old man' whom, Morgenthau writes, everyone liked but who 'could not rule his empire, for he had no preparation for such a difficult task'.[28]

While the CUP then implemented measures to shore up its powers and limit that of the sultan, it resumed the work of state-building, but was then interrupted by the counter-revolution. To its credit, it enacted some measures that saw an improvement in conditions in the eastern provinces. It undertook reforms there, sacking former elites and replacing them with more competent administrative and judicial officials who immediately took steps to return land taken from Armenians, curtail depredations by Kurds, and restore some semblance of security of life and property.[29] The CUP also benefited from these measures, as many of the sacked officials were old adherents of the Hamidian regime and thus potential impediments to CUP policies.[30]

However, in many regions in the east, little changed. CUP authorities were willing to overlook the usual abuses of Armenians by Kurds and Turks as they centralised administration of these provinces, in part by insisting that powerful Kurdish chieftains forgo some of their control and yield it to government bureaucrats. This did not prevent a sense of alienation and bewilderment from spreading among the Kurds, who felt betrayed by the state and its gestures of support for the Armenian population, even though state officials assured the Kurds that they would not be required to return land to Armenians.[31]

III. ACCOUNTABILITY FOR THE ADANA MASSACRES

In the wake of the tragedy in Adana, the state did step in to bring a swift close to the whole affair. Though 43 people, including three Armenians, were convicted of crimes and sentenced to death by hanging, many were disappointed with the rulings.[32] If the post-coup CUP government gave little public attention to the '31 March incident', others, including the Turkish-language press, blamed, unfathomably, the Armenians, as they had blamed them for the Hamidian massacres a decade before. Doctors Nâzim

[27] Reynolds, *Shattering Empires*, 58–60.
[28] H Morgenthau, *Ambassador Morgenthau's Story* (Garden City, NY, Doubleday, Page, 1919) 17.
[29] Reynolds, *Shattering Empires*, 56.
[30] Kaligian, *Armenian Organization and Ideology under Ottoman Rule*, 43.
[31] Reynolds, *Shattering Empires*, 58–60.
[32] Kévorkian, 'The Cilician Massacres, April 1909', 365–68.

and Şakir, by now prominent members of the CUP central committee, argued that the Armenians provoked the massacres in order to invite European intervention.[33]

Months later, the government appointed a new governor of Adana Province, Djemal Pasha, the future minister of the navy and wartime commander of the Ottoman Fourth Army. In his postwar memoir, Djemal blamed Bishop Mushegh Seropian, the chief Armenian prelate of Adana Province, for the massacres because he had encouraged Armenians to arm themselves. The bishop would later bear the brunt of Turkish and foreign criticism for having exhorted Armenians to import weapons into Adana.[34] In the eyes of the CUP and others, his actions directly implicated him in fomenting sedition against the Ottoman state.

Not all Ottoman statesmen parroted this narrative. In August, Grand Vizier Hüseyin Hilmi Pasha sent out a remarkable circular acknowledging the Armenians' just cause in the face of discrimination and their contributions to the establishment of constitutionalism. He blamed the Adana massacres on the Muslim populace who had assumed that false intentions lay behind Armenians' enthusiasm for the constitution's restoration. Sent to the governors of all the *vilayets*, it read:

> Under the old regime ... certain classes of the Armenian community were undoubtedly working toward political ends. Whatever the forms their activity took, however, it had but one aim: to put an end to the intolerable misdeeds and harassment of a despotic government ... it has been observed that, in the recent past, the Armenians have done a great deal to help this nation obtain the Constitution, thereby demonstrating their sincere attachment to the Ottoman fatherland. Convinced, above all, after the restoration of the Constitution, that their nation could find neither salvation nor happiness outside the context of allegiance to the Ottoman Constitution, they concentrated their efforts on working on a common accord for the nation's welfare. Hence there is no grounds for the false opinion that leads those ignorant of the truth to suspect the Armenian community of nursing blameworthy political aspirations.[35]

The special commissions formed to investigate the Adana massacres concluded that the 'events were the last, deplorable vestiges of the days of an absolutism that wished to stamp out all feelings of patriotic fraternity'.[36] This wishful explanation ignored the primary factor Der Matossian has singled out for the bloodshed, that the Armenians' public embrace of the constitution had triggered Muslim fears about the future and anxieties over eventual Armenian political and economic supremacy in the region.[37] The Muslims feared that the restoration of the constitution, and the equality it promised to the Armenians, would only lead them to attempt to establish dominance over them. Armenians and the Armenians' demands for fairness in the administration of justice would thus compromise their own rights and freedoms. All in all, the reforms threatened Muslims' core identity, sense of personal security and collective superior status in relation to the Armenians.

[33] T Akçam, *A Shameful Act: The Armenian Genocide and the Question of Turkish Responsibility* (New York, Metropolitan Books, 2006) 62.

[34] Der Matossian, 'From Bloodless Revolution to Bloody Counterrevolution', 159–60, 169–70.

[35] Kévorkian, *The Armenian Genocide*, 79.

[36] AMAE, Correspondence politique Turquie, ns, vol 283 ff 164/22-23v, reprinted in (1909) 42 *Azadamard*, as cited in Kévorkian, *The Armenian Genocide*, 79.

[37] See Der Matossian, *Shattering Dreams of Revolution*, 25–26, 164.

Some Armenians persisted in looking past this further tragedy in the hope that a better future lay just ahead. In May 1909, before a large crowd gathered in Istanbul, the noted Armenian feminist Zabel Asadur (Sybil) assured her audience that the massacres in Adana marked the last gasp of the Hamidian regime, closing 'for good an era of cries and sobbing and augur[ing] a new period under the mantle of the august constitution'.[38] She and the special commissions were close to a single mind on this.

The post-counter-revolutionary period marked yet another moment when the state could have fostered trust between the Armenians and the Muslim population. An honest and full acknowledgment of what had happened in Adana could have enabled the government to mend the long-frayed relationship. The elements responsible had to be brought to justice, but weren't, a matter that Grand Vizier Hilmi's statement did not address.

In parliament, Zohrab called attention to the state's fidelity 'to the long-standing tradition of denying the facts, as in the case of the Adana events'.[39] Four years later, in another session of the Chamber of Deputies, he observed: 'It would be somewhat naive to believe that, in this country, simply proclaiming the constitution could change the general attitude of the Ottoman population [in whose eyes] Christians can never be the equals of Muslims, the only ones who have rights'. He went on to say that the real failure after Adana was the state's bringing 'only ordinary participants in the massacres to justice, while continuing to provide cover for the main organizers of these atrocities'.[40] According to Kévorkian, the 'Young Turks [were now so] overwhelmed by ultra-nationalist circles', that Zohrab feared 'a general massacre of the Armenians could erupt at any moment'.[41]

IV. BEHIND THE FAILURE OF THE ARF-CUP ALLIANCE

Deputy Vahan Papazian, an ARF leader from the eastern city of Van, characterised Zohrab's views as 'a true definition of the psychology of this country, its Turkish population, and its leadership element'. He quoted Zohrab's sentiments expressed during a session of the Chamber of Deputies:

> Compatriots, know this: that the revolution that was ushered in with the proclamation of the Ottoman Constitution is far from a perfect enterprise … [T]he Muslim element, filled with hatred, continues its criminal divisiveness – this is an indication that the Turkish element has not matured enough for the constitutional system …[42]

In protest, CUP officials pressed the Armenian deputies to understand how constrained they were by their commitment to maintain the political loyalty of Muslims, and

[38] 'Azganver Hayuhik', *Amenun Taretsoyts* (1909) 126, 129, cited in A Manuk-Khaloyan, unpublished manuscript.

[39] (2 July 1909) 9 *Azadamard* 2 records of the 104th session, cited in Kévorkian, *The Armenian Genocide*, 109.

[40] Kévorkian, *The Armenian Genocide*, 115–16.

[41] Kévorkian, *The Armenian Genocide*, 116.

[42] Papazian, *Im hushere*, 126.

especially Kurds, in the sensitive border regions with Russia.[43] Privately they expressed more ominous sentiments. At a secret meeting with CUP members in 1910, Talât reportedly said:

> You are aware that by the terms of the Constitution, equality of Mussulman and Ghaiur [infidels] was affirmed ... [T]his is an unrealizable ideal ... [T]he Ghiaurs ... stubbornly resist every attempt to ottomanize them ... [and thus] present an impenetrable barrier to the establishment of true equality ... There can therefore be no question of equality, until we have succeeded in our task of ottomanizing the Empire.[44]

A year later, at the ARF general congress in Istanbul, time had run out. Party members concluded that the alliance with the CUP had failed:

> The CUP has gradually withdrawn from constitutional and democratic principles. The CUP has failed to take steps to combat and cleanse itself of right-wing elements which, increasing their numbers over time, have developed a preponderant influence. That no results have been realized from the numerous negotiations and agreements the ARF has undertaken thus far with the CUP and its government ... That ... they have found it sufficient to leave their promises unrealized ... And also, that despots, ravishers, and corrupt elements have been left unpunished and have been encouraged to continue the looting, the massacres, and the marauding.

The declaration concluded:

> We note with sorrow that, despite a series of hopeful initiatives, in the three years of constitutional rule the government policies ... have generally given way to creating distrust between peoples and the denial of national rights.[45]

For most Armenians, betrayal, continuing injustice and a disinclination among some Ottomans to live under a constitution brought down the unlikely alliance and renewed deep distrust. Some Turks attributed the failure of the alliance to Armenians' refusal to 'Ottomanise', while for others it was refusal to Turkify.

V. SUBSTITUTING OTTOMANISM WITH TURKIFICATION

A year before the outbreak of the First Balkan War, Dr Nâzım was only one among a number of important CUP members beginning to see Ottomanism as an increasingly unviable political ideology. Its central tenet, that all the diverse ethnic groups of the empire unite behind a single national identity, was, in his view, at odds with reality. In the eyes of the CUP, the 1908 Revolution had failed to restore political order and curb secessionist tendencies in the Balkans and the Levant. The facts on the ground remained well short of the promises embodied in the *Tanzimat* and the Ottoman constitution. If the state was to be saved, then, Nâzım and others believed, it would have to be done by relying on the dominant Muslim-Turkish element of the empire. Some conservative CUP members came to reject Ottomanism out of a desire to limit

[43] Kévorkian, *The Armenian Genocide*, 108.

[44] Report by Arthur Geary to Gerald Lowther, 28 August 1910, in *British Documents on the Origins of the War*, vol 9, pt 1, enclosure to no 181, 208.

[45] Kaligian, *Armenian Organization and Ideology under Ottoman Rule*, 86.

whatever equality non-Muslims still enjoyed. By this time even Talât had accepted, in Kévorkian's words, that 'general Turkification was a necessary condition for the adoption of the principle of equality for all Ottoman subjects'.[46] This meant that Ottoman subjects would be equal if they accepted assimilation, and now that was coming to mean being culturally Turkish.

Kurdish sociologist Ziya Gökalp thought as did Nâzım. By 1910 he had established a reputation as an influential ideologue within the CUP, especially with Enver, who at this time held the post of Ottoman military attaché in Berlin. He outlined a vision that departed from the multiethnic model of imperial rule to one based on Turkic nationalism, rewriting the understanding of Ottomanism as 'nothing other than a covert beginning of the Turkification process'.[47] For Gökalp, Turkish culture and a pan-Turkic identity formed the basis of the future Ottoman state, not Islam or Ottomanism. He viewed the true marker of the Turkish identity of the Ottoman Empire to be language, not religion. Over the next three years, many in the CUP rallied around the idea that all imperial subjects had to accept cultural Turkification and the political and economic dominance of a Turkish-speaking elite.[48] Turkism and/or Pan-Islamism would replace Ottomanism.

VI. MUSLIM ALBANIANS' REFUSAL TO 'TURKIFY'

On the western flank of the Ottoman periphery, the CUP government faced further challenges. Rebellion brewed in Albania. The Ottoman elite had long taken the loyalty of the Muslims in Albania for granted. Their sons had provided the sultan's honour guard. In 1911 the Albanians refused to comply with cultural Turkification laws imposed by the centre. The reaction of Dr Nâzım, an increasingly prominent CUP leader, was to characterise Albanians and other peoples as a fatal 'annoyance' that 'will have to disappear'. He confessed that their 'separatism' and that of others would mean the death of the empire:

> The pretensions of various nationalities are a capital source of annoyance for us. We hold linguistic, historical and ethnic aspirations in abhorrence. This and that group will have to disappear. There should be only one nation on our soil, the Ottoman nation, and only one language, Turkish. It will not be easy for the Greeks and Bulgarians to accept this, although it is a vital necessity for us. To bring them to swallow the pill, we shall start with the Albanians. Once we have gotten the better of these mountaineers, who think they are invincible, the rest will take care of itself. After we have turned our cannons on the Albanians, shedding Muslim blood, let the *gävurs* beware. The first Christians to move a muscle will see his family, house and village smashed to smithereens. Europe will not dare raise its voice in protest or accuse us of torturing the Christians because our first bullets will have been expended on Muslim Albanians.[49]

[46] Kévorkian, *The Armenian Genocide*, 122.

[47] Z Gökalp, *Türkleşmek, İslamlaşmak, Muasırlaşmak* (Istanbul, 1988) 39–40, cited in Akçam, *A Shameful Act*, 79.

[48] On the CUP's efforts to build a 'national economy' in the empire, see the original study by Z Toprak, *Türkiye'de 'Millî iktisat' 1908–1918* (Ankara, Yurt Yayınları, 1982).

[49] S Lévy, 'Les Méfaits de Comité Union et Progrès IV: La Perte de l'Albanie' (1913) 39(5) *Mècheroutiette, Constitutionnel Ottoman* 27, as cited in Kévorkian, *The Armenian Genocide*, 120–21.

Dr Nâzım's threats did not halt the insurrections that followed in the Balkans and elsewhere.

In Istanbul, the rules for governance were first bent, and then broken. The CUP government did not accept the election of a member of the generally secular, pro-decentralisation Liberal Union Party, the splinter group from the CUP led by Prince Sabahaddin. When it won a seat to the Chamber of Deputies in a by-election at the end of 1911 by a single vote,[50] the government refused to accept the vote because it signalled that their popularity within their own party was waning and presaged another counter-revolution. Its response was to engineer the dissolution of parliament, forcing a general election the following spring.

During the election campaign, CUP member groups planted misleading stories in the press, limited free public discussion, threatened violence against opponents, gerrymandered electoral districts, and probably fixed the voting. This would later come to be known as the election with the 'big stick' because of the CUP's thuggish tactics.[51] The results were predictable: out of 284 seats, the CUP-aligned bloc won 270.[52] Despite its victory, the CUP's manoeuvres had cost it its legitimacy among the broader political elite. Some historians identify this as the moment when Ottoman parliamentary politics came to an end, so shortly after its much-heralded restoration.[53]

The Ottoman military leadership found the CUP's activities so odious that in mid-1912, it orchestrated its own coup against the government, forcing its members to resign at the point of bayonets. The Saviour Officers, as the leaders of this coup were known, thereby engineered Prince Sabahaddin's Liberal Union Party into power. The new cabinet was composed of elder statesmen who were thought capable of bringing the nation together.[54] But the new office-holders themselves violated due process in prosecuting CUP leaders. Patterns of governance were being established that would lay down the template of modern Turkish politics today.

Doubtless the most jarring event in the empire's last years, just before the outbreak of the world war, was the smaller conflict that exploded in the Balkans in the autumn of 1912. In October, the Balkan League, an alliance consisting of Bulgaria, Greece, Serbia, and Montenegro, launched a surprise attack against the Ottomans, scoring devastating lightning victories in a matter of weeks. The Ottoman armies were pushed back across all fronts in the Balkans. The Ottoman government was in disarray. The CUP saw its chance to regain power. In January 1913, Talât and Enver, assisted by other army officers, stormed the government offices in Istanbul, taking the Liberal Union cabinet members unawares. All but one cabinet member were told to resign or be shot. Nazım Pasha, the Ottoman war minister and a well-known opponent of the CUP, was not given a choice. One account has Enver himself shooting and killing him. The grand vizier Mehmed Kâmil Pasha was among those who chose to resign. The new minster of war and the nominal head of the Ottoman military

[50] Zürcher, *Turkey*, 102.

[51] Zürcher, *Turkey*, 103.

[52] A Kansu, *Politics in Post-revolutionary Turkey, 1908–1913* (Leiden, Brill, 2000) 445–97.

[53] For example, M Şükrü Hanioğlu, *A Brief History of the Late Ottoman Empire* (Princeton, NJ, Princeton University Press, 2008) 156.

[54] Zürcher, *Turkey*, 103.

was now Enver himself. The Balkan armies in the meantime continued their advance, overrunning one city after another in rapid succession. Even Edirne, once the capital of the empire, of timeless symbolic importance and only 150 miles from Istanbul, was occupied.

VII. THE EMOTIONAL ROLLER COASTER

Excessive excitement during and after the viciousness of the big-stick election and entry into war likely put many CUP members, especially the senior leadership, in a state of emotional dysregulation. They would have swung from audacity and exhilaration to disbelief and terror at so many losses – territorial, military, constitutional and human – in so short a time, and finally to wild hope because things could not possibly get worse. Dysregulation may explain why, in late June 1913, a few weeks after the signing of a humiliating treaty and the formal end of hostilities, the CUP government gambled and entered into a second Balkan war to take advantage of post-war disputes over territory between Bulgaria and her erstwhile allies.

Balkan States and the Empire

Source: Mehmed Nail Bey Collection, www.turkeyswar.com/prelude/balkan.html.

This Second Balkan War lasted less than two months. Bulgaria was pitilessly pummeled by her former allies, Greece, Montenegro and Serbia, fighting over the spoils.

A brilliant offensive led by Enver punched across the battle lines and led to Edirne's deliverance. The victory mattered greatly, both symbolically and practically. Nonetheless, from 1911 to 1913, the Ottoman Empire had lost a third of its original territory and a fifth of its population. Its finances were in disarray. Retaking Edirne offered hope that the losing trend could be reversed and also served as a psychological defence against accepting the humiliating reality of the empire's rapid decline. In historian Vahakn Dadrian's assessment, the 'disastrous outcome [of the Balkan Wars] … left the very survival of that empire hanging in the balance'.[55]

The war resulted in an exodus of poverty-stricken and severely traumatised Balkan Muslims from the former Ottoman Balkan territories. While the social and emotional impact of and on 400,000 refugees streaming from the Balkans, especially Bulgaria, cannot be measured, it probably mattered as much as the territorial loss. The Balkan League armies had swept through and spread terror among the local Muslim population, who left behind everything they possessed as they fled for their lives and from their homeland.[56]

After first passing through Istanbul, many of the refugees were then settled in rural areas, including eastern Anatolia. Zürcher notes the 'severe outbreaks of typhus and cholera and a very high mortality rate' among refugees, and that, overall, their 'resettlement caused enormous problems [with] many spen[ding] the next few years in squatter towns'.[57] Arnold Toynbee, a leading historian on international affairs in the early twentieth century, coined the powerful phrase '[a]n unexampled tension of feeling' to characterise the fraught atmosphere that arose between refugees and settled populations in the aftermath of the Balkan Wars.[58]

VIII. THE DEVELOPMENT OF TURKISH NATIONALISM

In the face of losses in the Balkans and the misplaced hopes in Ottoman constitutionalism, Gökalp proposed a particularly extreme vision of Turkish nationalism, Turanism. He claimed that Turan was at once 'the mythical homeland of the Turks and cradle of their history', complete with a heroic mythical figure, 'obscure and vague for the scholar' but 'familiar and clearly known', as he wrote, 'to my heart'. Turan would be centered in Anatolia but also extend to the east, in territory that was then part of the Russian Empire, reimagined as part of a Turkic homeland. Pursuit of this invented homeland would be used as a rationale to punish those whom they could hold – non-Muslims, especially Armenians – as being responsible for the decline of the empire. For the politically prominent CUP members who adopted the ideology, Turanism would have served as a compensatory, if seemingly fantastical, collective

[55] V Dadrian, *The History of the Armenian Genocide: Ethnic Conflict from the Balkans to Anatolia to the Caucasus* (New York, Berghahn Books, 2003) 185.

[56] See J McCarthy, *Death and Exile: The Ethnic Cleansing of Ottoman Muslims, 1821–1922* (Princeton, NJ, Darwin Press, 1995) 135–78.

[57] Zürcher, *Turkey*, 108–109.

[58] A Toynbee, *The Western Question in Greece and Turkey: A Study in the Contact of Civilisations* (London, Constable, 1922; repr New York, H Fertig, 1970) 139.

psychological defence against the change of status. One of Gökalp's poems extolled the legendary leader among the medieval Turkic tribes:

> In me he still lives in all his fame and greatness
>
> Oghuz Khan delights and inspires my heart and causes me to sing psalms of gladness
>
> The fatherland of Turks is neither Turkey nor Turkestan: but the broad,
>
> eternal land of Turania ...[59]

Gökalp did not suppose that Turan would be realised immediately. For now, he was content with a cultural synthesis among Turkic peoples:

> ... the Turkmens of Azerbaijan, Iran and Khwarezm like the Turks of Turkey belong to the Oghuz strain. Therefore, our immediate ideal for Turkism must be Oghuz or Turkmen unity. What would be the purpose of this unity? A political union? For the present, no! We cannot pass judgment on what will happen in the future, but for the present our goal is only cultural unity of the Oghuz peoples.[60]

Turanism as conceptualised by Gökalp and other ideologues would encompass a region that included parts of the Russian Caucasus and Central Asia inhabited by Turkic peoples. These lands would be seized as compensation for the Ottoman territories that had already been lost or were likely to be lost in the near future. Turanism would be the true equaliser, because everyone in Turan would be of ethnic Turkic heritage. Islam, however, had to change in line with the growing strength of national thought and ideas. Both Turanism and what would become Islamism remained ill-defined, serving primarily as a contemporary defensive call to unity against the threat of the powerful force of politically liberal modernisation. Yet pan-Turkism's implications could appear ominous, suggesting almost physical destruction for those who did not conform to linguistic and religious conversion.

Enver was an early follower of Gökalp and become an ardent proponent of his Pan-Turkic vision.[61] Arif Cemil, a secretary in the CUP, later recalled:

> The objective took such immense shape in the minister of war's imagination until finally, [he envisioned] himself as the ruler of a resurrected Ottoman empire, one which, after uniting the Turks and Muslims of Asia and winning back the countries we had lost in Europe, would stretch from the Adriatic Sea to the waters of India ...[62]

Thus, according to Cemil, for Enver, Turkification was desired as much to save the Ottoman Empire as to cast it in a different form, that of a Turanian empire. He and other like-minded CUP officials had realised that further territory would be needed, because the Ottoman Empire was shrinking and would soon comprise little more than a rump state with Anatolia at its core. In line with Göçek's statement quoted at the start of this chapter, Akçam writes, 'Turkish national identity developed amid pronounced and continuous anxiety over the Turks' future and their very existence'.[63]

[59] JM Landau, *Tekinalp, Turkish Patriot 1883–1961* (Leiden, Uitgaven van het Nederlands Historisch-Archaeologisch Instituut te Istanbul, 1984) 111.

[60] Z Gökalp, *The Principles of Turkism*, trans R Devereux (Leiden, EJ Brill, 1968) 17.

[61] Akçam, *A Shameful Act*, 93.

[62] Akçam, *A Shameful Act*, 93.

[63] Akçam, *A Shameful Act*, 55.

IX. TO FIGHT, FLEE, OR FREEZE

Ottomanism remained a contested, evolving concept well into the years leading up the First World War. At its most basic level, it proposed a supranational identity for all Ottoman citizens. Empire-wide reform was associated with the efforts to construct, or reconstruct, an Ottoman identity. The Armenian community's attachment to their homeland, and assumption that they would continue to reside there no matter how difficult the political and social conditions, underlay their hopes and beliefs that change for the better was sure to come. But Armenians had witnessed the state drag its feet to enact reforms, first under Abdülhamid II and now from the CUP, for four decades. What had sustained those hopes had been the concrete promises of reform embodied in the *Tanzimat*, then Article 61 of the Berlin Treaty, the 1908 Revolution, and some candid acknowledgments of past wrongs and injustices. Following the revolution, there was an overweening hope and wary trust placed in the new constitutional regime and the state's ability to address the problems in the Armenian-populated provinces. The ARF, the preeminent Armenian political party after 1908, had expressed that trust by allying with the CUP.

However, in the six years following the restoration of the constitution, the CUP increasingly ignored the constitution and failed to enact changes. The ARF and many other Armenian political figures and others gave up on their hopes for constitutionalism under the new Ottoman governing class, shattered by multiple betrayals. They evinced fears about their community's future. Many emigrated, as had thousands before them during the massacres of the 1890s.

Embattled Ottoman leaders lurched from one crisis to another. Some Armenians wistfully held out hope that Europe, or specifically imperial Russia, would institute change from without. CUP members and the more chauvinistic Turkish intellectual class thought that if only they could do away with or reduce the power and influence of the Ottoman Christians, whom they blamed for inviting European intervention, they could save their empire. All the losses, threats, and turbulence led the CUP itself to splinter further, creating inner tensions and conflicts. Covert paramilitary forces that the CUP employed continued to threaten and murder their political opponents and hostile journalists.[64]

Being fearful, angry and trapped individually or collectively is traumatising. It is common, writes leading trauma expert Judith Herman, 'to displace … anger far from its dangerous source and to discharge it unfairly on those who did not provoke it', often a weaker target perceived as provocative and therefore blameworthy.[65] The Ottomans' hold in Europe and elsewhere was vanishing in a breathtakingly short space of time. Simon Zavarian, one of the founding members of the ARF, advised similarly fearful, angry and trapped, but infinitely much weaker, Armenians to respond cautiously to the Ottoman losses, 'for, if the Turks are defeated, they will naturally seek to avenge themselves on the Armenians, who constitute the weakest group and cannot defend themselves'.[66]

[64] See GW Gawrych, 'The Culture and Politics of Violence in Turkish Society' (1986) 22 *Middle Eastern Studies* 307.

[65] J Herman, *Trauma and Recovery: The Aftermath of Violence – From Domestic Abuse to Political Terror* (New York, Basic Books, 1992) 104.

[66] H Dasnabedian (ed), *Simon Zavarian: On the Occasion of the Seventieth Anniversary of His Death*, vol 3 (Beirut, 1992) 118–19, cited in Kévorkian, *The Armenian Genocide*, 137.

Much is made of the senseless destruction of World War I. Far less is made of how the Ottoman state might have sidestepped the devastation of World War I to a great extent, preserved the empire, and left the Armenians undisturbed in their homeland. It would have required a sincere enforcement of the equality clauses in their own constitution. Instead, throughout these years, new ideologies, including Turkish nationalism proved more attractive and ripened in response to the deteriorating imperial situation. Frightened by the threat to their entitlement, these Ottoman elites envisioned the future Ottoman Empire as Muslim Turkish, and no longer multiethnic. For some, the new ideas took a more extreme form. To reclaim the glory of grand imperialists, they wished to establish an enlarged, entirely Turkic empire, Turan. In 1913, Stepan Sapah-Guilian, like Zohrab, could sense the rumblings of a march towards a general massacre:

> Turkish nationalism, which, today, has the government of the country in its grip, will, without hesitation, ruthlessly massacre the Armenians … It is also plain that the old and new representatives of Turkish nationalism have no desire whatsoever to accept the idea of the existence, development and vitality of the Armenian people.[67]

[67] S Sapah-Guilian, 'Preuves et rèalitè' (1913) 3 *Hnchak* 6, as cited in Kévorkian, *The Armenian Genocide*, 134.

8

Five Men's Traumatisation before they Acquired Power

[The Balkans] were the richest and most developed provinces and a disproportionate part of the Ottoman ruling elite hailed from them.

Erik J Zürcher[1]

McCarthy's work [draws] … attention to the oft-unheeded history of Muslim suffering and embattlement that shaped the mindset of the perpetrators of 1915.

Donald Bloxham[2]

[I]t was precisely those people who, having only recently been saved from massacre themselves, would now take a central and direct role in cleansing Anatolia of 'non-Turkish' elements.

Taner Akçam[3]

FIVE MEN ARE widely held as being most responsible for the conception and implementation of the Armenian genocide. All five, or one or both of their parents, were born and raised in the Balkans (Rumelia), then part of the Ottoman Empire. There, at the time of their births and childhoods, tension was rising between Christians and Muslims, with many nationalists among the former wanting to break free from Ottoman rule. Each experienced traumas, mostly early in their lives, relevant to their later conduct and interaction with the Armenians. All were CUP members. Mehmet Talât, İsmail Enver, and Ahmed Djemal held important portfolios in the Ottoman government. The other two, Selanikli Nâzım and Behaeddin Şakir, occupied centrally appointed but unofficial positions from which they exercised power to shape policy and carry out the genocidal measures, especially in the eastern Anatolian provinces, in the midst of the First World War. The two oversaw the Special Organization, a paramilitary outfit trained for unconventional warfare. As early as 1910, some of them had already spoken of finding a permanent solution to the Armenian Question. Over the next few years, they all came to believe

[1] EJ Zürcher, *Turkey: A Modern History*, 3rd edn (London, IB Tauris, 2004) 108–109.
[2] D Bloxham, *The Great Game of Genocide* (New York, Oxford University Press, 2005) 210.
[3] T Akçam, *A Shameful Act: The Armenian Genocide and the Question of Turkish Responsibility* (New York, Metropolitan Books, 2006) 87.

that the Armenian presence in the empire should be reduced to the point that it no longer posed a threat to Ottoman sovereignty nor endangered the continued physical existence of the core national group of the empire, namely, the Turkish-speaking Muslim population.[4] The policy of genocide and the orders to carry it out were not decided in any one place, by any one group, or by any one of them alone. In a back-and-forth process, the policy was developed and supported by local provincial leaders charged with carrying out the measures in their jurisdictions.[5]

These men, like others who occupy top decision-making roles, are often called 'leaders'. But for Ronald Heifetz, the Harvard Kennedy School's specialist on leadership, individuals in such roles are not automatically leaders. They became leaders, whether or not they have formal authority, when they take responsibility for consulting with and responding to relevant constituencies and then work to enable those over whom they have influence to adapt to new realities of the times, such as today to climate change. These five Ottomans were not 'leaders'.[6]

A Demographic Map of the Balkans Circa 1880 (from Ernst Ravenstein's *Ethnographical Map of Turkey in Europe*)

Source: Élisée Reclus, *The Universal Geography: The Earth and its Inhabitants*, vol 1, edited by EG Ravenstein (London, JS Virtue & Co, Ltd, 1876).

[4] On core nationalism, see E Lohr, 'Politics, Economics and Minorities: Core Nationalism in the Russian Empire at War' in J Leonhard and U von Hirschhausen (eds), *Comparing Empires: Encounters and Transfers in the Long Nineteenth Century* (Göttingen, Vandenhoeck & Ruprecht, 2012) 518–29.

[5] T Akçam, 'When Was the Decision to Annihilate the Armenians Taken?' (2019) 21 *Journal of Genocide Research* 457.

[6] RA Heifetz, *Leadership without Easy Answers* (Cambridge, MA, Harvard University Press, 1998).

Both a witness to and a player in the events that were to come, was one who exercised leadership in his ambassadorial role. In late 1913, at age 57, Henry Morgenthau took up his first assignment in international politics as the American ambassador to the Ottoman Empire, its representative to the Sublime Porte, as the Ottoman government was known. In his post-war memoir *Ambassador Morgenthau's Story* and in other reflections in *All in a Lifetime*, Morgenthau wrote that the leaders of the new CUP government faced a task of the greatest magnitude that would 'test the strength of the ablest statesmen of any country'.[7] But he concluded that after ascending to power in 1908, these young men changed and abandoned the values that had propelled them into politics. He recorded his witnessing of the tragic result, the very opposite of broadening the democratic base and regeneration:

> I soon discovered that four years of so-called democratic rule had ended with the nation more degraded, more impoverished, and more dismembered than ever before. Indeed, long before I had arrived, this attempt to establish a Turkish democracy had failed. The failure was probably the most complete and the most disheartening in the whole history of democratic institutions.[8]

Morgenthau cared passionately about the ideas and principles embodied in the newly restored imperial constitution. As an immigrant to the United States from Germany at a time when European anti-Semitism was becoming more pronounced, he held the values enshrined in the US Constitution as sacred and saw the opportunity for the Ottomans to bring their country up to the same standards as those of his adopted homeland.

I. MEHMET TALÂT

Mehmet Talât, born in 1874 in Edirne, would become the most powerful member of the CUP. His father, Ahmed Vasif, came from a humble family of Pomaks from the village of Çepleci in the district of Kırcaali, in the eastern part of the Rhodope mountains of Rumelia. In his 1919 memoir, Talât disavowed his Pomak identity, because, according to biographer Hans-Lukas Kieser, 'he wanted to be, and to show himself, as a "pure Turk", in accordance with his embrace of Turkism'.[9] From April 1876 to 1878, local Bulgarian Christians rose in rebellion against Ottoman rule and were brutally repressed by Ottoman troops and *başıbozuk* irregulars, resulting in some 10,000–15,000 Christian deaths. Perhaps as many as 1,000 Muslims were killed during these disturbances.[10] Although the worst of the violence did not spread to the eastern reach of the Rhodope mountains, it struck not far from Çepleci, which lay in the path of the Russian army's advance on Edirne in 1877, undertaken in part to protect the Christians.

As the Russians approached, Talât and his family fled to Istanbul, returning to Edirne a year later.[11] Talât was a toddler during the two years of the violence and a boy in its aftermath. He would have sensed the fear that forced his family to flee, a threat

[7] H Morgenthau, *All in a Lifetime* (New York, Doubleday, 1923) 198.

[8] H Morgenthau, *Ambassador Morgenthau's Story* (Garden City, NY, Doubleday, Page, 1919) 12.

[9] Personal correspondence, 25 November 2018.

[10] See J McCarthy, *Death and Exile: The Ethnic Cleansing of Ottoman Muslims, 1821–1922* (Princeton, NJ, Darwin Press, 1995) 64.

[11] H-L Kieser, *Talaat Pasha: Father of Modern Turkey, Architect of Genocide* (Princeton, NJ, Princeton University Press, 2018) 41.

that probably would have been particularly vivid to his father, whose village was close to the sites of the worst violence. His family and social surroundings surely transmitted to him a growing unease as well as the disturbing impact of the violence as he matured into late boyhood and developed awareness that other members of the Muslim collectivity were his people. It is likely that this situation implanted in him an inchoate fear early on, one which as he grew older turned into directed but not carefully considered 'fight' action to preserve what remained of the empire.

Talât's unassuming origins probably led him to take his first job as an assistant at the post office.[12] From there he rose to the directorship of Salonika's postal and telegraph office and joined the Salonika branch of the CUP before the revolution of 1908.[13] In the first parliamentary elections held that fall, he was voted into the Ottoman Chamber of Deputies as the representative for Edirne. A year later, he was appointed to the cabinet as minister of the interior, where he remained, with a brief interruption, until 1917, participating in the turbulent first years of governance under the restored constitution in 1909–1913 and witnessing the devastating impact of the Italo-Ottoman and Balkan Wars. In his memoir, Morgenthau took note of Talât's great physical strength and charismatic personality, perceiving that, although not highly educated, he was a 'natural genius', genial, insightful about people, and possessed great mental focus, determination, courage, and quickness of mind.[14] In his view, it was these qualities that had led to his ascent to the leadership of the government.

Talât Pasha, circa 1917–20
Source: Library of Congress, LC-B2-5301-7.

[12] Kieser, *Talaat Pasha*, 42.
[13] M Şükrü Hanioğlu, *Türkiye Diyanet Vakfı Islâm ansiklopedisi*, sv 'Talat Paşa' (Istanbul, Türkiye Diyanet Vakfı, Islâm Ansiklopedisi Genel Müdürlüğü, 2010).
[14] Morgenthau, *All in a Lifetime*, 185.

Talât would reach the pinnacle of his power during the First World War. In his position as interior minister, he was the figure most responsible for the Armenian genocide. Talât's mastery and continual use of new communication technology – he famously kept a telegraph machine in his home – extended his reach to the far corners of the Ottoman Empire and enabled him to direct others in carrying out the crimes against the Armenians. In early 1917, Talât became the grand vizier (prime minister). In October 1918, as Allied armies barrelled down on Istanbul from the west, he and the rest of the CUP cabinet resigned and fled into exile. From 1918 to 1921, his former German wartime partners shielded him, even as an Istanbul court sentenced him to death in absentia. He would meet his end in March 1921 in an affluent part of Berlin, gunned down by a young Armenian, Soghomon Tehlirian (see Chapter 2).

Morgenthau found Talât both likable and terrifying, reporting instances of Talât enjoying his exercise of power as much as any autocratic sultan. Talât's traumatic background and limited education did not encourage him to grapple with the challenges of implementing the principles embodied in the Ottoman constitution. Instead, he seemed to have expected that this massive change would take place rapidly and automatically without preparation or management. Talât, Morgenthau wrote, complained of the 'great disappointment which he and his fellow revolutionists felt with their people' that this did not happen:

> Having lived for so many years in a state of subjection, the masses seemed completely cowed and did not respond in the least to any suggestion of progress or improvement. He also blamed the Sheikhs and feudal chiefs who were still extorting tributes and using most exasperating methods in collecting taxes.[15]

Morgenthau observed that it did not occur to Talât to consider a variety of methods for overseeing the broad changes the constitutional revolution promised.

II. İSMAIL ENVER

İsmail Enver was born in 1881 and grew up in Stambul, the old quarter of the capital on the European side of the city. His father was a Gagauz Turk, the name of a small ethnic community in what is now Ukraine that practised Eastern Orthodox Christianity. His mother held the most lowly of occupations in the empire – laying out the dead – and was of Albanian origin. Enver was raised a Muslim. At age 12 he entered the military academy in Monastir in Macedonia, where he rose to the rank of major at the age of 25.[16] While stationed in Salonika, he joined the local CUP branch and in 1908 led the successful march against the sultan. His stature only continued to grow when he was dispatched to Berlin to serve as military attaché at the Ottoman embassy. During his tenure in that post from 1909 to 1911, he became an admirer of the professionalism, dedication, and efficiency of the German military.

[15] Morgenthau, *All in a Lifetime*, 197.

[16] ŞS Aydemir, *Enver Paşa Makedonya'dan Ortaasya'ya, 1860–1908*, vol 1 (Istanbul, Remzi Kitabevi, 1970) 250–57.

Not long after returning to Istanbul, Enver volunteered to fight in Ottoman Tripolitania, which Italy had invaded in October 1911. A little more than a year later, now with the rank of lieutenant colonel, he led his men in the First Balkan War. By January 1914, Enver had become minister of war and chief of staff of the Ottoman army (the sultan remained the titular commander-in-chief). In spite of his humble origins, Enver rose in the sultan's retinue and that same year married the niece of Sultan Mehmed V.[17]

By then Enver had experienced first-hand both the humiliations of the Italo-Ottoman and Balkan wars and the triumphant recapture of Edirne, which he had personally led. Enver deeply identified with the Balkans, a region of central importance to the Ottoman Empire since the fourteenth century. He and many other Ottomans regarded this eastern region as the cradle of the Ottoman homeland.[18] Until it was eclipsed by the conquest of Constantinople in 1453, Edirne had served as the capital of the early expanding Ottoman principality. In a speech in 1913, Enver eulogised the Ottomans' loss of most of Rumelia and what it signified for him personally:

> How could a person forget the plains, the meadows, watered with the blood of our forefathers, abandon those places where Turkish raiders had hidden their steeds for six hundred years, with our mosques, our tombs, our dervish retreats, our bridges, and our castles, to leave them to our slaves, to be driven out of Rumelia to Anatolia, this was beyond a person's endurance. I am prepared to gladly sacrifice the remaining years of my life to take revenge on the Bulgarians, the Greeks and the Montenegrins.[19]

Enver's language reveals that in addition to grief he was offended and humiliated by this loss because it had been brought about by 'our slaves', that is, the empire's former Balkan Christian subjects. His intention to seek vengeance was a fight response to the trauma of the offending loss. In a letter to his fiancée on 8 May 1913, between the two Balkan wars, he wrote, 'revenge, revenge, revenge, there is no other word'.[20]

Possibly adding to his feelings over the loss of territory was concern for the Muslim population of the Balkans. The two wars turned some 400,000 of them – Turks, Pomaks, and Bosniaks – into refugees, who fled to or were settled in Anatolia and the Near East.[21] Enver himself may have experienced 'the unexampled tension of feeling' Toynbee identified in the aftermath of the Balkan Wars (Chapter 7). Perhaps he felt it more strongly than other CUP members. As a senior army commander, he played no small role during the two disastrous Balkan Wars and may have felt shame and responsibility for the refugees' plight. At the same time Enver's great ambition, apparent high self-regard and confidence, and willingness to act without as much

[17] Most of the information about Enver's family and early career comes from Aydemir's biography on Enver.

[18] MA Reynolds, *Shattering Empires: The Clash and Collapse of the Ottoman and Russian Empires 1908–1918* (Cambridge, Cambridge University Press, 2011) 39.

[19] Akçam, *A Shameful Act*, 115.

[20] M Şükrü Hanioğlu (ed), *Kendi mektuplarında Enver Paşa* (Istanbul, Der Yayınları, 1989) 240–42, cited in Reynolds, *Shattering Empires*, 39.

[21] EJ Zürcher, 'Greek and Turkish Refugees and Deportees, 1912–1914' *Turkology Update Leiden Project* (January 2003) 1, www.transanatolie.com/english/turkey/turks/ottomans/ejz18.pdf (accessed 21 July 2020).

thought as his colleagues might wish (see next chapter and Part III), would have shielded him from consciously feeling shame and responsibility deeply.

Ottoman War Minister and Commander-in-Chief Enver Pasha

Source: Library of Congress, LC-USZ62-77293.

Enver retained his daring ambition when he sought to carve a new path for the empire's regeneration. Upon the imminent collapse of the Ottoman armies in 1918, he joined the other Unionists to flee to Europe. Even Mustafa Kemal suspected his former comrade-in-arms was a potential political rival and barred him from returning to Turkey.[22] In 1919, Enver was sentenced to death in absentia by the Istanbul courts-martial. He made his way to Russian Turkestan and ultimately died in an armed skirmish with Red Army forces in 1922.

[22] Ş Yılmaz, 'An Ottoman Warrior Abroad: Enver Paşa as an Expatriate' in S Kedourie (ed), *Seventy-Five Years of the Turkish Republic* (London, Frank Cass, 2000) 40–69.

III. AHMED DJEMAL

Ahmed Djemal was born in 1872 on the island of Lesbos, then part of the Ottoman Empire (now of Greece), just off the Aegean coast of Anatolia. His father's side, writes his grandson Hasan Cemal, 'was uprooted and cast to Istanbul from the Balkans … [m]y father's mother, from Serres in the present day Greek Macedonia'.[23] His mother's Circassian family had first fled to Anatolia from Moldavia in the mid-nineteenth century during the Russian Empire's violent ethnic cleansing of some half a million Muslims from Transcaucasia, the North Caucasus and the Crimea. Many resettled on the northern shores of the Black Sea of the Ottoman Empire with great difficulty and showed considerable resentment towards their new Christian Greek and Armenian neighbours.[24] The trauma of the expulsion and flight from one empire to another was transmitted to Djemal and his mother. Cemal recalls its repetitious retelling, as traumatic experiences, once articulated, often are:

> I thought about my own family roots. They had also been extirpated from all corners of a huge empire. I vaguely recall from my childhood how the sufferings were recounted in conversations by the wood stove with sighs … My mother's side was dispersed from Caucasia and came to Istanbul. Her Georgian and Circassian roots go back to Northern Caucasus.[25]

Before assuming twin postings in World War I as army commander and governor-general of the Greater Syrian provinces, Djemal occupied a number of important positions, including military governor of Istanbul, governor of Adana, and minister of the navy. Djemal arrived in Damascus in November 1914, where he established his wartime headquarters. Simon Sebag-Montefiore reports on Djemal's many-sided personality.

> [He was the] … effective dictator of Greater Syria and supreme Commander of the Fourth Ottoman Army … [F]orty-five years old, squat and bearded, always protected by a camel-mounted squadron of guards, [he] combined brutish, paranoid cruelty with a weakness for pomp and circumstance … he had a sense both of his own greatness and of his own absurdity. [An observer] thought Jemal 'a strange man and one to be feared', but also 'a man of dual personality' capable of charm and kindness. Once, without anyone seeing, he gave a diamond-studded medal to a little girl whose parents found her with it when they returned home. One of his German officers … simply judged him 'an extremely intelligent oriental despot'.[26]

As governor-general of the Greater Syrian provinces from 1915 until the end of the war, Djemal acquired a notorious reputation as a ruthless and imperious overlord presiding over his own fiefdom. He is still remembered with bitterness for his order to have some two dozen Arab nationalists in Beirut and Damascus hanged in May 1916.

[23] H Cemal, *1915: The Armenian Genocide* (Istanbul, Hrant Dink Foundation, 2015) 54.
[24] O Figes, *The Crimean War: A History* (New York, Metropolitan Books, 2010) 424–25.
[25] Cemal, *1915*, 54.
[26] S Sebag-Montefiore, *Jerusalem: The Biography* (New York, Random House, 2012) 413–14.

Yet Djemal left another legacy, uncommon in his time and place, in advocating an expanded role for women in Ottoman society. 'I believe firmly in the important part which woman is called upon to play not only in social life, but also public affairs', he wrote proudly in his post-war memoirs.[27] He claimed credit for the growth of the feminist movement during the Second Constitutional Era and pronounced his belief in the ultimate emancipation of women not only in the Ottoman Empire but other countries as well. While almost universally reviled in the Arab world, among some Armenians his memory remains mixed with some. At the meeting at Harvard University in 2009 (see Preface), an elderly Armenian in the audience tearfully expressed his gratitude to Cemal that his grandfather had spared the life of the man's own grandfather, a doctor who treated Ottoman soldiers serving in Syria. As grandson Cemal sees it, '[H]e protected, sheltered Armenians in Adana and Beirut', where he also founded a school for Armenian orphans (see Chapter 17).[28]

Like other CUP elites, Djemal's foremost concern on the eve of World War I was how to go about preserving and maintaining the empire. In his memoir Cemal related how Talât asked Djemal for his opinion about an alliance with Germany, to which he answered, 'I should not hesitate to accept any alliance which rescued Turkey from her present position of isolation'.[29] His other ambitions during the war are less clear. An early sympathiser of the CUP cause, Djemal worked strenuously to improve the social infrastructure and the military readiness of the Ottoman Empire. Most incredibly, indirect evidence surfaced after the end of the war to suggest that Djemal was interested in overthrowing the CUP. In December 1915, just over a year after the Ottoman Empire entered the war in alliance with the Central Powers, he allegedly reached out to Hakob Zavriev, a Russian Armenian member of the Dashnak party, who claimed to have important connections with Russian state officials and with whom Djemal had established a rapport. At that time, Zavriev 'informed the Russians that [Djemal] ... was dissatisfied with the government, and would probably like to overthrow it'.[30] Russian officials promised to treat the issue seriously and take up the matter with their French and British allies.[31] In exchange for overthrowing the CUP and surrendering Istanbul and the Straits to Russia, Djemal supposedly proposed the creation of a separate state with himself as sultan. In the end, however, the scheme was thwarted by the French and the British because it conflicted with their post-war plans to divide up the empire. Given the lack of supporting evidence, many historians dispute that Djemal had any real intention to defect to the side of the Entente and that, in fact, no such overture had ever even occurred.[32]

[27] D Pasha, *Memories of a Turkish Statesman, 1913–1919* (New York, George H Doran Company, 1922) 18–19.

[28] Cemal, *1915*, 36–37.

[29] Cemal, *1915*, 108.

[30] F Kazemzadeh, *The Struggle for Transcaucasia, 1917–1921* (New York, Philosophical Library, 1951) 28–29.

[31] Kazemzadeh, *The Struggle for Transcaucasia*, 28–29; and D Fromkin, *A Peace to End All Peace: The Fall of the Ottoman Empire and the Creation of the Modern Middle East* (New York, Henry Holt, 1989) 214–15.

[32] See S McMeekin, *The Russian Origins of the First World War* (Cambridge, MA, Harvard University Press, 2011) 198–201; and U Trumpener, *Germany and the Ottoman Empire, 1914–1918* (Princeton, NJ, Princeton University Press, 1968) 151.

Djemal Pasha, with German Officer Captain von Frankenburg, Commander of the Asien Korps, during World War I

Source: Library of Congress, LC-B2-3435-4.

Djemal's country, linked with Turkishness, was of the greatest value to him, for which no sacrifice would be too great. Before leaving on a long trip in 1920, Djemal wrote a long letter to his son, then studying in Hungary. The letter reads as if it is his last testament to this son. It was unmitigated by second thoughts, such as about leaving him or carrying out murderous policies and actions during the war:

> I am going on a longish trip [as a military adviser in Afghanistan]. Chances are I will not see you for a long time. And again chances are you will not hear from me for a long time. And here with this letter I will give you some counsel … Let the love of country, the love

> of Turkishness be your most valuable jewel. Love your country and Turkishness more than everything. Do not refrain from any sacrifice for these two.
>
> After I die, follow the exact path I have up to now.[33]

'In the family it was believed that Djemal Pasha was different from Enver and Talât', writes Cemal, in that he used his considerable power less than the others did to carry out violence against those designated as enemies. Yet in his own memoir written after the war, Djemal exhibited an early form of denial over the Armenians' fate when he spoke about the amicable relationship prevailing between the Armenians and Turks over the centuries, without mentioning the brutal conditions under which Armenians had come to live and then to die. Cemal indicates that the rest of the family still perpetuates Djemal's disavowal:

> [I]t was said that 'Pasha Grandpa' was not responsible for 1915. And whenever I said, 'but he was responsible politically' in response, I would cause a slight stir. Though not too loud, I would witness some negative voices rising against me in the family.[34]

Djemal was assassinated in July 1922 in an act of rough justice and revenge. Like his colleague Talât's fate, the assassination was carried out as part of Operation Nemesis, the covert postwar campaign devised by Armenian political operatives to track down and kill key CUP leaders implicated in the genocide.

On three occasions I heard Cemal emphasise in his public speeches about how important it is 'to understand and share one another's pain'. In legal venues and history classes, comparisons of suffering are necessary, but there is a place elsewhere for simply understanding another's pain. Cemal made his point without comparing the Muslims' and Armenians' pain – or anyone else's. He was pointing out the importance of recognising the pain of others as well as one's own and of the commonality that provides. When he did so, I heard some in the audience muttering, seemingly believing that he was placing Armenian and Muslim pain on an equal plane.

IV. BEHAEDDIN ŞAKIR

Behaeddin Şakir was born in 1874, the same year as Talât, and in Bulgaria, where he, too, would have grown up amidst the tensions between Ottoman Christians and Muslims as well as fears of – if not encounters with – the Russian Army. By 1891 Şakir, a young medical student, was banished by the sultan's government to Erzincan in northeastern Anatolia for his association with the burgeoning Young Turk movement. From there he managed to flee first to Egypt and then to Paris, where he assisted the CUP leadership and met Selanikli Nâzım. Together the two, with Ahmed Rıza, provided the CUP with 'a sound organizational basis, with branches in many parts of

[33] Cemal, *1915*, 33–34.

[34] Cemal, *1915*, 37. For a detailed study on Djemal's policies during the war, see M Talha Çiçek, *War and State Formation in Syria: Cemal Pasha's Governate during World War I, 1914–1917* (New York, Routledge, 2014).

the empire and adjacent countries and an effective secretariat and communications'.[35] After the 1908 Revolution, Şakir returned to the Ottoman Empire, devoting himself to CUP party activity and organisation.[36] In 1913 he and Nâzım created a paramilitary unit called the Special Organization, headed by Enver.[37]

Early in the war, Şakir was almost killed on the Caucasus Front, and the traumatic experience 'coloured his actions' during its remainder.[38] Thereafter he authorised the cruellest measures against Christians. A 1919 report by the Armenian Patriarchate identified him as the CUP 'Central Committee member responsible for carrying out the liquidation of the Armenians'.[39] He was one of the main individuals tasked with overseeing the implementation of the genocide, employing Special Organization members to be 'butchers of men'.[40] In the post-war courts martial in early 1920, the prosecutor declared in his concluding statement that

> ... Bahaeddin Şakir organized battalions of butchers ... and coordinated all the crimes committed in this region. The state was complicit in these crimes. No government official, no judge, no gendarme ever stepped in to protect the population subject to these atrocities ... Traveling in a special automobile, he went from one local center to the next to communicate orally the decisions made by the Party for Union and Progress and the directive dispatched by the various sections of the party and the heads of government ... in these localities ... The atrocities that were committed, on a premediated plan and with absolutely premeditated intent, were ... organized and ordered by delegates of the Party for Union and Progress and its highest bodies and then carried out by the leaders of the governorships, ... pliant tools serving the designs and desires of this organization, which knew no law and had no scruples.[41]

Also during the war Şakir was implicated in brutal acts of violence and ethnic cleansing against thousands of ethnic Greeks, organising their removal from parts of Anatolia and resettling them in the homes of recently removed Armenians:

> [F]rom his arrival in the region [the Black Sea coast, a major centre of ethnic Greeks in the Ottoman Empire] in December, 1916, the [removal] process took on a much more systematic character; by the end of the month, at least eighteen villages were completely emptied. During the first month of 1917, some eight notables of Samsun were arrested and four thousand inhabitants were deported.[42]

[35] Zürcher, *Turkey*, 89.

[36] F Ahmad, *The Young Turks: The Committee of Union and Progress in Turkish Politics, 1908–1914* (Oxford, Clarendon Press, 1969) 179.

[37] UÜ Üngör, 'The Armenian Genocide in the Context of 20th-Century Paramilitarism' in A Demirdjian (ed), *The Armenian Genocide Legacy* (New York, Palgrave MacMillan, 2016) 15; and Akçam, *A Shameful Act*, 93–94.

[38] Akçam, *A Shameful Act*, 203.

[39] APC/APJ, PCI Bureau Ջ 947–50, file of Bahaeddin Şakir, 1–2, as cited in R Kévorkian, *The Armenian Genocide: A Complete History* (London, IB Tauris, 2011) 199.

[40] 'First Session of the Trial of the Unionists, 27 April 1919, Abstract of the Report of Vehib Pasha', *Takvim-ı Vakayi*, 5 May 1919, quoted in Kévorkian, *The Armenian Genocide*, 186.

[41] APC/APJ PCI Bureau Հ 172- Հ 182, a deposition written in Ottoman Turkish, as cited in Kévorkian, *The Armenian Genocide*, 187.

[42] T Akçam, *The Young Turks' Crime against Humanity: The Armenian Genocide and Ethnic Cleansing in the Ottoman Empire* (Princeton, NJ, Princeton University Press, 2012) 112.

Like his other CUP colleagues, Şakir escaped at the end of the war. Like Talât and Djemal, he ended up slain in Berlin by an ARF assassin.

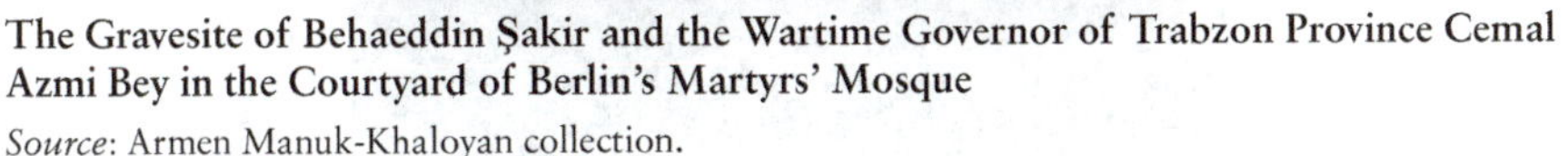

The Gravesite of Behaeddin Şakir and the Wartime Governor of Trabzon Province Cemal Azmi Bey in the Courtyard of Berlin's Martyrs' Mosque

Source: Armen Manuk-Khaloyan collection.

V. SELANIKLI NÂZIM

The man who would partner with Şakir in crime was Selanikli Nâzım, born in 1870 in Ottoman Salonika into a *dönme* (crypto- or hidden Jewish) family.[43] Before the First Balkan War, while employed as the director of a hospital in his native town, he joined the Young Turk movement. After the Greek army captured Salonika in 1912, Nâzım was imprisoned in Athens for his Turkish nationalist connections for nearly a year. There, prison guards lied to him, saying that all his family had been killed. That, as well as the torture that reports say he was subjected to, certainly would have traumatised him.[44] After his release and relocation to Istanbul, he wrote about the atrocities committed against Muslims in the Balkans and swore revenge against the

[43] On the *dönme*, see MD Baer, *The Dönme: Jewish Converts, Muslim Revolutionaries, and Secular Turks* (Stanford, CA, Stanford University Press, 2009).

[44] UÜ Üngör, *The Making of Modern Turkey: Nation and State in Eastern Anatolia, 1913–1950* (Oxford, Oxford University Press, 2011) 45, citing A Eyicil, *Ittihad ve Terakki Liderlerinden Doktor Nâzım Bey 1872–1926* (Ankara, Gün, 2004) 130–32, 153.

Ottoman Christians. According to historian Uğur Ümit Üngör, Nâzım was transformed 'from a patriotic doctor into a rabid, vindictive nationalist'. Üngör's words well describe the effect of traumatisation on this man.[45] Once World War I began, Nâzım, in his position of influence, used his power in the Special Organization to exercise his vindictiveness over Ottoman Christians. In early 1915 he is said to have called for a new wave of violence to be unleashed against the Armenians, one that would 'produce total annihilation', remarking that it would be 'essential that no Armenian survives'.[46]

Doctor Nazım Bey
Source: Wikimedia Commons.

VI. WITNESSES OF THE LOSS OF HOME AND HOMELAND

These five important CUP members were born within 11 years of one another, from 1870 to 1881, in the midst of the Great Eastern Crisis. At least one of them fled

[45] Üngör, *The Making of Modern Turkey*, 45.
[46] S Totten and PR Bartrop, *Dictionary of Genocide*, sv 'Nazim, Dr. Mehemed' (Westport, CT, Greenwood Press, 2008).

with his family and presumably others, to Anatolia for safety, with likely moments of being been flooded with fear and excitement.[47] Even though as children they would scarcely have understood the symbolic meaning of the threats to the land they resided in and to their people, these early experiences of witnessing and hearing about terrors, hardships, and losses would have inspired fear of losing the world they knew.

By the time of the Hamidian massacres, four of these men had reached early adulthood, and the fifth, Enver, was an adolescent. All were at an age when the influence of their peers and social conventions was at its greatest (see Chapter 16).[48] They may at this point have read or heard of the blame levelled against the Armenians for the massacres of Adana in 1909 and the resulting censure of Abdülhamid II by Europeans. They would have known of the societally approved impunity enjoyed by the perpetrators of these massacres and the Adana massacre, the deflection of the role played by state authorities, and the responsibility for the violence being assigned to the Armenians.

The long, tense period in Ottoman Rumelia extending over these men's entire childhood, adolescence, and early adulthood culminated in 1912 with the outbreak of the First Balkan War in which some of them were notably involved. 'The visceral emotional reaction [of Ottoman Turks] to the Balkan Wars whitewashed and annulled any serious rational reflection',[49] writes sociologist Fatma Müge Göçek. The unerasable humiliation is part of the background of the CUP's later policy decisions towards Ottoman Christians. Failing to bring considered thought and reasoning to making and executing their inhumane decisions was accounted for in part by their experience of the collective trauma after the Balkan Wars exacerbated by earlier memories of trauma.

Historian Donald Bloxham points out the significant effect of the scale of suffering of Muslim cleansings and migrations and 'the indifference of the outside world to it'.[50] This was in great contrast to the concern, however instrumental, expressed in Europe for the Armenians' suffering. From the mid-nineteenth century to the early twentieth, the expanding Russian Empire forced more than a million Muslims from their homes in the Caucasus into Ottoman territory. That massive wave of refugees was followed by the substantially larger one from the Balkans. Little notice was paid to the loss of hundreds of thousands of lives.[51] Bloxham observes that this indifference reinforced Sultan Abdülhamid's tacit approval of the massacres of the 1890s, 'providing a model of the "solution" of population problems and accentuating an already brutalised ethos of state demographic policy in the region'.[52] His phrase,

[47] For an analysis of these men born and raised in the Ottoman periphery, see EJ Zürcher, 'The Young Turks: Children of the Borderlands?' (2003) 9 *International Journal of Turkish Studies* 275.

[48] For example, see R Kegan, *The Evolving Self* (Cambridge, MA, Harvard University Press, 1982) 95 ff.

[49] F Müge Göçek, *Denial of Violence: Ottoman Past, Turkish Present, and Collective Violence against the Armenians, 1789–2009* (New York, Oxford University Press, 2015) 234.

[50] Bloxham, *The Great Game of Genocide*, 63.

[51] See D Quataert, *The Ottoman Empire, 1700–1922* (Cambridge, Cambridge University Press, 2005) 117–19.

[52] Bloxham, *The Great Game of Genocide*, 63, citing Fikret Adanır's then unpublished manuscript, 'Non-Muslims in the Ottoman Army and the Ottoman Defeat in the Balkan War of 1912/13'.

'brutalised ethos', describes a collectively traumatised, morally injured society that might even have interfered with any arousal of pity at the sight of streams of impoverished Muslim refugees. For some of them, this would have triggered recollections of their parents' similar journeys. Conscious or unconscious, these emotional remembrances often help account for attitude formation and subsequent behaviour.

In sum, these five men, three with senior official portfolios and two with non-official posts in the CUP regime, bore witness to the gradual dismemberment of the Ottoman Empire at the hands of the Great Powers, and to the losses of their homelands and dangers to their own lives – provoking humiliation, terror, horror, sadness, and grief. Under immense stress, the CUP's dominant coping mechanism was to consolidate control over the government at first by intimidating and threatening their opponents. Later they released their fearful offence and grief-filled anger in vengeance. Their coping mechanisms were demonstrated in sequential manifestations of heedless bravado and disturbed, costly judgment, taking form, to name a few examples, in resisting change in the Balkans, collective murder, the pursuit of new homelands elsewhere, and the creation of a homogenous state, one cleansed of its diverse ethnic elements. The internal phenomena of '[f]eelings of rage and murderous revenge fantasies', writes Judith Herman, 'are normal responses to abusive treatment'.[53] Pretty much everyone would have them. But, especially when persons do not or cannot separate inner mental, highly emotional activity from considered judgment with regard to taking action, individuals with power may act on that mental activity, and recklessly enact their revenge fantasies.

The CUP leaders perhaps sensed that a double standard had been applied to their families' and other Muslims' hurts and humiliations, that their people had been unseen, neglected, and thus insulted by the Great Powers. I wonder if they asked themselves if they had recognised the suffering of the Armenians and other Christians. These men did not show any evidence that they had outgrown looking for others to blame in order to make sense of events. They did not look within themselves and their political or social class for any responsibility for their situation. Instead, they cultivated their revenge, and its link with honour.[54] I write this in order to try to understand them, not to excuse them from responsibility for their acts.

The five most prominent members of the CUP, unlike many of their colleagues, had not spent extensive time abroad, such as in Paris and London. There, like Murad, Sabahaddin, and Rıza, they would have been exposed to people and ideas from other places, to help them understand the profound currents of change of the period. Apart from their personal histories in the tense, uncertain, and dangerous Balkans, their differences of class, and (regarding Talât) education, there is another factor that may help explain why they did not work with men such as Murad, Rıza, and Sabahaddin, with whom the three shared concerns about the problematic sultan and the empire – not that they were all great heroes, but at least those who had spent extensive time abroad seemed not to be ruled by passions for revenge. Talât, Enver, Djemal, Şakir, and Nâzım were alike in that their traumatisation at least partially accounts for

[53] J Herman, *Trauma and Recovery: The Aftermath of Violence – From Domestic Abuse to Political Terror* (New York, Basic Books, 1992) 104.
[54] Akçam, *A Shameful Act*, 86.

their not opening themselves to new ideas and ways of thinking, and being unable or unwilling to manage their compulsions for revenge. That is, the strong emotions generated by real existential fears about the collapse of the empire would have contributed to strengthening the desire for revenge, itself stemming from their involuntary reaction to their traumatisation. As the leading heads of the Ottoman Empire, they had achieved the power to exact that revenge, even if they did not have the power to save the empire. If their reactions to early traumatisation played a part in how they connected with others, it also limited their capacity to nurture and prepare for the changes required for regeneration.

Morgenthau offered unusually bold advice to Talât in February 1914, six months before the outbreak of the war. It did not take account of his traumatisation or desire for revenge. Morgenthau's advice, akin to Zohrab's and Sapah-Guilian's admonitions, was to adopt the goal of a pluralism like America's:

> In Turkey I have shown you the wonderful, national rug that we have produced in the United States. It was woven by the millions that inhabit our land, natives and foreigners, whites and blacks, people from the North, South, East, and West, men and women, and from materials produced in our own soil and imported from all countries … it makes a fine, harmonious whole …

Morgenthau looked through rose-tinted glasses when he claimed quite so much success for his own country. His belief in the self-evident rightness of America's liberal values, and his personal experience as a well-assimilated Jewish immigrant, may have prevented him from perceiving that the CUP leaders' initial enthusiasm for constitutional principles and ideas first formulated during the *Tanzimat* era remained, even into 1914, in Şükrü Hanioğlu's word, 'romantic' and thus shallow.[55] Furthermore, he lacked familiarity with the culture that had produced such men as Talât and the other CUP leaders.

The five top CUP officials had been socialised within the moral culture of their communities. It did not dictate specific policies and actions. If they had to accept a shrunken Ottoman Empire, it would be one in which the welfare and rights of Muslims, the dominant group, took absolute and murderous precedence over Armenians and other non-Muslims. They only possessed a dim understanding of constitutional politics and governance, but they well understood that they had power that they could and did choose to exercise in its most extreme and ruthless form. They looked to the destruction of the Armenians and Armenian culture to secure their collective existence in a distinctly Muslim-Turkish state. They could and did frame such policies, and see that they were carried out, though, only because they possessed the power to do so – power that they exercised, unsupported and unrestrained by any moral considerations.

[55] M Şükrü Hanioğlu, *The Young Turks in Opposition* (New York, Oxford University Press, 1995) 31.

9

The Armenian Genocide

> [T]he Turkish authorities ... were merely giving the death warrant to a whole race; they understood this well, and, in their conversations with me, they made no particular attempt to conceal the fact.
>
> Ambassador Henry Morgenthau[1]

FROM THE MIDDLE of the nineteenth century until the end of the first decade of the twentieth century, the Ottoman Armenians had taken seriously the assurances embodied in the *Tanzimat* reform program for greater political and legal rights in governance, opportunities for social and economic mobility, and wider scope for fairer internal administration in the empire. At times, the Great Powers supported the Armenians in these aims, such as when they included Article 61 in the 1878 Treaty of Berlin. They thereby acknowledged Armenian grievances on the record, creating an 'Armenian Question'. But after decades, what Ottoman Armenian community leaders, already deeply engaged in the matter, had only clearly succeeded in was elevating their concerns to the intermittent, if often self-interested, notice of foreign diplomats.

The Ottoman governments formed after the 1908 Revolution were not up to the work of solving the major problems confronting the empire. They were neither able to correct the free fall of the Ottoman economy nor address adequately the empire's other serious structural and social woes. Ottoman economic weakness was compounded by the continued exploitation by the Great Powers of the much-resented capitulatory system, which reduced the Ottoman Empire to 'semicolonial status' in relation to Europe.[2]

The Great Powers had formally accepted responsibility for the difficult task of implementing Article 61, and had not followed through;[3] Sultan Abdülhamid II had also begrudgingly agreed to implement it and then resisted.[4] After 1908, conservative Ottoman statesmen felt that the constitution, rather than the foreign-imposed Article 61, would form the basis of further reform. No wonder, then, that after the Hamidian and Adana massacres, the breakdown of ARF-CUP relations and the

[1] H Morgenthau, *Ambassador Morgenthau's Story* (Garden City, NY, Doubleday, Page, 1919) 309.
[2] EJ Zürcher, *Turkey: A Modern History*, 3rd edn (London, IB Tauris, 2004) 112.
[3] D Bloxham, *The Great Game of Genocide* (New York, Oxford University Press, 2005).
[4] CJ Walker, *Armenia: The Survival of a Nation*, rev 2nd edn (New York, St Martin's Press, 1990) 121–26.

CUP's own authoritarianism, by 1913–1914, many Armenians had lost trust in the Ottoman state and, in the east particularly, lived in dread of ongoing discrimination and persecution. Nonetheless, until the very start of the genocide in 1915, Armenians continued to hope for a brighter future.

I. THE YENIKÖY ACCORD

In 1912, Armenian leaders in both the Ottoman and Russian empires approached their respective governments with a new reform scheme for Anatolia. The first outline of this program, drafted by Russian diplomats, called for the creation of a new land commission, the restriction of Muslim refugee settlement in the Armenian-populated provinces, and the establishment of a large general inspectorate that would administer the region.[5] These terms did not carry the weight that they would have had had the Armenians had military force behind them, though it was widely perceived that Russia would leverage its strength in order to coerce the Ottomans to implement the plan.

None of the other Great Powers, however, were entirely comfortable with the level of influence Russia stood to wield in the eastern provinces, and so in mid-1913 their representatives met to renegotiate its terms. The conference was held at the summer residence of the Austro-Hungarian ambassador in Yeniköy, a suburb of Istanbul. After months of negotiations, the references to land issues and Muslim refugee settlement found in the original plan were dropped and it was agreed that the general inspectorate be divided into two administrative units, to be headed by representatives of neutral countries. Finally on 8 February 1914 the Ottoman and Russian governments signed the agreement at Yeniköy (also known as the Armenian Reform Plan or Armenian Reform Agreement).

In effect, Russia committed itself to championing the plight of the Armenians, while safeguarding its own geopolitical interests. An international agreement would forestall precipitous moves by the other powers to intervene and seize territory in case the Anatolian provinces in the Ottoman Empire should experience further turmoil and chaos, preventing at once an early collapse of the Ottoman Empire and the capture of the Straits by another foreign power.

However, leading CUP members who had not been consulted reacted with 'ire and fury', raging against the involvement of other countries, and convinced that this would spell the end of the empire.[6] They regarded Armenian collaboration with outsiders as yet another form of European colonialism, challenging Ottoman sovereignty.[7] They saw the Yeniköy Accord's terms as merely a first step, which would be followed by the Russian Empire joining with Armenians to leverage an independent Armenian state,

[5] H-L Kieser et al, 'Reform or Cataclysm? The Agreement of 8 February 1914 Regarding the Ottoman Eastern Provinces' (2015) 17 *Journal of Genocide Research* 291.

[6] V Dadrian, *The History of the Armenian Genocide: Ethnic Conflict from the Balkans to Anatolia to the Caucasus* (New York, Berghahn Books, 2003) 185.

[7] MA Reynolds, *Shattering Empires: The Clash and Collapse of the Ottoman and Russian Empires 1908–1918* (Cambridge, Cambridge University Press, 2011) 75.

'just as similar earlier agreements in the Balkans had been preludes to secession'.[8] The educated Muslim public, too, thought the reform plan threatened the empire's territorial integrity, thereby reinforcing fears of Armenian separatism.[9] Furthermore, the CUP members appeared to be as much incensed by what they saw as insolence on the part of the Armenians in making this demand as they were by its substance.[10] Thus, the Young Turks' prior liberalism had now come to mean that they must make concessions, imposed on them, to the other, rather than honour their commitments on upholding the liberal principles they had earlier espoused.

Many Armenians greeted the signing of the Accord with limited enthusiasm.[11] But for those who came to view it as a positive step forward, the Accord represented the culmination of their long struggle to attain political and legal rights and avenues for redress for Armenians in the eastern provinces.

The Yeniköy Accord, however, was never implemented: the outbreak of the war gave the CUP the perfect excuse to shelve it on 31 December 1914.[12] It was another lost opportunity that might have saved a people in their homeland and preserved an empire, providing an honourable, forward-looking foundation for a state inclusive of its diverse citizens. Had the CUP leadership been willing to work sincerely with the Armenians, Russia would perhaps not have been seen by Ottoman Armenians as their sole protector. Now, instead, many CUP leaders viewed the Armenians as 'a serious and permanent threat to the empire's continued existence'.[13]

Years before the war, some CUP leaders allegedly spoke of a solution to their 'Armenian problem'. They did not use the word 'genocide',[14] which was coined decades later, but it was expressed in sufficiently definitive terms that outsiders felt sure of their intentions. In mid-1913, for example, in the midst of the Russian-led negotiations on the new reform package for the Armenian-populated provinces in Anatolia, the British military attaché in Istanbul, Major William Tyrrell, saw clearly that if outside powers pushed the Ottoman government to bring about reforms and award autonomy, mass slaughter would ensue. Louis Mallet, an assistant under-secretary of state at the British Foreign Office, summarised Tyrrell's view accordingly:

> [I]f it is really proposed by the Powers to enforce the autonomy of Armenia on Turkey without even consulting her or taking her own reform scheme into consideration, the men at present in power at Constantinople would sooner set all the Provinces ablaze and go down fighting than submit. If the Russian proposal is adopted it will be the signal for massacres all over the country.[15]

[8] Ara Sanjian, private correspondence.

[9] See Y Turkyilmaz, 'Rethinking Genocide: Violence and Victimhood in Eastern Anatolia, 1913–1915' (PhD thesis, Duke University, 2011) 63–64.

[10] R Kévorkian, *The Armenian Genocide: A Complete History* (London, IB Tauris, 2011) 76.

[11] Turkyilmaz, 'Rethinking Genocide', 68–69.

[12] Kieser et al, 'Reform or Cataclysm', 299.

[13] T Akçam, *Young Turks' Crime against Humanity: The Armenian Genocide and Ethnic Cleansing in the Ottoman Empire* (Princeton, NJ, Princeton University Press, 2012) 131.

[14] The word was coined by Raphael Lemkin during World War II.

[15] George Buchanan (St Petersburg) to Edward Grey (London), 6 July 1913, in *British Documents on the Origins of the War, 1898–1914*, vol 10, part 1: *The Near and Middle East on the Eve of War*, (London, HMSO, 1936) no 542, 483.

II. THE WAR BEGINS AND ARMENIAN SECURITY VANISHES

World War I would encompass four long years of fighting between the Triple Entente (later, the Allies, after the United States joined them) and the Central Powers. The Ottomans would face multiple fronts that stretched from the Dardanelles to Anatolia and the greater Middle East. The CUP had anticipated a new conflict with the Balkan states prior to the outbreak of World War I, but a new front in Thrace never materialised (indeed, Bulgaria would join the Central Powers in October 1915).[16] Until then, in an isolated corner diplomatically, the CUP was desperately in need of a reliable ally among the Great Powers. In the year leading up to the war, the CUP considered an alliance with Germany as most beneficial for the long-term interests of the Ottoman Empire, but the Germans did not initially reciprocate. Spurned, the Ottomans considered approaching even Russia's principal ally, France, with Navy Minister Djemal travelling to Paris in the summer of 1914 to propose an arrangement and receiving a polite refusal in turn.[17]

It was only in July 1914 that relations between Germany and the Ottoman Empire were set. In fact each's search for allies was accidentally facilitated by a decision by the British government. The Ottomans had commissioned two state-of-the-art warships from British shipbuilders, paying for them in part with funds raised by public subscription, but now the Admiralty under Winston Churchill decided to requisition them for the Royal Navy's use, rejecting, cheating, and publicly humiliating the CUP government. At this moment, with Europe on the cusp of war, Germany, having rebuffed earlier Ottoman requests, now looked favourably towards an alliance with the Ottoman Empire. The parties signed a secret alliance on 2 August 1914. On that same night, the Ottoman government suspended parliament (it would not reconvene until a year later), announced martial law, and ordered general military mobilisation in a policy that came to be called 'armed neutrality' – preparing for war without actually entering it.[18] The alliance gave the Ottomans what they had sought for so long: an iron-clad guarantee for the security of the empire and a long-term partnership with the most formidable military power on the continent.[19]

Even so, the CUP government displayed some hesitancy before committing to any concrete military action.[20] Incredibly, minister of the interior Talât and Enver secretly approached Russia's ambassador and military attaché. They proposed that the Ottomans throw their military weight behind the Entente in exchange for territorial guarantees, Russian withdrawal of support for the Armenian Reform Project, and restoration of the lands lost in the Balkan Wars.[21] Perhaps just as surprisingly the

[16] M Aksakal, 'Not "by those old books of international law, but only by war": Ottoman Intellectuals on the Eve of the Great War' (2004) 15 *Diplomacy & Statecraft* 507–44.

[17] Reynolds, *Shattering Empires*, 103–104.

[18] M Beşikçi, *The Ottoman Mobilization of Manpower in the First World War: Between Voluntarism and Resistance* (Leiden, Brill, 2012) 72.

[19] U Trumpener, *Germany and the Ottoman Empire, 1914–1918* (Princeton, NJ, Princeton University Press, 1968) 15–23; and M Aksakal, *The Ottoman Road to War in 1914: Ottoman Empire and the First World War* (Cambridge, Cambridge University Press, 2008) 93–104.

[20] Aksakal, *The Ottoman Road to War passim*.

[21] Aksakal, *The Ottoman Road to War*, 127–35.

Russians seriously considered the Ottoman proposal before declining it. Among other factors, historian Mustafa Aksakal finds that they refused to give up their support for the Armenian Reform Plan.[22] The threat of a separate Armenian state, with Russia committed to it, thus became even more immediate to the CUP government.

As war officially got under way in Europe in August 1914, the Ottoman and Russian empires soon engaged in their own 'undeclared war' all along the Anatolian-Caucasus frontier.[23] Large numbers of Armenians living on each side of the imperial borders were caught in the middle. The ARF addressed this dilemma at its Eighth General Congress, which convened in Erzurum in July 1914, and resolved that, should war break out, Armenians in the Ottoman and Russian empires would carry out their respective military duties with steadfast loyalty and dedication.[24] In Erzurum, just 50 miles from the Russo-Ottoman border, Ottoman authorities immediately expressed doubts about the loyalty of the Armenians and worries about the presence of Russian Armenians there. According to Reynolds:

> [T]he deputy governor of Erzurum … questioned the sincerity of Armenian promises to take up arms for the empire but … noted that the town's Armenians were maintaining cordial relations with their Muslim neighbors. Five days later, however, Erzurum's gendarmerie confirmed that Russian Armenians in the town were sending their families back across the border to Aleksandropol. Three Russian soldiers who defected explained that Armenian activists were conducting anti-Turkish propaganda among Russian soldiers and distributing arms to their compatriots along the border. [Soon] Enver informed the command of the Ottoman Third Army that Hnchak and Dashnak revolutionaries had agreed with the Russians to provoke Ottoman Armenians to rebel.[25]

Ottoman officials put the Armenian population in the east under intense surveillance.[26]

Despite misgivings, the CUP government next sought to revive its alliance with the most unlikely of partners. In August 1914, Bahaeddin Şakir approached ARF leaders and offered autonomy for the Armenians in an enclave in eastern Anatolia and Russian Armenia in exchange for siding with the government against the Russians, fomenting uprisings in the Caucasus and helping the Ottomans in their quest to conquer the region.[27] The ARF refused.[28] In Reynolds's view, 'The [CUP] had thin credibility to begin with and, given their commitment to centralized rule, the sudden offer of autonomy probably struck the revolutionaries as fantastic'.[29]

After months of goading from its German ally, in late October 1914 the Ottoman Empire finally entered the fray by launching a surprise naval attack against Russian installations and commercial shipping along the northern Black Sea coast.

[22] Aksakal, *The Ottoman Road to War*, 129–30.

[23] Akçam, *Young Turks' Crime against Humanity*, 148.

[24] Y Pambukian (ed), *Niwter H. H. Dashnaktsutean patmutean hamar*, vol 11 (Beirut, Hamazkayin, 2015) 110–26.

[25] Reynolds, *Shattering Empires*, 116.

[26] Akçam, *Young Turks' Crime against Humanity*, 139.

[27] DM Kaligian, *Armenian Organization and Ideology under Ottoman Rule: 1908–1914* (Piscataway, NJ, Transaction Publishers, 2009) 219–22.

[28] See Kévorkian, *The Armenian Genocide*, 175.

[29] Reynolds, *Shattering Empires*, 117; cf Kaligian, *Armenian Organization and Ideology under Ottoman Rule*, 219–22.

Russia and her Entente partners in turn declared war against the Ottoman Empire. In mid-December 1914, the Ottoman army under Enver's direction, against the counsel of his German advisers, embarked on a military campaign to strike deep into the Russian Caucasus. With stalemate on the Western Front, his aim was to restore the momentum in the war, but as his forces marched on the Russian town of Sarikamish in freezing weather, they encountered stout resistance by the Imperial Russian Caucasus Army. The ill-equipped Ottoman Third Army was unable to last longer than a month in the field before experiencing a humiliating rout. Casualties were high on both sides, with disease, hunger, severe winter weather, and bullet wounds taking a heavy toll on the men, but the Ottomans suffered especially grievously. Some 72,000 of the 100,000 men of the Third Army did not return when the order for withdrawal was given.

At the Sarikamish battle, the loyalty of the Armenians serving in the Ottoman Empire's forces was put to the ultimate test when they faced Armenians serving in the Russian Army. During the last months of 1914 and first months of 1915, an unknown number of Ottoman Armenians crossed into the Russian lines. This generated resentment among Ottoman Muslim troops, who turned their wrath on the Armenians in their ranks.[30] Though War Minister Enver privately acknowledged the great courage Armenian troops showed at Sarikamish,[31] he also accused the Armenians of collaborating with the Russians during the battle.[32] The experience at Sarikamish led to his decision in February to issue an order to disarm almost all Armenians (and other non-Muslims) in the Ottoman military and relegate them to service in labour battalions to work in the war economy in factories, railways, and farms.[33] Many were thereafter murdered at will, but many others died from overwork or massacre by the members of the Special Organization.[34] Troubling signs had appeared, though, even before Enver's decision. During the fighting at Sarikamish, Armenian soldiers were being murdered so frequently by their comrades-in-arms that one Muslim soldier, who intensely disliked them, reflected in his diary that 'if it goes on like that, there won't be any Armenians left in the battalions in a week'.[35] The Russian Empire's victory at Sarikamish may have halted the Ottoman drive into Transcaucasia, but this Russian-held territory became a place of refuge for Ottoman Armenians able to flee from the genocidal massacres (not yet quite underway) even knowing that the government would punish their families.[36]

[30] E Rogan, *The Fall of the Ottomans: The Great War in the Middle East* (New York, Basic Books, 2015) 108, 162.

[31] VN Dadrian, *Warrant for Genocide: Key Elements of Turko-Armenian Conflict* (New Brunswick, NJ, Transaction, 1999) 114.

[32] RG Suny, *'They Can Live in the Desert but Nowhere Else': A History of the Armenian Genocide* (Princeton, Princeton University Press, 2015) 243.

[33] Beşikçi, *The Ottoman Mobilization of Manpower in the First World War*, 131–32.

[34] EJ Zürcher, 'Ottoman Labour Battalions in World War I' in H-L Kieser and DJ Schaller (eds), *Der Völkermord an den Armeniern und die Shoah* [*The Armenian Genocide and the Shoah*] (Zurich, Chronos, 2002) 187–96.

[35] Rogan, *The Fall of the Ottomans*, 108. Rogan is quoting from the diary of a corporal in the medical corps, Ali Rıza Eti, who served on the Caucasus Front. Eti sarcastically remarked that in each unit three or four Armenian soldiers were shot by 'accident' every day. He wondered what would happen to Armenians after the war after witnessing the Armenian desertions.

[36] Akçam, *Young Turks' Crime*, 149.

Shortly after Sarikamish, it was another confrontation between Armenians and Turks that set in motion a series of events that would lead to the crystallisation of the Ottoman wartime policy against the Armenians. Centred on the eastern province of Van and its eponymous administrative centre, this region, with its mixed Kurdish, Turkish and Armenian population, represented the cradle of Armenian civilisation.[37] Since the 1890s Van had been a site of revolutionary politics and seen widespread killings and material destruction during the Hamidian Massacres. At the time the British vice-consul had reported to his ambassador, 'Generally speaking the situation is very bad; the Armenians are everywhere in a state bordering on panic'.[38] The situation in Van remained tense into the early twentieth century and on the eve of World War I.

In early 1915, the CUP government appointed a new military governor for Van, Cevdet Bey, Enver's brother-in-law and a man whose reputation for cruelty and hostility towards Armenians preceded him.[39] Upon his appointment, he immediately carried out a violent intimidation campaign against the province's Armenians. He ordered police to search for the weapons Armenians had imported from Russia and Persia, arrest their owners, and set fire to Armenian villages. In April, Cevdet's men attacked the Armenian civilians of Van, who organised a citywide defence, fought back, and, against overwhelming odds, managed to hold off collective slaughter. After two long, costly weeks, their deliverance arrived in the form of advancing Russian troops, with Armenian volunteer units leading the way. Even as Cevdet prepared to evacuate the city's Muslim population, he issued a command, according to an Ottoman army officer, 'to exterminate all Armenian males of twelve years of age and over'.[40] This order was carried out just as Ottoman forces withdrew in the face of the numerically superior Russian force. A joint Russian-Armenian/ARF administration took over the running of affairs in what was left of the town, but in short order authorities sanctioned the systematic looting and burning of Turkish homes.[41] The administration was short-lived; the Russians abandoned Van in August 1915 when the Ottomans returned in full force, necessitating a frenzied and arduous retreat back to the 1914 Russo-Ottoman border. Control of Van would shift back to the Russian Empire in 1916, and the city remained under occupation until the complete disintegration of the Causasus Army following the October Revolution and Bolshevik takeover.[42]

Van's devastation during the First World War was emblematic of the extinction of a once-thriving Armenian culture in eastern Anatolia. Like so many treasured villages

[37] RH Hewsen, '"Van in This World; Paradise in the Next": The Historical Geography of Van/Vaspurakan' in RG Hovannisian (ed), *Armenian Van/Vaspurakan* (Costa Mesa, CA, Mazda Publishers) 1.

[38] Dadrian, *The History of the Armenian Genocide*, 133.

[39] P Balakian, *The Burning Tigris: The Armenian Genocide and America's Response* (New York, HarperCollins, 2003) 179, 200–201.

[40] Dadrian, *Warrant for Genocide*, 116–17.

[41] See Turkyilmaz, 'Rethinking Genocide', 283–88.

[42] 'The major role played [in the genocide] by "the" Kurds ... turns out, upon examination, to be much less clear-cut than has been affirmed. Indeed, it comes down to the active participation of nomadic Kurdish tribes and only rarely involves sedentary villagers, who were encouraged by the Special Organization [see reference to Şakir below] to take what they could from deportees already stripped of their most valuable assets' (Kévorkian, *The Armenian Genocide*, 810).

and towns that had housed flourishing Armenian communities, Van never recovered. Mere traces of the old town remain near a new town built along the eastern shore of the lake after the Turkish republic came into being. With the exception of the tiny, poignant medieval church on Aghtamar Island, it remains an enduring exhibit of the material destruction of a civilisation by collective traumatic events. Even the somewhat heavy-handed restoration of the church recently undertaken by the Turkish government captures something of the state's own ambivalent attitude toward its painful past, oscillating from passive neglect to deliberate disrespect, if not – elsewhere – outright destruction.[43]

III. THE GENOCIDE

Matters came to a head in the spring of 1915. The Ottoman leadership faced mounting crises on all fronts. In February, the Entente powers commenced naval operations in an ambitious but ultimately unsuccessful campaign to force the Straits and knock the empire out of the war. Around the same time, another Armenian uprising broke out in Zeytun, a town located on the northeastern littoral of the Mediterranean. In April, British Commonwealth and French troops prepared to launch an amphibious assault on the Gallipoli peninsula. The CUP feared only the worst from the Armenians and their alleged sympathies with the imperial powers. On 24 April, it ordered a carefully planned decapitation strike against the Armenian elite in Istanbul. Under the cover of night, the police arrested some 240 artists, bankers, musicians, physicians, politicians, and priests from their homes and gathered them at the city's main police station.[44] They transported them to Haydarpaşa, an imposing railway station on the Asian side of Istanbul, and sent them to destinations many, sometimes hundreds of miles away. Of those arrested, four-fifths would eventually be murdered.[45] Armenians today commemorate 24 April 1915 as the day the genocide began.[46]

The next step in this cumulative process took place in May, when the state issued a 'temporary law' that gave it the legal mandate to enact extreme measures – deportations and violence – to ensure security in zones affected by war conditions. In effect, this gave the state permission to move against the Armenian population.[47]

[43] See the trenchant criticism by architectural historian Steven Sim in 'A Politically-inspired Restoration', VirtualANI, 14 February 2007, www.virtualani.org/aghtamar/2005restoration.htm (accessed 2 August 2020).

[44] D Bloxham, 'The First World War and the Development of the Armenian Genocide' in *A Question of Genocide*, 260–75; H-L Kieser, *Talaat Pasha: Father of Modern Turkey, Architect of Genocide* (Princeton, NJ, Princeton University Press, 2018) 235–38.

[45] Ara Sarafian, 'What Happened on 24 April 1915? The Ayash Prisoners', *Submissions*, Gomidas Institute, 22 April 2013, www.gomidas.org/submissions/show/5 (accessed 21 July 2020).

[46] Many identify the Ottoman defeat at Sarikamish and the beginning of the Gallipoli campaign as leading to the decision on the Armenian genocide. Recent research by Akçam argues that the Ottoman decision to destroy the Armenians was made even earlier. See T Akçam, *The Killing Orders: Talat Pasha's Telegrams and the Armenian Genocide* (Cham, Switzerland, Palgrave Macmillan, 2018).

[47] H-L Kieser and D Bloxham, 'Genocide' in J Winter (ed), *The Cambridge History of the First World War*, vol 1 *Global War* (Cambridge, Cambridge University Press, 2014) 606.

Talât's Interior Ministry expressed optimism about the likely success of the plan that Talât and the CUP had set in motion. Akçam has found a note from the ministry dated 26 May 1915 to the grand vizierate stating that the deportation of Armenians created the opportunity for 'eliminating [the Armenian problem] in a manner that is comprehensive and absolute'.[48] The largest massacres would end in 1916 but the genocidal measures against the Armenians would continue well into 1918 and beyond, when the Ottomans would advance into Transcaucasia. All these actions were accompanied by efforts to conceal the role of the CUP and the state, though they would never be able convincingly to distance themselves from the fate they imposed on the Armenians.[49] Historian Timothy Snyder, writing about how the Nazis persuaded the citizens of Zhytomyr in Soviet Ukraine to collude with them in blaming Jews for deaths that the People's Commissariat for Internal Affairs (NKVD) had carried out prior to the occupation, sums up: 'Here as everywhere, the lies and the killing were intimately connected'.[50]

The CUP had laid in place an astonishingly sophisticated state apparatus capable of carrying out its policies against the Armenians. Everything from the forced removal and massacres of the population, the confiscation, tabulation, and transfer of their wealth, as well as the confinement and surveillance of surviving deportees, came under the purview and direction of the state. The principal agents who were employed to carry out violence were the members of the Special Organization, directed by Şakir and Nâzım.[51] The Special Organization was a paramilitary outfit that had no clear command structure and hence could provide the state plausible deniability over what was to happen to the Armenians. Şakir and Nâzım had filled its ranks with convicts recently released from prisons. Snyder's observation that 'the production of lawlessness was an appropriate way to find murderers who could be recruited for organized actions' is also apt in this context.[52] While the Special Organization is widely held as the key instrument in the violence against the Armenians, the Ottoman Gendarmerie Corps, regular army units, as well as illegal bands and Kurdish marauders, would all assist in the killings.

The masterminds of the genocide made full use of the state's resources to implement the genocide as efficiently as possible.[53] Deportation – or death marches – might have been the most efficient in terms of numbers eliminated. On very short notice Armenian women, children, and the elderly were ordered by authorities to leave their homes and communities, carrying what they could, while simultaneously being

[48] Akçam, *Young Turks' Crime*, 132.

[49] Akçam, *Young Turks' Crime*, xxiii–xxiv.

[50] T Snyder, *Black Earth: The Holocaust as History and Warning* (New York, Tim Duggan Books, 2015) 183.

[51] To date, there still is no satisfactory study dedicated to the Special Organization. For a brief overview, see UÜ Üngör, 'Paramilitary Violence in the Collapsing Ottoman Empire' in R Gerwarth (ed), *War in Peace: Paramilitary Violence in Europe after the Great War* (New York, Oxford University Press, 2012) 168–70.

[52] Snyder, *Black Earth*, 168.

[53] Akçam, *Young Turks' Crime*, 228.

assured that they would eventually return to their homes and properties even as the deportation caravans made their way southwards.[54] Those who survived walked in long columns for weeks, through mountain and desert, to the final destination, Dayr al-Zur.[55] Men who were not shot on the spot were expelled with everyone else. Almost all are thought to have died en route from murder, starvation, thirst, disease, or torture carried out by Kurdish tribesmen or the soldiers accompanying them. Deportation meant permission for any Muslim to victimise the weak, helpless, and defenceless. Countless Armenians committed suicide in grief and madness from the horror they endured,[56] while some, despite the brutality of the marches, survived, more than the authorities may have counted on. They were gathered in several concentration camps established across the Syrian desert. Large numbers of the survivors were later massacred in Syria in 1916.[57]

The thinking behind the deportations was a complete 'demographic engineering' of the empire.[58] Akçam identified its guiding principle to be the '5 to 10 per cent criterion'.[59] This meant that if, at the place of origin, Armenians constituted more than 5 to 10 per cent of the total population, they would be expelled and deported to a region where they would not be permitted to exceed one-tenth of the total Muslim population.[60] Reductions were intended to be drastic enough to strip Armenian communities of their viability, community by community. A very small number of Armenian-populated villages were simply overlooked and left undisturbed.

The massacres began in earnest in late June of 1915, and all followed much the same pattern. Armed gangs would sweep into the towns and villages of Anatolia, round up the physically able Armenian men and young boys, lead them out of view, and then shoot, stab, or beat them to death. After searching homes for weapons and

[54] Such references abound in the primary source literature. For one contemporary account from Adapazarı, a town just east of Istanbul, see *The Treatment of Armenians in the Ottoman Empire, 1915–1916*, 420.

[55] See S Dolbee, 'The Desert at the End of Empire: An Environmental History of the Armenian Genocide' (May 2020) *Past and Present* 197. Like other contemporaries, Ambassador Morgenthau strongly believed that the Ottoman strategy of enforced deportation for dealing with undesirable populations was German in origin. 'The violent shifting of whole peoples from one part of Europe to another, as though they were so many herds of cattle, has for years been part of the Kaiser's plans for German expansion'. Morgenthau further asserts that the Ottomans adopted this approach 'under Germany's prompting' (Morgenthau, *Ambassador Morgenthau's Story*, 49). The chief Ottoman ally played one or more roles in the Armenian genocide, but it is less clear than what Morgenthau said and how significant it was. For a recent evaluation, see ED Weitz, 'Germany and the Young Turks: Revolutionaries into Statesmen' in RG Suny et al (eds), *A Question of Genocide: Armenians and Turks at the End of the Ottoman Empire* (Oxford, Oxford University Press, 2011) 175.

[56] See references to such acts in the collection of eyewitness testimonies in DE Miller and L Touryan Miller, *Survivors: An Oral History of the Armenian Genocide* (Berkeley, University of California Press, 1993) 20, 80, 96, and 103–105 for analysis. See also Balakian, *The Burning Tigris*.

[57] See Kévorkian, *The Armenian Genocide*, 625–98.

[58] Akçam, *Young Turks' Crime*, 95.

[59] Akçam, *Young Turks' Crime*, 228.

[60] Akçam, *Young Turks' Crime*, xvi.

assaulting and frequently raping the women, they would remove and arrest or simply shoot the remaining householders. In some instances, they herded entire communities into churches or barns and set them alight, or into caves, where they were asphyxiated by brush fires. Cases of resistance were rare, but in some places, such as Van, Urfa, and Musa Dagh, locals banded together in self-defence.

Cultural assimilation, rape, and other traumatic acts of sexual violence were major components in the program for genocide. Rape allowed for sexual release generated by the excitement of violence and was permitted, perhaps encouraged, as a way for the 'humiliation, intimidation, and dehumanization of the immediate victim, the victim's male relatives', and Armenians as a group.[61] One woman from Muş recounted how 'it was a very common thing for [Kurdish guards] to rape our girls in our presence. Very often they violated eight or ten-year-old girls ...'[62] Along with rape, forced assimilation was another common element of the genocide. Girls were usually kidnapped from their villages or along the deportation routes to the Syrian desert. To survive, some abductees converted to Islam and became servants or slaves in Kurdish and Arab households, while others were integrated into family units and, not uncommonly, generally well treated. Forced assimilation also took on other forms. In Ayntura, in present-day Lebanon, the state converted a Jesuit high school into an orphanage for Armenian and Kurdish boys and enforced a strict Turkish cultural assimilation program (see Chapter 17).

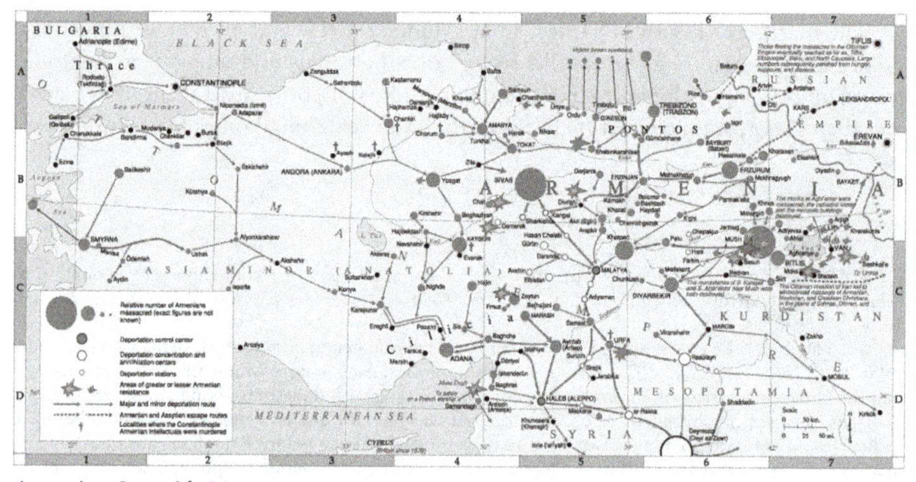

Armenian Genocide Map

Source: Robert H Hewsen, *Armenia: A Historical Atlas* (Chicago, University of Chicago Press, 2001) map 224.

[61] See M Bjørnlund, '"A Fate Worse than Dying": Sexual Violence during the Armenian Genocide' in D Herzog (ed), *Brutality and Desire: War and Sexuality in Europe's Twentieth Century* (New York, Palgrave Macmillan, 2009) 16, 29.

[62] See A Sarafian (ed), *The Treatment of Armenians in the Ottoman Empire, 1915–1916: Documents Presented to Viscount Grey of Falloden by Viscount Bryce*, uncensored edn (Princeton, NJ, Gomidas Institute, 2000) 128.

Armenians Being Deported on Train Wagons along the Berlin-Baghdad Railway
Source: Deutsche Bank AG, Historisches Institut.

Morgenthau received harrowing reports from American consular officials and other foreign representatives on the ground. In conversations with Talât, he learned of the interior minister's attitude towards the killings: prevention of future revenge by Armenians:

> 'Those who are innocent to-day might be guilty to-morrow';
>
> 'It is no use for you to argue … we have already disposed of three quarters of the Armenians; there are none at all left in Bitlis, Van, and Erzurum. The hatred between the Turks and the Armenians is now so intense that we have got to finish with them. If we don't, they will plan their revenge';
>
> 'No Armenian can be our friend after what we have done to them'.[63]

The Armenian communities in western Anatolia fared slightly better than those in the eastern provinces of the empire, but many towns and villages were not spared from either deportation or massacre.[64]

Throughout the genocide, there were instances of righteous Turks and Arabs extending help to the Armenians. Born in Lebanon of survivors, genocide scholar Greg Sarkissian's grandmother, great-aunt, and aunts and uncles were rescued and protected by a family friend for a year. Sarkissian relates:

> Haji Khalil, a devoted Muslim and a righteous Turk, was my grandfather's business partner. He had promised my grandfather he would care for his family in case of misfortune.

[63] Morgenthau, *Ambassador Morgenthau's Story*, 231, 232, 233.

[64] On these communities and the deportations in general, see RG Hovannisian and A Manuk-Khaloyan, 'The Armenian Communities of Asia Minor: A Pictoral Essay' and S Payaslian, 'The End of the Armenian Communities of Asia Minor', both in RG Hovannisian (ed), *The Armenian Communities of Asia Minor* (Costa Mesa, CA, Mazda Publishers, 2014) at 9–88 and 271–310 respectively.

> When the disaster greater than anything either of them could have imagined struck, my grandfather, Krikor, was hung just for being an Armenian. But Haji Khalil kept his promise. He hid my grandmother, her sister and their seven children in the attic of his house in Urfa for almost a year. He fed and cared for them and saw them to safety to Aleppo. He did this knowing well that whoever saved Armenians could have shared their fate of death and destruction.[65]

There are also documented instances of Ottoman officials refusing to go along with the CUP's plans. The Armenian communities in İzmir and Kütahya, for example, were largely spared thanks to the principled stand of Ottoman officials. In Diyarbekir Province two district governors who chose not to implement the deportation orders, Nesimi and Sabit Beys, are believed to have been ordered to be assassinated by their superior, governor Mehmed Reşid Pasha.[66] There were precious few individuals who decided to take a stand against the inhumanity that was unfolding before their eyes. Most were by-standers.

IV. HOW TWO SURVIVED

Two of the Armenians deported from Istanbul on 24 April 1915 were priests. One was Komitas Vardapet, who was also an accomplished musicologist, composer, and ethnographer. Before the war he had travelled to remote villages to record indigenous Armenian folk music and then toured Europe with an Armenian choir, performing these songs as well as his own compositions. He was deported on 24 April, and the ordeal he endured over the next few weeks shattered him completely. One fellow deportee, Grigoris Balakian, recalled how 'Father Komitas … thought the trees were bandits on the attack and continually hid his head under the hem of my overcoat, like a fearful partridge. He begged me to say a blessing for him ("The Savior") in the hope that it would calm him'.[67] Highly placed friends persuaded Talât to arrange for his return to Istanbul, where an observer later reported seeing him 'frozen; he could not move'.[68] He was admitted to the Hôpital de la Paix in the Şişli district of Istanbul, a sanitarium then run by the Ottoman military. A biographer of Komitas writes that he was haunted and 'wracked by guilt, images of the innocent trapped, tortured, and exiled'.[69] Komitas remained fully traumatised and after the war was moved to a mental institution, the Hôpital Villejuif, near Paris, where he died in 1935.

Balakian, a priest and community leader himself, fled from one horrifying situation to the next after being deported from Istanbul alongside Komitas. He retained

[65] KM Greg Sarkissian, 'The Centennial Commemoration Is about Truth, Memory and Justice, Not Hatred' (Zoryan Institute, 1 January 2015), https://zoryaninstitute.org/1481-2/ (accessed 18 August 2020).

[66] H-L Kieser, 'From "Patriotism" to Mass Murder: Dr Mehmed Reşid (1873–1919)' in *A Question of Genocide*, 142.

[67] G Balakian, *Armenian Golgotha*, trans P Balakian with AG Sevag (New York, Alfred A Knopf, 2009) 66.

[68] A Andonian, 'Komitas Vartabed qksori metch: Inch baymanneru dag haydnevetsav ir mdkin daknabe [Komitas Vartabed in exile: The conditions under which his mental distress appeared]' (1946) (15 Dec) *Arevmoudk* (Paris) 7, quoted in R Soulahian Kuyumjian, *Archaeology of Madness: Komitas, Portrait of an Armenian Icon*, 2nd edn (Princeton, NJ, Gomidas Institute, 2001) 135, fn 80.

[69] Kuyumjian, *Archaeology of Madness*, 132.

his sharp wits and showed endless courage and strength, physical and psychological. His powerful mind, the clarity of his memory, and his determination to expose the injustices to which the Armenian people had been subjected, enabled him to write down many of these experiences at the time, while committing to memory all he could not.[70]

In his memoir, Balakian offers his own graphic descriptions of what he had been told, remarking, for example, that '[t]ens of thousands of Armenian males, lashed together with … rope, were mercilessly butchered along all the roads'.[71] But mostly he recorded his own experiences, including terrifying escapes. In an internment camp in Çankırı near Ankara, he and others were held before beginning the 600-mile trek to the primary destination of the deportees, the Syrian desert town Dayr al-Zur. Balakian writes that their funds had all but been depleted in bribing officials or peasants for food, hiring carriages for transport, and paying gendarmes to accompany them to 'answer nature's call' away from the others.[72] On the journey, they spent one night near Yozgat and were awakened by a small group of Kurdish tribal chiefs searching their saddlebags for money. The chiefs informed the prisoners that they would kill them. But Captain Shukri, the chief of the Yozgat military police, and 11 of his men were responsible for looking after the Armenians and forbade the chiefs from carrying out their intentions.

Balakian and the others then set off, but before going much farther, the little group of Armenians received a visit from 'a few Armenian youths – Russian citizens who had been exiled from Istanbul'.[73] Balakian tells us that the youths, although Armenian, did not fear for their lives because they had Russian passports that provided them protection.[74] Shukri and his men accompanied Balakian's group further and explained how the bones he, Balakian, saw along the road got there:

> The police soldiers who accompanied us would … boast to some of us about how they had committed tortures and decapitations, cut off and chopped up body parts with axes and how they had dismembered suckling infants and children pulling apart their legs, or dashing them on rocks.[75]

They related how, after carrying out the massacre, a mob accompanying the gendarmes robbed the dead.

> When the carnage was over, the mob stripped the murdered and dismembered thousands in order to take their clothes …. Then it was the turn of the dogs, wolves, and jackals, which picked up the scent of blood and came from all directions to complete the job started by the Turks. Left in open air, the bodies then began to swell, rot, and decompose.[76]

[70] Balakian, *Armenian Golgotha*. On the works of other authors from the 'witness' genre, see A Frank, *Diary of a Young Girl* (New York, Alfred A Knopf, 2010); P Levi, *Survival in Auschwitz* (New York: Touchstone Books, 1996); J Kosinski, *The Painted Bird* (New York, Grove Press, 1995); and A Ornstein, *My Mother's Eyes: Holocaust Memories of a Young Girl* (Cincinnati, Emmis Books, 2004).

[71] Balakian, *Armenian Golgotha*, 135.

[72] Balakian, *Armenian Golgotha*, 132.

[73] Balakian, *Armenian Golgotha*, 133.

[74] Akçam, *Young Turks' Crime*, 148.

[75] Balakian, *Armenian Golgotha*, 145.

[76] Balakian, *Armenian Golgotha*, 149.

Captain Shurki told Balakian matter-of-factly:

> [Y]ou know that they [the deportees] had swallowed many pieces of diamond jewelry … the Turkish villagers, particularly the women, roamed for days among these thousands of stinking corpses, slitting their intestines and finding a considerable amount of jewelry, which they subsequently bought and sold.[77]

Shukri then assured Balakian that he and all the other Armenians would soon be murdered. That was why, he explained, he had told him so much, as he was under instructions to ensure their safety only so far. Balakian added that he was trying to 'extort us without resorting to violence'.[78]

V. REVENGE, EXPROPRIATION, PLUNDER

At the outbreak of war, the influx of mostly penurious refugees from the Balkans and Transcaucasia into the Ottoman Empire had greatly exacerbated the empire's financial woes. The assistance given to them had strained the coffers of the Ottoman state. With the outbreak of the war, the state resorted to desperate measures. In early August 1914, it seized crops, livestock, and horses, and raised taxes by up to 70 per cent.[79] The poor conditions of daily life were worsened by an Entente naval blockade established after the Ottoman entry into the war, and by government mismanagement. From early on, everyone felt the effects of food shortages and other material goods.[80] The requisitioning had been conducted with astounding, self-defeating recklessness. Morgenthau was shocked:

> The requisitioning that accompanied the mobilization really amounted to wholesale looting of the civilian population. The Turks took all the horses, mules, camels, sheep, cows and other beasts that they could lay their hands on … This system of requisitioning … had the inevitable result of destroying the nation's agriculture, and ultimately led to the starvation of hundreds of thousands of people.[81]

By early 1915, Morgenthau observed, the situation for Ottomans had led to conditions where very widespread collective traumatisation was inevitable:

> [A]ll over Turkey thousands of the populace were daily dying of starvation; practically all able-bodied men had been taken into the army, so that only a few were left to till the fields; the criminal requisitions had almost destroyed all business; the treasury was in a more exhausted state than normally … and the increasing wrath of the people seemed likely to break out against Taalat [sic] and his associates.[82]

Most Muslim refugees who had fled from the fighting in the Balkans had arrived in the empire only with what they had brought with them. As they struggled for

[77] Balakian, *Armenian Golgotha*, 157.
[78] Balakian, *Armenian Golgotha*, 140.
[79] Rogan, *The Fall of the Ottomans*, 59.
[80] MS Tanielian, *The Charity of War: Famine, Humanitarian Aid, and World War I in the Middle East* (Stanford, Stanford University Press, 2018).
[81] Morgenthau, *Ambassador Morgenthau's Story*, 64.
[82] Morgenthau, *Ambassador Morgenthau's Story*, 186.

a second time in their lives to cope under the conditions of war, many acted out impulses for revenge, as officials turned a blind eye, not on those who had forced them to flee but, in displacement, on Armenians and other defenceless Ottoman subjects, according to historian Berna Pekesen: 'Often, Muslim refugees, who had themselves been victims of forced displacement, also participated in the attacks on Christian villages'.[83] According to Zürcher,

> On lower levels, in the ranks of the Special Organization … that played an important role in the massacres, immigrants, especially Circassians, made up the main component. Even if we have no contemporary evidence from 1915 to show that revenge was the primary motive for these people, the overrepresentation of refugees among the killers is striking.[84]

When they ordered the deportations, the CUP authorities had assured the Armenians that after the war they would return to their homes, properties, and possessions, which in the meantime they would assume protection over. In fact, the removal of the Armenians from the villages and towns of eastern Anatolia meant that their property was left unattended and available for the taking. The opportunity was not allowed to pass. All of the Armenians' personal and communal property was confiscated by the state or individual actors. The state even attempted, unsuccessfully, to obtain the proceeds of victims' life insurance policies.[85] Jewellery, livestock, machinery, furniture, houses, farms, inns, businesses, bank accounts, and communal property – such as churches and the religious objects therein – were expropriated.[86] Everything was designated to go to Muslim Turks and Muslim refugees. In assessing the perpetrators, Kévorkian has observed that the Armenians in the Ottoman Empire served as scapegoats for Muslim refugees from the Russian Empire just as they had served for Muslim refugees from the Balkans. The latter identified Armenians with the Christians of the Balkans, while the former identified them with their Christian Russian oppressors.

> On the basis of an inventory of those chiefly to blame for this genocide, whether civilian and military officers or local notables, it can be affirmed that the individuals who were the most deeply implicated in the mass violence often came from the most marginal social groups and, it must be emphasized, were members of minorities with roots in the Caucasus … who … had accounts to settle with their painful history and were easily led to identify the Armenians with their Russian oppressors.[87]

In addition to the refugees, Akçam and Kurt point out that 'the Muslim bourgeoisie, the Ottoman army … the government, the state's own infrastructure and militia

[83] B Pekesen, 'Expulsion and Emigration of the Muslims from the Balkans', European History Online (EGO), published by the Leibniz Institute of European History (IEG), Mainz, (7 March 2012), www.ieg-ego.eu/pekesenb-2011-en (accessed 21 July 2020).

[84] EJ Zürcher, 'The Late Ottoman Empire as Laboratory of Demographic Engineering' (paper presented at the conference 'Le Regioni multilingui come faglia e motore della storia europea nel 19.–20. secolo', Naples 2008), quoted in Pekesen, 'Expulsion and Emigration of the Muslims from the Balkans'.

[85] HS Karagueuzian and Y Auron, *A Perfect Injustice: Genocide and Theft of Armenian Wealth* (New Brunswick, NJ, Transaction Publishers, 2009); and MJ Bazyler, 'From Lamentation and Liturgy to Litigation: The Holocaust-Era Restitution Movement as a Model for Bringing Armenian Genocide-Era Restitution Suits in American Courts' (2011) 95 *Marquette Law Review* 245.

[86] Ü Kurt, 'Legal and Official Plunder of Armenian and Jewish Properties in Comparative Perspective: The Armenian Genocide and the Holocaust' (2015) 17(3) *Journal of Genocide Research* 305.

[87] Kévorkian, *The Armenian Genocide*, 810.

organizations all benefitted'.[88] The hope was to use this plundered wealth to build up a Muslim Turkish middle class in the new Ottoman state.[89] Legislation was drafted with great care to ensure that Armenians could never return to claim what was formerly theirs. Other laws protected the new owners from any future claims. Moreover, bureaucratic procedures were codified to block any source of redress Armenians might seek.

During a session in parliament in October 1915, Ahmed Rıza (see Chapter 6) spoke out against the expropriations:

> [T]hey [the Armenians] are wandering in the mountains at this very moment, in a state of misery and bafflement. I appeal to the sense of misery and justice of the government to either send them back to their towns or to settle them wherever it is that they have been deported, before the winter makes itself felt.[90]

Later that month he raised the issue again:

> It is also not legal to classify the goods mentioned by the law as abandoned goods because the Armenian owners did not abandon them willingly, they were exiled, expelled forcefully ... If this law is enforced, these people will have been tyrannized once more ... This is why ... I had proposed an amendment. [But] the law was left as it was and it is being enforced. If it is true that this country has a constitution and that it is a constitutional state, it is also true that what is happening is cruelty. Pick up someone, expel him from his village, and sell his goods and property; this can never be considered to be permissible. This can be accepted neither according to the conscience of Ottomans, nor according to the Law [Constitution].[91]

Rıza's words, of course, were ignored.

VI. THE MEETING OF MINDS OF OTTOMAN LEADERS AND CITIZENS

There is no question that the Ottoman state planned and executed the genocide of the Armenian people. The CUP government was under enormous pressure due to loss of territory, threats of further losses, an influx of refugees, financial collapse, military defeats and an impoverished treasury. As the leaders' anxiety mounted and the situation grew more dire, the CUP government had unsuccessfully looked for outside stabilisers in the form of alliance partners. When it scapegoated and then murdered groups it held as hostile to its rule, the state could rely on a Muslim populace that

[88] T Akçam, *'Ermeni meselesi hallolunmuştur': Osmanlı belgelerine göre savaş yıllarında Ermenilere yönelik politikalar* (İstanbul, İletişim Yayınları, 2008) 223–36; and Akçam, *Young Turks' Crime*, 356–71, cited in Kurt, 'Legal and Official Plunder', 309. With the establishment of the Republic of Turkey in 1923, President Mustafa Kemal took no steps to restore the confiscated properties to their Armenian or Greek and Assyrian owners but upheld the process and continued to distribute goods and other belongings to his closest followers and members of the old CUP regime. The 'Kemalist movement ... could move towards appropriation as a matter of fact', writes Ümit Kurt. 'This distinction between confiscation and appropriation is a matter of active versus passive expropriation'.

[89] M Aksakal, 'The Ottoman Empire' in *The Cambridge History of the First World War*, 464.

[90] F Dündar, *Crime of Numbers: The Role of Statistics in the Armenian Question (1878–1918)* (New Brunswick, NJ, Transactions Publishers, 2010) 122–23.

[91] Dündar, *Crime of Numbers*, 123.

had undergone radicalisation in a time of total war. The people and the government shared a sense of entitlement, superiority, and power over others, and the conviction that Armenians threatened to betray and endanger the empire.

As important as it is to know the historical record and understand Ottoman motives and actions in their context, it is equally important to know that that knowledge and understanding may or may not justify actions taken. How to judge claims to justification? Among independent sources of judgement for justifications on this subject is the UN Convention's unambiguous clarity that no Ottoman fears and anxieties could have justified the genocide that its government heads carried out against its Armenian citizens.

VII. THE EFFECT OF GALLIPOLI

In the long, drawn-out battle of Gallipoli, which concluded after nearly a year in January 1916, Turks and Arabs in the Ottoman army fought brilliantly and courageously under the same banner. Mustafa Kemal proved himself to be a highly effective commander. According to Morgenthau, the containment and ultimate expulsion of Entente forces from the Gallipoli peninsula restored a sense of confidence among CUP leaders.

> I can hardly exaggerate the effect which the repulse of the Allied fleet produced upon the Turks [in the Dardanelles] ... The leaders of the Union and Progress Party [CUP] ... now began to have a determining effect upon Turkish national life and Turkish policy ... And now that the fortunes of war were apparently favoring the empire, I began to see an entirely new Turk unfolding before my eyes. The hesitating and fearful Ottoman, feeling his way cautiously amid the mazes of European diplomacy, and seeking opportunities to find an advantage for himself in the divided counsels of the European powers, gave place to an understanding, almost dashing figure, proud and assertive, determined to live his own life and absolutely contemptuous of his Christian foes.[92]

What motivates the pursuit of power, or the tenacity to hold on to it once obtained, at all costs? The answer offered in the chapters of Part II is that it is primarily the maintenance of collective status, however defined, and the rejection of equalisation or of human rights for all, which logically follows from it. Another question is whether the possession of great power causes something like addiction in its possessors. Is a decision to commit genocide the result, at least in part, of an addiction, a *compelled* 'fight', *compelled* action, in response to traumatic fears, old and new, as well as the acquisition of power? Chapters 1, 2, 3, and 8 have shown how trauma leads to distorted perception and meaning making in those with and without power. Dysregulated individuals with power are likely to be constantly primed for aggression or 'fight'.

Morgenthau identified emotional dysregulation among the CUP and other Ottoman elites when he described their rapid transition from 'hesitating ... fearful, etc' before the Gallipoli campaign to being 'proud and assertive' after the Ottoman

[92] Morgenthau, *The Ambassador's Story*, 274.

victory – 'an instance of reversion to type … determined to live his own life and absolutely contemptuous of his Christian foes'. In sum, the hard-fought victory at Gallipoli reawakened and reinvigorated what Morgenthau saw: the CUP leaders' sense of inherited, not genetic, superiority and entitlement and their ability to act with impunity and without fear of retribution.

The CUP leaders demonstrated a deficit of rational and moral imagination when they conceived of solving their 'Armenian problem' by genocide. They externalised all responsibility for it and often spoke of themselves as the victims of the Great Powers and of those they saw as their pawns, the Armenians. By blaming Armenians, they could even the score they tallied with them, strike back for their hurt pride, terrify and destroy Armenians as a way of overcoming their own fears, manifest power over them to prove to themselves that their own failing potency was not real, and distract themselves from their own failed efforts to save the empire. The kind of adaptive leadership that might have allowed them to regroup and prosper had been proposed by Prince Sabahaddin, but they did not choose that. They saw the Armenian Reform Agreement of 1914 and the early military defeats as the end of their empire, even of the nascent nation-state. The victory at the Dardanelles and elsewhere revived their hopes.

Thus, it does not appear that the CUP leaders analysed or conceived of an alternative strategy, or seriously considered the views of the CUP faction led by Prince Sabahaddin, with whom they had publicly broken, or asked themselves whether reaching an agreement with the Armenians might avoid further violence and partition and help to save the empire. From a behavioural and social-psychological perspective, a near-classic groupthink process characterised their decision-making.[93] And, in part, the CUP's limited imagination was framed by past and present traumatic threats that limited development and exercise of their more complex and humane mental capacities.

Acting out their compulsion for revenge did not preserve the empire. The genocide stained the republic, which replaced the empire in 1923, with this dishonour from its very foundation.

[93] IL Janis, *Groupthink: Psychological Studies of Policy Decisions and Fiascoes*, 2nd edn (Boston, Houghton Mifflin, 1982).

Part III

Violent Entitlement Carried into Armenian-Azerbaijani Relations in Transcaucasia

10

Enemies or Allies? Armenian–Azerbaijani Relations, 1850–1915

Azerbaijanis and Armenians turned their cosmopolitan city [Baku] into a medieval war zone.

Tom Reiss[1]

Thousands of dead lay in the streets and covered the Christian and Mussulman cemeteries. The odor of the corpses stifled us. Everywhere women with mad eyes were seeking their children, and husbands were moving the heaps of rotting flesh.

An Armenian woman in Baku, 1905[2]

Remarkably, the leaders of the Difai tried to blunt the edge of the intercommunal conflict. Aghayev sternly lectured the crowds in a Ganja mosque that even 'wild animals do not devour their own kind' and reminded them that the Muslims and the Armenians had for centuries lived in peace before the coming of the Russians.

Tadeusz Swietochowski[3]

WHEREAS PART II of this book focused on Armenian–Turkish relations in Anatolia, Part III concentrates mostly on early-twentieth-century relations between the Armenians and Azerbaijanis of Transcaucasia, today's South Caucasus, and on these two peoples' connections to the Ottoman and Russian empires.[4]

For centuries, the region of Transcaucasia, widely known as such well into the twentieth century, had been the crossroads of three empires – Ottoman, Persian, and Russian. Each empire ruled the region (or parts of it) at different times. In the wars

[1] T Reiss, *The Orientalist: Solving the Mystery of a Strange and Depressing Life* (New York, Random House, 2005) 14. This book is my source for biographical information about Lev Nussinbaum.

[2] Reiss, *The Orientalist*, 3. The statement was recorded by an Armenian woman who had been a young girl at the time of the violence in Baku.

[3] T Swietochowski, *Russian Azerbaijan, 1905–1920: The Shaping of a National Identity in a Muslim Community* (Cambridge, Cambridge University Press, 1985) 44, citing N Keykurun, *Azerbaycan İstiklâl mücadelesinin hatıraları* (Istanbul, Azerbaycan Gençlik Derneği, 1964) 14.

[4] Prior to the founding of the Azerbaijani Republic in 1920, most Azeris in Transcaucasia were referred to as Tatars. A significant ethnic Azeri population also exists today in northern Iran, and so when speaking of Azerbaijanis it is usually done so in reference to the citizens of that republic. This book has tried to remain consistent with respect to this gradual evolution in Azerbaijani identity.

of 1805 and 1828, the Russian Empire wrested Transcaucasia away from the Qajar rulers of Iran and over the next century consolidated its hold over it. Today the South Caucasus remains the homeland of peoples of varying ethnic backgrounds, as well as the site of their historical and current conflicts.

Unlike their Ottoman neighbours to the west, the vast majority of Azeri Muslims belonged to the Shia, rather than Sunni, branch of Islam. National identity prior to 1918 remained largely undefined, and until that date they might variably identify as Turks, Iranians, or Muslim subjects of the Russian Empire.[5] Russian imperial policies in the nineteenth century opened up new opportunities for Transcaucasian Muslims in the fields of higher education, commerce, and the military, but they could also become so repressive that many fled to the Ottoman Empire. Transcaucasia was also always host to a significant Armenian population from ancient times. Under Russian rule, they formed large and culturally active communities in the cosmopolitan cities of Tiflis and Baku.

Part III focuses on the Armenians' and Azeris' frequent conflicts in this period and moments of hope and opportunity for positive relations. Today a conscious awareness of the history so infused with collective trauma and transmitted trauma is needed, while that of some of those opportunities not taken then might inspire today. Awareness of both, plus intention and will, could change the still traumatising relations between the two peoples especially played out over Nagorno-Karabakh.

I. RUSSIAN TRANSCAUCASIA

In the mid-nineteenth century, Russian imperial authorities consolidated their administrative hold on the region with the creation in 1845 of the Caucasus Viceroyalty in Tiflis (modern-day Tbilisi). In 1867, the Transcaucasus was divided into five separate provinces (Kutaisi, Tiflis, Erevan, Elisavetpol, and Baku), an arrangement that would remain largely intact until the dissolution of the Russian Empire.[6]

The Russian census of 1897 established that Transcaucasia's population stood at about 5.7 million, of whom 1.6 million were 'Tatars' and 1.2 million Armenians.[7] Although the region's 'peripheral location and mountainous terrain' stood in the way of 'complete assimilation',[8] and while most Transcaucasians were poor, industrious and tradition-bound peasants and artisans, over time Transcaucasians internalised aspects of the cultures of all its peoples, producing a distinct Caucasian ethos and some sense of unity.

Ethnic Russians settled in increasing numbers in the region's two growing cities, Tiflis and Baku. Schools and institutions of higher learning were opened and available to the local population with the promise of professional careers in the civil

[5] T de Waal, *The Caucasus: An Introduction*, 2nd edn (Oxford, Oxford University Press, 2019) 26–28.

[6] Kutaisi and Tiflis lie in what is now Georgia, Erevan in Armenia, and Elisavetpol and Baku in Azerbaijan.

[7] RG Suny, *Looking toward Ararat: Armenia in Modern History* (Bloomington, Indiana University Press, 1993) 82; R Pipes, 'Demographic and Ethnographic Changes in Transcaucasia, 1897–1956' 13 (Winter 1959) *Middle East Journal* Table 2, 49.

[8] A Saparov, *From Conflict to Autonomy in the Caucasus: The Soviet Union and the Making of Abkhazia, South Ossetia and Nagorno Karabakh* (Abingdon, Routledge, 2015) 11.

service and army. At the same time the sense of being a nation with their own national identity was incubating in Transcaucasian Muslims, along with desires for independence from what was, for this substantial group, the heavy Russian hand. Historian Wayne Vucinich states that they regarded the Russians as 'foreign oppressors, people of another language and religion', and 'anti-Muslim'.[9]

The Armenians of Transcaucasia adapted to Russian rule far better than their Muslim neighbours. They were educated and successful, quick to adopt European intellectual modes of thought and cultural tastes and figured prominently in local government and business, especially in Tiflis.[10] By the late nineteenth century, Tiflis had become the most vibrant political and cultural centre for the Armenians of the Russian Empire.[11] Their visibility in the local political and economic spheres, however, engendered resentment among many Georgians, Azeris, and tsarist authorities.

II. BAKU

By the late 1800s, Baku had become the most important city in Transcaucasia after Tiflis. Located on a windswept peninsula that jutted out into the Caspian Sea, it possessed vast oil reserves that were as valuable as gold. From a dusty town in the early nineteenth century to a booming city at the turn of the twentieth, Baku attracted international fortune-seekers, labourers, revolutionaries, and immigrants.[12] By 1903 Baku's population stood at 206,000, up from 14,000 in 1863. Its diverse population, growing size, and hustle and bustle made it something of an 'alien enclave' in the region.[13]

Tsarist-appointed officials directly and closely oversaw the administration of the promise of mammon in Baku, reducing the city to semi-colonial status.[14] By the early twentieth century, there were some 167 oil companies in operation owned by Armenians, Georgians, Jews, Muslims, Russians, and others.[15] The affluent ruled in this Wild West–like frontier town where men were armed and hired personal bodyguards.[16] Yet most of Baku lived in near-uninhabitable dereliction. According to one visitor:

> Baku, considering its immense wealth, is one of the worst managed cities in the world. The lighting is inadequate, the wretched horse-tram service pitiable, the sanitary arrangements appalling; vast spaces are left in the middle of the town, drinking water is only supplied by sea water distilled, the few gardens are arid and thin, the dust is ubiquitous – fine and penetrating dust that gets into every nook and cranny.[17]

[9] From the foreword to A Altstadt, *The Azerbaijani Turks* (Stanford, CA, Hoover Institution Press, 1992) xii.

[10] RG Suny, 'Eastern Armenians under Tsarist Rule' in RG Hovannisian (ed), *The Armenian People from Ancient to Modern Times*, vol 2 of *Foreign Dominion to Statehood: The Fifteenth Century to the Twentieth Century* (New York, St Martin's Press, 1997) 43.

[11] Suny, 'Eastern Armenians under Tsarist Rule', 126.

[12] A Altstadt-Mirhadi, 'Baku: Transformation of a Muslim Town' in MF Hamm (ed), *The City in Late Imperial Russia* (Bloomington, Indiana University Press, 1986) 283.

[13] Swietochowski, *Russian Azerbaijan*, 22.

[14] RG Suny, *The Baku Commune, 1917–1918* (Princeton, NJ, Princeton University Press, 1972) 7–8.

[15] Swietochowski, *Russian Azerbaijan*, 39, gives the figures for the percentages of owners; Suny, *The Baku Commune*, 9.

[16] Suny, *The Baku Commune*, 27.

[17] L Villari, *The Fire and Sword in the Caucasus* (London, T Fisher Unwin, 1906) 181–82.

The city's unskilled labour force, about 70 per cent of whom were Muslim, worked in the oil industry or agriculture. They were particularly susceptible to the miserable, lawless, and unhealthy conditions, notably so even for this Dickensian period.[18] The oil dust and 'the danger of assault kept men armed and women indoors', recalled one socialist revolutionary who visited the city.[19] The 'development of the oil industry' had turned Baku into 'a capitalist city in a feudal land, a proletarian oasis surrounded by a peasant population … poor and completely uneducated', according to historian Ronald Grigor Suny.[20] The Baku branch of the Russian Social Democratic Workers' Party (RSDWP) publicised these conditions, raising awareness among labourers that they need no longer endure such hardship. Demonstrations and general strikes became common, with the Armenian and Russian labourers advancing their claims most vocally.

The Russo-Ottoman Border, 1878–1914

Source: Richard G Hovannisian (ed), *The Armenian People from Ancient to Modern Times: Volume II: Foreign Dominion to Statehood: The Fifteenth Century to Twentieth Century* (New York, St Martin's Press, 1997) map 3.

III. ARMENIANS AND THE RUSSIAN STATE, 1884–1905

Until the assassination of Tsar Alexander II, in 1881, relations between Armenians and the Russian state had been relatively amicable. But Alexander II's son and

[18] Altstadt-Mirhadi, 'Baku: Transformation of a Muslim Town', 289–93.

[19] E Broido, *Memoirs of a Revolutionary*, trans and ed V Broido (New York, Oxford University Press, 1967) 74, as cited in Suny, *The Baku Commune*, 31. The organisation referred to here is the Organization of Workers of Balakhany and Bibieibat, the Social-Democratic group led by the Shendrikov brothers in 1904–05.

[20] Suny, *The Baku Commune*, 7.

successor, Alexander III, believed that his father's reform policies had only encouraged popular dissent against the Romanovs and so issued a raft of decrees in the 1880s that curbed the privileges and local powers of the ethnic groups in the empire. Russian Armenians came under particular scrutiny because of the rise of Armenian revolutionary activity along the Russo-Ottoman borderlands, and their agitation on behalf of their compatriots in the Ottoman Empire. Suspicion and fear led many Russian officials to assume the worst of Armenian nationalist intentions.[21]

In the 1880s and 1890s, the Russian security organs began to crack down on Armenian revolutionary organisations. They increased surveillance against groups that they believed harboured subversive tendencies and interdicted individuals who launched armed expeditions across the Russo-Ottoman frontier territory to punish Kurds who had committed violence against Armenians.[22] Tsarist officials associated the growth of Armenian nationalism with separatism and the weakening of the imperial order. They closed down hundreds of Armenian schools, and also confiscated and banned publications that promoted Armenian national ideas. The imperial Russian authorities seemed unable to grasp the purpose and aims of the Armenian revolutionary committees and community organisations, whose gaze until the turn of the twentieth century was fixed towards the west and the plight of the Ottoman-Armenian peasantry.

By 1903, anxieties about the intentions of the Armenians led Tsar Nicholas II (r 1894–1917) to take further strong measures against them. Prince GS Golitsyn, the Russian governor-general of the Transcaucasus (the viceroyalty had been abolished in 1883), continued the policy of closing parochial Armenian schools but now oversaw the seizure of Armenian church property as well.[23] To further counter Armenian influence, he limited the number of Armenians in the civil service and replaced them with Muslims,[24] winning him their favour.

Armenians felt betrayed, offended, and deeply threatened. They organised demonstrations and formed committees of self-defence throughout Transcaucasia. The ARF and Hnchaks, the two main Armenian political organisations in the Russian as well as in the Ottoman Empire, found these activities insufficient to move tsarist officials. Before the repressive measures the tsar took against the Armenian church property and schools, their members had managed to keep their organisations and activities in the two empires separate, focusing mainly on the suffering of the Ottoman Armenians. But now they shifted their focus to events closer to home and began a secret assassination campaign targeting senior imperial administrators, police officials, and local collaborators.[25] In partnership with other Russian revolutionary parties, they intended to force the hand of imperial authorities.

[21] SB Riegg, 'Claiming the Caucasus: Russia's Imperial Encounter with Armenians, 1801–1894' (PhD thesis, University of North Carolina, 2016) 284–90.

[22] Riegg, 'Claiming the Caucasus', 290–302.

[23] RG Hovannisian, 'Russian Armenia: A Century of Tsarist Rule' (1971) 19 *Jahrbücher für Geschichte Osteuropas* 40.

[24] Swietochowski, *Russian Azerbaijan*, 40.

[25] See O Önul, *The Tsar's Armenians: A Minority in Late Imperial Russia* (London, IB Tauris, 2017) 15–35.

IV. THE RUSSIAN EMPIRE UNDER SIEGE

In January 1905, deteriorating socioeconomic conditions in the empire and Russia's humiliating losses in the war against Japan spilled over into popular discontent and brought a crowd of 150,000 to the streets of St Petersburg. Led by an Orthodox priest they approached the Winter Palace with a petition for greater political rights. The tsar's troops fired, killing scores and wounding hundreds more. The force with which the monarchy came down on these demonstrators, and the immense human losses it inflicted, inflamed Russian society throughout the empire.

The protests that now took place set off the 1905 Russian Revolution. Civil disturbances and workers' strikes convulsed the country in a revolt that cut across both class and ethnic lines. Peasants rebelled against the semi-feudal conditions prevailing in the countryside, organised rent strikes, and attacked the gentry. The effects of what soon became known as Bloody Sunday fed into the spate of killings that had broken out across Baku's Armenian and Muslim neighborhoods, their immediate cause, according to Simon Sebag-Montefiore, being the death by gunshot of an Azeri by an Armenian.[26]

Recognising the need to have competent officials to bring order to the chaos, Nicholas replaced the administrative head of the imperial government in Transcaucasia with Count Illarion I. Vorontsov-Dashkov, with whom Armenians had once enjoyed a harmonious relationship. Soon the decree ordering confiscation of Armenian church property and closing of schools was repealed.[27] The move reconciled most Armenians with the tsar. The fact that those Armenians seemed to forgive him spoke to Armenians' relief but also to their need to trust and be protected by the person and office of a self-proclaimed defender of Ottoman Christians. The moment produced '[s]pontaneous demonstrations of rejoicing, gratitude, and fidelity surg[ing] through many Transcaucasian cities and villages'.[28]

In October 1905, the tsar begrudgingly conceded limited political and civil rights for achieving justice, fairness, representation, and participation to the Russian people. His October Manifesto ordained the creation both of a parliamentary body (the State Duma) elected on a democratic franchise and Russia's first constitution. A new political culture began to take shape as political meetings were held on the street, new periodicals appeared, and political exiles began to return. There was a general sense of hope among the tsar's subjects that a bright future now awaited the empire.

However, relations between Muslims and Armenians in Transcaucasia had spun out of control. From 1905 until late 1906 they were so violent as to become known as the Armeno-Tatar War. Beginning in the east, wanton murders and pillaging spilled out onto the streets of Baku, in full view of the city's police force and Cossack cavalry, with Azeri mobs from the city's outlying districts scouring residential blocks in their hunt for Armenians. From Baku, the inter-ethnic bloodletting rippled across other Transcaucasus cities, rocking Tiflis and Yerevan in late February 1905,

[26] S Sebag Montefiore, *Young Stalin* (New York, Alfred A Knopf, 2007) 128.
[27] Suny, 'Eastern Armenians under Tsarist Rule', 134.
[28] RG Hovannisian, *Armenia on the Road to Independence, 1918* (Berkeley, University of California Press, 1967) 21.

Nakhichevan in May, Shusha/Shushi in June, Baku again in August, and Elisavetpol and Tiflis again in November.[29] Based on first-person accounts of the killings, it is clear that one or the other ethnic group often unleashed the violence on whoever was locally less powerful. Sebag-Montefiore notes that it was ARF fighters who led the massacres of Muslim villagers outside Baku in August in response to the killings earlier in the year.[30] The imperial authorities' inaction or, worse, responsibility for inciting inter-ethnic tension, earned them the ire of both Armenians and Azeris. Baku governor Prince MA Nakashidze was blown to pieces by a bomb in May 1905 for his alleged role in the affair.[31]

Estimates of numbers killed in the Armenian–Azeri war range from as low as 3,100 to as high as 10,000. According to historian Tadeusz Swietochowski, '[A]ll the available data suggest that the Muslims, who were usually on the attack, suffered greater losses than the Armenians, though not overwhelmingly so'.[32] A tally by an ARF Party stalwart, Khachatur Malumian (who went by the pen name of Eduard Aknuni), counted 128 Armenian and 158 Tatar villages despoiled and devastated.[33] Added together, overall property losses were staggering, estimated at over 40 million rubles (or about $548,537,296 today).[34]

V. MUSLIM–ARMENIAN RELATIONS IN MOUNTAINOUS NAGORNO-KARABAKH

Nagorno-Karabakh is the focus of today's active violence in the South Caucasus and today's primary manifestations of the region's unhealed and unprocessed collective trauma. Situated in the centre of the South Caucasus, Nagorno-Karabakh is a land blanketed by forested mountains and ancient churches and monasteries. Once ruled by Armenian princely dynasts and Muslim khans, by the turn of the twentieth century the region had been a part of the Russian Empire for close to a century. Its Armenian and Azeri population consisted of peasants and craftsmen in rural areas and a burgeoning bourgeoise class and nobility based in the town of Shusha/Shushi. Just to the east of the region lay Elisavetpol (now Ganja), a city of 30,000, with Muslims comprising two-thirds of the inhabitants, and Armenians around a quarter.[35] The Armenians of Nagorno-Karabakh were generally better off, more likely to embrace opportunities for education and prospects for material improvement, and to adopt Western modes of behaviour and thought. Most, but not all, Muslims lived more traditionally. Nomadic Muslims took their livestock to graze

[29] Swietochowski, *Russian Azerbaijan*, 41.

[30] Montefiore, *Young Stalin*, 142.

[31] Montefiore, *Young Stalin*, 128; Document 4, 'Report to the Department of Police on the Make-up of the ARF Central Committee in Tiflis' in V Yeghiayan, *Armenians and the Okhrana, 1907–1915* (Los Angeles, Center for Armenian Remembrance, 2016) 10.

[32] Swietochowski, *Russian Azerbaijan*, 41.

[33] E Aknouni, *Armenian Prisoners of the Caucasus (A Page of the Tzar's Persecution)* (New York, np, 1911) 30 fn 6.

[34] Hovannisian, *Armenia on the Road to Independence*, 21.

[35] NA Troinitskogo (ed), *Pervaia vseobshchaia perepis' naseleniia Rossiskoi Imperii, 1897 g*, vol 63 (St Petersburg, Tsentralnyi Staticheskii Komitet, 1904).

in mountain pastures in the summer and drove them down to the lower plains during the hard winters.

Shusha/Shushi was the crown jewel of the region. Called 'Little Paris' and the 'Jerusalem of Karabakh', the town, nestled atop a mountain looking out on the surrounding valleys rounded by sheer-drop cliff edges, must have had great charm.[36] Isolated and thriving, it was the cultural, intellectual, and commercial centre of Nagorno-Karabakh. The Ghazanchetsots Cathedral, completed in 1887 through funds raised by the local Armenian parishioners, towered proudly above the other edifices of the town. Yet even this prosperous, delightful little city was not spared the ravages of the 1905 disturbances and saw intense fighting break out between its two communities in August of that year. It would neither be the first nor second time that the town would fall victim to inter-ethnic violence in the twentieth century.

VI. AZERBAIJANI POLITICAL PARTIES FORM, UNITE, AND DIVIDE

The conclusion of the 1905 disturbances brought about an apparent realignment in Russian imperial policy in Transcaucasia. No sooner had Vorontsov-Dashkov rolled back Golitsyn's repressive measures against the Armenians than he began a campaign against the region's Muslims. In addition to confiscating their religious property, Muslim clergy were imprisoned, Russian settlements expanded in Transcaucasia, and Muslim homes, land and garden plots seized.[37]

In the midst of the disturbances in Tiflis, Vorontsov-Dashkov authorised the arming of the Social Democrat militia, a Russian left-wing revolutionary political organisation, as a way to keep the Azeris in check. The resulting Russian-Armenian détente gave rise to a movement among the different Muslim political groups in Transcaucasia to unite and begin cooperating with one another for the first time. Elisavetpol became a site of fervent political activity among the Muslim organisations. The Difai (Defence) Party was founded with the aim of defending the rights of Muslims in Transcaucasia. It denounced Vorontsov-Dashkov's close ties with the ARF, but stopped short of provoking renewed intercommunal strife. It blamed the recent tensions in Transcaucasia on the imperial administrators and began waging its own terrorist campaign against Russian officialdom.[38]

The Difai was not the only mainstream Muslim political party to form at this time. The Himmat was founded in 1904 and led by the local Muslim intelligentsia.[39] They promoted an agenda that closely mirrored the RSDWP's program but also sought to foster a mass movement among Transcaucasia's Muslim population. In their clandestinely published newspaper, they denounced the tsarist bureaucracy and called for the establishment of a modern education system and the betterment of the status

[36] S Mkrtchian and S Davtian, *Shushi: The City of Tragic Fate* (Yerevan, Amaras, 1999); and T De Waal, *Black Garden: Armenia and Azerbaijan through Peace and War* (New York, New York University Press, 2003) 185.

[37] E Ybert, 'Islam, Nationalism and Socialism in the Parties and Political Organisations of Azerbaijani Muslims in the Early Twentieth Century' (2013) 1 *Caucasus Survey* 45.

[38] Ybert, 'Islam, Nationalism and Socialism', 44–46.

[39] Swietochowski, *Russian Azerbaijan*, 51–52.

of women.[40] One of their members, Prokofiy Dzhaparidze, would go on to become a prominent political activist in Baku and close associate of the Bolshevik Armenian leader Stepan Shaumian. In 1906, the members of the young Himmat Party joined with members of Baku's Bolshevik Party to create a labour union for the city's oil workers, in turn giving the Bolsheviks a substantial power base in the city.[41]

While the Azerbaijanis and the Armenians in eastern Transcaucasia clearly lacked a history of sustained political cooperation, around the time of the 1905 Revolution, some progressive Azeri community and political leaders came to understand that 'Muslim development and Muslim-Armenian reconciliation were imperatives for social-democratic unity', according to historian Michael G Smith.[42] Members of the Himmat Party spoke about reaching an understanding on Muslim–Armenian relations, blaming the Russians for the violence between the two groups.[43] In the recently established State Duma, deputy Ismail Ziyatkhanov spoke at length about the imperial authorities' alleged provocations of civil conflict:

> We, the Muslims, were told by the administration: you have been economically enslaved by the Armenians. They are arming themselves and plan to create their state; one day they will do away with you. The Armenians were told that the idea of Pan-Islamism had put down deep roots in all strata of the Muslim community, and one day the Muslims would massacre them. Such was the pattern of the provocation … Then, it was said that the clashes had occurred on the ground of national enmity. I declare that there had never been any enmity between us the Muslims and the Armenians on economic grounds alone. We had been living as good neighbors and liked each other … In the past there had not been any armed clashes and if cases of murder happened, they were single exceptions and had never assumed any large proportions.[44]

Ziyatkhanov's words, spoken in the new political atmosphere ushered in by the 1905 Revolution, hint at what the two communities might aspire to return to and build on.

VII. THE JOINT EFFORT OF THE DIFIA, THE ARF, AND PRINCE SABAHADDIN

The Difai considered the possibility of a union of the Transcaucasian peoples, an idea that was first mooted in Elisavetpol by the Muslim organisations. Difai members took a major step in this direction when they shared the idea with the liberal factions of the ARF and with Sabahaddin's League of Decentralization, according to Swietochowski.[45] The ARF, a transnational organisation made up of both Ottoman

[40] Swietochowski, *Russian Azerbaijan*, 52.

[41] MG Smith, 'Anatomy of a Rumour: Murder Scandal, the Musavat Party and Narratives of the Russian Revolution in Baku, 1917–20' (2001) 36(2) *Journal of Contemporary History* 215–16.

[42] Smith, 'Anatomy of a Rumour', 215. Instances of intercommunal cooperation in Transcaucasia during the 1905 disturbances are also discussed in greater detail in L Sargent, 'The "Armeno-Tatar" War in the South Caucasus: Multiple Causes, Interpreted Meanings' (2010) 4 *Ab Imperio* 143.

[43] Smith, 'Anatomy of a Rumour', 215.

[44] Swietochowski, *Russian Azerbaijan*, 44.

[45] Swietochowski, *Russian Azerbaijan*, 45–46.

and Russian Armenians, agreed to work with Prince Sabahaddin's faction of the Young Turks to advance its goals of decentralisation and autonomy in the Ottoman Empire. Sabahaddin hoped to foster rapprochement between Muslims and Armenians in Transcaucasia as well as in the Ottoman Empire.[46] He believed that such rapprochement would gain European support and invite their intervention either to replace the sultan or force a change in the rules of governance. In Transcaucasia, according to Hanioğlu, Sabahaddin's spokesman appealed to the Muslims 'to come to terms with the Armenians'.[47]

This Armeno-Azerbaijani-Ottoman collaboration was based in the eastern Ottoman frontier town of Van, a poorly governed region in the imperial borderlands where lawlessness prevailed over order. It made sense as a place for revolutionaries to defy the official policies of the government in Istanbul in pursuit of cross-border goals. A group of Armenian and Azeri intellectuals jointly published and disseminated a bilingual journal across the border representing the views of the Armenian-Azerbaijani League, a body founded by Armenian members of the RSDWP's Baku branch and the Himmat Party.[48] Its publication succeeded in raising new hopes for reconciliation between Young Turk and Armenian organisations.[49]

Within Transcaucasia, the Muslim and Armenian political groups 'found a common ground in the idea of emancipation from Russia through the unity of the Transcaucasian peoples'.[50] The informal talks between the Difai and the ARF took place at exactly the same time as the alliance between the CUP and the ARF in the Ottoman Empire materialised. Their idea of Transcaucasian unity appeared to be in the form of a federated republic linked to Russia yet entirely free in the administration of its internal affairs, a seemingly constructive, empowering, and forward-looking progressive possibility in a torn land. At the same time, Difai leaders also took proactive measures, forming militias to defend the Muslim community against the tsarist officials' discriminatory measures against them and carrying out attacks against tsarist officials and suspected Muslim collaborators. According to historian Édith Ybert, the party's target lists never included Armenians.[51]

These progressive activities failed in both empires, yet surely left a their mark within each, along with the disturbances. Kévorkian surmises that the war that began in 1905 in the Caucasus 'probably had a greater impact on Young Turk circles than has previously been supposed' and that 'Turkish-speaking circles perceived it as a Turkish-Armenian conflict for control of the South Caucasus';[52] unsurprisingly, Sabahaddin's proposals for decentralisation and cross-border cooperation ran into opposition. An important voice against them was Behaeddin Şakir, by then a senior

[46] M Şükrü Hanioğlu, *Preparation for a Revolution: The Young Turks: 1902–1908* (Oxford, Oxford University Press, 2001) 95.

[47] Hanioğlu, *Preparation for a Revolution*, 95.

[48] A Bennigsen and C Lemercier-Quelquejay, *La presse et le mouvement national chez les musulmans de Russie avant 1920* (Paris, Editions de l'Ecole des Hautes Etudes en Sciences, 1964) 121, as cited in Hanioğlu, *Preparation for a Revolution*, 96.

[49] R Kévorkian, *The Armenian Genocide: A Complete History* (London, IB Tauris, 2011) 43.

[50] Kévorkian, *The Armenian Genocide*, 45.

[51] Ybert, 'Islam, Nationalism and Socialism', 48.

[52] Ybert, 'Islam, Nationalism and Socialism', 48.

member of the top CUP circle. He wrote privately that 'those Armenian revolutionaries … are enjoying themselves by offending humanity', referring to their alleged 'encroachments' on the rights of Caucasus Muslims.[53] This was the same letter, cited above, in which he also suggested 'putting an end to Armenian wealth and influence in the Caucasus' (see Chapter 6) and having Transcaucasia's Muslims unite with the Ottoman Empire.[54]

VIII. MAKING SENSE OF THE TRAUMATIC ARMENO-TATAR CLASHES

The Armeno-Tatar clashes might be seen as resulting primarily from latent ethno-religious animosities between the two peoples, exacerbated by the inaction of tsarist officials and police.[55] The legal authorities allowed ethnic tensions to boil up, such that, as Smith notes, 'Armenians and Azerbaijani Turks killed each other for the first time in the modern era because of who they were, how they looked, what faith they worshipped, or what tongue they spoke'.[56] This was certainly how contemporaries such as Abraham Giulkhandanian, an ARF member and resident of Baku, saw it. He remembered that rumours had circulated there months and days before the violence broke out. Once it did,

> … the police viewed the criminal acts that were being committed right before their very eyes in broad daylight with indifference and never desired to intervene … In our memories, all the events were, one by one, being drawn as if according to some carefully thought-out plan whose end goal was to stir animosity among Baku's various peoples and to pit one against the other for any price so that Baku could enjoy no peace.[57]

Giulkhandanian recalled reports of pamphlets and other materials being circulated that year, calling on the Muslims to take up arms because the 'Armenians were going to slaughter them' and purporting that they had already massacred a number of Muslims on the streets of Baku, although no proof of this accusation ever surfaced.[58] From greater distance Hovannisian attributes the violence to many factors, starting with the charged atmosphere in Russia, in which all pre-existing differences of ethnicity, religion, class, and education 'exploded into fierce combat'.[59]

The effects of the 1894–96 massacres in the Ottoman Empire had reverberated in Transcaucasia and must have played a role as well. News about them had reached across the Ottoman-Transcaucasian border, as would word of the impunity that the perpetrators had enjoyed, surely enraging many Russian Armenians, who in Transcaucasia were better able to organise and mount attacks against those who

[53] Hanioğlu, *Preparation for a Revolution*, 158.

[54] Hanioğlu, *Preparation for a Revolution*, 160.

[55] See Sargent, 'The "Armeno-Tatar" War in the South Caucasus', 144–45, for a brief review of the literature.

[56] MG Smith, 'Traumatic Loss and Azerbaijani National Memory', published in Russian as 'Pamiat' obutratakh i Azerbaidzhanskoe obshchestvo' in D Furman (ed), *Azerbaidzhan i Rossia: obshchestva i gosudarstva* (Moscow, Sakharov Institute, 2001) 90.

[57] A Giulkhandanian, *Hay-tatarakan undharumnere*, 2 vols (Paris, Haratch, 1933) 1:14, 17.

[58] Giulkhandanian, *Hay-tatarakan undharumnere*, 1:21–22.

[59] Hovannisian, *Armenia on the Road to Independence*, 21.

would perpetrate against them than their compatriots across the Ottoman border, as acknowledged in 1906 in an Armenian-American publication:

> The view of the Armenians as harmless sheep uncomplainingly stretching their necks to the slaughter is not borne out by the facts … It is also untrue that the Armenians have always been the chief sufferers. Although in Baku and Nakhichevan this was the case, at Erivan and Etchmiadzin they remained the victors. At Shusha and Baku in September they suffered heavy material losses, but otherwise they fully held their own and paid the Tartars in their own coin.[60]

IX. MEANINGS MADE OF THE ARMENO-TATAR WAR

When imperial authorities finally restored order in the Transcaucasus in 1907, Armenian leaders in both the Russian and Ottoman empires, having found they had dispelled 'the myth of Moslem invincibility', realised that 'their consciousness as a nation had risen … Armenians had once again learned to fight'.[61] With a friendlier administration in place in Tiflis and at the court in St Petersburg, Armenians felt confident in pressing the Russian state and the other Great Powers to renew their commitment to reforms in the Ottoman Empire, though perhaps at the risk of further alienating their neighbours in the Transcaucasus. At the 1907 ARF Party Congress, delegates agreed that socialist aims were to be subordinated to nationalist objectives. 'An Armenian who was not a dedicated patriot could not be a true socialist', writes Hovannisian.[62] But he observes that Armenians lost sight of the bigger picture, a psychological process he calls the 'blurring' of Armenian political judgement. '[I]n the zeal to liberate … the "real homeland" [the Armenian provinces of the Ottoman Empire] … the political comprehension of the Armenians revealed its greatest naiveté and weakness. The entire nation was easily aroused by the prospect of foreign intervention'.[63] There was a sense that the Armenians regarded themselves as being dependent on outsiders to achieve their nationalist aims.

For the Azeri Muslims of Transcaucasia, Swietochowski points out that their losses at the hands of Armenians in the war brought their community together, providing an impetus to educational and political development. The resulting solidarity

> … among Muslims in a cause transcend[ed] local or sectarian loyalties, and from now on these divisions ceased to be a serious impediment to political action. The symbol of unity was still the green banner of the Prophet, but the religious appeal functioned mainly as a traditional means of mobilizing the Muslim. A distinct, national, Azeri identity was in the making.[64]

However, the tsar's display of entitled autocratic imperial power squashed expression of both Azeris'– and Armenians' – hopes. The State Duma had given Muslims

[60] A Stone Blackwell, 'Outbreak in the Caucasus: Tartars and Armenians' (1906) 4 *Armenia* 30–31.
[61] Hovannisian, *Armenia on the Road to Independence*, 21, 23.
[62] Hovannisian, *Armenia on the Road to Independence*, 22.
[63] Hovannisian, *Armenia on the Road to Independence*, 23.
[64] Swietochowski, *Russian Azerbaijan*, 42.

hopes of fair processes and free expression of their interests. But in 1905 and 1906, at three all-Russian Muslim congresses, attended by a relatively conservative group of lawyers, teachers, landowners, businessmen, and clerical officials of liberal leanings, to consider political association and representation, the leaders were careful to articulate a position that would not provoke the tsar into taking repressive measures against them. The delegates from Transcaucasia, however, declined to participate in these deliberations, choosing rather to focus on the regional politics of Transcaucasia.[65] Then, in 1907, the proportion of non-Russian representation to the Duma was cut such that only a single deputy came to represent Transcaucasia's Muslims. This proved to be a fatal blow for many Azeri liberals.[66]

X. AZERIS DURING THE BALKAN WARS AND WORLD WAR I

In 1911–12, members of Baku's Azeri intellectual class split from the Himmat Party to form the nationalist and pan-Islamist Musavat (Equality) Party.[67] Its platform stressed rights for Muslims, 'the resurrection and unity of the Muslim world', progress in education and economic life, and 'the establishment, as need might arise, of contact and exchange of opinion with foreign parties which have the well-being of humanity as their aim'.[68] The Musavatists, like the ARF members, now prioritised the development of a national consciousness among the Muslims of the Russian Empire. In this, they earned no plaudits from the more socialist-leaning revolutionary parties. The Bolsheviks, who had emerged from the RSDWP split in 1903, regarded the Musavat as backward, treacherous, and religiously fanatical – characterisations that had some merit, Smith writes, but were very partial and self-serving, as is evidenced by the evolution of the Musavat Party.[69] The Musavat became the largest and most important Muslim party, with members drawn from all classes, operating initially in complete secrecy to avoid the scrutiny of the tsarist state.[70]

At the time of its founding, the Musavat Party's branches had raised funds to support the Ottoman Empire during the Balkan Wars, demonstrating solidarity with them at a time when the latter lacked political allies.[71] According to Ybert, the Musavatists soon came around to embrace the tenets of Turkish nationalism rather than pan-Islamism.[72] The Shia–Sunni divide with the Turks now lost any remaining significance to most Azeris, who more widely shared with Turks the greater commonality of Islam as well as a Turkic language.

[65] Swietochowski, *Russian Azerbaijan*, 48.
[66] Swietochowski, *Russian Azerbaijan*, 51.
[67] F Kazemzadeh, *The Struggle for Transcaucasia, 1917–1921* (New York, Philosophical Library, 1951) 20.
[68] See Kazemzadeh, *The Struggle for Transcaucasia*, 21.
[69] Smith, 'Anatomy of a Rumour', 218.
[70] Ybert, 'Islam, Nationalism and Socialism', 51.
[71] Ybert, 'Islam, Nationalism and Socialism', citing IS Bagirova, *Politicheskie partii i organizatsii Azerbaydzhana v nachale XX veka, 1900–1917* (Baku, Elm, 1997) 195–96.
[72] Ybert, 'Islam, Nationalism and Socialism'.

XI. THE FADING POSSIBILITY OF MUTUAL COOPERATION BETWEEN ARMENIANS AND MUSLIMS

After 1907 a new but somewhat uneasy calm settled over Transcaucasia. The trappings of intercommunal harmony seemed to have returned to their pre-1905 state. Elites mixed in Baku, where photographs show children of Armenian, Jewish, and Muslim oil barons playing together. Armenian and Muslim hopes and confidence in a better future were expressed by the 1911 construction of a magnificent opera house, the Mailov Theatre, the contribution and conception of the three Armenian Maylian brothers in the oil business and the Muslim magnate Zeynalabdin Taghiyev. Its opening reflected the city's recovering multiethnic social and cultural life.[73]

By May 1913, the relations between the Armenians and the Russians seemed to have returned to their high-water mark under the reign of Alexander II. Talks between Ottoman Armenian leaders and European diplomats on the reform program in the Ottoman Empire's eastern *vilayets* (administrative provinces) were underway. Like other observers cited in earlier chapters, Vorontsov-Dashkov was alarmed about the plight of the Armenian peasantry in eastern Turkey. In a May 1913 telegram to Russian Foreign Minister Sazonov, he reported on a meeting with Russian-Armenian leaders in which he underscored the tsar's promise of action on their behalf:

> Russia will … compel Turkey to undertake the long-awaited reforms [for] Turkey's Armenian subjects so that the latter would finally be able to live comfortably and peacefully and busy themselves with their work …

He wrote of the peril's immediacy:

> News regarding the violence committed against the Armenians is received more and more frequently … The [Armenian] delegation asks that the imperial government not to refuse to the Armenians of Turkey the surreptitious supply of the weapons necessary for self-defense … Russia, which has sworn to stand in the defense of the Turkish Armenians and has required their patience, should not deny the request of those … who have long awaited for the moment Russia's vigorous steps would put an end to their perpetual fears for life and property.
>
> Finally, the Armenians wait with trepidation for the Muslim refugees from Macedonia who will be settled on their lands at their expense …[74]

After the Balkan Wars, the tsar won Armenian loyalty and cooperation by his endorsement of the Yeniköy Accord (see Chapter 9). From now on the harmonisation of Russo-Armenian relations stood primarily in contrast to Russia's relations with Transcaucasian Muslims. During the early war years, some Transcaucasian Muslims would express their desire for an independent state, secretly seeking Ottoman

[73] M Suleymanov, 'Dni Minuvshie' (1989) 9 *Literaturnyi Azerbaidzhan* 70.

[74] MG Nersisyan and RG Sahakyan (eds), *Hayots tseghaspanutyune Osmanyan kaysrutyunum: Pastatghteri yev nyuteri zhoghovatsu* (Yerevan, Hayastan, 1991) 312–15, translation from A Manuk-Khaloyan, 'Viceroy of the Caucasus to Foreign Minister Sazonov, May 2, 1913', www.academia.edu/3758494/Viceroy_of_the_Caucasus_to_Foreign_Minister_Sazonov_May_2_1913 (accessed 21 July 2020).

support, though not necessarily wanting to fall under their orbit.[75] Swietochowski writes:

> [T]the first project on record for an independent state of Transcaucasian Muslims was conceived in the circles of former Difai members. Their emissary ... secretly crossed the lines and arrived at Enver Pasha's Erzerum headquarters in February 1915 ... to obtain Ottoman endorsement for the formation of a republic that would include the *guberniias* of the [sic] Baku, Elizavetpol, and Erivan, as well as Daghestan and Terek.[76]

The emissary's visit coincided with the massacre and deportation of perhaps several thousand Muslims by the Russian army during the course of military operations in Chorokh Valley in the spring of 1915 because they had purportedly welcomed the brief Ottoman occupation of this region in December 1914.

From then on developments between the Armenians and the Azeri Muslims were shaped by wartime conditions and the policies pursued by the two empires. Swietochowski, for one, indicates that at this point Enver Pasha and the Turanist ideologues were imagining that Trasnscaucasian territory would become Turan, part of future Ottoman territory.[77]

In 1915, Vorontsov-Dashkov was replaced by a new viceroy, the commander in chief of the Caucasus Army, Grand Duke Nicholas Nikolaevich, who, in contrast to the favouritism shown by his predecessor, was inclined to adopt a much less indulgent attitude toward Armenian interests. The occupation and the effective prosecution of the war were to take precedence over all other considerations.

The relationships between three pairs of groups – the ARF and the CUP faction led by Sabahaddin; Ottoman and Transcaucasian Muslims; and Ottoman and Transcaucasian Armenians – speak to the transnational connections of the Transcaucasians with actors in the Ottoman Empire. The failure of those who tried to bring unity between Muslims and Armenians in either empire indicates that their leadership may have lacked sufficient grounding and scope to rechannel existing traumatic tensions and fears stimulated by and serving the perceived interests of the powerful imperial rulers.[78] The peace builders were outmatched by more longstanding and entrenched elites.

Could the efforts of those peace builders have succeeded? One constraint against their realisation was the lack of any preparation. There had not been widespread discussion of what peace and unity could provide. Traumatic relations were familiar and perhaps accepted as inevitable. If in this period both Ottoman and Russian constitutionalism failed, the ideology of nationalism increasingly validated otherwise unmet demands for provision of safety from ongoing collective traumas and the possibility of expression of those basic identity units within these empires.

This chapter's narrative stresses the experience of the Russian Armenians and Azeris at the moments when progressive Azeri leaders in two parties proposed productive cooperation with Armenians. Today's descendants of both peoples, marked by events in the first 15 years of the twentieth century, as they were, might benefit

[75] Swietochowski, *Russian Azerbaijan*, 81.
[76] Swietochowski, *Russian Azerbaijan*, 80.
[77] Swietochowski, *Russian Azerbaijan*, 77.
[78] Hanioğlu, *Preparation for a Revolution*, 103.

from understanding and processing this traumatic history, how each was, at one or another time, seduced by hopes and promises of the beneficence of the imperial powers between whom they were caught. Past hurts and injuries have been transmitted to them and continue to be acted out in further major collective traumatic events, primarily in the dispute over Nagorno-Karabakh, a situation that apparently suits the two inheritors of those imperial states. It is where the greatest amount of unprocessed hurt from the relations between long-traumatised peoples renews and spreads itself, creating new hurts and even more damage.

11

A Kaleidoscope of Armenian–Muslim Relations in the Intense Dynamics of Transcaucasia and Baku in 1917

WORLD WAR I opened on the Western Front in August 1914. Two months later, the Ottoman Empire formally entered into combat on the side of the Central Powers by striking at its eastern neighbour and nemesis, the Russian Empire. Russia drafted 250,000 men out of its approximately two million Armenian subjects.[1] They would serve as regulars in the Russian army alongside those Armenians who would choose to enrol in the seven volunteer battalions raised by the newly formed Armenian National Bureau based in Tiflis.[2] Both the Imperial Caucasus Army and the volunteer units were augmented by Ottoman Armenians fleeing from service in the Ottoman army – and, later, the genocide – to Transcaucasia, as well as men from the United States and Europe. From the 1890s on, many of those in the latter group had been distant witnesses of the Armenian massacres, travelling long distances to fight for their people's survival hoping to see their land finally liberated from Ottoman rule.

I. TRAUMA AND TRANSMITTED TRAUMA IN THE BORDERLANDS

In the decade after the Hamidian massacres, relations between the Armenians in the eastern provinces and the Ottoman state grew tenser and more violent. Clashes between armed Armenian groups and the forces of the Ottoman state were a recurrent phenomenon and frequently spilled into the borderlands region with Russia.

[1] YG Sargsian, 'Hayeri masnaktsutyune paterazmin yev kamavorakan sharzhume' in TP Aghayan et al (eds), *Hay zhoghorvrdi patmutyun*, vol 6 (Yerevan, Haykakan SSH Gitutyunneri Akademiayi Hratarkachutyun, 1981) 547.

[2] RG Suny, 'Eastern Armenians under Tsarist Rule' in RG Hovannisian (ed), *The Armenian People from Ancient to Modern Times*, vol 2: *Foreign Dominion to Statehood: The Fifteenth Century to the Twentieth Century* (New York, St Martin's Press, 1997) 121, 136; Sargsyan, 'Hayeri masnaktsutyune paterazmin yev kamavorakan sharzhume' 547. The size of these volunteer battalions at this time probably did not exceed 7,000. Not all Armenians served on the Caucasus Front; many also took part in the campaigns on the Eastern Front against Germany and Austria-Hungary.

In describing the situation in the borderlands region during the war years, Reynolds evokes Thomas Hobbes's famous criteria of perhaps the least desirable life: 'Disease and starvation ravaged the population. Refugees, bands of deserters, and nomads wandered the land in desperate search of shelter and sustenance. [Life] was uncertain and competition for scarce resources harsh'.[3] As military operations began in late 1914, the first instances of mass violence began against Armenians (marking, according to Akçam's recent research, the true beginning of the genocide[4]) well before the episodes at Sarikamish and Van in the first months of 1915 (see Chapter 9). The Russo-Ottoman borderlands turned into a charnel house during the years of the most intense fighting on the Caucasus Front.

Individuals tend to project memories of threats personally experienced, or of past threats recounted in their people's narratives, onto current experiences, when they are reminded by a present experience of one in the past. The ranks of the Russian Imperial Army were reinforced by thousands of Ottoman-Armenian men who fled to the relative safety of the Russian lines both before and during the genocide. Their number included the survivors of the Adana massacre of only five years earlier. Their harrowing experience, as Zabel Yesayan documented it, would have exercised tremendous force on their decision to join the war effort against the Ottomans and on their behavior on the ground:

> The fear inhabiting those little children had been so great that, when they saw anybody at all, they shivered like someone in the grip of a fever. In the imaginations of those tender innocents, grown-ups all looked the same. They saw a criminal in every adult male, were deluded by terrifying resemblances, imagined ghastly scenes and wanted to flee – panicked, horror-stricken, stupefied, and shocked. Their young minds were deranged, because, for days, they had seen criminals brandishing knives or rifles in their hands, eyes burning with a lust for evil, mouths contorted by curses and threats. Blood had poured down like rain around those children, and for hours the pupils of their eyes had been wide with the terror inspired by the flames.[5]

Russian diplomatic posts around the world were inundated by requests to grant Armenians passage to Russia to serve in the Caucasus. One letter to the Russian ambassador to Washington informed him that a group of Adana Armenians then residing in the United States would incur all the expenses involved in travelling to Russia and kitting out for combat.[6] Thus would the prospect of fresh massacres and acts of violence against their kinsmen have triggered recent memories of the Hamidian and Adana massacres of 1894–96 and 1909, respectively, contributing to the actions of those many traumatised Armenians who resorted to indiscriminate violence against Muslim civilians during the war.

[3] MA Reynolds, *Shattering Empires: The Clash and Collapse of the Ottoman and Russian Empires 1908–1918* (Cambridge, Cambridge University Press, 2011) 155–56.

[4] T Akçam, 'When Was the Decision to Annihilate the Armenians Taken?' (2019) 21 *Journal of Genocide Research* 457.

[5] Z Yesayan, *In the Ruins: The 1909 Massacres of Armenians in Adana, Turkey*, trans GM Goshgarian (Boston, Armenian International Women's Association, 2016) 25.

[6] M Karapetyan, *Haykakan kamavorakan khmbere ev azgayin gumartaknere Kovkasyan razmachakatum (1914–1917 tt)* (Yerevan, HH GAA Gitutyun Hratarakchutyun, 1999) 40.

Military operations in the Chorokh Valley region in the Russian province of Batum assumed such an aspect in the spring of 1915. There, the pre-war population of 52,000 Muslims dropped to an estimated 7,000 in a matter of months.[7] The violence carried out against these subjects of the Russian Empire was ordered by the Russian general Vladimir Liakhov. His forces returned to the region in April, following a brief Ottoman occupation. He charged the area's Muslims with 'treachery', accusing them of having aided Ottomans during the occupation, and commanded 'his Cossacks to attack Muslims on sight and burn every mosque and village … to a cinder'.[8] Ottoman documents allege that 'Armenian militias' also took part in these atrocities.[9]

Many of the Armenians implicated in these attacks would have seen Muslims as legitimate targets, identifying them with the very Turks and Kurds who had carried out past massacres against Armenians. By late 1915, the disorderly conduct of some of the Armenian units had become such a liability to the Russian effort in the occupied zones that Russian commanders decided to dissolve them and integrate the men into the regular army.[10] The fog of war would only have added opportunity for more moral injury among already traumatised individuals of all ethnicities.

The Russians went on to achieve a string of military successes against the Ottomans in 1916, capturing the strategically important cities of Trabzon, Erzurum and Erzincan within months of one another. The Caucasus Army, composed primarily of Russian soldiers, with smaller numbers of Armenians, Georgians, and others in the ranks, had swept through a broad swath of eastern Anatolia and extended a new occupation regime over the Ottoman *vilayets*.

II. THE FEBRUARY REVOLUTION

For all its military successes against the Ottomans, by February 1917, Russia stared deep into an abyss. Food shortages grew more acute, soldiers serving on the Eastern Front against Germany and Austria-Hungary began airing their dissent with commanders and the conduct of the war, and social conditions deteriorated. What began on 23 February as a protest against inadequate food provisions in Petrograd

[7] Reynolds, *Shattering Empires*, 144; D Lang, *A Modern History of Soviet Georgia* (New York, Grove Press, 1962) 185.

[8] See the account in M Philips Price, *War and Revolution in Asiatic Russia* (London, G Allen and Unwin, 1918) 223–24. General EV Maslovskii confirms this in his memoirs, *Mirovaia voina na Kavkazskom fronte, 1914–1917 gg* (Paris, Vozrozhdenie-La Renaissance, 1933) 150. More generally, see P Holquist, 'The Politics and Practice of the Russian Occupation of Armenia, 1915–February 1917' in RG Suny et al (eds), *A Question of Genocide: Armenians and Turks at the End of the Ottoman Empire* (New York, Oxford University Press, 2011) 159.

[9] Reynolds, *Shattering Empires*, 144.

[10] JA Sanborn, *Imperial Apocalypse: The Great War and the Destruction of the Russian Empire* (Oxford, Oxford University Press, 2014) 90; Reynolds, *Shattering Empires*, 156–58. It is worth noting that a number of Armenian military leaders were also in favour of their dissolution. See Document 144 in V Yeghiayan (ed), *The Armenians and the Okhrana: Documents from the Russian Department of Police Archives, 1907–1915* (Los Angeles, Center for Armenian Remembrance, 2016) 184–87. For a spirited defence of the volunteer battalions and their activities during the war, see A Khatisian, 'Kaghakapeti me hishataknere' (1932) 10 *Hairenik Amsagir* 155.

(St Petersburg was renamed Petrograd at the start of World War I) spilled over into a full-fledged revolution. Tsar Nicholas II, an incompetent wartime leader, tried to put down the demonstrators with force until he was led to understand that the entire city had turned on him. He abdicated on 2 March, bringing an end to the 300-year-old Romanov dynasty. A group of liberal and centre-right deputies from the State Duma assumed power as members of the new Provisional Government and the newly christened Russian Republic.

The news of the February Revolution was received with '[d]elirious demonstrations' of joy in Transcaucasia. With Nicholas's abdication, Armenians especially looked forward to the end of arbitrary, manipulative and unfriendly practices by the tsarist administration.[11] They demonstrated relief from traumatic threat, as they had in 1905 when Nicholas had rescinded the decrees directing the seizure of Armenian church properties and the closing of Armenian schools.

The Russian Empire's Muslim political parties had supported the Russian war effort back in 1914. They welcomed the February Revolution, too, and saw it as an opportunity to secure further legal and cultural privileges. Whereas in 1911 the nationalist and politically conservative Musavat Party, with its branches in Russia as well as Transcaucasia, had aimed to unite with all the empire's Muslims, after the February Revolution, the Musavatists and their associates in the more liberal Himmat Party supported the Provisional Government in their bid for greater local rule. By spring 1917, 'all of Russian Islam had settled on federalism as its national political goal'.[12] Like the Armenians, the federalist solution promised them the chance to enjoy the rights they wished for and felt entitled to.

The Provisional Government had to see to the needs of a large, ethnically diverse, and destitute population while prosecuting a war on three fronts. Its liberal policies were not enough to earn the public's full trust and confidence. The massive toll on the Russian people after three years of total war left many anxious for immediate relief, partly saddling the Provisional Government with some unrealistic expectations. The situation played into the hands of the Bolsheviks, who, seeing their opportunity, began scheming to topple the Provisional Government and take power. The radical peace slogans articulated by the Bolsheviks and other antiwar groups were sinking in.

In spite of the challenges, the Provisional Government performed well in certain areas: they did away with the death penalty, abolished discriminatory legislation against Jews and implemented a program for the internal reorganisation of the old Russian empire. It was no longer a monarchy but its status would not be determined until the convening of a constituent assembly. In the meantime, the progressive elements in the Provisional Government ensured that due consideration would be given to the grievances of the most disaffected elements in the empire.[13] For Transcaucasia, this meant that the government in Petrograd would exercise authority via a newly created executive body, the Special Transcaucasian Committee (known by its Russian

[11] RG Hovannisian, *Armenia on the Road to Independence, 1918* (Berkeley, University of California Press, 1967) 70.

[12] RG Suny, *The Baku Commune, 1917–1918* (Princeton, NJ, Princeton University Press, 1972) 85–86.

[13] O Figes, *A People's Tragedy: The Russian Revolution, 1891–1924* (New York, Penguin Books, 1998) 371–78.

acronym *Ozakom*), which replaced the viceroyalty and would administer certain regional affairs while devolving others to local authorities. Throughout Russia, more local democratic governing bodies were established, including in Petrograd itself, where the Provisional Executive Committee of Workers' Deputies (the Petrograd Soviet) would emerge as a rival power base to the Provisional Government.

To succeed in Transcaucasia, a new federated arrangement would have had to unite the leadership of all the major ethnic groups of the region, with each retaining some degree of independent decision-making. Such possibilities evaporated over the next several months. Living in uncertainty and fear, collectively traumatised and anxious about the future, each group nurtured the known comfort and supposed safety and strength of their own group and hoped that the external supporters they looked to might help them achieve security for their people and national political expression. Armenians and Muslims each began making separate (as if a law of nature) contingency plans. They did not anticipate that, within just a year, failing to go through the difficult and maturing process of establishing a democratic, unified Transcaucasian identity and entity would subject them to decisive control by those very fearsome imperial powers between which they were sandwiched.

The new institutions allowed for some autonomy and self-determination in Transcaucasia. But among Armenians, there seemed to be a consensus that, as Hovannisian put it, 'Transcaucasia had been given "rulers" but not "rule"'.[14] But for all Transcaucasia's groups there were big unanswered questions: What was to be the relationship between the central government and the non-Russian-populated regions? What of Russia's continued participation in the war in alliance with the Allies? The conservative Ozakom officials in Tiflis, who represented the Petrograd government, simply tried 'to slow the pace of agrarian and political revolution'.[15] Given the uncertainty of the times, the Armenians formed a body, the Armenian National Council, in October 1917 to manage local matters in the region (see below).

That very same month, the Bolsheviks struck. Their supporters took over key sites in Petrograd on the night of 25 October and dispersed the Provisional Government. A new Bolshevik-dominated cabinet pulled Russia out of the war. The Bolsheviks' policies bewildered Transcaucasian leaders, who saw all the gains achieved on the battlefield and the streets during the revolution evaporate in an instant.

III. BAKU MUSLIMS IN 1917

The February revolution had stimulated important political changes in Baku. Its Muslims had generally believed and hoped that the revolution provided 'the opportunity to redress the wrongs they felt had been done to their people, to lift [them] to the level of their Christian neighbors, and to gain for them their proportionate share of … political power'.[16] The liberal Azerbaijani intellectual elite, especially, pushed

[14] Hovannisian, *Armenia on the Road to Independence*, 88–89.

[15] RG Hovannisian, 'Armenia's Road to Independence' in Hovannisian, *The Armenian People from Ancient to Modern Times*, 276, 283.

[16] Suny, *The Baku Commune*, 20.

for equal rights and opportunities, as had Armenians around the time of the 1908 Revolution in the Ottoman Empire. The Marxists among them followed the Russian revolutionary doctrine far more closely than did the nationalist Muslims, who felt an affinity with the Ottoman Empire. Like the Armenian socialist political parties, the Azerbaijani political parties struggled to agree on a common agenda. Above all, their hopes were pinned on the Provisional Government delivering on its promises for further liberalisation and the introduction of local rule.

Yet such changes did not materialise. The Baku municipal legislative body, the duma, for example, continued to operate according to rules created in the nineteenth century. These stipulated that no more than half its members could be non-Christian, while only male property owners qualified to vote in duma elections.[17] The newly established Baku soviet also failed to reflect the diverse ethnic make-up of the population as it might have because its members were elected by workers and the soldiers garrisoned in the city. As late as May 1917 a Musavat-aligned newspaper in Baku complained that no Muslims held positions in important local organisations and that the few who did in the less important ones amounted to 'a meaningless minority'.[18]

IV. BAKU'S ARMENIANS DURING THE PROVISIONAL GOVERNMENT

Although Armenians formed a distinct minority in Baku – 63,000 compared with the 90,000 Russians and 95,000 Muslims – they wielded disproportionate influence in local governance and the oil industry, and overall were wealthier than their Russian and Muslim neighbours.[19] During the war, they organised charities, took part in fundraising, and opened their homes to those fleeing from the genocide. The stories of refugees from the Ottoman Empire would have reinforced the tendency to contract within their own ethnic group. Zabel Yesayan, the sole woman CUP authorities had chosen for deportation on 24 April 1915 (see Chapter 9), had escaped, first to Bulgaria, then to Tiflis, and in 1917 made her way to Baku, where she wrote for a local paper. Although Baku was removed from the battlefront, tensions between Armenians and Azeris in the summer and fall of 1917 unsurprisingly persisted as the central government seemed to teeter on the brink of collapse.

V. MISSED OPPORTUNITIES IN BAKU

After the Armeno-Azeri war of 1905–07, St Petersburg had established a tight administrative regime in Baku, the centre of the most bitter fighting. The tsar had declared a state of emergency and appointed a new official to represent the central

[17] Suny, *The Baku Commune*, 8. Women in Russia were given the vote under the Provisional Government of the Russian Republic and Muslim women were among those who exercised the privilege.

[18] Article from the Musavatist newspaper, *Achiz-soz*, reprinted in *Kaspii*, 30 May 1917, no 117, and quoted in Suny, *The Baku Commune*, 140.

[19] Suny, *The Baku Commune*, 20.

government on all municipal matters. By 1917, Baku's viscous black oil remained in endless supply and was highly profitable for the powerful local and foreign investors living in their seaside mansions. The city was the industrial heart of all Transcaucasia. Fierce competition pervaded 'Petrolopolis', as some called it, amid the din and clamour of the city's shops and bazaars while a good part of the city's major ethnic groups still subsisted in great squalor.

Baku's famous marketplace was the city's cultural core, a Transcaucasian *agora*. People crowded there, not just for shopping but for entertainment and discussion. Kurban Said, the pen name of Lev Nussimbaum, the most likely author of *Ali and Nino* – the book Azerbaijanis today call their national novel – moved with his family as a child to Baku from their native Kiev and recalled his memories of the city where everyone mingled. 'The cosmopolitan Caucasus on the eve of [the October] revolution [was a place where] … a hundred races and all the major religious groups fought together only in battles of poetry in the market place', according to Tom Reiss, whose *The Orientalist* attempts to establish the disputed identity of *Ali and Nino*'s author.[20]

Yet the marketplace formed only one strand of the urban fabric. Social, intermingling across ethnic lines occurred primarily among old families of the elite. Within that stratum, it was characterised by an ethnic hierarchy, as in other classes. Even before the war, 'Muslim industrialists experienced condescension from Armenian, Russian, and foreign capitalists', indicative of the low regard non-Muslims held of Muslims, writes Suny.[21] Worker relations did cut across ethnic and class lines but according to the type and level of skill. Thus, the vast majority of Baku's labouring classes 'occupied the bottom of the labour hierarchy' extracting and processing the oil, and were very poorly paid.[22] The majority of the industry's better-paid skilled workers were Russian and Armenian. With the uncertainties brought about by revolution and war, the multicultural atmosphere may have only partially concealed the underlying train of events that was to overwhelm the city's inhabitants. In the months after the February Revolution, things in Baku went from bad to worse.

All the same, the city's contradictions and contrasts might have provided some basis for a cooperative and productive Christian and Muslim future. In the early 2000s, Zuleika Asadullayeva, the surviving daughter of the wealthiest Muslim oil baron in Baku during the pre-war period, recalled her memory of the tolerance of Muslim elites for certain differences:

> To be a Muslim like my family were Muslims was to have a universal religion, a respect for tradition but never dogma … not like today, with … fundamentalists who are as bad as the Nazis or Bolsheviks.[23]

Until the war came to Baku in September 1918, the city remained a place where the elite continued to lead privileged lives. Then, had community leaders been willing to take on more responsibility, they might have ensured a different future. Tellingly,

[20] T Reiss, *The Orientalist: Solving the Mystery of a Strange and Depressing Life* (New York, Random House, 2005) xv.

[21] Suny, *The Baku Commune*, 21.

[22] Suny, *The Baku Commune*, 21.

[23] Reiss, *The Orientalist*, 35.

today Asadullayeva cannot speak for Baku's wealthy Muslims who might agree because such opinions might invite reprisal from the government.

VI. STEPAN SHAUMIAN: EMBODIMENT OF THE HISTORICAL MOMENT'S POTENTIAL

The workers' tireless champion and leader in Baku was Stepan Shaumian. Born in Tiflis to an Armenian family, Shaumian mixed in social revolutionary circles as a university student in St Petersburg, Riga and Tiflis, eventually making his way to Switzerland in 1903, where he fell in with Lenin. Shaumian returned to the Caucasus in 1907 to work as a labour organiser and activist, earning him the nickname of the 'Caucasian Lenin'.[24] He was popular with workers of all ethnicities and advocated on their behalf as they went on strike for better conditions.

Stepan Shaumian

Source: L Lezhava and G Rusakov (eds), *Pamiatnik bortsam proletarskoi revoliutsii pogibshim v 1917–1921 gg* (Moscow, Gos. Izd-vo, 1925) 683.

[24] Eg, see Suny, *The Baku Commune*, 341.

With the onset of war, the Russian Empire required that Baku run smoothly in order to keep on tap 'the precious fuel which lubricated the war machine'.[25] Thus, when Shaumian's organising led to a strike that threatened disruption, tsarist authorities arrested and exiled him to Saratov in western Russia. After the February Revolution, he was released and allowed to return to Baku. In his absence, the local Mensheviks had taken power in the city. The warm welcome that he, a committed and known Bolshevik, received from them upon his return demonstrated the high regard in which he was still held. It is surely one of the reasons that he was subsequently elected to the Baku soviet.[26] He and the Mensheviks together represented the mood of cooperation and solidarity invested in the revolution as well as the hopes that would be realised under Shaumian's leadership.

Shaumian's ideological principles did not curb his commitment to the workers' interests nor to the spirit of cooperation with others, at least not right away. In Baku the Bolshevik Party was associated with the left-wing, worker-oriented Himmat Party, in contrast with the Himmat branches elsewhere, which were supported by the Mensheviks.[27] Shaumian and his comrades intended to keep the sympathetic Bolshevik workers' constituency together irrespective of their differences on Marxism and opposition to the ARF, which placed national issues on a higher plane than social class struggles.[28]

In the wake of the February Revolution, the Provisional Government had begun disassembling the vestiges of autocracy by widening the scope of democratic decision-making at the local level. In Transcaucasia the state's devolution of authority to local structures might have but did not, however, translate into closer intercommunal ties between Christians and Muslims or more popular government. The Bolsheviks capitalised on popular discontent, and in Baku this led to the dissolution of the Ozakom and the creation of a power vacuum that the local Bolsheviks sought to fill. Over time, they felt more confident in forcing the pace of change, combining class and national struggle in a way unique to Baku.

VII. THINGS FALL APART

Food shortages in Transcaucasia and Russia remained a serious problem throughout 1917. The Provisional Government was unable to ensure timely deliveries of essential foodstuffs and goods. One reason was the scarcity of labour due to the conscription of hundreds of thousands of peasants into the Russian army, which received the lion's share of whatever was produced. But most of the grain produced in the Volga for distribution never left the region due to its clogged road and railway networks.[29] In Baku the poor inhabitants received significantly less grain allotments than the city's rich.[30]

[25] Suny, *The Baku Commune*, 58.
[26] Suny, *The Baku Commune*, 75–76.
[27] T Swietochowski, *Russian Azerbaijan, 1905–1920: The Shaping of a National Identity in a Muslim Community* (Cambridge, Cambridge University Press, 1985) 87–88.
[28] Suny, *The Baku Commune*, 207.
[29] LT Lih, *Bread and Authority in Russia, 1914–1921* (Berkeley, University of California Press, 1990).
[30] Suny, *The Baku Commune*, 111.

The shortage was worsened by the fact that local farmers refused to sell grain to buyers whom they understood would only then charge exorbitant prices to the poor.[31]

Over time, the limited supplies of essential goods caused inflation to increase, while the oil industry faced erratic demand. The local economy contracted, and wages did not keep up with higher costs.[32] The price of bread went up by 100 per cent, sugar 51 per cent, milk 205 per cent, and eggs 292 per cent.[33] The predominantly Muslim farmers who supplied the city complained of bad terms for both food producers and consumers. Better-off Muslims, who were suspected of hoarding grain, became the objects of spontaneous searches by the Baku authorities. Bungled efforts by officials to correct the situation exacerbated the medical, psychological, social, and political impact of hunger.[34]

Within a few months of the revolution, the traumatic spectre of starvation haunted the region. In Baku's Freedom Square, civilians and soldiers of different ethnicities and political persuasions met and listened 'to anyone not afraid to take the podium'. They discussed and argued for hours on end. Suny assesses these public and serious 'oratorical battles on Freedom Square … as decisive as any other part of the political struggle in Baku, for they would ultimately decide which party would win the support of the Baku garrison', the garrison being the sole professionally armed unit in the city that held the threat of violent intervention.[35]

By the end of the summer, the authority of all three of Baku's governing bodies had vanished.[36] Some 3,000 Muslims demonstrated in the streets to complain about unfair food distribution in August. The scenes of political agitation were signs of leftist ascendancy, as the Bolsheviks' antiwar platform attracted greater levels of support from the downtrodden segments of the city's population.[37] The duma, which contained bourgeois elements, seemed to reclaim its authority in the autumn, but by December it was close to bankruptcy, and local bankers, suspicious of Bolshevik intentions after the October Revolution, refused to bail it out.[38]

Due to the impressive efforts of voluntary organisations, the city managed to cope. But the situation remained tenuous. A large strike of workers over management and ownership of the oil industry remained unsettled. Promises and agreements that workers had wrested from industrialists were broken. The soviet was dominated by non-Muslims, which led its Muslim members to lose patience with the majority's refusal to respond to latter's concerns about consistent underrepresentation.[39]

[31] Suny, *The Baku Commune*, 102.

[32] Suny, *The Baku Commune*, 62–63.

[33] Suny, *The Baku Commune*, 62.

[34] Reynolds's powerful description tells us that in much of Anatolia, Muslim civilians were also living in a veritable hell: 'In the Anatolian countryside tribesmen roamed without clothing and were reduced to eating grass, mud, and coal. Starvation stalked even Istanbul, where prices for essentials were soaring uncontrollably and the possibility of bread riots loomed. The empire, as a whole, [like the Russian Empire], was exhausted, worn down, and bankrupt. Only the onset of an unusually severe winter, which brought combat operations to a halt on the Caucasian front, preserved what remained of the army and prevented military collapse' (Reynolds, *Shattering Empires*, 167).

[35] Suny, *The Baku Commune*, 137.

[36] Suny, *The Baku Commune*, 110.

[37] Suny, *The Baku Commune*, 112.

[38] Suny, *The Baku Commune*, 182.

[39] Suny, *The Baku Commune*, 139.

Finally, chaos overtook Baku. There was rioting, rampant thievery, looting, and multiple deaths and injuries. The traumatic situation produced only more tension, suspicion, and animosity between Armenians and Muslims and the population at large, doubtless exacerbated by bitter memories of the mutual bloodletting of 1905–07. At a time when nearly everyone lacked regular provisions for food, the inequalities stood out: Armenians and Russians were relatively better off than Muslims, occupied more positions of political responsibility in Baku, and had greater access to food. Muslims were the hungriest.

The Muslims blamed the Armenians for these realities. Suny's judgement is that the two groups made sense of all their frustrations and disappointments in terms of ethnic differences: 'No matter how complex or diffused the causes of the material crisis, the nationalities expressed their anger and frustration in the traditional hostility toward their ethnic enemies'.[40]

Under such distressing conditions, people would have constricted even more into their nationally defined groups. Dismayed and frustrated, many of the men under arms, especially those in the Baku garrison, felt betrayed by the anarchic dysfunction around them and lost confidence in the Provisional Government. They withdrew their support for the Mensheviks and for the war, and threw their support behind the antiwar Bolsheviks. The Musavat Party, too, voiced their opposition to the war and aligned with the Bolsheviks. The sole military support municipal authorities could truly rely on boiled down to the garrison's officer corps and volunteer Armenian units.[41]

VIII. TRANSCAUCASIAN MUSLIMS COME UNDER SUSPICION

The Provisional Government's continuing commitment to the unpopular war helps explain its short lifespan. The new republic's government faced a host of challenges in the summer of 1917 that, in addition to food shortages and material privation, included Bolshevik agitation and a failed march on the capital by the rightist Russian general LG Kornilov. The allegiances of the people of Baku, as in the rest of Russia, were tested. The Bolsheviks tapped into the mood 'of isolation and growing alienation' and heightened resentment among Muslim politicians.[42]

The Musavat, by now the most important Muslim political party in Baku, settled on a platform for autonomy for Turkic-speaking Transcaucasians.[43] Having united with the recently formed Turkic Federalist Party – 'an organisation of feudal landlords' – the Musavatists nevertheless were divided among themselves on fundamental questions about their organisation as a collectivity and their relationship to their two large, powerful neighbours. Some members felt their true affinity and loyalty to be with the Ottoman Turks, others with Transcaucasia's Muslims. Still others advocated for an alliance with the Bolsheviks, reciprocating the latter's antiwar position,

[40] Suny, *The Baku Commune*, 115.
[41] Suny, *The Baku Commune*, 138.
[42] Suny, *The Baku Commune*, 94.
[43] Hovannisian, *Armenia on the Road to Independence*, 72.

although the Bolsheviks did not return the sentiment, always viewing the Musavatists as traitors and advocates of pan-Islamism.[44] Transcaucasia's Muslims must also have felt the weight of suspicion of non-Muslim neighbors as the threat of an Ottoman invasion of Transcaucasia became an increasingly distinct reality.

In the autumn of 1917, the Transcaucasian Muslim party organisations held a congress in which they argued their different positions. The Musavatists, attracted by Lenin's call for 'self-determination for all nationalities', reaffirmed their interest in a federated Transcaucasia.[45] Others advocated political unity with the Ottoman Empire. Since Muslims were still barred from serving in the Russian armed forces except as volunteers, they agreed as a whole to the idea of creating Muslim military units. The Provisional Government reluctantly granted them permission to serve in the army without issuing them arms.

IX. THE COMPLICATED SITUATION IN THE BORDERLANDS

By late summer 1917 the Russian army had held the upper hand in the fighting on the Caucasus Front for over a year. The army stood triumphant over the Ottomans, occupying a large swathe of the eastern provinces. Armenians in Transcaucasia and elsewhere saw the increasing possibility of a Russian victory, and even hoped that it would allow them to reclaim their homeland. In September 1917, the Armenian National Congress, attended by representatives of the Russian Armenian political parties, confidently met in Tiflis to outline the map of the postwar settlement of the territories. The ARF delegates also staked out the future boundaries within which their people would live in a unified, federated Transcaucasia, a plan roughly reflecting existing ethnic and topographic divisions in the region, thus aiming 'to foster harmonious relations with Georgian and Moslem workers', with the ARF insisting that 'regional progress and peace depended on international cooperation'.[46]

Meanwhile, tens of thousands of Armenian refugees. who had fled from the massacres and survived by escaping into Transcaucasia, had been returning to their homes and lands. This seemed like a plausible decision because, in spite of the weakening Provisional Government and growing unpopularity of the war among Russians generally, the Caucasus Army had by and large managed to maintain discipline and its own cohesiveness along the Anatolian front. Thus did Armenian refugees begin to return to their 'devastated towns and villages … [looking] feverishly [to rebuild] their homes and sowing their fields in time for an autumn harvest'.[47]

However, in response to Bolshevik anti-war and anti-Provisional Government propaganda, as well surely as physical exhaustion, the Russian troops began to manifest a breakdown of morale and authority, and to desert.[48] In mid-November the

[44] Smith, 'Anatomy of a Rumour', 216–17.
[45] Suny, *The Baku Commune*, 142.
[46] Hovannisian, *Armenia on the Road to Independence*, 88.
[47] Hovannisian, 'Armenia's Road to Independence', 284.
[48] S McMeekin, *The Russian Origins of the First World War* (Cambridge, MA, Harvard University Press, 2011) 227–28. On the October Revolution's effects on the Caucasus Army, see GS Melikian, *Oktiabrskaia revoliutsiia i Kavkazskaia Armiia* (Yerevan, Aiastan, 1989).

breakdown speeded up exponentially with the shattering Bolshevik Revolution and the armistice that was signed a month later. The party's slogan, 'Peace, Land, Bread', had its intended effect on the Russian troops as the full implications of Russia's withdrawal from the war became evident. They deserted from their units in the occupied territories and headed home, leaving massive gaps along the front. This was a gift like no other to the astonished Ottomans. They would soon be well able to exploit it.[49]

The delegates to the Russian Armenians' congress did not anticipate the Bolshevik Revolution or Russian withdrawal from the war. Once it happened, the Ottoman army of course saw the Transcaucasus as again open to them and prepared to march. Within weeks, in the face of a new advance by Ottoman troops to reoccupy the very lands to which they had returned, the Armenian refugees were seized with fear and panic, knowing that they would again be subject to violence or outright murder.

X. DELIBERATING ARMENIAN IDENTITY

The congress of the Armenian political parties that gathered in Tiflis in the autumn of 1917 engaged in profound deliberations. They asked themselves why Armenians had been slow to develop a national consciousness. Hovannisian summarises their answers:[50]

— Their lack of cohesion came from living scattered from one another rather than in dense concentrations.

— The 'constant friction' among them 'hindered Armenian progress'.[51]

— Nearly a millennium before, the Armenians had lost their own 'tradition' of governing, in contrast to the Georgians and Azeris of Transcaucasia, who 'were accustomed to rule and received the patronage of the Russian government'.[52]

— 'Living for centuries under foreign lords, each more abhorrent than the other, the Armenians had come to associate government with evil. Even when presented the opportunity to rule, they shunned the responsibility and suspected any of their own people who attempted to rise in the administrative hierarchy. The psychology of the Armenians, in sharp contrast with that of the Georgians and Tatars, was that of a subject people'.[53] This seemed to show awareness of fear of taking initiative and responsibility for their actions, which they understood as compelled by another.

— Armenian intellectuals had neglected Transcaucasian affairs and concentrated their attention on Armenians' problems in the Ottoman Empire. 'Moreover, imbued with strong nationalistic tendencies, they had not produced individuals of all-Russian and international significance'.

[49] Hovannisian, *Armenia on the Road to Independence*, 113.
[50] Hovannisian, *Armenia on the Road to Independence*, 89.
[51] Reynolds, *Shattering Empires*, 89.
[52] Reynolds, *Shattering Empires*, 89.
[53] Reynolds, *Shattering Empires*, 89.

— Necessity had now reduced their focus to physical survival rather than development of a national consciousness.

— With the Provisional Government embroiled in crisis, during its last session the congress elected to create two representative entities that would handle Russian-Armenian–related affairs. The first, the Armenian National Assembly, was a legislative body made up of 35 members, while the 15-member National Council was tasked with executive functions. The latter would declare Armenia's independence in May 1918.

In raising and discussing these matters, Armenians were close to processing their history, traumatic and non-traumatic, and its impact on their collective identity, although the discussion did not and could not have included an understanding of collective trauma as such. This was a needed discussion given their perhaps more hopeful than reasonable assumption that they would in the immediate future have options to consider regarding returning to their Ottoman homeland. But these renewed hopes were again shattered. Within a month, the Bolsheviks' revolution would herald momentous changes across not only Russia, but the entire world.

12

Bolshevik Decrees and Anarchy in the Borderlands, Late 1917–Early 1918

> Russians and Armenians saw themselves caught in a deadly vice between advancing Turkish troops ... and the ... local Muslim populations. Muslim civilians saw the retreating [Russian] troops as advancing against them.
>
> Michael G Smith[1]

IN THE WAKE of the major changes that followed the 1917 October Revolution, Transcaucasia saw episodes of localised, murderous anarchy, mixing terror, hope, and immense uncertainties. After the Bolshevik coup in Petrograd, a number of prominent liberal politicians, including the Provisional Government head, Alexander Kerensky, fled abroad. Lenin led the formation of a Bolshevik-dominated cabinet government, the Council of People's Commissars (the *Sovnarkom*), and proclaimed the establishment of the Russian Soviet Republic (Soviet Russia). He immediately began to issue a series of major decrees.

In November and December 1917, the new government concluded an armistice with the principal members of the Central Powers: one between Soviet Russia and Germany and Austria-Hungary, and the other – without the input of *Sovnarkom* authorities – between the provisional Transcaucasian ruling authority, the Commissariat, and the Ottomans.[2] Erzincan, an Ottoman town that had been taken by Russian forces in their drive into Anatolia in 1916, served as the site of the negotiations. The truce signed on 18 December brought hostilities to a close and forbade both sides from building up their forces along the lines of contact. Nevertheless, the Ottomans shuffled troops along the front and strengthened their main force opposite the Russian lines. Truces or no truces, with desertions, disruptions to supply lines, and inter-ethnic massacres, chaos and anarchy spread behind the Russian lines well before a final treaty was concluded.

[1] MG Smith, 'Anatomy of a Rumour: Murder Scandal, the Musavat Party and Narratives of the Russian Revolution in Baku, 1917–20' (2001) 36(2) *Journal of Contemporary History* 223.

[2] RG Hovannisian, *Armenia on the Road to Independence, 1918* (Berkeley, University of California Press, 1967) 109–10.

Meanwhile, negotiations between the Central Powers and Soviet Russia opened on 22 December 1917 at the German Army Eastern Front headquarters in Brest-Litovsk. On 3 March 1918, the Brest-Litovsk Treaty would formally end the conflict between Germany and Russia and between Russia and the Ottoman Empire.

I. GIFT GIVING TO THE PEASANTS AND OTTOMANS

In late October, Vladimir Lenin's first decree, the Decree on Peace, was issued and adopted by the Second Congress of the Soviet of Workers', Soldiers', and Peasants' Deputies. It announced Russia's immediate withdrawal from war as a way of attaining 'peace without victory'.[3] The decree spoke to the nature of the peace the Bolsheviks intended, one 'without annexations and indemnities'.[4] A Decree on Land was also adopted by the Congress on 26 October, abolishing private property and redistributing the use of land in large estates among the peasantry.[5] These two decrees in effect legitimated and gave impetus to Russian demobilisation. Russian conscripts began to stream back home so that they could be present for the great land redistribution. By early January 1918, the Caucasus Army had melted away, leaving only a few thousand troops to man a 300-mile-long front.

The decrees and dissolution of the Russian army set the Bolsheviks up for the rawest possible deal from the Ottomans as they began to negotiate a peace treaty in Brest-Litovsk. Russian withdrawal was an 'unimagined' gift to the Ottomans and could scarcely have come at a better time.[6] The CUP could now decide to pursue multiple cherished objectives: to take back the provinces that had been occupied by the Russian army, to protect Muslims from retreating Armenian troops, and to retake territory in Transcaucasia seized by the Russian Empire 40 years earlier. As their early offensives succeeded, the Ottomans revisited old aims while formulating new ones: to weaken the Armenians in Transcaucasia; to seize control of the oil in Baku; for some CUP ideologues, to realise a Turan homeland; and to find a way to keep Russia off Ottoman turf for good. The impediments to just marching in to attain these objectives were the signatures on the paper truces and the pressures of negotiations.

[3] L Engelstein, *Russia in Flames: War, Revolution, Civil War, 1914–1921* (Oxford, Oxford University Press, 2017) 239–40.

[4] This decree was issued on 26 October 1917. See JW Wheeler-Bennett, *Brest-Litovsk: The Forgotten Peace, March 1918* (London, Macmillan, 1938) Appendix 1, 375–78.

[5] A Rabinowitch, *The Bolsheviks in Power: The First Year of Soviet Rule in Petrograd* (Bloomington, Indiana University Press, 2007) 19 ff.

[6] R Kévorkian, *The Armenian Genocide: A Complete History* (London, IB Tauris, 2011) 702.

II. WHO WERE TRANSCAUCASIANS AND WHAT WAS TRANSCAUCASIA?

The Russo-Ottoman Borderlands, 1914

Source: adapted from Robert Hewsen, *Armenia: A Historical Atlas* (Chicago: University of Chicago Press, 2001) Map 164.

One week after the coup, Lenin and the *Sovnarkom* issued a new decree outlining their stance on the future composition of the Russian state. The Declaration of the Rights of People granted Russia's various nationalities with the right to self-determination 'even to the point of separation and the formation of an independent state'.[7] The decree was met with scepticism in Transcaucasia. The socialists who dominated Transcaucasian politics thought the scheme impractical. The federalist model originally proposed by the Provisional Government was far more preferable than Lenin's offer of separation from Russia. As Reynolds writes, Transcaucasian socialists believed 'Democratic union, not ethnic separatism, would best serve the peoples of the empire, including their own'.[8] Moreover, they abhorred the Bolshevik party program and the violent means they had employed to seize power. They refused to recognise their authority but at the same time found themselves in a vulnerable position as the Caucasus Front was denuded of men and matériel. Though they would not have known it, the new decree was part of a broader strategy by Lenin to gain the upper hand in his negotiations with the Central Powers. Clearly, though, Lenin's move threw Transcaucasia's future into doubt.

[7] F Kazemzadeh, *The Struggle for Transcaucasia, 1917–1921* (New York: Philosophical Library, 1951) 56–57; MA Reynolds, *Shattering Empires: The Clash and Collapse of the Ottoman and Russian Empires 1908–1918* (Cambridge, Cambridge University Press, 2011) 192.

[8] Reynolds, *Shattering Empires*, 192.

The Bolshevik stratagem took on more elaborate form when, in early January, the *Sovnarkom* summoned representatives from across Russia to reconvene the Constituent Assembly in Petrograd. The Constituent Assembly had been held up since the February Revolution as the one national democratic governing institution that could properly represent the wants and needs of the people. The delegates met for the first and only time at the Tauride Palace in Petrograd on 5 January 1918 amid scenes of pandemonium and defiance. The Bolsheviks would not have any of it: on arrival the following day, members were barred from reentering by a locked building. They instead called for the convening of the All-Russian Congress of the Soviets, whose countrywide membership was elected solely from their own party and the Left Socialist Revolutionaries. It would serve solely to rubber-stamp the Bolsheviks' decisions.

Blindsided by the Bolshevik withdrawal from the war, the three main ethnic groups of Transcaucasia came together in Tiflis to form a new, interim regional executive governing body, the Commissariat. The Commissariat articulated an agenda that took into account prevailing political, social, and economic exigencies, agreeing to take steps to stabilise the military front, end class privileges, and revamp the local economy. These challenging objectives, however, proved too ambitious in theory and near impossible to implement in practice.[9] Transcaucasian leaders could not bring themselves to agree to any number of political matters, including the all-important question of the region's relationship to Russia.

From the very outset of the October Revolution, local bodies like the Transcaucasian Soviets had proclaimed their belief in the Constituent Assembly as the sole legitimate entity able to decide on the fate of 'our dear mother land'.[10] The Commissariat's leaders adhered to this position, but, as that body was considered to be only temporary, Transcaucasia's delegates to the Constituent Assembly in early 1918 decided to create a new regional authority, the Seim, which would be vested with 'sufficient power to impose revolutionary order and inaugurate needed reforms'.[11]

The Seim's newly elected representatives, too, remained loath to define its political status in relation to Russia. Most hoped and believed that the Bolsheviks would not hold on to power for long and that the Constituent Assembly would reconvene to lead a government representative of all of Russia's peoples.[12] Thus, although Lenin had exhorted the non-Russian regions of the former empire to seek self-determination, the Seim made no decision but remained paralysed by inaction. Not wanting to wait on the Seim to make up its mind, individual Armenian, Georgian, and Azeri groups began to form their own militias and local governing bodies. Thus, Transcaucasia made little, if any, progress towards unification.

[9] Hovannisian, *Armenia on the Road to Independence*, 107–08.

[10] 'Resolutions of the Army Committee and of the Regional Center of Soviets', 26 October 1917 [8 November 1917], Republic of Georgia, *Dokumenty i materialy po vneshnei politike Zakavakaz'ia i Gruzii* (Tiflis, Tipografiia pravitel'stva Gruzinskoi respubliki, 1919) 1–2, as cited in Reynolds, *Shattering Empires*, 192.

[11] Hovannisian, *Armenia on the Road to Independence*, 125.

[12] Hovannisian, *Armenia on the Road to Independence*, 106–108.

III. ORDER IN TRANSCAUCASIA AND MUSLIM MILITIAS

Throughout 1917, traditional law enforcement and order keeping in Transcaucasia unsurprisingly broke down. The dissolution of the gendarmerie and legal authority left a vacuum that ethnic militias and armed bands would soon fill.[13] In the race to secure arms and form self-defence units, the Muslims of Transcaucasia, among all the region's ethnic groups, proved slowest to act and take measures to protect their community.

During the war, Russia's Muslim population had not been subject to conscription, having long been excluded from military service except as volunteers. Although on the eve of the October Revolution Kerensky had authorised the Muslims of the empire to organise and arm, his government had not provided them with weapons, as it had earlier to the Armenians and Georgians.[14] Then, in late 1917, the British and French, dreading an impending Ottoman offensive along the Caucasus Front, supported financing and arming the Armenian and Georgian units but not the Muslims, even as they encouraged 'the Azerbaijanis "to take weapons of Russians going through Azerbaijan"'.[15]

Warily watching their neighbours arm themselves, Transcaucasia's Muslims sought out arms wherever they could be found. They raided trains to confiscate weapons from demobilising troops making their way through Transcaucasia. These confrontations sometimes turned violent. The most notorious incident took place in January 1918 when a Muslim militia, acting on the authority of the Tiflis government, attacked deserting Russian soldiers who were travelling home by train along the Tiflis–Baku railway line. They halted the train near the village of Shamkhor, some 25 miles west of Elisavetpol, disarmed the soldiers, and murdered perhaps 1,000 of them. 'Shamkhor shocked Baku, embarrassed Tiflis, and strengthened the Transcaucasian Muslims, who had proven that they had the single most effective military force in the area', writes Suny.[16]

The incident acted 'as a signal for concerted Moslem movements in Erevan [Province]', setting off a series of violent encounters between Armenians and Muslims. In the first months of 1918

> ... [t]hroughout the province [of Erevan], wherever mixed Armeno-Tatar hamlets existed, the weaker national element fled from fear or by force ... Only immediate joint action by the Armenian and Muslim councils spared the city from going up in flames ... [A contemporary commission report] painted a sad picture of anarchy and mutual Muslim-Christian atrocities. Scarcely a single depot was operative along the entire railway, which was continually sabotaged by armed bands. Armenians decried Tatar violence in one district, while, in another, Muslims bewailed the loss of hundreds of their innocent brothers at the hands of ruthless Armenians ... [N]o positive action was taken to relieve the crisis.[17]

[13] A Altstadt, *The Azerbaijani Turks* (Stanford, CA, Hoover Institution Press, 1992) 83.
[14] RG Suny, *The Baku Commune, 1917–1918* (Princeton, NJ, Princeton University Press, 1972) 198.
[15] Altstadt, *The Azerbaijani Turks*, 83–84.
[16] Suny, *The Baku Commune*, 200.
[17] Hovannisian, *Armenia on the Road to Independence*, 143–44.

The uncertainty, need, and overall abject conditions on the Caucasus Front contributed to the general state of anxiety and escalating acts of violence. The terms of the Erzincan Truce were more honoured in the breach than the observance, and the prospect of a vengeful, rampaging invasion army made the scenario all the more frightening. Coupled with the painful memories and fears resulting from the mutual butchering of Christians and Muslims in 1905–07, the civilian populace was triggered again and again in the violent reenactments in these encounters. In this unconstrained environment, Muslims and Armenians took revenge against the innocent, as well as the guilty, to protect, regain, and preserve what they could. Armenian and Muslim alike avenged injustices against those perceived to be perpetrators. The distinction between collective victim and collective perpetrator became blurred.

IV. THE DECREE ON 'TURKISH ARMENIA'

As noted above, the departure of Russian troops from the occupied Ottoman provinces marked the final disintegration of the Caucasus Army, leaving a large vacuum of power and security. This interim not only provided a much-needed reprieve to the battered Ottoman military but paved the way for a new offensive to be launched in the coming spring. The recovery of the Russian-occupied provinces was indeed vital for the Ottoman government's 'reputation and success'.[18]

On 29 December 1917, Lenin and the People's Commissar for Nationalities, Joseph Stalin, issued a decree titled On Turkish Armenia, recognising 'the Armenians' right to self-determination' and proclaiming the right of all Armenian refugees 'to return to their lands' in the Ottoman Empire.[19] To ensure the physical safety of the Armenians and facilitate their return, the decree called on Armenians to create their own militia.[20] In Austria-Hungary and Germany, newspapers buzzed with the possibility of a plebiscite being held in the region.[21] Unaware of the Bolshevik logic behind the decree, the Ottomans would have read it as the Yeniköy Accord all over again. The Ottomans saw the threat to their interests and aims. At Brest-Litovsk they objected to the arming of the Armenian population as conflicting with Lenin's decrees about withdrawal from the war and no annexations.[22]

Were Lenin and Stalin sincere in their exhortations for a liberated Armenia? The Bolsheviks' early decisions no doubt sowed a great deal of confusion throughout Russia, but their foremost concern proved to be the preservation of their hold on power. They 'authorised' a temporary governing body in Turkish Armenia, with the appointment of Lenin's old friend, Stepan Shaumian, as its head. In effect, Shaumian was being asked to hold fast to the gains that Russia had attained in the war until such

[18] Reynolds, *Shattering Empires*, 179.

[19] USSR (Union of Soviet Socialist Republics) 'Dekret soveta narodnykh Komissarov o "Turetskoi Armenii"' in *Dokumenty vneshnei politiki SSSR* vol 1 (Moscow, Politizdat, 1957) 74–75; Reynolds, *Shattering Empires*, 179.

[20] Reynolds, *Shattering Empires*, 179.

[21] Reynolds, *Shattering Empires*, 179.

[22] Reynolds, *Shattering Empires*, 180.

time as the *Sovnarkom* could divert more men and resources to bring the region back into Soviet Russia's fold. However, offering rhetorical support to the self-determination and arming of the Armenians signified nothing less than the Armenians' sacrifice on the altar of Bolshevik political objectives. It was hoped that they would, at best, slow an anticipated Ottoman advance into Transcaucasia.[23] The Russian Civil War, which would last for almost three years, arguably began after the dissolution of the Constituent Assembly, and the *Sovnarkom* was consequently keen on marshalling as many troops as possible to defend the new regime. The promises and decree were intended to preserve Soviet power rather than offer protection and ensure fair justice for Armenians.

V. ACTS OF VENGEANCE AS THE OTTOMAN ARMIES MOVE EAST

Parties who sign truces consent to bringing a temporary halt to fighting. To maintain the ceasefire concluded at Erzincan, both parties agreed to control and punish unofficial actors. This meant that, on the Transcaucasian side, the military authorities would treat irregular armed bands, such as Kurdish tribes and militias, as illegal formations operating outside the bounds of traditional rules of warfare. The Ottomans likewise agreed to rein in the Kurds and ensure their compliance with the truce. But the scale of the anarchic violence was evidence perhaps of the ceasefire's unrealistic terms. The Ottomans exploited this reality to justify their military build-up close to the lines, even though the Erzincan Truce stipulated that there was to be no such activity. Ottoman commanders prepared to commence operations at the slightest pretext.

In early January 1918, shortly before the Armenian and Russian Christmas holidays, which fell in the first week of the month, the Ottomans encouraged Kurdish tribes to probe and harass Armenian frontline positions near Erzincan. The Armenians incrementally drew back and gave ground to their adversaries. The Ottomans' luck held out. It was a very harsh winter, and Ottoman troops were close to 'irreparable catastrophe', exhausted after years of fighting, hunger, lack of supplies – traumatised – when they happened upon plentiful stores of food, clothing, weapons, and ammunition abandoned in eastern Anatolia by deserting Russian troops.[24]

For Armenians, Russian withdrawal from the war, the Ottomans' growing confidence, and now the Russians' surrender of precious caches of arms and munitions, had the makings of a new, monumental disaster. Armenian forces were small and, without the once-formidable presence of the Caucasus Army, stood no chance against the Ottomans. The return of Armenian refugees to eastern Anatolia morphed into a tragedy of immense proportions, forcing the thousands who were able to to follow the army back into the Caucasus. As the Ottomans intended, the Armenians' future in the Ottoman half of their historic homeland was quickly vanishing.[25]

[23] Reynolds, *Shattering Empires*, 180.
[24] Hovannisian, *Armenia on the Road to Independence*, 121.
[25] Hovannisian, *Armenia on the Road to Independence*, 137.

What remained of the Caucasus Army at the end of 1917 was made up of a hodgepodge of regular soldiers and men who had emerged from almost three decades of waging guerrilla warfare against the Ottoman state. At the height of the chaos, many of these men seized the opportunity to settle scores with old foes. They preyed upon Kurds, exacting upon them what had been done to their people over recent decades in the Armenian-populated provinces of eastern Anatolia, committing 'episodic massacres [of innocents, the elderly, children, women] … extorting "taxes", expelling them from their homes, and settling others in their place … pillaging Kurdish villages … stealing … cattle, [and committing] ceaseless assaults upon Kurdish women'.[26]

Within a week of the signing of the truce, Murad of Sivas (Sebastia), an Armenian fighter who has alternately been called an outlaw and a revolutionary,[27] and his fedayee band were accused of wreaking horrific atrocities against the local Muslim population. Murad's behaviour was judged by Ottoman general Vehib Pasha as egregious disregard for the rights of the Turkish and Kurdish inhabitants, a judgement that local Muslim representatives gave credence to.[28] Murad had earlier been condemned to death in absentia by the Ottoman government and was now held as the source of the deaths of thousands of Muslims who lost their lives at the hands of 'lawless bands' of Armenians.[29]

The atrocities committed by Armenian troops and bands outraged the senior Ottoman military leadership. Although the violence was of the sort his government had been inflicting or permitting for years against innocent Armenians, on 12 February 1918, days after breaking the truce, Vehib issued a note of protest in a language imbued with all apparent righteous innocence to his counterpart, Caucasus Army commander IZ Odishelidze. Vehib justified the recommencement of hostilities by explaining that he was acting 'in the name of humanity and civilization':

> Despite my convincing appeals and your sincere promises, the crimes and atrocities in the areas evacuated by your troops, instead of ceasing, have passed all bounds and have created such a situation that it is thoroughly impossible for me to hold my troops in the role of silent spectators, since they hear and are aware that their parents, children, wives, and relatives are doomed to annihilation. Therefore, considerations based on humanity and civilization demand the improvement and rectification of this situation by taking decisive and undelayable measures in the evacuated areas. It is only for this reason that I am compelled to push forward parts of the military units from the two armies under my command. However, I hasten to add that this does not constitute an enemy act against the Russian Army … I warmly and sincerely assure you that the … truce continues in force except for the paragraph respecting the demarcation lines, which, because of the withdrawal of the Russian troops, automatically loses its significance.[30]

[26] Reynolds, *Shattering Empires*, 194.

[27] This matter provides a very concrete example of differences between academics. Hovannisian accepts that Murad committed excesses, while Kévorkian assesses them to be 'on the order of a psychological feint'. See Hovannisian, *Armenia on the Road to Independence*, 121; and Kévorkian, *The Armenian Genocide*, 702.

[28] For example, see Reynolds, *Shattering Empires*, 198.

[29] Hovannisian, *Armenia on the Road to Independence*, 123.

[30] *Dokumenty i materialy*, 48–49, cited in Hovannisian, *Armenia on the Road to Independence*, 122–23.

In another part of this communication (from a partially different Turkish text of the same document), Vehib wrote:

> The Armenians are determined to destroy and annihilate the Ottoman Muslims by way of crimes such as burning homes, massacres, looting of property, and the 'rending of honor' [rape], about which there is no doubt that the Armenians are committing and will be committing as part of an organized plan.[31]

The Caucasus Army commander replied to Vehib that he was exaggerating but did not deny that the Armenians had been forced to take 'preventative steps' to curtail Muslim band activities, explaining them as reactions to Turkish and Kurdish predations.

The Ottomans thus made sure to prepare both the military and political grounds for the midwinter offensives. Enver Pasha, in his capacity as minister of war, issued orders in early January to his commanders to advance past the truce lines. However, on the sidelines at Brest-Litovsk, Mehmet Talât conferred with one of his diplomats about possibly countering Armenian violence against Muslims by inciting Russia's Muslims and was 'cautioned … that little could be expected from Russia's Muslims [because they] were not organized and were too divided politically, and the poor state of communications in Russia blocked the dissemination of information'.[32] Vehib and fellow commanding general Musa Kâzim Karabekir's armies promptly began their march on Erzincan and Trabzon. In light of their massive numerical and material superiority, the makeshift Armenian and Georgian units had no option but to retreat.

VI. THE CIVIL WAR IN TRANSCAUCASIA

In the uncertainties brought about by this new revolutionary situation, Transcaucasians and Russians grew increasingly distressed and alarmed by the methods and objectives of the Bolsheviks and were desperate to reinstate the Constituent Assembly. Not only had the Bolsheviks seized power by force, but they were, in the words of the Tiflis Territorial Center of Soviets, bent on ensuring 'the triumph of [their] counter-revolution and destruction of the freedoms gained'.[33]

Civil war erupted throughout the land between the newly formed Bolshevik Red Army and their opponents, which was made up of many factions and known as the White Army. The Bolsheviks and their supporters fought to secure their ideological agenda against an assortment of monarchists, conservative landowners, ethnic nationalists, Cossack warlords, moderate socialists, and liberal politicians unified only by their opposition to the Bolsheviks. In Transcaucasia this conflict took on a form of a clash between both classes and nations.[34]

[31] Reynolds, *Shattering Empires*, 197–98.
[32] Reynolds, *Shattering Empires*, 181, citing Söylemezoğlu, *Hariciye Hizmetinde*, vol I, 442–43.
[33] Suny, *The Baku*, 172.
[34] L Riga, *The Bolsheviks and the Russian Empire* (Cambridge, Cambridge University Press, 2012) 186.

The new realities that opened in 1918 presented a frightening spectacle for Russia and the world. The Bolsheviks had initiated enormous revolutionary political and social changes. Each of the three major ethnic groups in Transcaucasia had formed their own separate militias and bands for deployment against one another and the two Ottoman armies advancing at breakneck speed into the region. Central authority had collapsed, leaving a power vacuum that anarchic violence filled. Armenian refugees were subjected to violence a second time around by the Ottomans. And now the prospect of civil war loomed. Reynolds' invocation of Hobbes's famed picture of life in a state of nature continued to apply. In this vacuum of authority, law, order, and any certainty, all were perpetrating and all were being victimised. For much of the time, dread and alarm swamped hope for everything except survival.

13

How World War I Ended in Transcaucasia: Betrayal, New Republics, Race Murder

After the reports of the day were over, Halil Pasha [Enver's uncle] ... would unfold his favorite theme of a Pan-Turkish Empire ... Turan .... The closely related Tatar tribes of the Caucasus must naturally join this union. Armenians and Georgians, who form minority nationalities in that territory, must either submit voluntarily or be subjugated. The Armenian question had approached solution in the course of the war; for all the Young Turks were determined that this people should be exterminated. It was embarrassing that the Georgians, fearing a similar fate, had appealed to Germany, and that the German Government was officially protecting them.

Lieutenant Colonel Ernst Paraquin, Officer in the Imperial German Army and Chief of the General Staff of the Ottoman Sixth Army[1]

THE MEMBERS OF Transcaucasia's regional legislature, the Seim, represented the region's three major ethnic groups. Although they sought to ensure a degree of continuity and security in Transcaucasia, the three never could unite to answer fundamental questions they could only answer jointly: Should Transcaucasia form a single political entity independent of Russia, and, if not, what form then should Transcaucasia assume? The answers largely depended on each group's attitude to the unstable political situation in Russia. The Musavat Party members of the Commissariat sympathised with the Menshevik position. They were not yet averse to working with the Bolsheviks, but they were not ready to throw their support behind them. The Georgian members overwhelmingly belonged to the Menshevik faction that preferred to remain within a democratic Russian state or, in the extreme scenario, carve out a Menshevik authority in Transcaucasia independent of a Bolshevik-controlled Russia.[2] The few pro-Bolshevik members of the Seim could not persuade their colleagues to subordinate Transcaucasian authority to the central Soviet government.

[1] E Paraquin, 'Politik im Orient', *Berliner Tageblatt*, 24 January 1920, translated into English and republished as 'Turkish Dreams and German Blunders' (1920) 304 *The Living Age* 763. Ernst Paraquin was a German army officer who was part of the military mission advising and training the Ottoman army in Transcaucasia.

[2] RG Suny, *The Making of the Georgian Nation*, 2nd edn (Bloomington, Indiana University Press, 1994) 192–94.

The result of the Commissariat not reaching agreement was that the Transcaucasian leaders pressed neither for formal unity among themselves nor for a final break with Petrograd. Instead, they trusted that the Bolsheviks would in time be swept from power. For members of the ARF and other left-leaning Armenian political parties, this was really not the most pressing question. Their foremost concern was the liberation of the Ottoman Armenian homeland, and the Bolshevik rhetoric they had now become discouraging.

As noted in Chapter 12, the Erzincan Truce, signed in mid-December 1917, was followed a month later by the opening of peace talks between the Bolsheviks and Central Powers at the German Eastern Front headquarters in Brest-Litovsk. The Central Powers and the Soviet Republic invited representatives of the Transcaucasian government to attend, but the leaders of the Commissariat ignored the summons. Ottoman leaders refused to accept their absence and urged Transcaucasian leaders to proclaim an independent government. Any negotiating partner the Ottomans dealt with had to possess the legal authority to conclude and enforce international agreements.[3]

I. THE OTTOMANS' OPPORTUNITY

Russia's exit from the war had handed an immense, unexpected gift to the Central Powers. For the Ottomans in particular, as already emphasised, it provided a needed respite for the armies on the Caucasus Front and a chance to reclaim formerly occupied territory, the lands that the Russian Empire had taken several decades earlier. The advance back into Transcaucasia would also bring them into closer contact with other Turkic-speaking Muslims, presenting the desired opportunity to build a *cordon sanitaire* between themselves and Russia. At the same time this would be the most propitious moment and opportunity for pursuing Turan. Finally, Ottoman commanders sought to protect local Muslims from the depredations of Armenian and Russian forces. By January 1918 Ottoman forces were massed and ordered along the line of contact, and faced the now-thinned ranks of what was left of the Caucasus Army.

II. WOULD TRANSCAUCASIAN MUSLIMS SUPPORT OTTOMAN AIMS IN TRANSCAUCASIA?

Mehmet Talât Pasha, now the grand vizier of the CUP government, led the Ottoman delegation to the talks at Brest-Litovsk. It was during the negotiations there that he first learned of Lenin's decree on 'Turkish Armenia'. For Talât and other CUP ministers, the decree cast a pall over Ottoman efforts to reestablish authority in the occupied eastern provinces. They feared the decree was a tangible statement of support for an Armenian state constructed on 'our occupied territory.' In reality it

[3] RG Hovannisian, *Armenia on the Road to Independence, 1918* (Berkeley, University of California Press, 1967) 119.

was a tactical manoeuvre by Lenin to withdraw Russian forces temporarily in order to save his embattled government.[4] Apparently unaware of this, and hoping to pressure the Bolshevik government to reconsider, Talât wired his highly placed diplomat, Galip Kemali, then in Petrograd, for advice on possibly inciting the Muslims of Russia to pressure the Bolsheviks to reconsider their support for the Armenians. But Kemali advised against this, as 'little could be expected from Russia's Muslims … They were not organized and were too divided politically, and the poor state of communications in Russia blocked the dissemination of information'.[5]

III. OTTOMAN AIMS IN TRANSCAUCASIA

In mid-February 1918, Leon Trotsky, who led the Soviet delegation at Brest-Litovsk, abruptly and without explanation quit the negotiations and left for Petrograd. Unwilling to entertain his antics, having correctly perceived his departure to be a gambit to foment workers' revolutions in central Europe, the Germans resumed the war and advanced hundreds of miles deep into western Russia in the span of a few days. Significantly, the Ottomans began their first advance into eastern Anatolia at around the same time. For Hovannisian the Ottomans' timing was notable, coming two days after Trotsky's departure from Brest-Litovsk and the authorisation of an offensive by the German High Command.[6] The Ottoman armies' overwhelming superiority in numbers under generals Mehmed Vehib and Kâzım Karabekir choked off the meager resistance of the Russian, Armenian and Georgian troops, who retreated back to their original defensive lines along the 1914 Russo-Ottoman border. Erzincan, Erzurum, and Van soon fell in rapid succession to this two-pronged assault devised by the Ottoman commanders.

Historians differ over whether the pursuit of Turan was an important factor, or even a factor at all, in shaping Ottoman ambitions in Transcaucasia. Reynolds, evaluating the internal correspondence between senior Ottoman officials and military leaders, argues that the CUP's objective was not the unification of Muslims as such, but the creation of a strong, reliable barrier in Caucasia to block a future resurgent Russia.[7] But he does point out that Enver favoured 'an independent Caucasian state [that] … could potentially neutralize the Armenians if it was based on a dominant coalition of Caucasian Muslims and Georgians'.[8] Kévorkian points to German and Armenian sources also alleging a deliberate effort on the part of Ottoman commanders to expand eastwards in order to neutralise the Armenians of Transcaucasia, Persia, and the North Caucasus.[9] Both Kévorkian and Hans-Lukas Kieser argue that the

[4] MA Reynolds, *Shattering Empires: The Clash and Collapse of the Ottoman and Russian Empires 1908–1918* (Cambridge, Cambridge University Press, 2011) 181.

[5] Reynolds, *Shattering Empires*, 181. Reynolds is citing Galip's memoirs in GK Söylemezoğlu, *Hariciye Hizmetinde Otuz Sene*, 4 vols (Istanbul, Şaka Matbaası, 1949–55) vol I, 442–43.

[6] Hovannisian, *Armenia on the Road to Independence*, 123.

[7] See MA Reynolds, 'Buffers Not Brethren: Young Turk Military Policy in the First World War and the Myth of Panturanism' (2009) 203 *Past and Present* 137–79.

[8] Reynolds, *Shattering Empires*, 195, and especially fn 21.

[9] See R Kévorkian, *The Armenian Genocide: A Complete History* (London, IB Tauris, 2011) 704–12.

CUP targeted Armenians and other Christians for persecution during the Ottoman advance into the region. Testimony such as that given in 1920 to French naval intelligence by Lieutenant Colonel Ernst Paraquin, an officer of the Imperial German Army and chief of the general staff of the Ottoman Sixth Army, affirms that the destruction of the Armenians of Transcaucasia was tied to territorial Pan-Turkic expansion (Paraquin does not use the word 'Turan').

> Halil [Pasha Enver's uncle] … noted that 'the Armenian question' was on the 'verge of being solved … through … annihilation of the Armenian race. All the interested Turkish departments are working to this end with implacable resolve'. The German officer's [Paraquin's] account emphasizes … that the Young Turk leaders were prepared to make every sacrifice to achieve their Pan-Turk project, including abandoning their Arab possessions.[10]

What has been imparted in this book prior to this point about Ottoman interest in establishing Turan has persuaded me that Turan had been and remained an objective, among others, for some of the important CUP decision makers. But the mix of the immediate historical context with psychological forces was also likely to have been compelling in the minds of CUP actors. The immense opportunity provided by the Russian pull-out had to have revitalised grandiose determination to take the Russians' place and rule the Transcaucasia as they wished, thereby replacing the loss of imperial territory elsewhere. As an extension of Ottoman lands, it would have to be free, if not of all Christians, certainly of Armenians as a collective force. Given CUP wartime measures against Armenians, it is difficult to imagine that Christians allowed to reside in these newly acquired lands would have been granted cultural rights or access to schools and communal institutions.

IV. THE TREATY OF BREST-LITOVSK

With the Germans on their doorstep, a civil war underway, their armies on all fronts having fully disintegrated, the Bolsheviks now came under overwhelming siege. Lenin decided it was time to give in. On 3 March 1918, the two parties signed the Treaty of Brest-Litovsk. In it the Russians had to capitulate to the extraordinarily draconian peace terms dictated by the Central Powers. They had forced Russia, Lenin said, to 'that abyss of defeat, dismemberment, enslavement and humiliation'.[11] The terms were so harsh, according to historian Spencer Tucker, they 'shocked even the German negotiator'.[12] Russia was to cede to the Central Powers 1,260,000 square miles of former imperial territory inhabited by a third of its population (about 55 million people), of which some 10,000 square miles of Transcaucasia (with a population of 650,000) were specifically awarded to the Ottoman Empire. Russia would also cede

[10] Quoted in SHAT, Service Historique de la Marine, Service de reseignements de la Marine, Turquie, 1BB7 235, doc no 1992, Constantinople, 16 April 1920, 'La politique pantouraninne', by E Paraquin, 3–4, cited in Kévorkian, *The Armenian Genocide*, 704; and H-L Kieser, *Talaat Pasha: Father of Modern Turkey, Architect of Genocide* (Princeton, NJ, Princeton University Press, 2018) 367–69.

[11] VI Lenin, *Selected Works*, vol 2 (Moscow, Foreign Languages Publication House, 1947) 443.

[12] SC Tucker, *The Great War, 1914–18* (Bloomington, Indiana University Press, 1998), 156.

most of the country's coal and iron deposits, and much of its industrial capacity.[13] Baku remained the only strategic city in Transcaucasia the Soviets refused to relinquish. Further exactions would come in August of that year in a supplemental treaty in which the Soviet Republic would agree to pay six billion rubles to Germany as compensation for the damage and destruction inflicted by the Russian armies during their wartime occupation of German territory.

V. THE TRABZON TALKS

Throughout the course of the war, the Armenians had held out hope for an eventual Entente victory. They had optimistically gathered at clubs, cafés, and taverns in Tiflis, Yerevan and elsewhere to discuss the likely establishment of an autonomous administrative authority over occupied Ottoman territory. But this was not to be. The Seim had halfheartedly listed autonomy for Ottoman Armenia as one of its preconditions for talks with the Ottomans, but the signing of the Treaty of Brest-Litovsk, which had been negotiated almost solely between the two principal powers, had rendered the matter moot.[14] Any proposal that questioned the territorial integrity of the Ottoman state was impermissible for the CUP leadership.

The Armenian members of the Seim met with their colleagues in Tiflis two days before the conclusion of the Brest-Litovsk negotiations to agree to the terms specifying the turnover of the formerly occupied eastern provinces to Ottoman control. They could not have known of the treaty's secret provision in which Russia also agreed to demobilise and dissolve any irregular units (referring directly to the meager formations the Armenians had put together after the departure of the Russian troops).[15] Thus, Russia, now under its new Bolshevik rulers, again betrayed the Armenians, much as it had when, along with the other Great Powers, it had failed to enforce the terms of the 1878 Treaty of Berlin.

In fact, the Transcaucasians as a whole were ignorant of the terms that were then being concluded at Brest-Litovsk. Without that knowledge, they agreed to the preconditions, including restoration of the pre-war boundaries, offered for new talks between themselves and the Ottoman Empire at the Black Sea coastal port of Trabzon. But before the peace delegation even departed from Tiflis, on 2 March they were greeted with word that Russia was relinquishing not only the formerly occupied provinces, but Kars, Ardahan, and Batum (the *Elviye-i Selâse*). It was another important and traumatic betrayal. Aleksandr Khatisian, a member of the Transcaucasian deputation and future premier of Armenia, remembered the Armenian delegates receiving the news with 'great astonishment and disappointment'.[16] The Brest-Litovsk Treaty

[13] JW Wheeler-Bennett, *The Forgotten Peace: Brest-Litovsk, March 1918* (New York, William Morrow, 1939) 269–75; J Bunyan and HH Fisher (eds), *The Bolshevik Revolution, 1917–1918: Documents and Materials* (Stanford, CA, Stanford University Press, 1934) 523–24; and Hovannisian, *Armenia on the Road to Independence*, 199.

[14] Hovannisian, *Armenia on the Road to Independence*, 130.

[15] See 'Russko-Turetskii Dopolnitelnyi dogovor k mirnomu dogovoru' in USSR (Union of Soviet Socialist Republics), *Dokumenty vneshnei politiki SSSR*, vol 1 (Moscow, Politizdat, 1957) 200.

[16] A Khatisian, *Hayastani Hanrapetutian tsagumn u zargatsume* (Beirut, Hamazkayin, 1968) 38.

stipulated that the immediate evacuation of Russian troops from the three provinces would precede plebiscites that would be held to determine their ultimate fate.[17] The Transcaucasians publicly denounced the ceding of the territories but, shorn of any good options could but sullenly board the ship that would sail for the scheduled talks at Trabzon on 7 March.

When the talks opened, the Ottomans insisted that the Transcaucasians clarify the region's legal status. This demand splintered the Transcaucasian delegation, which had already left Tiflis on divided terms. The Georgian position underwent dramatic change. Over the strenuous objections of their Armenian colleagues, the Georgian delegates were ready to see the two primarily Armenian-inhabited provinces of Kars and Ardahan go to the Ottomans, because they would retain control over the port of Batum, where the terminus points of both railway and oil pipelines originating from Baku were located.[18] As a concession, the Georgians signalled their support for a proposal they had worked out with their Armenian colleagues to establish an autonomous Armenian enclave in eastern Anatolia, in which up to 400,000 Armenian refugees would settle.[19] The Georgians' commitment, however, was not all it appeared to be. The Georgian foreign minister of Transcaucasia, Akaki Chkhenkeli, confided to Hüseyin Rauf Bey, head of the Ottoman delegation, that support for the initiative was lukewarm among himself and the other members of the delegation and arose only out of his own desire to prevent the Armenians from 'sowing anarchy inside Transcaucasia'.[20]

The Trabzon conference adjourned temporarily without resolution. On the sidelines of the talks, the Muslim members of the Transcaucasian delegation were accused of divulging the content of its deliberations to the Ottomans. The Ottomans thereby gained a sense of the weak ties between the Georgians and Armenians and exploited the differences to forestall the formation of a Georgian–Armenian coalition.[21] Because the Ottomans continued to pressure their Transcaucasian counterparts for prompt acceptance of the Brest-Litovsk terms, the conference reached an impasse.[22] The Azeri delegates also became increasingly impatient. In a session of the Seim back in Tiflis, Azeri deputy and future first prime minister of Azerbaijan Fathali Khan Khoiski identified the logic behind the Ottoman position, namely, that since the Ottomans still considered Transcaucasia a part of Russia, the Transcaucasians had 'to fulfill the terms accepted by Russia'.[23] It had every obligation to fulfill the terms it

[17] Wheeler-Bennett, *The Forgotten Peace*, 405–406; Hovannisian, *Armenia on the Road to Independence*, 151.

[18] Hovannisian, *Armenia on the Road to Independence*, 179.

[19] AN Kurat, *Türkiye ve Rusya XVIII: yüzyıl sonundan Kurtuluş Savaşına kadar Türk-Rus ilişkileri (1798–1919)* (Ankara, Türk Tarih Kurumu Basımevi, 2011) 471–72, argues this proposal emanated from the Armenian side. Khatisian, however, offers a different account in his memoir. He says that the idea to allow 300,000 Armenians to move back to Anatolia was first floated by Rauf Bey, who in the same breath proposed that '300,000 Tatars' also be permitted to settle in the region. This proposal was rejected by the delegation because, Khatisian says, 'it would have deprived us of the right to demand Turkish Armenia, which the Turks wanted to settle with Muslim elements from Transcaucasia' (Khatisian, *Hayastani Hanrapetutean tsagumn u zargatsume*, 45–46).

[20] Reynolds, *Shattering Empires*, 200–01.

[21] Reynolds, *Shattering Empires*, 202.

[22] Hovannisian, *Armenia on the Road to Independence*, 140–41.

[23] T Swietochowski, *Russian Azerbaijan, 1905–1920: The Shaping of a National Identity in a Muslim Community* (Cambridge, Cambridge University Press, 1985) 122.

had accepted at Brest-Litovsk. Even the Pan-Islamist element among the Azeri leadership came around to this view: though they opposed the notion of nationalism, they embraced independence and hence secession from Russia as a stepping-stone to eventual union with Turkey rather than as a move toward Azerbaijani statehood'.[24]

VI. 'THE UNREAL WORLD OF TRANSCAUCASIAN POLITICS'[25]

On 29 March 1918 the talks at Trabzon resumed.[26] The Ottomans again brought up the question of Transcaucasian independence, believing that if representatives of a separate Transcaucasian entity were to become the Ottomans' new legal international partners, they would approve the Russian territorial concessions awarded to them at Brest-Litovsk. But the members of the Transcaucasian delegation remained unwilling to make such a decision and tried in vain to 'persuade the Ottomans that their [undeclared] state could simultaneously be part of Russia and exempt from the treaty's terms.[27]

The Trabzon talks soon ended inconclusively because no decision had been taken on the question of independence or the final boundaries between the Ottoman Empire and Transcaucasia. The Ottomans issued one last ultimatum for recognition of the Brest-Litovsk terms. To increase the pressure General Vehib marched his forces in the direction of Batum. The Transcaucasians resorted to further recriminations while the Seim deliberated for more than a week on their dwindling options. During an emergency meeting held in Tiflis on 13 April, Seim representatives acknowledged the 'existence of a state of war' with the Ottoman Empire.[28]

Transcaucasia's makeshift army was composed mostly of Armenian and Georgian troops. In the wake of mass desertions following the October Revolution, the commanders of the Caucasus Army had agreed to the formation of Armenian and Georgian national units in an effort to plug gaps along the front facing the Ottomans. Before it was unseated from power, the Provisional Government had also agreed to transfer Armenians serving on the then-active Eastern Front to Anatolia. Only several thousand of the 35,000 men who received reassignment orders, however, made it to the Caucasus, and even then the farthest most of them got was Baku.[29] The fledgling Armeno-Georgian forces stood no chance as the Ottomans barrelled through them and drove up to occupy Batum on 13 April.

In the midst of the fight, the Georgian Social Democrats and Azeris had come to believe that independence remained the only answer to their predicament. The *Dashnaktsutiun* reluctantly agreed. On 22 April, the Seim finally took the momentous step of announcing the establishment of the Transcaucasian Democratic Federative Republic and sued for peace the next day.

[24] Swietochowski, *Russian Azerbaijan*, 122.

[25] Swietochowski, *Russian Azerbaijan*, 124.

[26] At this very time Armeno-Azeri tensions in Baku erupted into full-scale massacres of Muslims by Armenians (see Chapter 14). It is hard to imagine that word of the violence did not quickly reach the Transcaucasian delegates at Trabzon.

[27] Reynolds, *Shattering Empires*, 200.

[28] Hovannisian, *Armenia on the Road to Independence*, 153–55.

[29] Hovannisian, *Armenia on the Road to Independence*, 81.

Because of the failure to settle matters at Trabzon, changes on the ground and, suddenly, a new republic, a new round of peace talks was convened in Batum in early May. The Transcaucasian delegation, made up once more of Armenian, Azeri and Georgian members, arrived in the port town with the understanding that the Brest-Litovsk Treaty would serve as the basis of negotiations. They were quickly disabused of that notion when their opposite number in the Ottoman camp informed them that the concessions in Brest-Litovsk would no longer suffice: Kars, Ardahan, Batum, and significant parts of Tiflis and Erevan provinces were now also part of the list of Ottoman territorial demands, in addition to transit rights and other economic privileges. The Transcaucasian delegation recoiled from the demands and pleaded with the Ottomans to reconsider. But the latter were not interested in negotiating, and in order to pressure the representatives of the federative republic to sign the draft treaty they presented on 11 May, they authorised the Ottoman armies to return to the offensive.[30] Confronted by insurmountable political and military pressure, the Transcaucasia delegation bickered with one another and traded stinging barbs. They tried to drag out the talks as long as they could, but their only hope lay in intervention from outside. Unity was fast proving a farce and if any help was to be had it would have to be attained by each side separately and without the other knowing. The divisive scheming presaged the Transcaucasian Federative Republic's final demise.

Thus, the new Transcaucasian Republic's birth was overdue and all but stillborn. The Transcaucasians had squandered precious time when they might have worked on their differences to hammer out a common approach for negotiations and conditions for as good a peace as they might have obtained from the Ottomans. There were few precedents for confidence-building measures on the level required for a region the size of Transcaucasia, certainly nothing like the activities of the local councils in Erevan Province, which had successfully prevented violence from breaking out between Christians and Muslims earlier in the year, possible violence that surely in part would have been compelled reenactment of previous, unprocessed trauma from 1905–1907.

A better prepared Commissariat and Seim with stronger convictions might have been able to muster the forces, moral, legal, and military, to repulse the Ottomans and even confront Soviet Russia when it returned to conquer Transcaucasia two years later. However, their divisions remained in place and the Transcaucasian peoples and their leaders would continue to endure hunger, violence, anarchy, and a profound sense of uncertainty until the Soviets imposed their repressive peace in 1920–1921.

VII. TRAUMATIC FEARS AND THE IMPETUS FOR MUSLIM UNITY IN TRANSCAUCASIA

The peace agreements that were concluded in the spring of 1918 did not lead to improvements in relations between Muslims and Christians in Transcaucasia. During the peace talks held at Trabzon and Batum in May-June 1918, visiting Muslim delegations from both the North Caucasus and Transcaucasus approached the Ottomans

[30] Hovannisian, *Armenia on the Road to Independence*, 172–76; Reynolds, *Shattering Empires*, 206–10.

with the purpose of establishing closer relations with them and even asking that they be placed under their protection.[31]

The diverse agendas of the different groups from the Caucasus at the Batum conference were about to make clear, if it was not already transparent, the impossibility of forming a united front to conclude a single treaty. In what was about to become the Republic of Georgia, a petition

> in the name of the Muslim population of … [Akhaltsikhe and Akhalkalaki, which had large Armenian populations] pleaded for the territorial incorporation of [the two districts] within the Ottoman empire for the sake of 'rescuing the Muslims of the aforementioned districts from total extinction'.

Reynolds points out that 'the petition invoked the right to self-determination granted by the Russian Revolution':

> It observed that the two districts had been forcibly taken from the Ottoman empire in 1828 and claimed that their Muslim populations had never cut their spiritual ties to the Ottoman empire and that ethnic tensions in the region had escalated to a level that threatened the very existence of the Muslims.[32]

All this, according to the German military attaché present at Batum, Otto von Lossow, reflected 'the impact of Turkish propaganda' on the 'uneducated Muslim masses'.[33] Perhaps the Muslim deputations were drawn to the Ottoman Empire now that its star was again on the rise. Amid the tumult and disorder in the Caucasus, the Ottomans' projection of strength and confidence and the possibility of stability may have made their army's occupation welcome to the local population at large, not just the Muslims.[34]

VIII. THE ARMENIANS TRIUMPH OVER EXISTENTIAL THREATS

The Ottoman military carried out a second major incursion into Transcaucasia in May 1918. The Ottoman Third Caucasus Army under General Vehib wheeled south toward the Ararat plain and Erevan Province, the heart of Transcaucasian Armenia (Eastern Armenia). This region had become host to thousands of Armenian refugees who had survived the 1915 genocide and, under the Provisional Government, had eagerly returned to their homes in the occupied Ottoman provinces. With the beginning of the Ottoman offensive in February 1918, they had been compelled to abandon their homeland once again in a chaotic and dangerous retreat, accompanied back into the Caucasus by Armenian military forces.

[31] Reynolds, *Shattering Empires*, 200, 207; and Swietochowski, *Russian Azerbaijan*, 126. Interestingly, one delegation reminded Rauf Bey of their common Circassian heritage and urged him to adopt a more conciliatory attitude towards the Transcaucasian delegation. See Khatisian, *Hayastani Hanrapetutean tsagumn u zargatsume*, 46–47.

[32] Reynolds, *Shattering Empires*, 207.

[33] Swietochowski, *Russian Azerbaijan*, 126.

[34] E Forestier-Peyrat, 'The Ottoman Occupation of Batumi, 1918: A View from Below' (2016) 4 *Caucasus Survey* 165.

Thus, in late May, elements of the Third Caucasus Army appeared on the plains of Ararat, barely a day's march from Yerevan. In Batum, Ottoman representatives issued a 72-hour ultimatum to the Armenian deputation, by which time they must have informed the Ottomans whether the Armenians in Erevan Province intended to fight or submit. 'The very existence of the Armenian people seemed at an end', Hovannisian writes.[35] The Armenians' supplies had dwindled to nothing, they were hemmed in on all sides, and they faced an Ottoman invasion army with no place to retreat to. They looked ready to capitulate without a fight.[36]

The Armenians made what they felt might be their last stand. From 21–29 May, in the face of the threat of existential entrapment, they went into 'fight', not 'freeze', mode (see Chapter 2). Under the command of General Foma Nazarbekov, the Armenians prevailed in three separate engagements at Sardarapat, Bash-Aparan, and Karakilisa. In the midst of the fighting, division commander General Movses Silikian issued a passionate appeal to his people, exhorting them to pick up arms in the spirit of the Armenians' ancient ancestors:

> Armenians! Hasten to free the fatherland!
>
> The moment is at hand that every Armenian, forgoing his own person in the name of … the salvation of the fatherland and the defense of the honor of his wife and sisters – must expend their last bit of energy to strike the enemy … [He] … wants to exterminate our long-suffering nation. But if we are to be exterminated, would it not be better that we at least defend ourselves, with weapons in our hands? … Armenian women! Recall the noble women of the fifth century … follow their example! …. For the physical survival of a people that has suffered so much! …. Rise up! Toward holy war![37]

Remarkably, the Ottomans were beaten back. The Armenians' resistance was what led General Vehib to issue an order to retreat, acknowledging in a report that 'as long as their [the Armenians'] existence is in danger, they will prefer to die fighting'.[38]

IX. THE END OF A WARTIME ALLIANCE

Although the signing of the Treaty of Brest-Litovsk represented one of the high-water marks of the Ottoman-German alliance, there were signs that the partnership was beginning to fray.[39] In the summer of 1918, German and Ottoman strategic interests converged upon Transcaucasia, with each power eyeing this region as essential for the effective prosecution of the war. Germany sought to secure vital railway lines and oil and other mineral resources. In August, in a supplementary treaty to the Treaty of Brest-Litovsk, it permitted Baku to remain within the prospective borders

[35] RG Hovannisian, 'Armenia's Road to Independence' in Hovannisian (ed), *The Armenian People from Ancient to Modern Times* 295.

[36] See J Kayaloff, *The Battle of Sardarabad* (The Hague, Mouton, 1973) 58–59.

[37] S Vratsian, *Hayastani hanrapetutiwn* (Beirut, Mshag, 1958) 141.

[38] Reynolds, *Shattering Empires*, 211.

[39] See F Fischer, *Germany's Aims in the First World War* (New York, WW Norton and Co, 1967) 550–62; U Trumpener, *Germany and the Ottoman Empire, 1914–1918* (Princeton, NJ, Princeton University Press, 1968) 167–99.

of the Soviet Republic on condition that it provide Germany with a steady supply of oil. For their part, the Ottomans intended to build up alliances with friendly Muslim governments in the Caucasus as a way of safeguarding their vulnerable eastern flank. In so doing, they aimed to establish their influence and hegemony over the region at the expense of their senior ally.[40]

The acts of mutual sabotage began as early as May 1918, when Kaiser Wilhelm II's government authorised General Otto von Lossow to enter into secret negotiations with Georgian leaders. In exchange for physical protection, the leaders of the future Georgian republic were ready to put their country and its resources at Germany's disposal. The Ottomans meanwhile were busy recruiting men for a new military formation called the Army of Islam, to whose banners local Muslims were expected to flock to as the empire's forces advanced deeper into Transcaucasia. During the talks in Batum in May, Lossow had tried and failed to persuade the Ottomans to change their plans and hold back these forces. But Enver's half-brother, General Nuri, at the head of this invasion force, had already established his headquarters at Elisavetpol.[41] Its central objective was to march on to Baku, which was still under the control of Bolshevik forces (see Chapter 14). The German and Austro-Hungarian officers on the ground viewed the Ottoman advance with a mix of apprehension and anger, fearing that the Ottomans were seeking to crush the remaining Armenians rather than to aid their new ally, Azerbaijan, in securing its new capital.[42]

X. SACRIFICING THE ARMENIANS

During this period the Armenians were never safe from being persecuted by the forces that wanted to stamp them out of existence. The spectre of a revanchist Armenian state haunted CUP leaders well into the end of the talks at Batum. Writing to General Vehib Pasha on 21 May, for instance, Enver contended that the creation of an Armenian republic would be 'a big mistake'.[43] To the man whose homeland, Rumelia, had been, as he saw it, overrun by the former Christian slave-subjects of the empire, the Christian Armenians posed an overwhelmingly potent threat, again about 'to destabilize the Ottoman Empire', like a 'Bulgaria of the East'. A resurgent Armenian state, he continued, would be even worse than the Russian enemy because Armenia's interests, unlike Russia's, lay inside the Ottoman Empire's borders:

> If today in the Caucasus a small Armenia possessing a population of 500 to 600 thousand and sufficient territory is formed, in the future this government, together with the

[40] See Hovannisian, *Armenia on the Road to Independence*, 176–79; and S McMeekin, *The Berlin-Baghdad Express: The Ottoman Empire and Germany's Bid for World Power* (Cambridge, MA, Belknap Press of Harvard University Press, 2010) 318–39.

[41] WED Allen and P Muratoff, *Caucasian Battlefields: A History of the Wars on the Turco-Caucasian Border, 1828–1921* (Cambridge, Cambridge University, 1953) 478–79.

[42] For forceful arguments that expound this view, see V Dadrian, *The History of the Armenian Genocide: Ethnic Conflict from the Balkans to Anatolia to the Caucasus* (New York, Berghahn Books, 2003) 347–54; and Kévorkian, *The Armenian Genocide*, 702–13.

[43] ATASE, Enver to Vehib, 27 Mayıs 1334 [27 May 1918], K 2919, D 499, F 3-31, cited in Reynolds, *Shattering Empires*, 211.

> Armenians who will come mainly from America and from elsewhere, will have a population of millions. And in the east we will have another Bulgaria and it will be a worse enemy than Russia because all the Armenians' interests and ambitions are in our country. Consequently, in order to remove this danger, the formation of even the smallest Armenian government must be prevented. Land from the Muslims must not be given to the Armenians; rather, to the contrary, I prefer that the Muslims occupy provinces such as Yerevan.[44]

On 24 May, as the Armenian and Ottoman armies were waging fierce battles not far from the base of Mount Ararat, Talât wrote to Halil Bey, also expressing fears about the prospect of an Armenian state:

> A small Armenian autonomous [government] will five years later become a five million-strong Armenian state, it will dominate the Caucasus, and it will become the 'Bulgaria of the East'. All the Armenians in Iran and America will gather there and, as you describe, they will get every form of aid from the English and French, and in the future they will move against us with the Christian Georgians and also with great ease with the Iranians … Therefore, were it possible, the best thing would be to lance the boil … Since it is not possible, it is necessary that Armenia be formed in an extremely weak and unviable form.[45]

Ottoman thinking about the creation of a Turanian state with respect to an independent Armenia followed the same lines. For Ottoman ideologues, were an autonomous Armenian state to impede the territorial expansion of the Ottoman Empire, it would then endanger Ottoman suzerainty wherever and however it was composed. Thus, even after the immense massacres of Ottoman Armenians and the complete political and cultural uprooting of the Ottoman Armenian way of life, the state believed that its Armenian problem had yet to be resolved. The Armenians still posed a threat in their eyes, and they were convinced that sooner or later they would menace them again. Projection of one's own thoughts onto another is a common dynamic and very prevalent in traumatised (as well as narcissistic) individuals. It seems that the Ottomans could not comprehend that a people would want to live in peace rather than according to their own predatory modus operandi. The conditions the Ottomans imposed on the Armenian republic at Batum reflected the same exaggerated fears and misperceptions the Ottomans had had of Armenians when executing the genocide. The Ottomans, having been unable to defeat the Armenians just days earlier, now acted to confine them to a minuscule portion of the Transcaucasus. According to Hovannisian, this sacrifice was accepted by the neighbouring Georgians and Azerbaijanis as necessary for future peace with the Ottomans:

> A view pervading these discussions [held between the Georgian and Azerbaijani members of the Transcaucasian delegation in May 1918] was that one of the three constituent peoples of the Transcaucasian Federative Republic would fall victim to Turkish aggression but it was hoped that the other two, Georgians and Muslims, would maintain cordial mutual relations. It was anticipated that the Armenians would figure no longer in the politics of Transcaucasia.[46]

[44] ATASE, Enver to Vehib, cited in Reynolds, *Shattering Empires*, 211.
[45] Kurat, *Türkiye ve Rusya*, 661–62, cited in Reynolds, *Shattering Empires*, 210.
[46] Hovannisian, 'Armenia's Road to Independence', 296–97.

In Batum, Khatisian confronted the Georgian Menshevik Noi Zhordania on the Georgians' attitude toward the Armenians' future.

> Zhordania … expressed his sympathy for the Armenians, who were destined for the worst possible fate. He added, however, that the responsibility for the tragedy lay with the political party which directed the Armenian people [ie the ARF] … Zhordania … explain[ed] that, because Armenians continued to resist the Turkish forces and … the intolerable chaos in Transcaucasia, Georgia would be obliged to declare its independence. … he told his Armenian friend and associate of many years: 'We cannot drown with you. Our people want to save what they can. You, too, are obligated to seek an avenue for agreement with the Turks'.[47]

XI. THREE NEW REPUBLICS

On 26 May 1918 the Georgian Social Democrats announced in the Seim that Georgia was unable to pursue its interests in solidarity with its neighbours and declared their withdrawal from the federated republic. That very day, not mentioning their secret talks with Germany, Zhordania travelled to Poti, a Georgian port on the Black Sea, to meet with General von Lossow. Two days later, they signed an agreement formally bringing Georgia into the German fold. German troops took up positions in Tiflis and hoisted up the flag of the Kaiserreich.[48]

On 28 May the Azerbaijanis signalled their intention to leave the Transcaucasian Federation. Khan Khoiski, on behalf of the newly established Azerbaijani National Council, explained that the decision was the result of the collapse of the Russian Empire and the anarchy in Transcaucasia.[49] The proclamation did not espouse Azerbaijani nationalism or state pan-Turkism as a goal.[50] Rather, it declared Azerbaijan a democracy and professed its 'neutrality with regard to nationality, religion, and sex', key principles augured by the February Revolution.[51] Before the Azerbaijanis could look toward building their new state, however, they would have to take control of Baku, then still under the control of the Bolshevik-aligned city government. Fortunately for them, in the treaty that would be concluded at Batum, the Ottomans would agree to render them all forms of military assistance, setting the stage for a showdown in Baku.[52]

The declarations of independence issued by Georgia and Azerbaijan left Armenians with little option but to do the same. The Armenian National Council, a 15-member body created in October 1917 to carry out the executive functions of the Armenian National Bureau and represent the interests of the Armenians of Russia, issued a tepidly worded statement announcing the creation of the Armenian republic on 30 May. Later backdated to 28 May, its tone betrayed the Armenian political

[47] Hovannisian, *Armenia on the Road to Independence*, 184–85, citing the Armenian revolutionary ST Arkomed. In his memoirs, Khatisian once more recalls the conversation differently, with Zhordania laying the blame on the Armenians as a whole rather than just the ARF (Khatisian, *Hayastani Hanrapetutean tsagumn u zargatsume*, 81–82).

[48] Hovannisian, *Armenia on the Road to Independence*, 188–89.

[49] A Balaev, *Azerbaidzhanskoe natsional'noe dvizhenie v 1917–1918* gg (Baku, Elm, 1998) 204–205, cited in Reynolds, *Shattering Empires*, 213.

[50] See Swietochowski, *Russian Azerbaijan*, 129.

[51] Reynolds, *Shattering Empires*, 213.

[52] Swietochowski, *Russian Azerbaijan*, 130.

leaders' gloom.[53] 'In view of the dissolution of the political unity of Transcaucasia and the new situation created by the proclamation of the independence of Georgia and Azerbaijan', it plaintively began

> [t]he Armenian National Council declares itself the supreme and only administration for the Armenian provinces. Due to certain grave circumstances, the National Council, deferring until the near future the formation of an Armenian national government, temporarily assumes all governmental functions, in order to pilot the political and administrative helm of the Armenian provinces.[54]

Rather than heralding the triumph of a long-sought national rebirth, the leadership of the Armenian republic expressed little confidence in the future Armenia's prospects. The Armenians 'shuddered before the prospect of independence', writes Hovannisian, words conveying the traumatic shock of such unwanted independence.[55] While Georgia had Germany as a protector, and Azerbaijan had the Ottoman Empire, Armenia, without the protection of Russia, the country that could come closest to an ally, was 'abandoned and hurled upon the mercy of the same Turkish rulers who had annihilated the Armenians of the Ottoman Empire'.[56]

In the summer of 1918, the Ottomans organised plebiscites in Kars, Ardahan, and Batum in accord with the terms of the Treaty of Brest-Litovsk. The Armenians inhabiting these provinces had chosen not to find out what Ottoman occupation would entail and escaped eastwards or towards the North Caucasus. The majority of the remaining, largely Muslim, population opted to become part of the Ottoman Empire. Reynolds writes that the 'lopsided nature of the voting makes clear that the plebiscite's outcome was predetermined'.[57] Because the non-Muslim inhabitants had either already fled or were afraid to vote otherwise, fearing Ottoman reprisals, there is little reason to think that the outcome would have been any different. But holding plebiscites gave the Ottomans' annexation the veneer of compliance with the treaty.

XII. THE DEMOCRATIC REPUBLIC OF ARMENIA

On 4 June 1918, the Ottoman Empire concluded three separate treaties in Batum with Armenia, Azerbaijan, and Georgia, acknowledging the independence of these new states, drawing their respective boundaries, and recognising the Ottoman annexation of Kars, Ardahan, and Batum. The Ottomans assumed that these states would block

[53] According to Simon Vratsian, following Georgia's and Azerbaijan's declarations of independence on 26 and 28 May, respectively, the Armenian National Council decided to send a peace delegation to Batum with full authorisation to negotiate and agree to terms on behalf of an 'independent Armenia' (independence was one of the preconditions the Ottomans had set for the negotiations in Batum). Due to external pressures, however, the actual declaration did not come until two days later. On 29 May, members of the ARF met in session in Tiflis and decided that independence was the route that was to be taken. The declaration of independence was consequently issued by the Armenian National Council on 30 May, but backdated to 28 May, the day it was decided to send the peace delegation to Batum (Vratsian, *Hayastani Hanrapetutiun*, 152–54).

[54] Hovannisian, *Armenia on the Road to Independence*, 191.

[55] Hovannisian, *Armenia on the Road to Independence*, 186.

[56] Hovannisian, *Armenia on the Road to Independence*, 186.

[57] Reynolds, *Shattering Empires*, 244.

or absorb any future Russian incursion into Anatolia through Transcaucasia and thus achieve the desired *cordon sanitaire* they sought between themselves and their northern adversary.

Even as they made their peace with the Ottomans, the new republics had to contend with one another's territorial pretensions (the Batum treaties did not address the matter of borders between the Transcaucasian states). From 1918 until the Soviet invasion of the Transcaucasus, Karabakh (or 'Karabagh'), along with the adjacent regions of Zangezur and Nakhichevan, were flashpoints of interstate rivalry between Armenia and Azerbaijan.[58] In autumn 1918, Karabakh came under joint Ottoman-Azerbaijani control while chaos and internecine fighting broke out in Zangezur and Nakhichevan.

While the Ottomans were unsuccessful in smothering the young Armenian state, they did retain the ultimate say in what shape it would take. They dictated its tiny size and chose for it only dry, rocky land. The state they allowed to exist would be as unviable as they could make it. 'The land permitted to the Armenian Republic was obviously unable to support the nearly 300,000 refugees who had fled there over the course of the past three years', Hovannisian states.[59] Armenia's few fertile regions were to remain under Ottoman occupation. Without a secure alliance with a major power, the Armenian state could hardly pose a threat to them.

The obligations the Ottomans imposed on the new Armenian republic were just as harsh: Armenian officials were responsible for any behavior to which the Ottomans objected;[60] the Armenian army was to be reduced drastically in size; and they were 'to ensure the unhindered transit of Ottoman troops and supplies across the republic'. Furthermore, Armenia agreed to shoulder the responsibility of the national and cultural rights of its minorities in language absent from the agreements concluded with Georgia and Azerbaijan: the Muslim inhabitants of the state were to be granted 'full religious and cultural liberties'. The Ottomans retained 'the right to intervene' if Armenia broke any of the terms of the agreement.[61] The Armenians accepted all this in the belief that the alternative would have resulted in complete devastation and ruin.

The Ottomans came close to imposing what amounted to a continuation of genocidal policies. The Armenian people lacked food, medicine, and clothing. Starvation was widespread. The inhabitants' immune systems, already broken down due to the stresses of wartime conditions, hunger, and cold, were especially vulnerable to weakening in 1918 and into 1919 by the worldwide Spanish influenza. Already enormously reduced in numbers, one-fifth of the population of the new Armenian republic perished in the winter of 1918–1919.[62] The Germans made efforts to intervene, but their pleas for the Ottomans to ease the conditions in Armenia fell on deaf ears:

> The German representatives in the Caucasus urged their government to persuade the Turks to permit the return of the refugees [to the Ararat plain and neighbouring regions] … to harvest crops they had planted … [They] warned that, should they be denied this minimal

[58] RG Hovannisian, *The Republic of Armenia*, vol 1: *The First Year, 1918–1919* (Berkeley, University of California Press, 1971) 156–96.

[59] RG Hovannisian, *The Republic of Armenia*, vol 2: *From Versailles to London, 1919–1920* (Berkeley, University of California Press, 1982) 6.

[60] Hovannisian, *Armenia on the Road to Independence*, 196–97.

[61] Hovannisian, *The Republic of Armenia*, vol 1, 37.

[62] Hovannisian, *The Republic of Armenia*, vol 1, 130.

> favor, the Armenians would be annihilated by the end of the winter. [The] … officials complained that this extermination was fervently desired by Essad Pasha [a long-serving Ottoman officer of Albanian origin] who was intent on completing the project undertaken by General Vehib … [Thus the] crops, so vital to the Armenians, were carried away by the Turks or allowed to rot in the fields. The [Armenian] Republic's inhabitants subsisted on grasses and herbs throughout the summer and autumn, but by winter even these were gone … [m]ore than two hundred thousand orphans and refugees perished.[63]

Social historian Nora Nercessian cites a 1918 report revealing that the Ottomans went far beyond the demands they had extracted from the Armenians in the Batum treaty. In Aleksandropol (today's Gyumri), a town just to the northwest of Yerevan

> Turkish forces confiscated and transported to Turkey more than 50,000 large antlered animals, 100,000 heads of sheep, 5,000 horses, … 90,282,500 pounds … of wheat … tools, spades, and 80% of the carts in the province to prevent the future cultivation of lands to replace the wheat and barley the province had been stripped of. Stores were robbed, large quantities of furniture from homes were taken, and rugs and carpets along with large panes of glass, doors, window jams and roofing had been stripped off houses … and 12,000 individuals had been taken as slaves.[64]

It seems that the Ottomans could not even tolerate the presence of the Armenian people living in any part of their Transcaucasian homeland.

XIII. THE CUP'S TRAUMATIC FEARS AT THE TIME OF THE TURAN QUEST

General Kâzım Karabekir (during the Turkish War of Independence)
Source: Wikimedia Commons.

[63] Hovannisian, *Armenia on the Road to Independence*, 210.
[64] NN Nercessian, *The City of Orphans: Relief Workers, Commissars and the 'Builders of the New Armenia', Alexandropol/Leninakan, 1919–1931* (Hollis, NH, Hollis Publishing, 2016) 16, citing K Aleksanyan, 'Aleksandrapoli gavare 1920-i Turk-Haykakan paterazmi nakhoryakin' [the Province of Alexandropol on the Eve of the Turkish-Armenian war of 1920] (2012) *Haigazian Armenological Review* 402, n 35.

> 'Karabekir was a member of the generation including Enver and Atatürk, too, who fought forever. Their wars began before World War I and would not finish when it finished'.[65]

The photo shows a man with fixed, staring eyes, often a sign of trauma. His eyes may be reflecting the stresses of his years on the battlefield and overwhelming responsibility. The son of a general, he had fought Greeks and Bulgarians in 1906–07, served in the Balkan Wars, and had been a prisoner of war for six months. An extremely able individual and a great soldier, during World War I he saw action in different theatres before being assigned to command the Ottoman II Corps in Transcaucasia.

The fears felt by some Ottoman statesmen would have been heightened, not allayed, by the commission of genocide. They may have felt guilty about their crimes or for blaming outsiders for them and felt their condemnation. They may have been aware of and wishing to have been guided by the basic moral precepts they knew from childhood. The secrecy and cover-ups shrouding their activities, and their denial to those who witnessed and called attention to the wrongs, indicate consciousness of wrong-doing. Such exposure would have instilled anxiety and fear of outsiders' reactions to their crimes.

Guilt may partly explain why Talât and Enver claimed that the new Armenian state would become so powerful. To them such a possible state would have justified their mission to subjugate, if not destroy, the Armenians, simultaneously assuaging their guilt and bolstering their rationalisations. It would enable them to bury from consciousness their knowledge of the truth of their guilt, hiding it from themselves. From then on, they, the leaders, could and did lead their entire nation away from that knowledge and that guilt. The perpetrator punishes the victim for holding up a mirror to them that they do not want to look at, or dismisses the image in the mirror.

During this profoundly troubled period, some Transcaucasian Armenian and Muslim leaders had found room for future cooperation. As mentioned earlier, in Erevan Province a joint local council of both sides had prevented the outbreak of further massacres. When Armenia and Azerbaijan declared independence in May 1918, each extolled values ushered in by the February Revolution, including respect for the others' nationality, religion, and gender. At the time of their establishment, the Azerbaijani leadership expressed acceptance of, if not support for, the Armenian state. The two states exchanged ambassadors. Other areas where relationships could be mended or improved also emerged. Some are noted in the next chapter, which explores developments in eastern Azerbaijan during this brief period. But overall Armenian–Azerbaijani relations would remain cool, untrusting and tense over the course of 1918 and over the next two years occasionally erupt into unbridled animosity and bitterness.

[65] H Arslanbenzer, 'Kazim Karabekir: Primary Opponent of Ataturk', *Daily Sabah*, 31 March 2018. See also EJ Zürcher, *The Young Turk Legacy and National Building: From the Ottoman Empire to Atatürk's Turkey* (London, IB Tauris, 2010) 19–25.

14

Baku, 1917–1918: More Conflict, its Seeds Planted for Transmission

> This novel [*Ali and Nino*] ... made me discover the whole world that lay beneath my feet ... this Romeo and Juliet story at the height of the oil boom [1914–1920], between a Christian girl and a Muslim boy ... [It] tears away at the fabric which has covered me growing up here in Soviet Baku like a shroud, like a funeral veil dropped by the bloodiest version of the West, the inhuman Bolshevik Revolution, upon this fantastic world of the highest cultural and human aspirations – the hope of the total merger of East and West into something new and modern – which existed but for a moment in time. Can you imagine it?
>
> Fuad Akhundov,[1] speaking to Tom Reiss[2]

THE FEBRUARY REVOLUTION had inspired great hope among the Russian people. But within a short time the new government was unable to overcome the challenges the empire faced in the midst of war and great social upheaval. Food shortages continued, the economy worsened still further, and political and ethnic tensions rose throughout the huge imperial domains. Fear, chaos, and hardship threatened to overshadow hope and commitment for reform. By October 1917, the Bolsheviks had become the most vocal critics of the Provisional Government, blaming the country's woes on the government's decision to stay in the war. Their moment came and they seized power. Their coup, sudden withdrawal from the war, and dissolution of the Constituent Assembly gave rise to the White movement. Civil war erupted and spread across Russia.

Although Transcaucasia did not experience the massive set battles and resulting devastation that ravaged Russia from 1917 to 1920, a new wave of anxiety and unrest

[1] Fuad Akhundov, a Baku native, guides visitors around Baku, presenting its history as depicted in the novel *Ali and Nino*, urging us to imagine it then, a moment in time he regards as aspirational. The novel is an evocation of the city and its cultures before and during World War I. The three main characters are Ali, an Azeri Muslim, in love with Nino, a Georgian Christian, and Nacharyan, an Armenian and close friend of the lovers and, apparently, of their love. He is depicted as thoughtful and unattractive-looking, in contrast with the lovers' extreme attractiveness. Nacharyan desires Nino and forcibly abducts her, betraying both his friends. Before there is any indication of an abduction, Nacharyan tells Ali, 'If you should need any help – I'm at your disposal'. Ali then says, 'I pressed his hand warmly. It just showed: there really were decent Armenians. This was quite a disturbing thought' (K Said, *Ali and Nino: A Love Story* (New York, Overlook Press, 2016) 78).

[2] T Reiss, *The Orientalist: Solving the Mystery of a Strange and Depressing Life* (New York, Random House, 2005) xiv.

arose the Ottoman armies advanced on the Caucasus Front. Armenians, Muslims, and Russians underwent the breakdown of order that had been more or less kept by the Caucasus Army and the state, placing its peoples in what Smith graphically analogises to a 'deadly vice' – the Armenians and Russians seeing the Ottoman troops moving against them, and the Muslims perceiving the remnants of the Caucasus Army against them.[3] During the second half of 1917, as droves of Russian soldiers abandoned the front, large stores of supplies and weapons were abandoned. The acting Transcaucasian government in Tiflis armed Muslim bands and instructed them to prevent war matériel from falling into the Bolsheviks' hands. In eastern Transcaucasia, Muslim bands received arms from the French and British, who had a different aim in mind: preventing the Ottoman armies from reaching Baku.[4]

In Baku and the outlying towns and villages, as well as in Nagorno-Karabakh, Armenians and Muslims, and Muslims and Bolsheviks, each also backed by their own outlaw bands, fought over food, land and weapons. The Baku soviet raised its own forces to ensure the security of the Bolshevik government. With the collapse of legal authority, it seemed – in the natural, or even in the sociobiological, order of things – inevitable that peoples would increasingly contract into their own ethnic groups for security.

I. MUSLIM STRUGGLE FOR FEDERALISM

At least 30 Muslim political organisations had offices in Baku,[5] each with its own set of agendas and policies. They defied neat categorisation, and formulated platforms that combined some mix of Islam with nationalism, liberalism, or socialism.[6] Among the Muslim intellectual elite, for example, one could count socialists, democrats, moderate nationalists, and a handful of Bolsheviks. Theirs was a movement led by intellectual elites and workers. The vast majority of the Muslim peasantry were still politically 'inert'.[7]

According to Smith, the ideas espoused in the first secret discussions among the founders of the largest Muslim party, the Musavat, evolved from a purely pan-Islamist platform to a much more expansive agenda that celebrated pan-Islamism as well as social democracy and nationalism. By the time of the February Revolution, '[y]ears of agitation and propaganda [since its founding in 1905], not to speak of injustice and oppression, had indeed energized [its members] to social-democratic and class-conscious ideals'.[8] The Musavat Party now counted on the support of the Muslim poor and 'Muslim women [who were] voting for the first time'.[9] As strong backers of the democratic principles and socialist policies of the Provisional Government, their

[3] MG Smith, 'Anatomy of a Rumour: Murder Scandal, the Musavat Party and Narratives of the Russian Revolution in Baku, 1917–20' (2001) 36(2) *Journal of Contemporary History* 215, 223 (see Chapter 12).

[4] A Altstadt, *The Azerbaijani Turks* (Stanford, CA, Hoover Institution Press, 1992) 83–84.

[5] RG Suny, *The Baku Commune, 1917–1918* (Princeton, NJ, Princeton University Press, 1972) 85.

[6] E Ybert, 'Islam, Nationalism and Socialism in the Parties and Political Organisations of Azerbaijani Muslims in the Early Twentieth Century' (2013) 1 *Caucasus Survey* 43.

[7] Suny, *The Baku Commune*, 323.

[8] Smith, 'Anatomy of a Rumour', 224–25.

[9] Smith, 'Anatomy of a Rumour', 224–25.

liberal platform advocated 'an eight-hour day, and six-day week; special privileges for pregnant women and mothers; ... pay twice a month in cash; ... government insurance for lost work, and for inspections of workplaces and housing'.[10] In clear contrast to the Bolsheviks, the Musavatists promoted, according to Smith, 'not class polarization but ... class cooperation'.[11] They also held liberal positions on religion and national rights, applauding the Provisional Government's decision to repeal all laws that discriminated against Russian citizens on the basis of religion and nationality.[12] The party's membership grew greatly after the February Revolution.

Muslims took advantage of the new liberal atmosphere to express their identities and beliefs openly. The Russian historian LG Protasov, who reviewed the April 1917 records of the 48 Muslim deputies of the Constituent Assembly, found that all voiced their support for 'Turkification, Islamisation, Europeanisation'.[13] At the first All-Russian Muslim Congress in June 1917, deputies deliberated on the form that Muslim territorial autonomy should assume within the empire. Should it consist of a single territory inhabited by all Muslims or a collection of smaller, autonomous regions with substantial Muslim populations? Mammäd Amin Räsulzadä, the enthusiastic founder of the Himmat Party in 1911 and a creative, independent intellectual, would become president of the Democratic Republic of Azerbaijan in 1918, an office he held during its brief two years of existence.[14] Devoted to Azerbaijani independence with the aim of bringing the benefits of socialism to Muslims, which he felt had to be achieved through Muslims' self-rule,[15] he disputed the existence of a single Muslim nation. At the Congress he contended that such absence of unity also prevailed among Christians. 'There is no Christian nationality and likewise there is no Islamic one', he said, concluding, '[i]n this great Muslim house there must exist separate dwellings for Turks, Persians, and Arabs'.[16] The large majority of the Congress agreed, voting to transform 'Russia into a democratic republic based on national-territorial-federal foundations'.[17] They agreed to call on the Provisional Government to grant wider cultural autonomy to Russia's Muslims and establish a central Muslim administration to oversee their affairs.[18] The dissenting minority placed greater value in their historic and religious ties to other Muslims. For them, the more appealing idea was an abstract unity based on Islam.

[10] Smith, 'Anatomy of a Rumour', 218.

[11] Smith, 'Anatomy of a Rumour', 219.

[12] T Swietochowski, *Russian Azerbaijan, 1905–1920: The Shaping of a National Identity in a Muslim Community* (Cambridge, Cambridge University Press, 1985) 84.

[13] E Ybert, 'Islam, Nationalism and Socialism', 53.

[14] For years senior Bolsheviks treated him with more respect than they might have otherwise because it was believed that he had saved the life of the young Stalin. His political allegiances changed over his lifetime, although he always remained focused on what would work best for Muslim Transcaucasians. It appears that Räsulzadä's lack of enthusiasm for the new Soviet order forced him to flee to Turkey in the early 1920s. According to journalist Thomas Goltz, he died 'a broken man': see R Räsulzadä, 'Mammad Amin Rasulzade: Founding Father of the First Republic' (1999) 7 *Azerbaijan International* 22–23; and S Sebag Montefiore, *Young Stalin* (New York, Alfred A Knopf, 2007); T Goltz, *Azerbaijan Diary: A Rogue Reporter's Adventures in an Oil-Rich, War-Torn, Post-Soviet Republic* (London, Routledge, 1998) 18.

[15] Smith, 'Anatomy of a Rumour', 219.

[16] (1917) 10 *Der Neu Orient* 526–27, as cited in Świętochowski, *Russian Azerbaijan*, 92.

[17] SM Dimanshtein (ed), *Revolutsiia i natsionalnyi vopros* (Moscow, 1930) 3: 294, as cited in Swietochowski, *Russian Azerbaijan*, 92.

[18] See Swietochowski, *Russian Azerbaijan*, 91–93.

II. POLITICAL AND ADMINISTRATIVE STRUGGLES BEFORE AND IMMEDIATELY AFTER THE OCTOBER COUP

Overall, party politics in Baku increasingly split along ethno-religious lines. The leading members of Baku's Bolshevik party were disproportionately Russian and Armenian, while most Azerbaijani Muslims in the city and in Baku Province were either critical of Bolshevism or indifferent to it.

As noted in chapter 10, since its very founding, the Musavat Party had been caricatured by the Russian Social Democrats in 'imperial, orientalist terms, governed by the long-standing ideological categories of Muslim "backwardness", "treachery" and "religious fanaticism"'.[19] The Bolsheviks had further accused the Musavat Party of turning its back on the party's ideology in favour of pan-Islamism. This was a politically motivated charge that implicitly painted Muslims 'as a deviant and disloyal minority within the empire, manipulated by the traitorous Musavat'.[20] Russian progressives ignored the fact that they shared many of the same liberal positions as the Musavatists and could not accept even the most moderate Muslim political parties as equal working partners. However, by summer 1917 the Bolsheviks were able to swallow their pride and forge a 'tactical alliance' with the Musavatists in Baku based on mutual objectives and interests, including a common desire to see the war end.[21]

In that summer, Baku's soviet and duma failed to govern effectively, particularly failing to distribute food to the city's population fairly. For this they were harshly criticised across the political spectrum, including by an increasingly militant labour movement. In late September, more than 64,000 workers walked out after their leaders were unable to reach a settlement with their employers, bringing Baku to a standstill. The Bolsheviks capitalised on this situation by forming a strike committee intended to unify the city's working class and consolidate governmental authority under the soviet.[22]

Stepan Shaumian, leader and chairman of the Baku soviet, was widely trusted because of his prior success in mediating labour disputes on behalf of different ethnic groups and classes. To avoid provoking any repetition of the bloodletting between Armenians and Muslims in 1905–1907, Shaumian and other Bolsheviks made an effort to dispel fears of a violent takeover of the city by the party.[23] In the weeks following the strike, an intense pro-Bolshevik propaganda campaign was carried out by a Georgian member of the Baku soviet, Prokofiy Aprasionovich, as well as by Shaumian and other party stalwarts.[24] The campaign enhanced the prestige of the Bolsheviks among not only labourers but also the soldiers of the local garrison, most of whom were Armenians.

Shaumian hoped that his party's rising popularity would usher in a pro-Bolshevik majority in the elections for deputies to the Baku soviet in October 1917. But when

[19] Smith, 'Anatomy of a Rumour', 216.
[20] Smith, 'Anatomy of a Rumour', 217.
[21] Smith, 'Anatomy of a Rumour', 220.
[22] Suny, *The Baku Commune*, 213.
[23] Suny, *The Baku Commune*, 214.
[24] See Suny, *The Baku Commune*, 117–51.

the elections were held, the Musavat Party's candidates prevailed. In another election for the city duma, shortly after the October Revolution, the Bolsheviks lost badly, winning only 15 per cent of the vote. The Muslim national parties and the combined Socialist bloc each received about 25 per cent, while the Armenian national parties and the Kadets garnered the remainder.[25] In the autumn of 1917, then, Baku's populace sent two unmistakable signals that they remained unpersuaded by the relentless Bolshevik sloganeering.[26]

However, Baku's Musavat leaders, in conjunction with their more extreme leftist colleagues, issued a resolution outlining their aims once more. Protesting the imposition of Bolshevik governance, they reiterated that Baku's local 'government ought to be purely democratic and made up from the representatives of the revolutionary democracy without differentiation by nationality or party in accordance with the real strength of each party'.[27] They espoused support for a peaceful solution to conflicts between the city's pro- and anti-Bolshevik factions, counselling 'the whole democracy to join in the tactic of the conciliation'.[28] They also took a public stand on the nationality question. 'Nationalities not inhabiting defined territories', the fourth point of the Musavat's program read, 'should be granted the right of national and cultural autonomy'. Days later, from Petrograd, Lenin declared that all peoples of the former empire possessed the equal right to self-determination and that that right might take the expression of sovereign states.[29] A few weeks later, the Council of People's Commissars (*Sovnarkom*) adopted a statement addressed to the 'Toiling Muslims of Russia and the Orient', exhorting them to organise their 'national lives' as they so chose.[30]

Lenin's decree notwithstanding, Muslim leaders did not believe that the Bolsheviks in Petrograd would honour their pledges to allow the non-Russian elements of the empire to exercise their right to self-determination. Confronting official discrimination united most of the politically active Muslims of eastern Transcaucasia, regardless of where they fell on the political spectrum. While some leading Muslims worked actively for a federated Russian state under moderate socialist leadership, Swietochowski notes that the Musavat's 'main reaction to the overthrow of the Provisional Government' was 'to press forcefully the issue of autonomy'.[31]

As elsewhere in Russia and Transcaucasia, the situation in Baku kept deteriorating. Above all, hunger became even more widespread. In mid-1917, impoverished and starving Muslims protested en masse on Baku's streets, attacking an official working for the city's central food supply commission.[32] In response the soviet directed the garrison soldiers to distribute food and ordered searches of potential hoarders.

[25] Suny, *The Baku Commune*, 160.
[26] Suny, *The Baku Commune*, 159.
[27] Suny, *The Baku Commune*, 166.
[28] (1917) 82 *Bakinskii rabochii*, as cited in Suny, *The Baku Commune*, 166.
[29] For a brief overview on the Bolshevik conception of self-determination, see T Martin, *The Affirmative Action Empire: Nations and Nationalism in the Soviet Union, 1923–1939* (Ithaca, Cornell University Press, 2001) Chapter 1.
[30] Swietochowski, *Russian Azerbaijan*, 101.
[31] Swietochowski, *Russian Azerbaijan*, 99.
[32] Suny, *The Baku Commune*, 110.

But the soldiers ran roughshod over the civilians, wantonly requisitioning goods and so greatly overstepping the bounds of their authority over the next several months that, in December, thousands of Muslims marched in further protest over the lack of physical security, insisting that Muslim policemen patrol their neighbourhoods.[33]

In response, the executive committee of the soviet felt it necessary to call an emergency meeting to establish a 'military-revolutionary committee' with broad powers to restore and maintain order. But before deciding that a coalition government should instead take over,[34] an unscheduled session of the duma overrode them. A back-and-forth then ensued, as the duma and the Bolshevik-dominated soviet vied for power in the city. Of the two, the duma lacked the wherewithal to challenge the growing power of the Bolsheviks and their local allies in the military-revolutionary committee.[35] Only the committee seemed capable of maintaining order, and by the end of the year the duma acknowledged the futility of further resistance and the supremacy of the soviet. 'The Bolsheviks', writes Suny, 'had indeed succeeded in Bolshevizing the soviet'.[36] The balance of political power in Baku had shifted.

The members of the duma bore some responsibility for this transfer of power. As noted they had failed to mobilise and act in the spirit of the principles of the February Revolution and remained wedded to the rules dating to the institution's creation in 1878, in which the right to vote for duma members was limited to only 1.5 per cent of the total population, men of property. The percentage of members who were non-Christian could not exceed more than half (and would later be reduced to a third). Furthermore, the duma was insolvent. It could not feed or pay the soldiers, who by this time had in effect become the city's police. The duma's chairman, Fathali Khan Khoiskii, presided over a moribund institution in a disintegrating city.[37]

In this turbulent period of hope and fear, the city's ethnic and class-based tensions were never adequately addressed by the city's authorities. Violence directed against Muslims went unpunished. The city's failure to take measures in that regard contributed to the greater violence inflicted on the Muslims during the 'March Days', as the events soon to unfold came to be called.

III. HUNGER IN BAKU

Despite the triumph of the soviet, no single voice spoke on behalf of the city. Baku's Bolsheviks and Musavatists were at odds with and wary of each other's designs. The political acrimony led to a breakdown in basic city services. The police force was greatly reduced in numbers. Wages continued to drop precipitously, to about a third of pre-war levels.[38] As noted, extreme hunger had persisted for more than a year.

[33] Suny, *The Baku Commune*, 187–88.
[34] Suny, *The Baku Commune*, 188.
[35] Suny, *The Baku Commune*, 190.
[36] Suny, *The Baku Commune*, 192.
[37] See A Altstadt-Mirhadi, 'Baku: Transformation of a Muslim Town' in MF Hamm (ed), *The City in Late Imperial Russia* (Bloomington, Indiana University Press, 1986) 300–301.
[38] Suny, *The Baku Commune*, 178.

Grain deliveries from the North Caucasus were held up. When Shaumian intervened in the fighting between pro- and anti-Bolshevik elements in the North Caucasus, it backfired so spectacularly that it led to further delays in the shipment of foodstuffs.[39] Whatever food was available was so expensive that it was as good as unavailable: in 1917 alone prices had risen 125 per cent across the board.[40] While no social or national group was spared from the effects of hunger, privation, and want, Muslims – and especially Muslim oilfield workers – were particularly vulnerable.[41] The Musavat leaders were well aware that they lacked the political power that they, as Muslims, should have wielded in proportion to their numbers.

IV. GROWING FEAR AND POLARISATION

With the soviet emerging as the more powerful municipal body, Baku's Bolsheviks threw their weight around as they strove to establish their preeminence in the city. In their dealings with the ARF, they let the Armenian national party know that they rejected the latter's singular fixation on Ottoman Armenian matters, advising them to shift their focus to the plight of the city's working-class population.[42] The local Muslim population noticed unappreciatively that the soviet took weeks to seat representatives of the Musavat and Himmet parties. The Bolsheviks' actions proved so heavy-handed that many Baku Muslims waited impatiently for their deliverance from an outside force.

Shaumian tried to convince Muslim leaders that the Bolsheviks remained their best bet as reliable political allies. But many believed Shaumian and the Bolshevik Party had already reneged on many of their avowed principles. In February 1918, for instance, Räsulzadä published a column in *Bakinskii Rabochii* (a newspaper, the 'Baku Labourer') complaining of Bolshevik favouritism towards Armenians: 'Turkish Armenia receives a decree on self-determination, the Armenians approach their cherished dream, supported by the Dashnaktsutiun, but, for the Caucasian Azerbaijani federalists, the Baku Bolsheviks frighten them with [destruction]'.[43] Shaumian responded by defending the Bolshevik track record, claiming that they 'were opposed to all nationalists equally and would not permit national self-determination if it meant control by the nationalists'.[44] While many Muslims were not swayed by Shaumian's reasoning,[45] a considerable segment among the population, including many workers, remained supportive of him.

Yet both the soviet and the duma were fast losing the confidence of significant segments of Baku's population. Civic trust evaporated, and discord, hunger, ethnic

[39] Suny, *The Baku Commune*, 185–87.

[40] A Dubner, *Bakinskii proletariat v gody revoliutsii (1917–1920 gg)* (Baku, Azgnin, 1931) 52, as cited in Suny, *The Baku Commune*, 151.

[41] Suny, *The Baku Commune*, 346.

[42] See Suny, *The Baku Commune*, xi–xii.

[43] 27 *Bakinskii rabochii*, 17 February 1918, 143, quoted in Suny, *The Baku Commune*, 206–207.

[44] Suny, *The Baku Commune*, 207.

[45] Suny, *The Baku Commune*, 207.

discrimination and animosities, and the absence of legitimate authority enveloped the city and the wider region. The sense of foreboding was palpable, according to Suny:

> [U]nexplained shootings occurred daily; and a duel between the Moslem forces, still weak and underequipped, and the well-armed soviet and Dashnak forces was expected to break out at any moment ... [F]ear knew no national bounds. The Armenians and other non-Moslems of the city feared the growing aggressiveness they perceived in Moslems outside of the city and expected it to spread to Baku.[46]

A sense of being severed from the outside seemed to grip the entire city. The city's Muslims were cut off from their kin to the west and north. The Armenians and Russians were cut off from their coethnics and from the central government. All fell back on those around them who were familiar, being of the same ethnicity or political grouping.

V. ARMED CAMPS

The news of the rapid advance of the Ottoman armies on the Caucasus Front in late February reached the citizenry of Baku in no time. Although the more widespread fighting that the Russian civil war would bring to Baku's streets had not yet arrived, tensions between the Bolsheviks and their adversaries and between Muslims and non-Muslims continued to escalate.

To shore up the soviet's authority, Shaumian directed the disbanding of the city's garrison and had their weapons transferred to the newly created soviet militia, the Red Guard.[47] The soviet also raised a separate fighting force that would serve in a more professional capacity, the Red Army. Both of these forces drew their strength from the ranks of the formerly garrisoned troops of the Russian army and Baku's labour force. Of the Red Army's approximately 20,000 men, some 60 to 70 per cent alone were Armenian and Russian and just 10 per cent Muslim.[48]

The consolidation of soviet military power took place in tandem with the formation of national military units in Transcaucasia. The Red Army was merely one military faction created in the final months of 1917, joining separate Armenian, Georgian, and Muslim national units that had sought to fill the security vacuum left by the February and especially October revolutions.[49] The local Armenian national units in Baku, initially authorised by Tiflis when the Russian Caucasus Army began to disintegrate, were substantially enlarged by the arrival of regular uniformed Armenian soldiers from the Eastern Front who had originally been dispatched to reinforce the Caucasus Front. Severe winter weather and disrupted railway connections, arising from incidents like that in Shamkhor, had prevented them from leaving Baku. Now there were armed elements in the city primed and ready to react to provocations.

Many frightened Muslims left the city in massive numbers (the 'flight' response).[50] Others stayed, finding solidarity with those with whom they felt safest (a mix of the

[46] Suny, *The Baku Commune*, 214–15.
[47] Suny, *The Baku Commune*, 197–98.
[48] Suny, *The Baku Commune*, 270; Reynolds, *Shattering Empires*, 226.
[49] Suny, *The Baku Commune*, 197.
[50] Suny, *The Baku Commune*, 215.

'freeze' and 'fight' responses). These responses to traumatic threat underscored the shattering of any remaining working alliance between the city's mostly Russian and Armenian Bolsheviks and the Musavatists.

In the midst of panic and uncertainty, some Muslim leaders from Baku and other Muslim communities began seriously entertaining the creation of an independent state, not just an autonomous political entity within a federated state. By mid-March 1918, some Azeri members of the Seim in Tiflis were calling for Transcaucasian independence. Some imagined an independent Azerbaijan enlarged by the incorporation of parts of northern Iran and Dagestan in the North Caucasus.[51] One Muslim political leader, Nasib Ussubakov, questioned the soundness of the policy and how long a Muslim state would remain independent. It would require, he thought, its citizens' willingness to fight the Ottomans, and he doubted they would. He himself expressed no interest in union with the Ottoman Empire 'since Transcaucasia, owing to a hundred years of Russian rule, was more advanced than Turkey'.[52]

VI. THE MARCH DAYS MASSACRE

On 30 March 1918, the steamship *Evelina* docked at Baku's harbor, carrying members of the Caucasus Native Cavalry Division, better known as the Savage Division, a Russian military unit comprised largely of Kabardian, Chechen, Circassian, Tatar, and Dagestani servicemen and Russian and Georgian officers. They had travelled to Baku to attend a funeral for a fallen comrade, arriving fresh from a dispute over unfair grain distribution in nearby Lenkoran.[53] The men hailed from various North Caucasian Muslim tribes. Feared, crack equestrians, they had been ardently loyal to their division commander, the tsar's brother, who had lived with and like them. Men from noble Russian families served proudly as their officers. Beyond the anger over the immediate grain situation, this Cossack-like unity of Muslims who had fought for the ostensibly Christian Russian Empire, although indifferent to politics, felt betrayed by both the Provisional Government and the Bolsheviks. While they had remained loyal to the former, they refused to have anything to do with the latter.[54]

There are different versions of what took place, but not of the general course of events. When the *Evelina* docked, the soviet sent agents, possibly armed, to inquire about the purpose of their visit. One version has it that as the agents began to board

[51] Swietochowski, *Russian Azerbaijan*, 121. This rhetoric revived after the breakup of the USSR when some interested circles within Azerbaijan and the US advocated for a union between Azerbaijan and northern Iran (which by various estimates has more than 20 million Azeris).

[52] Swietochowski, *Russian Azerbaijan*, 121.

[53] MG Smith, 'The Russian Revolution as a National Revolution: Tragic Deaths and Rituals of Remembrance in Muslim Azerbaijan' (2001) 49 *Jahrbücher für Geschichte Osteuropas* 376. For the most recent appraisal of the March events, see MG Smith, 'Power and Violence in the Russian Revolution: The March Events and Baku Commune of 1918' (2014) 41 *Russian History* 197.

[54] Altstadt, *The Azerbaijani Turks*, 85. Information on the division may be found in AV Venkov and KB Mamsirov, 'Kavkazskaia Konnaia Tuzemnaia Diviziia i ee komandir Velikii Kniaz Mikhail Aleksandrovich v Period Pervoi Mirovoi Voine' (2014) 183 *Izvestiya VUZov Severo-Kavkazskii region* 38–45.

the ship, the soldiers of the Savage Division fired on them, wounding some and killing others. A group of Muslim and Armenian Bolshevik emissaries from the city were immediately sent to persuade the men to hand over their weapons. When news spread of the disarming of this honour guard, the city's Muslims demanded that the weapons be returned and that they themselves now be provided with arms. Word then went round the city that the soviet planned to concede to these demands. This might have concluded the incident had 'not the atmosphere in the city been saturated with the anxieties of the past months and the conviction that a national feud was overdue', according to Suny.[55] Instead, 'the city was turned into an armed camp'.[56] Soldiers of the soviet were reportedly fired upon on the streets. Negotiations between the soviet and local Muslim leaders to defuse the threat of civil war led nowhere.

The next day the soviet issued a declaration that the situation was out of control. It blamed the Musavatists for fomenting revolt, casting the events in a primarily anti-Bolshevik, rather than ethnic, light, and making note of the deep social, economic, and ethnic fissures that had split Baku apart in the previous six months. Within hours, fighting spread out across the city and the oilfields. Some of the soviet's members, Armenian, Muslim and Russian alike, again claimed that Muslims had planned an anti-Bolshevik counterrevolution and marshalled the power under their command to neutralise the threat.[57] The soviet's forces were joined by the Armenian militias and placed under the command of the newly created Committee of Revolutionary Defence. On the evening of 31 March, the committee's forces launched an assault on the relatively unarmed Muslim quarter of Baku. Their superior firepower quelled the uprising by the end of the next day. Negotiations were held with delegates from the Musavat Party, who capitulated to all of the soviet's demands.

The violence should have ended there. However, Bolshevik authorities did not, or could not, restrain the ARF militia and other armed Armenians. For the next 'day and a half they looted, killed, and burned in the Muslim quarter',[58] Suny writes:

> The Armenian soldiers ... were indiscriminate in their vengeance, killing even Moslems who were pro-Bolshevik. The Ismailie Building, one of the finest examples of Moslem architecture in the city, was burnt down ... Almost the entire upper part of the city, from the Bazaar to Chemberekend, was burning by the afternoon ..., and the battle continued on the mountain which rises in the center of Baku. Only toward the evening of [that day], after three days of fighting, did the battle come to a close and the looters take over the streets.[59]

'The relatively well-armed and disciplined Bolsheviks and Dashnaks succeeded in crushing the Musavat ... In the process they turned the Caspian port into a "redoubt of terror and pogrom" ... against Muslims as a whole', adds Reynolds.[60] Shaumian

[55] Suny, *The Baku Commune*, 216.

[56] Suny, *The Baku Commune*, 216.

[57] Suny, *The Baku Commune*, 218.

[58] Suny, *The Baku Commune*, 224.

[59] Suny, *The Baku Commune*, 223–24. Suny here is citing *Biulleten' komiteta revolutsionnoi oborony*, no 3 (6 April 1918); N Narimanov, *Stat'i i pis'ma biografcheskim ocherkom* (Moscow, 1925) 6.

[60] Reynolds, *Shattering Empires*, 200. The 'redoubt of terror and pogrom' (*Hort des Terrors und des Pogroms*) comment is originally from J Baberowski, *Der Fiend ist überall: Stalinismus im Kaukasus* (Munich, Deutsche Verlags-Anstalt, 2003) 138.

put the overall death count at 3,000,[61] while contemporary Azeri estimates claimed as many as 12,000 Muslim deaths.[62]

In the aftermath of the massacre, Baku witnessed the further exodus of the Muslim population. A few months later, more than 6,000 workers from a single plant threatened to leave if civil authorities did not make good on grain deliveries to the city.[63] According to both Suny and Reynolds, an utterly extraordinary '*one-half* of the city's Muslims fled to the countryside' (emphasis added).[64] Among those who fled were local council members and men serving in the Muslim militias. Suny adds that the Muslim political parties 'were not again to play a role until the Turkish army reinstated them. The Muslim National Council and Muslim military units simply disappeared'.[65] Historian Audrey Altstadt cites the observation of the British vice-consul in Baku that 'not a single Musulman of any importance remain[ed]'.[66] All important posts in Baku were now held by Armenians, Georgians or Russians. The exception was Nariman Narimanov, an Azeri educator and writer in charge of social welfare and a decade-long sympathiser of the Bolshevik cause.[67]

On 1 April 1918, a day after the conclusion of the violence, members of the Committee of Revolutionary Defense tried to reengage with Muslims but failed to coax them 'back into the fold of the "revolutionary democracy"'.[68] Muslims continued to leave the city in such numbers that by June, authorities in Astrakhan, on the northern end of the Caspian Sea, let it be known that they might turn away additional refugees.[69] The soviet may have intended to entice Muslims to stay, or to induce those who had left to return, but with the aim of bringing them around to the Bolshevik Party position. This offer was unpalatable for most Muslims, especially because the soviet had effectively given impunity to those responsible for the March outrages.

The Armenians who took part in the massacres and looting during the second phase of violence during the March Days were acting out of fear and vengeance, their feelings overdetermined by decades of unpunished crimes against their ethnic kin in the Ottoman Empire: the Hamidian massacres, the 1909 Adana massacre, the many smaller killings in the eastern Ottoman provinces, and the violence and losses in 1905–1907 in Transcaucasia, the genocide, and now the recent threat posed by the advance of the Ottoman army. All of this contributed to the climate of fear and mistrust in Baku.

[61] S Sef, 'Bakinskii Oktiabr' (1930) 11 *Proletarskaia Revolutsiia* 72, cited in F Kazemzadeh, *The Struggle for Transcaucasia, 1917–1921* (New York, Philosophical Library, 1951) 75.

[62] JH Sicotte, 'Baku: Violence, Identity, and Oil, 1905–1927' (PhD thesis, Georgetown University, 2017) 159.

[63] Suny, *The Baku Commune*, 297.

[64] Reynolds, *Shattering Empires*, 200.

[65] Suny, *The Baku Commune*, 225.

[66] Altstadt, *The Azerbaijani Turks*, 86, quoting from a report sent to the War Office and cited in AJ Plotke's unpublished manuscript, 'We Must Trust to What We Can Improvize [sic]: The British Empire and the Intelligence Operations in North and South Russia, 1918', 327.

[67] Ybert, 'Islam, Nationalism and Socialism', 43–58, 53.

[68] Suny, *The Baku Commune*, 223–24.

[69] Suny, *The Baku Commune*, 297.

VII. THE SIGNIFICANCE OF THE MARCH DAYS

The immediate political consequence of the March Days was the full consolidation of Bolshevik power in Baku. Shaumian declared the situation a 'victory' when he wired the Bolshevik government in Petrograd: '[W]e are the bosses of the situation in the full sense of the word'.[70] Exulting in the soviet's success in establishing Bolshevik pre-eminence in the city, Baku's Bolsheviks ordered the Armenian National Council in Baku to 'cease conducting searches, making arrests, and collecting taxes' and to 'merge its troops with the Soviet's forces'.[71] They decreed the closure of all 'bourgeois' newspapers. Yet the Bolsheviks did not risk further estranging the city's remaining population, especially the Armenians, whose support they relied on. Later Shaumian privately admitted that he and colleagues had deliberately sought to ratchet up tensions to bring on a showdown between the city's Armenians and Muslims.[72]

As is evident from the above, after the Bolshevik coup, Shaumian himself had changed. He loftily criticised Transcaucasia as a backward, 'petty-bourgeois country' plagued by rival nationalisms. He no longer cultivated the trust of non-Bolsheviks, as he had previously. He attacked both Mensheviks and Musavatists 'with insult'.[73] Sarcastically, he 'singled out those Muslims "who dream of making Baku into the capital of Azerbaijan". The name *Azerbaijan* in his mouth had the ring of a term of derision', Swietochowski notes.[74] He and Dzhaparidze, who had long been involved with progressive Muslim causes, instead showed 'contempt for the Muslims … [regarding them] as immature from the revolutionary viewpoint and culturally inferior'.[75]

For many Muslims, Bolshevism and Armenian nationalism were now indistinguishable: both carried negative connotations and were associated with each other, especially because of the Bolsheviks' reliance on the Armenian forces. Since Muslims saw that the Armenians shared power with the Russians, comments Altstadt, 'It is hardly surprising that Azerbaijani Turks regarded soviet power as Russian-Armenian rule'.[76] The only politically active Muslims still in Baku were the leftist Himmat members, and presumably even some of them had fled. From then on, writes Swietochowski, 'Azerbaijani leaders … placed their hopes no longer in the Russian Revolution but in support from Turkey'.[77]

On 13 April 1918, one week prior to the founding of the short-lived Democratic Federative Transcaucasian Republic and just over a month from the founding of the three new republics, Shaumian and his colleagues, taking into account the prevailing

[70] Suny, *The Baku Commune*, 227.

[71] Swietochowski, *Russian Azerbaijan*, 118–19.

[72] Swietochowski, *Russian Azerbaijan*, 115.

[73] On Shaumian's 'petty-bourgeois' comment, see Suny, *The Baku Commune*, 175. From *Bakinskii rabochii*, no 86 (18 November 1917), and Shaumian, *Izbrannye proizvedeniia*, II, 117–18; and Hovannisian, *Armenia on the Road to Independence*, 117.

[74] Swietochowski, *Russian Azerbaijan*, 114.

[75] Swietochowski, *Russian Azerbaijan*, 135, quoting Soviet historian Ia Ratgauzer in his *Revoliutsiia i grazhdanskaia voina*, 177.

[76] Altstadt, *The Azerbaijani Turks*, 87.

[77] Swietochowski, *Russian Azerbaijan*, 119.

disunity in Transcaucasia, dissolved the discredited duma and assumed full control of the city. They created a new authoritative body, the *Sovnarkom*, modelled on the government led by Lenin, though it would from thereon be referred to as 'the Commune', after the Paris Commune of 1871. Under this 'short-lived experiment in maximalist socialist administration', Shaumian now planned to extend Bolshevism over all of Transcaucasia.[78] The Baku Bolsheviks' newly attained power was sanctioned by the central government in Petrograd (Lenin and the others would relocate their offices to Moscow on 5 March 1918).

The Commune was subject to directives from Moscow. In April 1918, the Baku *Sovnarkom* decided to effectively sideline the ARF and the Right Socialist Revolutionaries from the political process.[79] Within weeks, the Commune enacted the maximalist Bolshevik vision in Baku: levying a massive tax on capitalists, taking real estate out of private hands, and nationalising the oil industry. Soon all these changes were modified or dropped. By this time, the Russian civil war was in full swing, though its physically destructive effects would not be felt for a few years' time. The approaching Ottoman Army of Islam posed the immediate danger to Baku's Bolshviks.

The embittered mass of Muslims showed little responsiveness to Bolshevik gestures. Afterwards, Azeri leaders spoke no longer of autonomy but rather of separation. They no longer placed their hopes in the Russian Revolution but in a resurgent and vengeful Ottoman army.[80] Contemporary reports about a political assassination that took place on Baku's streets, writes Smith, reflected the demonising stereotypes the Bolsheviks had expressed about Muslims. He points out that they have since been repeated in Soviet historiography, 'prefiguring and empowering the plot line of social polarization that has survived so tenaciously to this day'.[81] That traumatising discrimination was already in existence in 1917 and 1918 and was, as Smith points out, lastingly transmitted. The March Days marked a turning point after which, some scholars believe, reconciliation between Muslims and Armenians became impossible. But while it was a turning point, it was not perhaps the end point. At this moment in this narrative, we are in the middle of a long story of the basic struggle for the dignity of security and respect by but not yet for all parties, one held up in measurable part by each's own unprocessed collective trauma.[82]

[78] Suny, *The Baku Commune*, 214–15.
[79] Suny, *The Baku Commune*, 228–30.
[80] Swietochowski, *Russian Azerbaijan*, 119.
[81] Smith, 'Anatomy of a Rumour', 215, 240.
[82] For a discussion of the motivation for dignity, see D Hicks, *Dignity: The Essential Role It Plays in Resolving Conflict* (New Haven, Yale University Press, 2011).

15

World War I's End in Eastern Transcaucasia: War Fever Sparks the Turan Quest and Race Murder

By June 1918 Ottoman armies had retaken the formerly Armenian-inhabited provinces in eastern Turkey as well as Kars, Batum, and Ardahan and more in Transcaucasia. But they had not succeeded in eliminating the Armenians or an Armenian state. The Russian civil war in Transcaucasia between the Bolsheviks and the disparate parties making up the so-called White opposition had hardly begun. A vacuum of power still remained, making it a good moment for the Ottomans – in violation of the Erzincan Truce and the Brest-Litovsk Supplementary Treaty – to continue their offensive in Transcaucasia to Baku. For some of them, one object included establishing Turan.

With Allied victory over the Central Powers just a few months away, World War I was about to come to an end. The Allies would launch a massive offensive against the Central Powers in Europe across the Western Front and the Middle East along the Palestinian and Mesopotamian fronts. The Ottomans would retreat as British and French forces closed in from behind. By September, Bulgaria, which had joined the Central Powers in late 1915, would sue for peace and Germany would begin negotiations for an armistice with the Wilson administration.

The CUP leadership resigned on 8 October 1918, leaving a caretaker government to discuss an armistice with the Allies. On 30 October, aboard the British warship HMS *Agamemnon*, anchored off the coast of Mudros, a port town on the Aegean island of Limnos, Ottoman delegates and Allied officials agreed upon the following conditions: an immediate cessation of hostilities, the demobilisation of the Ottoman armies, the Allies' right to occupy any part of the empire's former eastern and south-eastern provinces – those in which Armenians had lived in their largest numbers – and the release of all Armenians who were held against their will by Muslim families. Several days later, a massive Allied fleet steamed up the Bosphorus, and Istanbul came under military occupation.

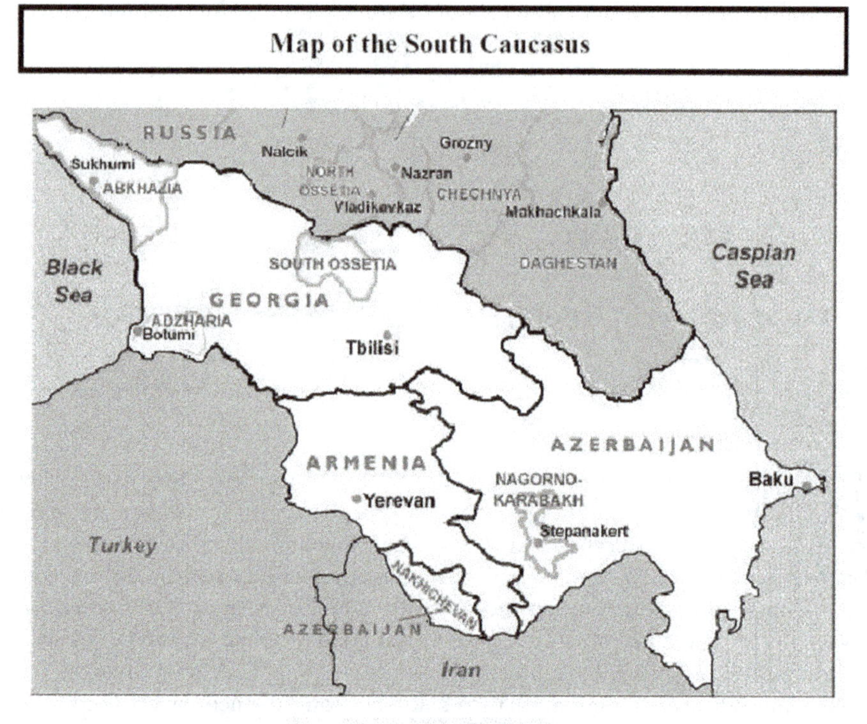

I. THE PURSUIT OF TURAN BEFORE THE BOLSHEVIK REVOLUTION

At the start of World War I, Ottoman statesmen adopted different approaches arising from historic Ottoman stratagems to prevail against the Entente. One effort intended to stir up pan-Islamic feelings and solidarity around the world. This formally began with Sultan Mehmed V Reşad issuing a proclamation from Istanbul for Muslims worldwide to rise up against their colonial oppressors. Another invoked race and territory to promote a vision of an expanded 'Turkish' state. Gökalp composed one poem in August 1914 that went, 'The lands of the enemy will be ruined! / Turkey will grow and become Turan … Each of its regions will be a new Balkan!'[1]

In the months preceding the Ottoman entry in the war, Talât had gathered a small circle of confidantes around him made up of provincial officials and committee leaders. Among them was Enver Pasha's cousin, Hasan Tahsin (Uzer), former CUP governor of Van and now of Erzurum, and an ardent proponent of further imperial

[1] E Köroğlu, *Ottoman Propaganda and Turkish Identity: Literature in Turkey during World War I* (London, IB Tauris, 2007) 122.

expansion to the east. Tahsin's influential office was located in a region close to the border with Transcaucasia. In September 1914, he telegraphed Talât to paint 'a rosy picture of pro-Istanbul sympathies [in the region], even in Northern Iran, along with unrest in Russian Azerbaijan' and boasted of having well-equipped paramilitary forces at his disposal.[2] In another communication he appealed to Talât to permit him to 'occupy and rule Azerbaijan'.[3]

The Special Organization, overseen by Doctors Şakir and Nazım, also directed its energies towards the east in late 1914, circulating propaganda leaflets calling for holy war. One such proclamation in Persia called on the faithful to 'oust the Christian enemy from our land'.[4] The American missionary, Clarence Ussher, recalled that the deputy governor of Van, Cevdet Bey, led 'bands of volunteers across the border to stir up the Persians against Russia and by destroying and plundering many Christian villages, to arouse their lust for blood so that they might be incited to join in a holy war'.[5]

II. WAR FEVER RELAUNCHES THE PURSUIT OF TURAN

As the Ottoman armies began to advance into Transcaucasia in February 1918, foreign observers sounded alarms over the impending danger to Armenians and other Christians in the region. The long-serving American representative in Transcaucasia, Consul F Willoughby Smith, fired off a number of frantic telegrams to his government about the likely consequences of a renewed Ottoman incursion into the Transcaucasus. He conveyed his belief that local Muslims were impatiently waiting for the Ottoman arrival 'in order to show their hand' and destroy the Christian population.[6] The US State Department admonished Smith to refrain from interfering in Russian affairs. Undeterred, Smith advised his country to clear out of Transcaucasia to enable the 'Christian races time to form an agreement with the Ottomans'.[7]

The dissolution of the Russian army on the Caucasus Front had reawakened grandiose imperial designs among Tahsin and other CUP ideologues. As Kieser puts it, 'A fever … had spread among ambitious parties who wanted to play a role in the scheme of conquest'[8] and who espoused an eagerness for the 'great cause'. Enver's defeat early in the war at Sarikamish had only set back the Ottomans' eastward dreams. The changed times found a deputy of Tahsin pressuring his CUP superiors to resume the

[2] H-L Kieser, *Talaat Pasha: Father of Modern Turkey, Architect of Genocide* (Princeton, NJ, Princeton University Press, 2018) 194.

[3] Kieser, *Talaat Pasha*, 200.

[4] AMAE, *Perse*, ns, vol 18, ff 112, 113, cited in R Kévorkian, *The Armenian Genocide: A Complete History* (London, IB Tauris, 2011) 225.

[5] CD Ussher, *An American Physician in Turkey: A Narrative of Adventures in Peace and in War* (Boston, Houghton Mifflin, 1917) 226. On Ottoman propaganda activities in Transcaucasia, see T Swietochowski, *Russian Azerbaijan, 1905–1920: The Shaping of a National Identity in a Muslim Community* (Cambridge, Cambridge University Press, 1985) 80.

[6] F Willoughby Smith to David R Francis, National Archives and Records Administration (NARA), College Park, MD, Record Group 84 (hereafter RG 84), vol 10, 3 January 1918.

[7] Paraphrase of Consul Smith's report of 7 January 1918, NARA RG 84, vol 10.

[8] Kieser, *Talaat Pasha*, 200.

campaign for Turan, writing, 'Hitherto, there was not the [necessary] seriousness, effort, and contribution to pursue vigilantly the road to Turan. I assure [you] that within two months Azerbaijan, including Tabris [sic], can be occupied without any illusion'.[9] Years later one Ottoman officer recalled in his memoirs: 'We went to Turan. We were to enter Iranian Azerbaijan to arm the Azerbaijani Turks, then to proceed to Turkestan [Russian Central Asia], to arm the Turks there. Thus we wanted to work for the great cause of Turan'.[10]

Renewed prospects in the east were discussed and given ample space in the press, and touted by state officials. Gökalp launched a new journal emphasising 'racial, religious, and economic – not political – unity', using words that Kieser characterises as resembling 'blueprints for European fascism'.[11] 'Gökalp's Turan', he writes, 'reemerged after its aborted 1914 boom and again proved its deathly potential, as it went hand in hand with the will to partially (Talât) or entirely (Major General Halil Kut, Enver's uncle) destroy the remaining Armenians in the Caucasus'.[12]

In preparing for a new military campaign in the east, Talât, as the head of government, took wider strategic risks into account. Shortly before the May 1918 battles in which the Armenians checked the Ottoman advances at Sardarapat and Karakilise, he spoke publicly, if cautiously, in favour of the creation of an Armenian state. If a negotiated settlement were to be had with the Allies that summer, Talât wanted to be in a position to argue that he had not been totally insensitive to the plight of the Armenians. This would soften international outrage over the Ottomans' treatment of the Armenians and thereby secure more advantageous terms at the negotiating table in the anticipated post-war settlement with the Allies.[13] In his biography of Talât, Kieser cites a telegram to Enver wherein Talât wrote, 'if, God beware, we failed [militarily] against the Armenians, this would be ugly in the eyes of the world and dangerous for our country'. Kieser adds what Talât did not explicitly articulate, namely, that failure to do so would mean that their 'crimes would then be revealed and entail political consequences'.[14]

Just as they had feared the 1914 Yeniköy Accord as a prelude to the partition of the empire, both Talât and Enver feared the emergence of an Armenian state on their eastern flank and intended to prevent its establishment. Failing that, the Ottomans had to weaken the Armenians lest 'a strong Armenia would have a strong international voice and make its case against Turkey'.[15] We know that on 27 May 1918 Enver had informed General Vehib of his fears:

> [i]f in the future a small Armenia is established, it will take orders from America … It would become a country of millions and again for us a kind of Bulgaria in the East, and a more harmful enemy than Russia, because all Armenian interests and wishes are focused on our country …[16]

[9] Kieser, *Talaat Pasha*, 256.
[10] Kieser, *Talaat Pasha*, 207.
[11] Kieser, *Talaat Pasha*, 368.
[12] Kieser, *Talaat Pasha*, 355.
[13] Kieser, *Talaat Pasha*, 369–76.
[14] Kieser, *Talaat Pasha*, 365–66.
[15] H-L Kieser, email message to the author, 15 January 2019.
[16] Kieser, *Talaat Pasha*, 366.

CUP policy evolved to neutralise the Armenians from ever forming a threat. During the May peace talks at Batum, Otto von Lossow, the German military attaché at the embassy in Istanbul, reported to the Foreign Office that

> [t]he aim of Turkish policy is the permanent occupation of the Armenian districts [of Transcaucasia] and the extermination of the Armenians. All of Talaat's and Enver's assurances to the contrary are lies. In Constantinople, the extreme anti-Armenian trend has gained the upper hand.[17]

However, having been unable to defeat the Armenians in the battles of late May 1918, the Ottomans opted for a policy of containment and, apparently, even proposed the idea of alliance. Just before the Batum treaty was signed, General Vehib made, to the incredulity of Armenian leaders, the astonishing proposal that they, the Armenians, join the Ottomans in a new offensive against the British in Persia.[18] The proposed alliance took advantage of the Armenians' weakness and isolation. The delegation turned Vehib down.

III. WHAT *DID* THE CUP WANT?

In September 1918, Kut, as he wrote in his memoirs, told Armenian leaders that he would 'not leave a single Armenian on the surface of the earth'.[19] Was the CUP seeking, or considering seeking, to extend the genocide into the former Russian imperial lands in Transcaucasia? Declarations and threats to that effect certainly were made. Or were they meant or intended to intimidate and cow the Armenians into submission?

IV. MILITARY AND POLITICAL PREPARATION FOR THE ASSAULT ON BAKU

In spring 1918, the newly created unit within the Ottoman army, the Caucasian Army of Islam, set up its main base of operations in Elisavetpol, the seat of the Azerbaijani government-in-exile. The army was ostensibly intended to strengthen the influence of Islam in the Caucasus and bring the Muslims of the region into a closer political and spiritual bond with the Ottoman state.[20] The 18,000 men that made up the Army of Islam were an unusual mix. Led by Enver's nephew, Major General Nuri Pasha, its officers included Ottomans, Germans, and Russians (the latter ex-POWs), the Christians among them far outnumbering the Muslims.[21] The troops came from

[17] Kieser, *Talaat Pasha*, 366–67.

[18] RG Hovannisian, *Armenia on the Road to Independence, 1918* (Berkeley, University of California Press, 1967) 196.

[19] H Bozarslan, 'L'extermination des Arméniens et des Juifs; quelques élements de comparaison' in H-L Kieser and DJ Schaller (eds), *Der Völkermord an den Armeniern und die Shoah/The Armenian Genocide and the Shoah* (Zürich, Chronos, 2002) 322–23.

[20] MA Reynolds, *Shattering Empires: The Clash and Collapse of the Ottoman and Russian Empires 1908–1918* (Cambridge, Cambridge University Press, 2011) 222.

[21] Reynolds, *Shattering Empires*, 223.

only somewhat less varied backgrounds – regular Ottoman troops, irregulars from Georgia, former soldiers of the Savage Division, members of Azerbaijan's nascent national forces, and, finally, local Azeris who were pressed into service and given little training. The men in this final category were expected to enlist in enthusiastic numbers, but they fell far short of Ottoman recruitment targets.[22] In September 1918, even as they were preparing for their final push onto Baku, Enver had to reassign more forces from the regular Ottoman army to reinforce the Army of Islam.

After the March Days, Baku's Bolsheviks had renamed and reconstituted their government along the lines of the 1871 Paris Commune. The Ottomans now aimed to topple it with their new army and restore Baku to the Azerbaijani government. All the same, the Ottoman command acted imperiously in their dealings with Azerbaijani leaders – more than the latter may have expected from their purported allies.[23] The Ottomans 'convinced' the Azerbaijani National Council to relocate from Tiflis to Elisavetpol and dissolve itself. A new cabinet of mostly non-Musavat ministers led by Fathali Khan Khoiskii weakened the nationalist party's position in relation to its opponents.[24] Ottoman leaders now had a pliable government from whom they could expect cooperation on every level.

V. CLOSING IN ON BAKU

The Army of Islam marched on Baku through territory mostly inhabited by Muslim peasants and nobles. To date the peasants had remained largely unmoved by Bolshevik appeals, and once the Army of Islam and Muslim political parties 'saturated [them] with Musavatist and nationalist propaganda', there remained few supporters for the 'Armenian–Bolshevik alliance in Baku' in the countryside.[25]

Shaumian's deputy, Dzhaparidze, likened the approaching Muslim forces to the 'closing [of] a counterrevolutionary circle' around the city.[26] The Commune's Red Army had at its disposal some 20,000 troops, enough men on paper to meet the Ottoman challenge. This numerical strength gave the Commune the confidence to dispatch its army westwards in early June 1918 in a bid to neutralise the nest of counter-revolutionary resistance centred in Elisavetpol.[27]

However, physical conditions were rough on the men, and most Azeri peasants remained unsympathetic, if not downright hostile, to the new Bolshevik regime. The Bolsheviks had delivered on the long-promised redistribution of land only a few weeks before, at a time when the peasants had already taken matters into their own

[22] Reynolds, *Shattering Empires*, 223.

[23] Swietochowski, *Russian Azerbaijan*, 131–32.

[24] RG Suny, *The Baku Commune, 1917–1918* (Princeton, NJ, Princeton University Press, 1972) 287.

[25] Suny, *The Baku Commune*, 323.

[26] Dzhaparidze, 'Telegramma v Tiflis', 9 April 1918, and 'Doklad na chrezvychainom zasedanii soveta rabochikh, soldatskikh, i matrosskikh deputatov bakinskogo raiona', 8 April 1918, 223–26 in Izbrannye stat'i, rechi i pis'ma; and AB Kadishev, *Interventsiia i grazhdanskaia voina v Zakavkaz'e* (Moscow, 1960) 84–89, cited in MG Smith, 'Anatomy of a Rumour: Murder Scandal, the Musavat Party and Narratives of the Russian Revolution in Baku, 1917–20' (2001) 36(2) *Journal of Contemporary History* 226–44.

[27] Reynolds, *Shattering Empires*, 224–26.

hands by launching a violent campaign against their landlords and private owners.[28] It was far too late to gain the peasants' trust or support.[29] The Commune troops did nothing to endear themselves to the local population, and even made

> … a mockery of the Commune's claim to champion the cause of the exploited peasantry, Muslim and Christian alike. As one Armenian Bolshevik lamented about the Communards, their hatred toward Muslims motivated 'requisitions, contemptuous treatment, and frequent shootings' and thereby unnecessarily alienated them.[30]

The Commune army disintegrated within weeks, not least because of the harsh conditions of the physical environment. The men lacked water, other basic supplies and had no local support. They were plagued by hot weather and dysentery. Under such conditions, the Commune forces stood no chance against the Army of Islam. In August its strength was completely shattered in an engagement near Kurdamir,[31] exposing the Armenian population in the region around Elisavetpol to attack and sparking the flight of thousands who sought refuge in Baku.[32]

VI. INTERNATIONAL COMPETITION FOR BAKU

Germany, Britain, and the Soviet regime in Moscow each had vested interests in not seeing Baku fall to the Ottomans. Ahead of the Army of Islam's advance, they took steps to frustrate the Ottomans' plans. Lenin, desperate to not lose control of the city's strategically vital oil fields, asked Germany for support in reining in their ally. The Germans obliged but demanded, as the price for their assistance, further concessions in the shape of territory and a 25 per cent share of Baku's oil's output. Yet the Germans overestimated the level of influence they could exert against the Ottomans. Enver issued dual sets of orders to conceal his true intentions from his ally. One, made public, dissembled and provided assurances of peaceful Ottoman objectives in Baku. The other, internal correspondence encouraged Ottoman commanders to hasten their advance. They outsmarted their German allies.

Since the Bolshevik Revolution, the British, too, had aimed to keep the Central Powers, as well as the newly established regime in Moscow, out of Baku. They intended to ensure the security of their own communication lines to Persia, Afghanistan, and India and put a damper on Pan-Turkic activity.[33] British major general Lionel Dunsterville of the Indian Army had received orders in December 1917 to lead a small force to deny the Germans and Ottomans access to Baku and, to the extent possible, the Transcaucasus. He was to encourage the consolidation of a broad regional alliance that would unite the three new republics against the Central Powers.[34] If necessary, his

[28] Y Murgul, 'Baku Expedition of 1917–1918: A Study of the Ottoman Policy Towards the Caucasus' (thesis, Bilkent University, 2007) 126.

[29] Murgul, 'Baku Expedition of 1917–1918', 126.

[30] Reynolds, *Shattering Empires*, 225–26.

[31] WED Allen and P Muratoff, *Caucasian Battlefields: A History of the Wars on the Turco-Caucasian Border, 1828–1921* (Cambridge, Cambridge University, 1953) 486–89.

[32] Suny, *The Baku Commune*, 292.

[33] Murgul, 'Baku Expedition of 1917–1918', 156–57.

[34] Murgul, 'Baku Expedition of 1917–1918', 156.

men were to occupy and burn Baku's oilfields, processing equipment, and port.[35] The British planned to support a 'uniting of Georgia, Azerbaijan and Armenia … under … a federation against the Germans and Turks'.[36]

VII. SHOWDOWN AND MASSACRE IN BAKU

In late summer 1918 the military threat combined with worsening living conditions added to the misery of Baku's long-suffering inhabitants. 'The principal diet of the people', notes Suny, 'was, of necessity, fish and caviar. Bread was mixed with nuts, and water was distributed by ration cards. Typhus and cholera made the citizens' plight unbearable'.[37] Citizens struggled with what to do. '[A] paralyzing fear [the "freeze" response] gripped the population of the city [and] drove them to grasp at the straw offered by the British'.[38]

The soviet convened to discuss the possibility of British aid, with support from both the left and right Socialist Revolutionary parties. As the Army of Islam got closer to the city, Moscow, wanting the British in Baku no more than they wanted the Germans, so informed the city's Bolshevik leadership. The prospect of British intervention was anathema to both Stalin and Lenin, who communicated to Shaumian their opposition to accepting help from 'a bunch of Anglo-French imperialists'.[39] Contempt also went down the social scale, and not for the first time. One Baku Bolshevik characterised the city's workers as having a 'petty fear for their own skins'.[40] During the proceedings Shaumian ultimately decided that the only way 'to save Baku for Russia' was to await reinforcements from the Red Army, though he was painfully aware that sufficient numbers would never arrive in time.[41]

After several repeat attacks, the Ottomans smashed through Baku's remaining defensive lines in late July 1918 and stood poised to land the final blow. Seeing no other way out, on 31 July, Shaumian tendered his resignation. Along with the city's other Bolshevik leaders, they made ready to sail out of Baku.[42] Shaumian wrote to Moscow:

> We could not be among those who placed themselves at the mercy of the Turkish pashas, who saved their skins by allowing the Bolsheviks and the Russian troops to be torn to pieces

[35] The activities of Dunsterville's forces in Persia and Baku are recounted in his memoirs. See LC Dunsterville, *The Adventures of Dunsterforce* (London, Edward Arnold, 1920). On British policy in the region more generally, see Suny, *The Baku Commune*, 278–79.

[36] Murgul, 'Baku Expedition of 1917–1918', 156.

[37] Suny, *The Baku Commune*, 304.

[38] Suny, *The Baku Commune*, 323. The Israeli writer, Amos Oz, described his experience as a child living in 1947 Jerusalem waiting to learn whether the General Assembly of the United Nations would vote to allow partition of Palestine between Jews and Arabs and hence allow a state, Israel, to come into existence. His words (*A Tale of Love and Darkness* (London, Vintage, 2004) 333) closely follow the atmosphere that emerges from the sources about what Baku's people would have felt at this time: 'But Jewish Jerusalem was … a … town, confused, terrified, swept by gossip and false rumours, at its wits' end, paralysed by muddle and terror'.

[39] Suny, *The Baku Commune*, 306–10.

[40] Suny, *The Baku Commune*, 310.

[41] Suny, *The Baku Commune*, 314.

[42] On this sequence of events, see Suny, *The Baku Commune*, 312–20.

> by Turkish bands, nor are [we] ready to surrender Baku to the English. We have decided to save the revolutionary troops we have which are loyal to the Russian Soviet government, in expectation of the troops coming from Astrakhan, together with which we will declare war on two fronts, on Turkish and English imperialism, to defend Baku for a revolutionary Soviet Russia.[43]

Shaumian and the others failed, however, in their bid to escape and were confined to a ship berthed in Baku's harbour. In the power vacuum left by the Bolshevik abdication, a newly formed government made up of Right Socialist Revolutionaries, Mensheviks, and Dashnaks assumed administrative duties in Baku, forming what they called the Centro-Caspian Dictatorship. The new city leadership immediately set to preparing Baku for a siege. On 31 July, the city's defending forces rallied to repulse a major assault launched by the Ottomans. Encouraged by this victory, the Dictatorship extended a formal invitation to Dunsterville, and over the next week the first British detachments started trickling into the Black City.

VIII. LAST CHANCES

Despite military setbacks elsewhere, the Ottomans still demanded that Baku capitulate. In a message to the Armenian National Council in Tiflis dated 3 August 1918, the commander of the Army of Islam had even promised safety to the Armenians on the condition that the city be surrendered immediately. But with the British entrenching themselves behind the city's battle lines, Baku's new leaders felt capable of holding out against the siege and so 'were no longer interested in surrender as they had been three days before'.[44] However, their confidence in British military might and resolve was misplaced. There were far too few men to reinvigorate Baku's defences. Within days of his arrival, Dunsterville privately acknowledged the hopelessness of the situation.[45]

In the final week of August 1918, Ottoman forces renewed their attack on Baku. Dunsterville withdrew with his men, throwing the Baku government into a state of panic. Their embarkation process began on 14 September. Baku fell to Ottoman forces the next day. General Nuri held back his men to allow the irregular Azerbaijani units of the Army of Islam and Muslim citizens to pillage and plunder the city without encumbrance. A new and immense massacre followed.

> The Christian population rushed toward the harbor, where they crammed into every available vessel. Nearly half of Baku's seventy thousand Armenians succeeded in escaping the Turkic vengeance by sailing to Enzeli, Astrakhan, or Krasnovodsk … On the morning of September 15, the Armenian Council and the Centro-Caspian Dictatorship departed on one of the last ships, as the Christian quarters were already shrouded in smoke.[46]

In two days some 9,000 Armenians were slain by Azerbaijani, as well as Ottoman, soldiers. Not even hospital patients were spared. General Nuri entered the city and

[43] Suny, *The Baku Commune*, 319–20.
[44] Suny, *The Baku Commune*, 326.
[45] Suny, *The Baku Commune*, 327–36.
[46] Hovannisian, *Armenia on the Road to Independence*, 227.

restored order on 16 September, though in a subsequent report to Enver he washed his hands of responsibility for what had ensued, claiming 'that the numbers of Armenians and Russians killed did not amount to 1 per cent of the number of Muslims killed in March', and that he had taken measures to prevent disturbances by carrying out executions of looters.[47]

Baku, Hovannisian notes, had fallen to the Ottomans in 'flagrant breach' of the Brest-Litovsk Supplementary Treaty.[48] The empire's Central Power allies had vainly exerted pressure on the Ottomans during the summer to refrain from pressing their advance on Baku. The city was claimed in the name of the Azerbaijan republic. Triumphant Ottoman troops marched through the streets, past the smoldering ruins of what had once been the second largest urban center of Transcaucasia.

The fate of Shaumian and the other communards was no less tragic. Allowed to depart for Bolshevik-held Astrakhan on 14 September on board the *Turkmen*, the ship was waylaid and docked at Krasnovodsk. There, they were promptly arrested and imprisoned by anti-Bolshevik White Russians. After some deliberation, the 26 commissars were taken out and executed, the bodies interred under the sandy dunes of Russian Turkestan.[49]

IX. ARMENIAN, TURK, AND TRANSCAUCASIAN MUSLIM RELATIONS AT WORLD WAR I'S END

Before Transcaucasia's descent into anarchy in 1917, relations between Armenians and the Muslims of Transcaucasia, especially the Azeris, had been marked by mistrust and fear, hurt and violence. Throughout the war, their relations had worsened.

When the Ottoman army crossed the prewar border in early 1918, it attempted to move as quickly as possible in order, as General Vehib put it, 'to deliver Muslims from the massacres'.[50] He complained to his Russian counterpart, General ID Odishelidze, that the Armenians were acting in concert to put an end to all Muslim civilisation in the region: '[T]he Armenians' apparent determination to annihilate the Ottoman Muslim population in the occupied territories as part of an organized plan', Vehib informed Odishelidze, 'required Ottoman forces to advance for the sake of "humanity and civilization"'.[51]

Reynolds finds no evidence of such a plan and that the Armenians, '[i]nstead of attempting to mount any form of defense ... preferred to withdrew [sic] and perpetrate "extraordinary acts" against the Muslim villages they passed through'.[52] Reynolds concludes that '[a]lthough the available evidence does suggest serial massacres, the

[47] Reynolds, *Shattering Empires*, 234.

[48] Hovannisian, *Armenia on the Road to Independence*, 227.

[49] Suny, *The Baku Commune*, 337–43 and F Kazemzadeh, *The Struggle for Transcaucasia, 1917–1921* (New York, Philosophical Library, 1951) 144–46.

[50] Reynolds, *Shattering Empires*, 198.

[51] Reynolds, *Shattering Empires*, 197, citing ATASE, To the Commander of the Caucasus Armies, General Przheval'skii, [nd], K 2930, D 5530, F 8.

[52] Reynolds, *Shattering Empires*, 197.

small Armenian forces were incapable of carrying out a program of annihilation'.[53] The Ottoman commanders, surely well-aware of the fighting capabilities of their adversaries, overstated the threat and scale of the Armenians' activities. This fit within a pre-existing practice of state-sponsored exaggerations and distortions about Armenians.

During the May 1917 All-Russian Muslim Congress, delegates had voted for a resolution that outlined a federalist model of political organisation in the then Russian republic.[54] But the Provisional Government had not delivered on that or on other matters important to them.[55] Soon after the Bolsheviks seized power in October 1917, it became evident to Azeris that the Bolsheviks were, to borrow Dunsterville's wording, 'malevolent'[56] and would exert their control over politics and society through force rather than consent. Thus, once the Bolshevik leaders in Petrograd dissolved the Constituent Assembly, they too failed to deliver the reforms to Russian Muslims for which the latter had long pressed. Much like the Armenians of the Ottoman Empire in 1914, Russia's Muslims lost faith that the reformed Russian state would accord them greater political and cultural autonomy and safety.

Indeed, after the March Days, 'the Musavat ... await[ed] their Turkish brothers who would reinstate them in the capital of Azerbaijan', even as they made clear their opposition to being absorbed into the Ottoman Empire.[57]

In mid-June 1918, a week after Azerbaijan declared independence, Khan Khoiskii, the newly elected prime minister, signed a 'friendship' treaty with the Ottoman government in Batum. Unlike its neighbours, the treaty granted Azerbaijan the right to request armed assistance from the Ottomans to ensure safety and order, a clause that was immediately understood at the time as a promise to supply military aid to fight the Armenians over control of Baku and elsewhere.[58] The treaty with the Ottoman Empire did not necessarily mean that the newly cemented Azerbaijani–Ottoman relationship was established on entirely amicable terms, however. Even as the two sides signed the new agreement, the Ottomans refrained from conferring official recognition upon Azerbaijan, 'offending [the] ADR leadership' and presumably renewing fears of Ottoman intentions, Audrey Altstadt has noted.[59] Feelings overall towards the Ottomans were mixed, both friendly and suspicious. The Azerbaijanis were grateful for Ottoman help, but they still sought to carve out an independent state and clearly did not want to be part of the Ottoman Empire.

[53] Reynolds, *Shattering Empires*, 198.

[54] Suny, *The Baku Commune*, 86.

[55] Swietochowski, *Russian Azerbaijan*, 96–97.

[56] General Dunsterville spoke of Bolshevism as a movement whose 'malevolent tendencies have permeated the blood of all the races in this part of the world ... the spirit is the old spirit of revolution, the spirit of men gone mad' (see Dunsterville, *The Adventures of Dunsterville*, 119).

[57] Suny, *The Baku Commune*, 348. See Swietochowski, *Russian Azerbaijan*, 130–31.

[58] A Altstadt, *The Azerbaijani Turks* (Stanford, CA, Hoover Institution Press, 1992) 90 and also Murgul, 'Baku Expedition of 1917–1918': 'The Fourth Article of this agreement was highly vital, because according to this article, Azerbaijan would have the right to request for Ottoman military support in order to guarantee her safety and order. The agreements made with Armenia and Georgia were in the form of peace agreement, whereas the agreement signed with Azerbaijan was in the form of friendship and cooperation'.

[59] Altstadt, *The Azerbaijani Turks*, 90.

The Armenians were terrified and 'to avoid extermination at the hands of ancient enemies ... were willing to ally with any force [ie the Bolsheviks] great enough to preserve their nation'.[60] But the alliance with the Bolsheviks did not save them from massacre by Azerbaijanis with the Ottomans' backing in September 1918.

With the signing of the armistice at Mudros, the Ottomans were finally forced to withdraw from the occupied regions in the Transcaucasus and return to the 1914 Russo-Ottoman border. Some Ottoman intelligence and military officers stayed behind to provide covert assistance to Azerbaijan. For the next two years, until the Soviets moved back in, they played leading roles in organising Azerbaijan's military and developing effective resistance networks in regions claimed by Armenia. Periodic conflict would break out between Armenia and Azerbaijan as they clashed over control of the regions of Nagorno-Karabakh, Zangezur, and Nakhichevan. These territorial disputes died down with the establishment of Soviet power in the South Caucasus in 1920–1921. Whatever dreams of expansion into eastern Transcaucasia or creation of a Turanian homeland Ottoman commanders and statesmen cherished were dashed – for the time being.

X. TRAUMA AND ARMENIAN–AZERBAIJANI RELATIONS

The collective psyches of the Transcaucasian Armenians and Azeris were traumatised during the intercommunal violence of 1905–1907 (see Chapter 10). The violence seeded long-term fear and deep mistrust, hurts, and resentments of unpunished crimes the two peoples had committed against each other. The deprivations and terrors of World War I again pushed these peoples to their limits. The Russian First World War, like the Ottoman First World War, unfolded within a single continuum of violence and tensions that extended beyond the strict temporal framing of the war. Traumatic experiences remained raw and triggerable in the psyches of affected individuals and were transmitted as such to the next generations. For the Armenians of Transcaucasia, trauma was also overdetermined, that is, multicausal. Knowledge of massacres of Armenians in the Ottoman Empire had informed the Transcaucasian Armenian psyche since at least the 1890s.

For a large segment of Azeris, the events of the March Days convinced them that the Bolsheviks and Armenians were working in tandem against them, while, doubtless, their own role in the massacre of Armenians in September had the similar effect of equating them with the Ottomans. Both peoples' prior trauma history with each other was reinforced. The events destroyed the trust needed on which to base productive coexistence. Trust can be rebuilt, but slowly. 'Trust but verify', wisely recommends the Russian proverb.

The threats and uncertainties of Bolshevism, even with its heralded exhilarating potential, and of Ottoman invasion also informed the Armenian and Azerbaijani psyches. While the final result of the Ottoman invasion was uncertain, what was

[60] Suny, *The Baku Commune*, 348.

certain for the Muslims, as for everyone else, was the prospect of further fear, violence, need, want, injury, loss, and death – more traumatic experience for all.

From 1918 to 1921, in Transcaucasia, as in all of Russia, no effective central authority existed. To fill the power vacuum and ensure the physical security of their respective communities, each political or national group utilised militias and other national armed units, alleviating some fears but raising others. The creation of separate militias epitomised the hostile psychological space that the Transcaucasian peoples inhabited. They seemed to represent the lack of any spirit of unity and cooperation among Transcaucasians that could have developed and made the Transcaucasian Democratic Federative Republic a viable reality. Since then, the peoples of the South Caucasus have kept the bit between their teeth.

Part IV

Analysing and Processing Collective Trauma: Is a Different Future Possible?

16

How People Make Meaning in General, and Illustrated by an Armenian and a Turk

THE PROFOUND UNDERSTANDING of meaning making relied on in this chapter was originally conceived and empirically tested by Robert Kegan.[1] Since the early 1980s, he and his many graduate students, including myself, have carried out in-depth research, both qualitative and quantitative, on many hundreds of individuals. At its heart is the understanding that all individuals begin to negotiate *how* they understand their experience, in all realms of life, from birth onward in an unconscious process, one that evolves naturally throughout the lifespan from one epistemology to another, more complex and inclusive epistemology for making meaning. These epistemologies organise and shape a person's experience. They function like out-of-sight, unconscious puppeteers who pull strings that react, evaluate, and shape experience as it is lived. Outside of conscious awareness, each epistemology builds on and incorporates the prior one, taking in and structuring experience according to whichever epistemology we currently make meaning in. As meaning making evolves into a more complex epistemology, it reshapes our understanding of, or meaning we ascribe to, our experience and produces perspectives on prior experience. This chapter presents this concept of meaning making, which explains and illustrates how, as our way of making meaning evolves, we acquire and adjust our narratives.[2]

Kegan's conceptualisation proposes a series of increasingly complex, nested epistemologies. At any given time, people tend to organise experience according to one epistemology or, also identifiably, in between two epistemologies for some years. Our minds do not jump from one to another. In the course of a lifespan, minds may evolve[3] gradually and sequentially from the simplest to the most complex. The time spent

[1] Kegan and then some of his graduate students constructed hypotheses for exploring differences among individuals' organising epistemologies. Determination of an individual's current organising epistemology in use is made only after someone with training carries out and analyses a specialised interview. Although trained and practiced in conducting and analysing such interviews, I have not interviewed Meline Toumani or Ece Temulkuran, whose published words I will analyse later in this chapter. Since I analyse their written words without having administered the interviews in which their way of making meaning could have been definitively determined, I refer to their way of making meaning as 'heuristics.'

[2] Eg R Kegan, *The Evolving Self* (Cambridge, MA, Harvard University Press, 1982).

[3] 'May' evolve because not everyone evolves through all the epistemologies.

evolving out of one epistemology and into another may be lengthy, and people evolve at different rates. However, most of us evolve in adolescence into the 'co-constructing' epistemology (explained below), but not necessarily further. The experience of trauma tends to impede or interfere with the evolutionary process (see Part I).

I. THE 'CONCRETELY SELF-CENTERED' EPISTEMOLOGY

Meaning making begins at birth. For example, babies and very young children organise their elders' approving and disapproving facial expressions or word sounds by associating them into patterns that indicate 'is permitted/good' or 'is not permitted/bad'. However, the discussion here starts not with meaning making at a very young age but with the 'concretely self-centered epistemology' (the names of the epistemologies used here are mine), which is generally characteristic of mid-childhood. In this epistemology, needs and desires are understood solely in concrete terms to be satisfied, such as 'I want chocolate ice cream'. In this epistemology, we can organise concrete things into categories of other concrete things – for example, baseball players into catchers, pitchers, and outfielders. We understand that doctors take care of what 'hurts' or 'bleeds', but we do not yet understand 'our health' – an abstract concept.

In this epistemology, when children categorise experiences as 'good' or 'permitted', or 'not good', they organise them into concrete behavioural rules that restrain their pursuit of concrete desires. Children understand 'Do unto others as you would have them do unto you' solely in terms of concrete admonitions, such as those against stealing and killing in the Ten Commandments. Similarly, relationships to others are instrumental and/or reciprocal in the service of satisfying concrete needs, desires, and interests. The satisfaction produces reasoning about what brings felt wholeness: 'My teacher was nice to me or praised me today' and therefore, 'I like her and I like school'. Alternatively, 'My teacher was mean to me yesterday'; therefore, 'I hate school. I won't go'.

Even though relationships to others are instrumental and/or reciprocal, they are not necessarily pursued unconditionally, such as when the meaning-maker runs into concrete restraining factors such as consequences for disobedience. As a partial result of constraints, children spontaneously invent fairness and compromise in their relationships to get what they want.[4] 'You did this, so now I do that as a consequence'. Concepts such as 'an eye for an eye', which in this epistemology is what fairness is understood to mean, begin to emerge. We do not altogether abandon this way of meaning making when we evolve into more complex meaning making. 'An eye for an eye' continues to stand for concrete revenge taking.

A large cohort of adults make meaning in this epistemology. They feel good and whole when they follow the rules learned earlier in achieving their ultimate goal, gaining desired ends while avoiding constraints or punishment. However, when they were children, some adults may not have developed practices of rule-following and getting-along-with-others, fairness and compromise. They may have got away with

[4] Kegan, *The Evolving Self*, 163.

rule-breaking, cheating, and lying. Their parents may have behaved similarly, thereby modelling what is sociopathic behaviour. When such children become adults, they may demonstrate sociopathic tendencies or become fully sociopathic. This means that any concerns they have about their effect on others remain the same as when they were children – a concern as to what affects *them* only. They are entirely instrumental. They may also see other people only single-mindedly pursuing their own interests. They align with others according to whether the others do or do not fulfil their interests. Their relationships hold if their needs or interests are satisfied, but they terminate those relationships that no longer provide the means to what they need.

II. THE 'CO-CONSTRUCTING' EPISTEMOLOGY

In the co-constructing epistemology, a qualitatively more complex major new ability is acquired (again without awareness). Our minds now organise experience in abstract terms and general concepts like 'health' or 'our people'. Whereas before we classified concrete objects only into concrete categories, we now classify them into abstract categories; for example, 'Health is what doctors and nurses look after'. This ability enables people to enter the process of socialisation outside the familiar concreteness of family and school. Our more evolved inner shaping or organising epistemology can internalise abstract concepts from external societal and cultural authorities in our 'psychosocial surround' (Kegan's phrase), be they people, books, groups, institutions, organisations, logical arguments, ideologies, laws, or social mores.

In the prior concretely self-centered epistemology, human relationships were personal and immediate, limited to concrete, known individuals. In the co-constructing epistemology, people now become capable of identifying psychologically with others they do not know and whose minds they can take in, minds they 'know' impersonally that they identify with, though, because they are part of and identified with themselves. Epistemologically we are, without being consciously aware of it, people pleasers in a critically necessary way. In this epistemology, we feel most whole not in having our concrete needs and desires met but in conforming to these internalised demands and expectations regarding abstract rules, roles, or values in our own social surround.

Co-constructing enables the existence of community and civilization. It enables us to know that we belong to society, and are part of larger groupings beyond the family and the personally known. One identifies with and experiences oneself as being part of and an agent for an external order – the demands and roles of a society, a culture, and a people. In this epistemology, individuals embody and thus advance their people's culture. By being alive in the culture, the individual is necessarily its keeper, its living continuance. It is Kegan's great insight that

> [t]hese are the first moments of a remarkable development in the evolution of meaning, for at this time the organism, which for so long has been cultured, begins itself to assume the function of culturing, a function critical to the continued survival and enhancement of that greater life community of which it is a part.[5]

[5] Kegan, *The Evolving Self*, 166.

Meaning making in the co-constructing epistemology is nonetheless limited and limiting. Co-constructing is adequate for understanding or resolving conflicting concrete wants or needs, but not for understanding conflicting abstractions, such as others' opinions and values. The limits are highlighted when individuals are faced with conflicting choices between internalised authorities. How does one choose independently if one's mind can only produce options that are enmeshed in others' authority? The mind needs to be independent of its internalised authorities in order to evaluate them independently. For example, a man deciding whether to divorce his wife may weigh the conflicting views and values imposed by various external authorities – wife, parent, therapist, lawyer, church, society. But the results of hundreds of lengthy interviews to determine individuals' meaning-making epistemology have demonstrated that this man cannot ask himself to decide *independently* of those whom he values and who matter to him. If he cannot differentiate his mind from others', he cannot manage or regulate their demands on his mind.

Struggling with such inner conflicts frequently spurs evolution to the next epistemology. If instead, however, individuals sidestep the struggle and conform to external authority (ie take 'the path of least resistance') because it *is* that authority (this motivation for conformity is determined in the special interview), they may not evolve beyond what for them is right because authorized by their authority.

III. THE 'SELF-AUTHORING' EPISTEMOLOGY

As noted above, evolution from one epistemology to the next occurs at different rates and hence at different times in people's lives. Only a minority of adults evolve out of co-constructing and into the epistemology in which they become their own authorities. And some of those individuals seem to evolve seamlessly into the next 'self-authorising' epistemology as early as their late 20s; more commonly this evolution is hard-won later in life, even much later.

In the early phase of evolution into this meaning-making epistemology, we often reject our internalised authorities, with whom we identified in our previous epistemology, just as we unconsciously rejected our first and nearest authorities, our parents, when we evolved into co-constructing. In the self-authorising epistemology, we become aware that our minds are separate from others' minds. This awareness alters our interior relationship with those minds and with all that we value in our psychosocial surround, even as we may still value and identify with it. The big difference is that we now regard its authority over us as distinct from our own authority over ourselves. We no longer feel ultimately bound or obligated by the norms and leaders of our community. By the time we have evolved fully into this epistemology, we have developed our own philosophy or system for decision-making. Each of us becomes his or her own inner system of authority.

In this more complex epistemology we acquire the new cognitive ability of systemic thinking enabled by our new separateness of mind, which enables us to have perspective, not just on demands from co-constructed realities, but on entire systems. We understand any one particular demand as being just one element in a whole system. Persons, groups, institutions, or sets of institutions can all be understood as systems.

Thus, we can engage with whole systems, coordinating, comparing, and regulating them in our minds and in our relationship to them. Loyalty to valued authorities outside ourselves becomes just one possible factor in our choice system, whereas in the previous epistemology, absolute loyalty to one or another authority was the unconscious determinant.

Our meaning making now occurs independently of neighbours, bosses, priests, colleagues, the Supreme Court, or any other external authority. We value what is important to us for reasons that we can articulate out of our own authority. We each become the source, the generator, of authority, of who we are, what we value, why we think and do what we do. We have created, internally and unconsciously, our mind's own meaning-making philosophy. From this we now construct systemic narratives and make systemic judgements.

To be self-evaluating and self-correcting demands an internal standard. Being able to separate ourselves from other systems and make meaning out of our own philosophy, our own authority, means that we think complexly in distinguishing between what we think and what they think. We have perspective not only on elements of our psychosocial surround but on other systems as well. Systemic perspective on our society and culture enables us to become critical observers of the inputs of the community that has shaped us and carry inside. As we mature in this epistemology, we can be both appreciative and critical of a person or an institution we hold dear, because we now recognise them as being independent from us.

In this epistemology, we may conform with others outwardly but not conform inwardly. If we do conform out of a loyalty, it is no longer the result of an unconscious, automatically compelled state of mind as in the prior co-constructing epistemology. We now consciously *choose* to act in conformity or not with the authorities of the society, whether people, texts, or ideals. That is, alignment with others, or whatever authority is for us, is no longer the ultimate satisfaction and value. Concrete goals and aligned relationships still matter, but honouring one's inner philosophy is now paramount. We enjoy the feeling and the results of having this self-authorising mind and are often successful and influential in the world, maybe with power and prestige, emanating from confident judgement, systemic thinking, and moving flexibly among systems. We are 'cultures unto ourselves'.[6]

However, this epistemology, too, is limited and limiting by virtue of the meaning-maker's unconscious identification with his or her own authoritative system or philosophy. Embedded in our own system, we lack perspective on it. If asked, we would probably explain that what we assert or believe is obvious. Unable to demonstrate perspective on our system, we would resist any challenge to the autonomy and self-control that it offers us, as mediator Jeffrey Seul observes.[7] Thus, individuals who are making meaning in this epistemology become reactive to perceived challenges and feel defensive, irritated, condescending, or contemptuous, out of unconscious identification with maintaining their own inner authority and unaware of it.

[6] Kegan, *The Evolving Self*, 166.

[7] JR Seul, 'How Transformative Is Transformative Mediation? A Constructive-Developmental Assessment' (1999) 15(1) *Ohio State Journal on Dispute Resolution* 148.

IV. 'ALWAYS-LEARNING' MEANING MAKING IN THE FLEXIBLE EPISTEMOLOGY

In this epistemology, we become willing, if faced with compelling evidence, to adjust our entire understanding to take in the greater wholeness of things, of recognising new elements in ourselves. Individuals can notice that what they find expressive of the full humanity of others, even when difficult, unbearable, or unacceptable, they find also (similar) expression of in themselves. By evolving into this epistemology, our meaning making becomes 'complexly flexible', because we become flexible in gaining perspective on ourselves as whole systems. As Seul describes it:

> An adult [in this epistemology is] … able to relativize, and thus evaluate, the assumptions, values, and historical and cultural circumstances that underlie [his or her previous epistemology] … one now may choose to serve moral epistemologies that do not accord with one's former ideological biases. [One's prior epistemology] now can be viewed *and treated* as one meaning making system among others. To say that epistemology is relativized is not to say, however, that it necessarily is disregarded. In most cases, it will remain an important source of meaning … One's conception of self and other is … not self/other (implying sharp division), but self-and-other (interpenetrating; distinct but not separate).[8]

In this epistemology, we may find ourselves dealing with conflicts between universal moral values without easy answers, such as when a conflict exists between pursuing justice versus pursuing peace. In this epistemology, we do not shift that which is our responsibility onto others who are less powerful, because we are in charge of ourselves, of what we do and how we would like our behaviour to be understood. When we condemn, it is on the basis of universal moral standards, while acknowledging the reality and complexity of ambiguity. At the same time, we hold that there must be constraints and punishments in the context of achieving justice, fairness, the rule of law, rather than enacting spite and revenge, getting even as in 'an eye for an eye'. At times we experience a contradiction in being both flexible and principled. We accept living with contradiction.

V. MEANING MAKING WITH TRAUMA

While being actively traumatised or when later triggered to the traumatic experience, individuals are unlikely to be able to access their most complex meaning-making ability. Trauma disables us from integrating traumatic experience into our narratives, which are composed and recomposed as our meaning making evolves out of whatever epistemology is in use at the time. With trauma, the mind kicks in with automatic reactions that compartmentalise the experience and seals it off. Traumatic experience remains locked within the epistemology in which meaning was made at the time of the trauma. Rather than being recast in the increasingly more complex forms made possible as the mind moves from one organising epistemology to the next, the traumatic experience

[8] See R Kegan, *In Over Our Heads: The Mental Demands of Modern Life* (Cambridge, MA, Harvard University Press, 1994) 104–105, 331; and Kegan, *The Evolving Self*, 104.

has been 'encapsulated', in psychologist Gil Noam's term,[9] disconnected from the wider meaning systems that one ordinarily creates for past and present experience as one develops.

In sum, traumatised people do not generally function as well as those who have not been traumatised, but in very different degrees and realms of life. When trauma shatters minds, it often interferes with the structuring by the more complex system across all of their subsequent life experience, while for others, it can disable or limit development of more complex meaning making solely in relation to the traumatic experience.

VI. AN ARMENIAN AMERICAN AND A TURK SEPARATING FROM CO-CONSTRUCTED COLLLECTIVE NARRATIVES

Meline Toumani published *There Was and There Was Not: A Journey through Hate and Possibility in Turkey, Armenia, and Beyond* in 2014, when she was a journalist with the *New York Times*. Turkish journalist Ece Temelkuran published *Deep Mountain* in 2010, when she was a journalist with *Habertürk* in Turkey. Thus, both books came out shortly before the 100th anniversary of the start of the Armenian genocide. Between 2008 and 2015, hope briefly existed for an official breakthrough in Armenian-Turkish relations. It was the period when US Secretary of State Hillary Clinton supported the signing of protocols between Armenia and Turkey, when Hasan Cemal accompanied Abdullah Gül to the football match in Yerevan,[10] there visited the genocide memorial and met with the grandson of the man who, as long understood, had been involved in assassinating his grandfather.

Each book sold well and drew praise and intense, deep criticism. Each book demonstrates the challenge of involvement in this relationship in which these authors were able, and did, question their own identity groups and did not necessarily identify with them in all ways. Toumani and Temelkuran are close in age, thoughtful and talented. They did not write in relation to each other, but each sought to test and expand her understanding of the other's people. For Toumani, it was the Turks; for Temelkuran, it was the Armenians in Armenia and the Armenian diaspora. In each's travels to the other's countries, each experienced, or projected, what was felt as an unpleasant inescapability – for Toumani, it was of predictably being seen by Turks only in her Armenianness before and after she was seen as anything else; for Temelkuran, it was of predictably being seen by Armenians only as a Turk before anything else. Both disliked the experience of being stereotyped. Each became worn out and disheartened

[9] GG Noam, 'The Self, Adult Development, and the Theory of Biography and Transformation' in DK Lapsley and FC Power (eds), *Self, Ego and Identity* (New York, Springer, 1988); GG Noam, 'Normative Vulnerabilities of the Self and Their Transformations in Moral Actions' in GG Noam and TEW Wren (eds), *The Moral Self: Building a Better Paradigm* (Cambridge, MA, MIT Press, 1993) 209; and D Elsayed et al, 'Anger and Sadness Regulation in Refugee Children: The Roles of Pre- and Post-Migratory Factors' (2019) 50(5) *Child Psychiatry and Human Development* 209–39.

[10] For an account of the moment, see M Toumani, *There Was and There Was Not: A Journey through Hate and Possibility in Turkey, Armenia, and Beyond* (New York, Henry Holt, Metropolitan Books, 2013) 255–70.

by the negativity of each group toward the other. Each wrote about crossing psychological as well as geographical boundaries between the two peoples shortly before the centenary of the Armenian genocide. In so doing each writer represents an important subgroup of her ethnic identity group.

Part of each's method for carrying out field research was the same – each travelled to places where the other people live. While travelling and writing, each found that she needed to understand her own identity better – Toumani's Armenianness in relation to Turks; Temulkuran's Turkishness in relation to Armenians. Both wanted to escape what they felt was the dominance of the issue of genocide recognition in all contacts between Armenians and Turks. Both write that growing up in their respective communities, they learned to hate the other community. Both wanted to escape from that.

Both books depict some groups of Armenians poorly. Toumani describes her visit to a home for century-old genocide survivors in Long Island without showing much empathy and is gratuitously critical of the look of impoverished Armenian Armenians. Temulkuran, in apparent ignorance, criticises Armenian Americans in Los Angeles for their strong interest in receiving reparations. She compares them negatively to Turks, suggesting that Turks are somehow above interest in money regarding Armenians (not recognising that during the genocide the Turks stole everything from the Armenians and that presumably many still live off the takings).

Both writers are critical of Turks, but not gratuitously. Toumani, speaking theoretically, and Temulkuran, partially so, describe the attacks on and suffering of past generations due to collective trauma. Each writes movingly about horrific collective traumas and asks herself important questions. Toumani is candid about the difficult process of stepping away from the ties to her own identity in order to examine it, and her relationship to it, for herself. Temelkuran is outspoken as she distances herself from how many Turks define 'Turkishness'. Each is courageously exploring a very difficult situation freshly with her evolved and evolving meaning making and allowing readers to accompany them as they open up their learning process. Both writers found that stepping away from their society's conventional wisdom would be misrepresented and endanger their relationship to many in their respective communities. Both writers reveal minds that have evolved to a complexity that allows them to be separate from their nationality. Both books hint at the earlier, less complex way of making meaning and the later, more complex way that each constructed her experience of her national heritage over time. Both have incurred intense public criticism.

Analysing their words with the meaning-making epistemologies makes it possible to contextualise how they were brought up, how they used to be, and how at the time of writing they were in the process of changing their relationships to their nationalities. One reviewer who gave Toumani's book a mixed judgement shows his recognition of her evolving learning process: 'The ultimate value of this book is that questioning what you are taught to find a logic in or, even, to prove it wrong, is important in intellectual development'.[11] His phrase 'intellectual development' applies to development in meaning making and fits both books equally.

[11] W Bairamian, 'Book Review: There Was and There Was Not', *The Armenite*, 26 December 2014.

Each writer reveals her own process of inner growth toward more depth and complexity. Such inner growth and perspective on conventional positions is essential to advancing the forward progress of the arc of justice. In constructing the world out of the same epistemology, both may have come to have more in common with each other, with an 'enemy', than with many co-nationals.

VII. MELINE TOUMANI'S MEANING MAKING AT THE TIME SHE WROTE HER BOOK

During her childhood in New Jersey, Toumani tells us, she learned at home about the Armenian genocide, learning that was then reinforced and expanded upon in her community. As she grew up, she found that being loyal to her community meant conforming with it, which for her was stifling and constricting. She had to reexamine her view of her community for herself. When she began the difficult process of separating herself from the truths previously co-constructed with her Armenian community and set off to explore the attitudes she had learned in it, she opened herself to the possibility of departing from some of her people's story. By 2014, Toumani's mind demonstrated abstract thinking about systems and considerable perspective, revealing a self-authorising capacity. She had come to understand that narratives differ over time and with different authors: 'There are very few stories that, once sifted through memory, research, philosophy, ideology, and politics, emerge unequivocal'.[12] She came to view critically some of the narrative on which she had been raised and accepted without question. Toumani demonstrates how her perspective on that narrative changed when writing about the Armenian driver Saro, who took her from Yerevan to Ararat to attend a soccer match between a team of Anatolian Armenians from Istanbul and a team of Russian Armenians from Rostov. The driver insisted to her that the players from Turkey were Turks, and she replied that they were Armenian players from Istanbul. The driver then said, 'Bring me a Turk so I can tear him to pieces'.[13] Toumani comments about the driver's rage:

> A Turk. When an Armenian in Armenia says, 'Turk', he usually means somebody from Azerbaijan. Sure enough, Saro proceeded to tell me that he fought in Karabakh against Azerbaijani soldiers. Next, he said, 'I cut off a man's ears. Just like that'.[14]

She became impatient with him, feeling that although Turks and Azerbaijanis sometimes call Azerbaijanis 'Turks', that shouldn't mean that Armenians should do so. She offers her reasoning:

> I found it maddening the way they used the label 'Turk' for people from Turkey as well as Azerbaijan. It's not that it was racist, exactly – Turks and Azeris sometimes did this, too. But for an Armenian to do so was like using an all-purpose word for 'enemy'. There were different enemies, specific enemies, and this mattered; each conflict had its

[12] Toumani, *There Was and There Was Not*, 5.
[13] Toumani, *There Was and There Was Not*, 215.
[14] Toumani, *There Was and There Was Not*, 215.

> own dynamics, its own governmental players, and its own geographic border. Eliding the differences only helped guarantee that nothing would change. I brought this up to anyone who would listen, but so far not a soul had agreed with me that the distinction was important.[15]

She would like her readers to share her understanding, including the moment she catches herself imposing, in her mind, a stereotype on a man she assumed was a Turk but who was not. She then reflects, 'How easily certainty took shape. How hard to dismantle'.[16]

When writing about female progenitors, Toumani asks some tough questions – how would she frame abstract choices, how to approach this history?

> [T]here are two things I know to be true. One: I know that if your grandmother told you that she watched as her mother was raped and beheaded, you would feel something was yours to defend. What is that thing? Is it your grandmother you are defending? Is it the facts of what happened to her that you are defending, a page in the encyclopedia? Something as intangible as honor? Is it yourself you are defending? If the story of the brutality that your grandmother encountered were denied or diminished in any way, you would feel certain basic facts of your selfhood extinguished … If somebody says no, what your grandmother suffered was not really quite as heinous as you're saying it is, they have said that your existence is not really so important. They have said nothing less than that you don't exist. This is a charge no human being can tolerate.[17]
>
> [The second thing I know to be true is] that if somebody tells you that you belong to a terrible group of people, you will reject every single word that follows with all the force of your mind and spirit. What if somebody says to you that your history is ugly; that your history is not heroic; your history does not have beauty in it? Not only that, you don't know your history.
>
> What you have been taught by your mother and your father and your teachers, it's false. You will retreat to a bomb shelter in your brain, collapse inward to protect yourself, because what has been said to you is nothing less than that your entire understanding of who you are is in danger. They will have said to you that your existence is without value. You, who wondered now and then about what the meaning of your life was, who made a soft landing place for those worries by allowing yourself to feel a certain richness about where you came from and who and what came before you, will be left empty. The story you thought you were part of does not exist. Neither do you exist.[18]

When faced with the Turkish denial of the genocide and accusations against the Armenians, Toumani is triggered and loses the perspective and complex meaning making she otherwise displayed. This particular brutality, from the outside, has constructed her identity and defines her reaction to it. Although this is not how she generally makes meaning, at this imagined moment of retraumatisation, she co-constructs her identity and her meaning in life with what Turks might have said.

[15] Toumani, *There Was and There Was Not*, 216.
[16] Toumani, *There Was and There Was Not*, 59.
[17] Toumani, *There Was and There Was Not*, 5.
[18] Toumani, *There Was and There Was Not*, 5.

VIII. ECE TEMULKURAN'S MEANING MAKING AT THE TIME SHE WROTE HER BOOK

Temelkuran's purpose and method in writing her book were almost mirror images of Toumani's. Temelkuran takes the reader with her as she travels to Armenia, France, and the United States to improve her understanding of Armenians and Armenian-Turkish relations. She quickly finds she would like to understand her own nation, the Turks, better. She grew up in a progressive, left-wing household. She reveals herself taking perspective on complex facts about the system of being a Turk, demonstrating a self-authorising epistemology:

> My leftist mother and her friends were tortured by men who called themselves Turks.[19]
>
> … from primary school through high school we'd assemble outside in the snow to hear rousing speeches praising our Turkishness;[20]
>
> … university classmates were beaten by young men [who were] convinced that the virtue of being Turkish outweighed all else, as were the armed men who … committed massacres in Anatolia in the name of Turkishness[21]

She continues reflecting on being threatened, with perspective on her identity, as she asks, 'Who are "we" Turks?'[22] 'Can I', she asks, 'still be a Turk but not be the same?' In other words, can she free herself from the co-constructed self-image?

> Threatening letters … arrive every time I write an article about the Kurds, the Armenians, or the army. … Does being a Turk mean you're 'one of them'? Is it possible to be a Turk without being part of any of that?[23]

The question leads her to tell us how she was raised: how, from the perspective of her current self-authorising meaning-making capacity, she took on co-constructing with her parents:

> Who told you that you must always defend good against evil, and when? As you take part in demonstrations at university you feel as though you're a continuation of your parents, doing your duty to defend good, just as they did. This is your duty to your mother, and to your father … In the same way I'm now compelled to write articles demanding an accounting for days I myself haven't experienced.[24]

Next she demonstrates ability to put herself in others' shoes with an empathic and analytic eye, as if she were replying to Toumani's plaintive despair about her hypothetical grandmother's fate:

> I ran through all the people I'd interviewed – the ones in Armenia, in Paris. In all cases, the stories they'd heard in childhood had become part of their own childhoods … The Diaspora was composed of [adult] children wishing to salvage their mothers' childhoods and trying to assuage unbearable pain. That was the source of the rage.[25]

[19] E Temulkuran, *Deep Mountain*, trans K Dakan (London, Verso, 2010) 25.
[20] Temulkuran, *Deep Mountain*, 25.
[21] Temulkuran, *Deep Mountain*, 25.
[22] Temulkuran, *Deep Mountain*, 158.
[23] Temulkuran, *Deep Mountain*, 25.
[24] Temulkuran, *Deep Mountain*, 122–23.
[25] Temulkuran, *Deep Mountain*, 132.

Like Toumani, she asks, 'If your mother had been robbed of her childhood, wouldn't you, too, advance into the arena with your sword drawn?'[26]

At the same time, she acknowledges that her process finds her also stepping back at a certain point. About being hated by Armenians, she writes, 'I've had my fill of posing questions to people programmed to hate me, and I doubt I'll ever do anything like this again'.[27]

Temulkuran's many questions about what it is to be a Turk demonstrate that she has perspective on how others' eyes see (the system of) being a Turk and that she experiences her own mind separately from theirs. At the same time, she admits that trying to answer these questions is hard, because it requires her to separate her view of herself from what she had co-constructed with the dominant environment of Turkish society in which she grew up, as well as from what she had taken in from the Armenian Diaspora about Turks:

> We joke among ourselves about the image of 'the Terrible Turk', but who do we mean when we say 'we'. Who are we? Getting away from the epic tales of the Turks we're fed at home; our defensive Third World response to the condescension we face abroad; the wrongs committed at home in the name of Turkishness; and the slights received abroad because of Turkishness: once we're disentangled from all that, who are 'we?'
>
> Suddenly, the shoe is on the other foot. I'd come here to understand Armenians, but I now realise that I first had to understand who 'we' were ... It was time to look past the flattering image Turks have of themselves, and past the terrible image of the Turk prevalent among the Diaspora. I would have to look past those twin distortions as I took a hard look in the mirror. Much harder than I expected.[28]

IX. THE MEANING MAKING FACTOR IN TRAUMA-INFORMED CONFLICT RESOLUTION

The three primary goals of this book are:

1. To demonstrate that collective trauma and collective transmitted trauma are historical realities that often have widespread negative post-trauma influence on collective psychological or mental capacities such as discriminating thinking, building or rebuilding trust, and knowing when to be flexible and when principled;
2. To advocate that these realities need to be included among other important factors in understanding and working with troubled inter-group relationships for their improvement; and
3. To contribute to improvement in Armenian, Turkish, and Azerbaijani relations.

The ability to develop and use such capacities in the complex situations that are this book's subject ideally requires that perspective on them, as in the self-authorising epistemology, be manifested in peoples (or other large, persistent, self-defined, identity

[26] Temulkuran, *Deep Mountain*, 132.
[27] Temulkuran, *Deep Mountain*, 76.
[28] Temulkuran, *Deep Mountain*, 159.

groups) as well as individuals. But the research is clear: most individuals remain in the co-constructing epistemology. However, if those individuals a people regards as its influencers or leaders minimally manifest the self-authorising epistemology *and* are principled, principled changes may occur. Better yet are a people led by flexibly-minded, as well as principled individuals. When unprocessed trauma interferes with the development or use of these capacities, it interferes with prospects for juster, less destructive activities and relations.

Given that:

- Individuals without trauma or transmitted trauma generally make meaning according to one epistemology or a place in between two epistemologies;
- Without processing and healing, traumatised individuals are likely to compartmentalise the traumatic experience and as a result make meaning of it in a less complex epistemology than the rest of their experience;
- The work of conflict resolution occurs on a ground filled with psychological landmines of triggerable traumatic memories, of emotions, thoughts, and body sensations, whether expressed aloud or not, when individuals do not (easily) have access to their most evolved mental capacities.

Thus:

- Conflict-resolution processes should be conducted to speak to individuals' different ways of making meaning;
- Leading and facilitating conflict-resolution processes, whether formally designated as such or not, will be helped if those individuals have evolved into the self-authoring epistemology.

Volkan's thesis, that a people's attachment to and love for their ethnic self's identity is not outgrown or forgotten, is a true but incomplete picture. It's not a matter of whether we continue to love our identity, but whether we have evolved to and make use of a capacity for complex and systemic thinking that leads to taking another look, to questioning, to discerning between this part of our identity and that part, and to apply principled judgement to actions taken in its name.[29]

[29] VD Volkan, 'The need to have enemies and allies: A developmental approach' (1985) 6(2) *Political Psychology* 219, https://doi.org/10.2307/3790902 (accessed 22 July 2020).

17

Meaning Making with Trauma and Relative Powerlessness in the Armenian People as a Whole

The crimes of massacre and genocide have become political weapons used against those aspiring for change and reform or seeking redress of grievances.

Gerard Libaridian[1]

IN 1936, ARMENIAN-AMERICAN writer William Saroyan famously challenged readers to take in the resilience and the determination of Armenians to persevere despite their long history of tragedy and persecution:

> I should like to see any power of the world destroy this race, this small tribe of unimportant people, whose history is ended, whose wars have all been fought and lost, whose structures have crumbled, whose literature is unread, whose music is unheard, whose prayers are no longer uttered.
>
> Go ahead, destroy this race. Let us say that it is again 1915. There is war in the world. Destroy Armenia. See if you can do it. Send them from their homes into the desert. Let them have neither bread nor water. Burn their houses and their churches. See if they will not live again. See if they will not laugh again. See if the race will not live again when two of them meet in a beer parlor, twenty years after, and laugh, and speak in their tongue. Go ahead, see if you can do anything about it. See if you can stop them from mocking the big ideas of the world, you sons of bitches, a couple of Armenians talking in the world, go ahead and try to destroy them.[2]

Sixty-seven years later, in 2003, Armenian sociologist Lyudmila Harutiunian observed, 'Fear of being destroyed, and destroyed not as a person, but destroyed as a nation, fear of genocide, is in every Armenian. It is impossible to remove it'.[3] Armenians as a collectivity today espouse, sometimes fearfully and defiantly but always proudly, the traditions that have made them a unique people, in the process manifesting fight, flight, or freeze at different times and ways. Some try to find productive routes forward, sometimes dissociating the politics of the past from the politics of the present.

[1] GJ Libaridian, *The Karabakh File* (Cambridge, MA, Zoryan Institute, 1988) dedication.
[2] W Saroyan, *Inhale and Exhale* (New York, Random House, 1936).
[3] Quoted in T de Waal, *Black Garden: Armenia and Azerbaijan through Peace and War* (New York, New York University Press, 2003) 79.

Since the genocide, the Armenian people's resilience and hard work have enabled its members to thrive as a diaspora in the United States and elsewhere. In the country of Armenia, located on a very small part of the Armenians' ancestral homeland in today's South Caucasus, at this moment in time they are on the road to building a democratic republic with important support from their brethren outside. At the end of World War I, Armenians fought successfully to establish an independent state and also strove, unsuccessfully, to unite with the neighbouring region of adjoining Nagorno-Karabakh. Fighting for Karabakh resumed after over 70 years of Soviet control came to an end in 1991.

Today's Armenia is a work in progress under conditions of great poverty, landlocked borders, a tough fight against ingrained corruption (like other ex-Soviet states), and a neighbourhood so unfriendly that Turkey and Azerbaijan even build regional roads and pipelines to skirt the Armenian republic. The Armenians' decades of traumatic experiences imprinted terror, horror, bottomless grief, anger, and awareness of the greatest injustice. In hopes of finding safety and improving their condition, the Armenians have transmitted their memories and search for justice to family, community, and the world.

Major traumatic experience changes and marks a people. This chapter speaks to some of the marks, or symptoms, in terms of the meanings made by some of today's Armenians of their past and present experiences of collective traumatic events. I look at today's conflict in Nagorno-Karabakh as the primary dynamic mark of unprocessed trauma, one suffered in common with and in need of processing also by Azerbaijan, Turkey, and Russia. Before addressing it and other symptoms, the context of the historical events referred to in Parts II and III above are recapped. (Russian symptoms are not discussed.)

I. STRIVING FOR SAFETY AND EQUALISATION

The Armenians constituted one among the many ethno-religious groups in the Ottoman Empire from the time of the conquest of Constantinople down to the 1915 genocide. For most of that period, as non-Muslims, they were not permitted to participate in political life. But within their community (*millet*), both on their ancestral lands and in other parts of the Ottoman Empire, they exercised governance over civil matters. In time, they established a large network of schools, and developed habits and practices of self-governance centred on religious and communal institutions. Most Armenians lived in the empire's eastern provinces where, outside the *millet*, they did not enjoy the same benefits and protection afforded by the law as their Muslim neighbours. Nonetheless, despite the discrimination, by the beginning of the twentieth century Armenians within every class were more broadly educated and better off than Turks and Kurds, inducing fear and resentment among the Muslim population.

In 1839, the Ottoman state initiated a series of reforms known as the *Tanzimat*, a purpose of which was to elevate the political and social status of non-Muslims in the empire. Less than half a century later, the *Tanzimat* resulted in a constitution granting full participatory rights to non-Muslims. However, after a few months of constitutional rule, Sultan Abdülhamid II set the constitution aside for the next three decades.

This allowed him to ignore the promises to the Armenians in the constitution as well as those in the Treaty of Berlin. Still hopeful, frustrated, and hurting, but determined to attain the promised equalisation, Armenians founded revolutionary political parties soon after the proroguing of the constitution and dissolution of parliament.

Ottomans concerned for the future of the empire under an incompetent sultan also soon founded their own revolutionary political committees, of which the CUP became the most important. The similar aim of fundamental change brought members of the revolutionary parties of the different ethno-religious communities together, inaugurating a period of informal cooperation between them. By 1908, the CUP successfully led a revolt against the sultan and reinstated the Ottoman constitution. Armenians could now participate in political life, but the solutions to the fundamental matters of their safety and establishment of an equal playing field receded ever more and the informal alliance (between the CUP and Armenians) fell apart.

The Yeniköy Accord of 1914, which would have introduced political and social reforms in the eastern provinces, represented the final effort to institutionalise equality for Armenians. But although the CUP agreed to the plan, they feared that it threatened to lead to loss of a large part of the Anatolian homeland and thus to the end of the empire. Yet if they did not agree, so the thinking went, then Armenians might pursue an agenda for independence anyway. When war came, the Armenians were unable to escape blame from the CUP authorities. The ruling elite was convinced that the vocal, if intermittent, rhetorical support by the European powers credibly encouraged subversion and disloyalty among the Armenians. They pointed to the transnational connections between the members of the Armenian revolutionary political parties as evidence of conspiratorial activity. That an unknown number of Ottoman Armenians did cross over to the Russian lines seemed only to confirm the worst fears of Ottoman political and military leaders. The CUP leadership ignored whatever international obligations the Ottoman state had agreed to vis-à-vis the Armenians over the past 40 years.

A few months into World War I, Ottoman forces suffered a near-catastrophic defeat at Sarikamish. Ottoman confidence was restored after 11 months of fighting and finally prevailing at Gallipoli. By then the CUP government had launched its genocidal program, obviating any question of Armenian rights as they murdered and deported this people, emptying towns and villages. Having assured Armenians that they would safeguard all their property and return it after the war, the authorities dropped all pretence and demonstrated that it never had any intention of doing so.

In the last year of the war, the Ottoman armies penetrated Transcaucasia and showed no regard for the welfare for the Armenians of the region or the hundreds of thousands of refugees who had gathered there after the massacres and deportations. The Armenians established a state in an insecure neighbourhood.

II. BENEFITS AND COSTS OF PRESSING FOR GENOCIDE RECOGNITION

Experience is traumatic when individuals or peoples are continually threatened or overwhelmed, disempowered, and deprived by a greater power. Post-trauma victims and survivors focus on safety and/or justice or revenge. If the threat remains, that focus remains constant, and may remain constant even without threat. Sometimes victims and survivors may reengage the perpetrator or a stand-in in the same kind of situation ('repetition compulsion'). Repetition may be an attempt to correct or change history by having a different experience, but repetitions retraumatise.

The Armenian people as a whole have righteously continued to focus on and push for Turkey's recognition of the genocide in the face of its continuous denial. Some have spent years in American and international courts seeking reparations, almost all unsuccessfully. According to Marc Mamigonian, a scholar of Turkish denial, the years of energetic struggle for recognition among Armenians and others has produced an impressive scholarly and popular literature of the genocide and accounts for the increasing worldwide recognition of the crimes committed. Some of this recognition has come from a number of non-official Turks, some of whom have done original scholarly work on the subject and manifested courageous, non-violent activism. These ways of pursuing recognition are productive coping strategies. Such non-violent 'fight responses' reduce the helplessness of traumatisation.

Frustrated at Turkey's decades-long denial, some Armenians in the diaspora pursued a different course, that of a violent 'fight response' in the form of a campaign of direct revenge against the Turks, which aimed for recognition of the genocide, reparations, and the provision of territory for a homeland. In the mid-1970s a group calling itself the Armenian Secret Army for the Liberation of Armenia (ASALA) carried out a violent campaign of assassinations and bombings against Turkish leaders, diplomats, and Turkish national businesses.[4] From its founding to its dissolution in the 1980s, ASALA killed some 40 diplomats, including some of their family members and bystanders. Other organisations also arose around this time. Armenian terrorism, as it became known, received a great deal of critical press, and the efforts of several national governments, infighting among organisation members and declining belief in their effectiveness ultimately led to their disbanding in the early 1990s. According to Armenian-American actor and writer Eric Bogosian, author of an account of the immediate post-WWI Armenian assassination campaign of CUP officials known as Operation Nemesis, the murders set back Turkish public opinion regarding genocide recognition. He believes that they greatly hindered moves to improved relations.[5]

In pursuit of genocide recognition by Turkey, many Armenians' hopes for healing have been dashed, another kind of cost. Those Armenians hoped and believed that should Turkey acknowledge the genocide, healing would take place. Some may also have hoped for sincere understanding, an apology, amends, and/or an assurance not ever to repeat. Although the official perpetrator party has not taken any of these steps in more than 100 years, a segment of the Armenian people remains focused on them for healing, especially on acknowledgment. While most Armenians would feel both relief and a measure of healing should Turkey recognise the Ottoman Empire's commission of genocide, those who focus exclusively on obtaining Turkey's

[4] See A Kurz and A Merari, *ASALA: Irrational Terror or Political Tool* (Boulder, CO, Westview Press, 1985).

[5] See Chapter 11 of *Operation Nemesis: The Assassination Plot that Avenged the Armenian Genocide* (Little, Brown 2015).

acknowledgment present themselves, and would unconsciously seem to think of themselves, as Turkey's hostages in this respect, dependent on Turkey in order to heal.

The sad dependency on the perpetrator party for healing was evident at a moving commemorative event a decade ago. In 1915, Djemal Pasha and the Turkish feminist Halide Edib gathered 1,000 Armenian children in an orphanage in Ayntura in modern Lebanon, where they were taught Turkish and converted to Islam, if necessary by methods of great cruelty, writes Maurice Missak Kelechian.[6] Kelechian, an Armenian-American from Lebanon, undertook a project to see that a memorial was built at the former orphanage in which the remains of these young Armenians would then be deposited. At the inaugural event in 2010, Kelechian spoke compassionately: 'Today's memorial will make the world aware of the impact of the irreversible pain and suffering inflicted by human beings onto others'. He expressed righteous rage:

> I was appalled and revolted by the realization that the Genocide did not stop with the killings, the drowning, the burning and the rapes, it rather continued to crawl beyond the deserts, the rivers and the caves; the final frontier of the Genocide aimed at annihilating the memory of what constituted 'Armenian culture'.[7]

Kelechian also, however, expressed the sense of being held hostage by Turkey as long as it withholds acknowledgement and regret. '[The memorial] will also tell the world that it is impossible for the Armenian people to heal and go on living with their heads held high when their colossal losses are categorically denied by the Turkish government'.[8]

Official Turkish recognition of the genocide would presumably end most of the denial of the genocide by ordinary Turks, reduce the offensiveness of encountering denial and end the focus on Turkey by those who look to its acknowledgment for healing. In 2015, on the centenary of the Armenian genocide, people living the world over spoke forthrightly about the 'genocide', even in Turkey (though not Turkish officials). Thereafter, some Armenians redirected their attention, like Bogosian, who declared that, in effect, the Turks' particular recognition doesn't matter: 'We [Armenians] don't need to ask for [genocide] recognition anymore. It is recognized'.[9]

My point is that what Turkey does, or does not do, does not have to mean that Armenians cannot 'heal and go on living with their heads held high'. It does not have to mean that, as Richard Hovannisian puts it, 'Armenians [have felt that they] … cannot fully overcome that blow [the genocide] until it is acknowledged through acts of contrition and redemption'.[10] Leaving aside '*fully* overcoming' the genocide – an impossibility – 'overcoming' refers to the limits imposed on Armenians by themselves when they claim dependence on the perpetrator party for recovery.

[6] A vivid first-person account of life in the orphanage is found in K Banian, *Goodbye, Antoura: A Memoir of the Armenian Genocide* (Stanford, CA, Stanford University Press, 2015).

[7] MK Kelechian, 'My Journey of Love, Turkification of Armenian Children in Antoura Lebanon – Inauguration of Khachkar and Bronze Statue' *MassisPort*, 29 September 2010.

[8] Kelechian.

[9] 'An Evening with Eric Bogosian', interview by Alex Dinelaris, Live Talks LA, Alex Theatre, Los Angeles, 5 May 2015.

[10] RG Hovannisian, 'Introduction: Confronting the Armenian Genocide' in RG Hovannisian (ed), *Looking Backward, Moving Forward: Confronting the Armenian Genocide* (New Brunswick, Transaction Publishers, 2003) 2.

Hovannisian observes that, for those Armenians, that dependency '*imprisons* them in the past' (emphasis added).[11] He then contends that the Armenian people's 'liberation' cannot occur while the Armenians' meaning making depends on what Turkey does. Like individuals, a people can benefit from compassionate, understanding connections with others to help enable healing, but that connection does not need to be with the perpetrator. Healing is more than helped, however, when the perpetrator party not only acknowledges the truth but gives credible reassurance that the crimes will not be repeated in the future.

After the Hasan Cemal event (described in the Preface), a young man who had attended wrote to me, as follows:

> We need to remember that Armenians are traumatized. Armenians do not choose this; our upbringing is structured in a way that by the time we become conscious, we are traumatized. It is a typical state of an adult Armenian. As an Armenian, you do not have the luxury of doing nothing and being normal. If you do nothing, you remain traumatized.[12]

He correctly stressed the need for conscious intention and action by the victimised party to overcome traumatisation and feel empowered. He contrasts being in that situation with growing up as a 'typical Turk' who in ignorance does not need to take such steps:

> It takes a conscious effort, and availability of adequate tools, to heal. In this sense, it is actually easier to be a typical Turk in this conflict, as your typical state is to be normal. You grow up knowing nothing. If you do nothing to change yourself, you are still a normal person.[13]

Many Turks are brought up in ignorance of this part of their history. What this young man did not address was the need for the perpetrator party to collectively come to terms with and heal from the traumatising commission of its crimes, especially self-inflicted traumatic moral injury (see Chapter 18).

Ultimately, by resigning themselves to waiting for an action by the perpetrator, Armenians give away much of their own consequential power and ability to heal themselves. The French-Armenian philosopher Marc Nichanian, a descendant of Armenians murdered during the genocide, reflects on Armenians' repetitious insistence on Turkey's acknowledgment. He writes, 'We claim all over the world that we have been "genocided": we relentlessly need to prove our own death'.[14] He acknowledges he feels shame when he and other Armenians ceaselessly appeal and dependently implore for a response from a supposedly 'civilised humanity'. 'I have always felt shame … as far back as I can remember … I have felt shame every time we spoke of ourselves'.[15] Speaking of this ceaseless appeal as repetition compulsion, he sees that it emanates from a place of inner disempowerment and unconscious submission.

[11] Hovannisian, 2.

[12] Email to the author, 2009.

[13] Email to the author.

[14] M Nichanian and D Kazanjian, 'Between Genocide and Catastrophe' in DL Eng and D Kazanjian (eds), *Loss: The Politics of Mourning* (Berkeley, University of California Press, 2003) 127.

[15] M Nichanian, *The Historiographic Perversion* (New York, Columbia University Press, 2009) 117 ff.

He favours instead the idea that Armenians speak to one another to process their trauma to heal and empower themselves together:

> For, each time we spoke *of* ourselves, we did not speak *to* ourselves. Each time, an appeal was made to a third party, to the West, to the 'observer', to … 'civilized humanity' … As survivors we have never ceased, in fact, to appeal to the external gaze.[16]

In looking to Turkey's recognition for healing, Armenians forgo the reward of empowerment that recovery brings. A primary part of that empowerment is the liberation of which Hovannisian spoke.

III. RESTRICTED CRITICAL THINKING

Individuals' involuntary physiological responses – hypervigilance, bodily tension, emotional dysregulation – are natural reactions to traumatic threat. But these involuntary responses interfere with critical thinking, meaning liberation of mind and self-empowerment, which is necessary for solving many kinds of difficult problems.[17] But few, if any, of us can think critically when reacting to traumatic threat or when triggered. We are choosing whether and how to fight, flee, or freeze.

In collectivities, one form that 'freeze' takes is that of a people huddling together for safety, withdrawing from interactions with outsiders, as well as for pleasure, comfort, and familiarity. Contracting into a huddle also helps psychologically to maintain the community. 'Huddling' can also lead to insularity, creating ignorance of the 'Other'. In the extreme, it may lead to further instability in relations with that Other, creating or reinforcing ignorance and breeding automatic rejection of outside influences and opinions. Not engaging with the Other makes it easier to project those fears, and derivative judgement, onto the Other. (See the 'contact hypothesis', Chapter 19).

IV. CAN ARMENIANS EXERCISE CRITICAL THINKING AND REMAIN LOYAL ARMENIANS, OR MUST THEY PRESENT A UNITED FRONT?

The Armenian people emerged immensely traumatised from the genocide. It matters to them that Turkey has 'got away' with it all, that many Turks live on their very property in their villages and live off what Armenians built over generations and hundreds of years, in a state built on top of their ashes. Over the decades of listening to Turkey's denial and discrediting of Armenians and their history, at times colluded with by Azerbaijan, many have understandably become impatient and defensive. Similarly, it matters that, seemingly out of a principle that does not apply to the situation, or simply out of habit rather than knowledge, commentators assume there must be a legitimate 'other side' as to whether there was 'genocide'.

[16] Nichanian, 117 ff.

[17] See discussion in R Heitfetz, *Leadership without Easy Answers* (Cambridge, MA, Harvard University Press, 1998) of three basic kinds of problems, one of which requires critical thinking.

A failure to process trauma disables the ability to gain perspective, that is, psychological space around one's attachments and loyalties on those difficult realities. But critical or independent thinking requires that perspective. For example, not thinking critically appears to account, or help to account, for overly defensive attacks by Armenians against other Armenians. When a backlash against both Armenian-American and Western scholars working in the field of Armenian Studies erupted in Armenia in 2009, *The Armenian Weekly* reported:

> … the Armenian government became so worried about the effects of accusations and intolerance by the wider Armenian community against prominent Armenian historians that it even prompted the interference of the president of the National Academy of Sciences of Armenia (NASA), academician Vladimir Barkhudarian: 'We condemn and find it imperative to end such name calling …'[18]

Barkhudarian's major concerns were that the manifestations of the intolerance of scholars in Armenia to differences with counterparts in the diaspora were not only unscholarly, but also interfered with cooperation among them and would give ammunition to adversaries.

> [This] … does not benefit our effort to form a united front against our adversaries and becomes an obstacle to the flourishing cooperation between academicians from the homeland and the diaspora.[19]

In other words, Barkhudarian's statement appears to condemn Armenian-American scholars' questioning of important matters if they give ammunition to those he calls 'our adversaries'. Thus, this attitude seems to suggest that overprotective insularity and at the same time suggests that Armenians cannot afford to disagree constructively and publicly with one another about relations with Turkey or Azerbaijan, perhaps because of Armenia's relative weakness. He seems to suggest that Armenians should back away from critically approaching sensitive national topics so as, for example, not to provide Turkey with material they might then use to bolster genocide denial and justify even greater hostility.

Critical thinking includes knowing the historical record and understanding known (or presumed) Ottoman motives and actions in their context. The men who carried out the genocide feared that if the Yeniköy Accord rolled out along its natural axis, Armenians might eventually find outside support to detach the eastern provinces. That was a reason for them to try to preserve the empire's territorial integrity, but not a justification for their method of genocide. Knowledge of reasons and understanding them gives events context but does not necessarily justify action taken. Reasons must be judged by a different standard. In this instance, a source of judgement is the UN Convention on the Prevention and Punishment of the Crime of Genocide, which gives no rationale for genocide at all. To repeat, the Convention makes it unambiguously clear that no Ottoman fears and anxieties could have justified what the Ottoman state carried out against its own Armenian citizens.

[18] A Khachatourian, 'Inappropriate Academic Discourse', *Armenian Weekly*, 19 February 2009, www.armenianweekly.com/2009/02/19/inappropriate-academic-discourse/ (accessed 22 July 2020).

[19] Khachatourian.

V. FRIENDLY OUTSIDERS AND LOYALTY

Another result of long-standing defensiveness is that some Armenians apply an unwritten loyalty code to non-Armenians who step outside certain bounds in discussion, followed by overly defensive attacks.

Today foreign policy expert David Phillips directs the Program on Peace-building and Rights at Columbia University's Institute for the Study of Human Rights. But when working under the US State Department in 2001, he initiated an effort to improve relations between Armenians and Turks in a Track 2 workshop: the Turkish Armenian Reconciliation Commission (TARC). Phillips reflected on part of the experience:

> TARC was accused of not being inclusive. So I made a point of meeting with its critics in the Dashnak Party, the People's Party, the National Democratic Union, and the National Unity Party. At a dinner they indicated that enlarging TARC's membership would make it more acceptable. However, their visceral hatred of Turks made it hard to envision them as members of TARC.[20]
>
> At a press conference …, I confronted a reporter from … the ARF's official publication. I deliberately chastised him for irresponsible journalism and spreading disinformation. The next day *Yekir* printed a photo of me on the front page with the headline 'Enemy of the Armenian Nation Visits Yerevan'. Soon thereafter, the European Armenian Federation announced that thirty-three groups had joined more than one hundred organizations in Greece, France, Italy, and Germany to condemn TARC.[21]

Around the time I was attempting to contribute to improving Armenian–Turkish relations in Track 2 problem-solving workshops and participating in the two events featuring Hasan Cemal, an Armenian interlocutor wrote to me in confidence:

> Armenians are really, really fed up with all the denial and the dirty games played by third parties, as in 'We'll recognize, no, we don't recognize, if you say this, we will recognize, I haven't changed my mind about 1915 and its big catastrophe etc. but I won't say the G word.' The whole endeavor may take a sour taste.

I am assured that many people, not just Armenians, felt that Phillips and I were inadequately prepared for our unconnected efforts. I can entirely understand why the Armenians of whom this interlocutor speaks feel this way. I believe they are partially correct about me. I realise now that, when I first involved myself in Armenian–Turkish matters, I was inadequately informed, especially about the depth of Armenian exhaustion, anger, and deep hurt from Turkish denial as well as the genocide.

Yet, I was then, and today remain, involved in the relatively new field of conflict resolution. The field has yet to realise its unique, indispensable potential (see Conclusion). My belief in that potential impelled me to write this book. Knowing what I now do, I regard my experience, and those of others, as that of pioneers conducting pilot projects; efforts for a peaceful and just coexistence must be more sensitive, sophisticated, and holistic. There is no recipe book. All involved have little choice but to experiment in this difficult, essential field, and learn.

[20] D Phillips, *Unsilencing the Past: Track Two Diplomacy and Turkish-Armenian Reconciliation* (New York, Berghahn Books, 2005) 98.

[21] Phillips, *Unsilencing the Past: Track Two Diplomacy and Turkish-Armenian Reconciliation*, 106.

VI. THE DEEP MARK OF TRAUMA IN TRANSCAUCASIA

In 1903, in Russian-ruled Transcaucasia, the tsar ordered the seizure of Armenian church property and closure of Armenian schools. In the midst of Russia's 1905 Revolution, he repealed the order. This was three years before the Young Turk Revolution. At the time, members of the Azeri intelligentsia had been pressing the tsar's government for greater civic and cultural rights, paralleling the push for rights by Armenians in the Ottoman Empire. The tsar simultaneously authorised repressive measures to be taken against Muslims. The Russian Empire was entering a period of civil strife during which authorities in the Transcaucasus did little to defuse to tensions between local Armenians and Muslims.

The violence wound down in 1907, and authorities this time managed to keep a tight lid on further disturbances until the October Revolution. The Bolshevik takeover set the civil war in motion. Four years of total war took a great toll on the people of the Russian Empire, and the civil war threatened to envelope Transcaucasia in further hardship, terrors, and anarchic conditions. Authorities were unable to keep order. Inter-ethnic violence and class strife intensified. Hunger was universal and Muslims went hungriest. Trauma in many forms was pervasive.

Within two months of Russia's withdrawal from the war, and with the Russian army in the Caucasus all but having vanished, the Ottomans invaded Transcaucasia. They tried but failed to prevent the establishment of an Armenian state. The Ottomans also dispatched the newly-created Army of Islam eastward to capture Baku. A month before its formation, the unexpected appearance of a shipload of armed Muslim soldiers at the city's port was the trigger for members of the Armenian community to embark on a massacre of thousands of local Muslims, destroying whatever trust remained between them. The crimes Armenians committed were overdetermined, not only by past unprocessed, retraumatising violence between them and Baku's Muslims, but also by desire for revenge on the Ottoman Muslims and by terror of the Ottoman advance. For three days, they displaced and acted out these fears and desires on their Muslim neighbours.

After the massacre, half of Baku's Azeri population fled to the countryside in terror, where they galvanised support for the advancing army. It finally arrived in August. In mid-September, it smashed through Baku's defences and permitted the Azeris to exact their vengeance for the March massacre. As many as 20,000 Armenians were killed before Ottoman commanders intervened and restored order. Muslims and Armenians were retraumatised. Righteous, intolerant and murderous nationalism followed, partial offspring of decades of unprocessed trauma.

VII. NAGORNO-KARABAKH: TRAGIC SYMPTOM

Nagorno-Karabakh, an enclave smaller than the state of Connecticut, is located within the legally-recognised borders of modern Azerbaijan. A region ringed by forests and mountains and broken in places by wide, green sweeps of cultivated land and pastures, it had been long a beloved home for ethnic Armenians and Muslims, the latter primarily Azeris. In the centuries before motorised travel, isolated Nagorno-Karabakh had been a crossroads for traders from the Persian, Russian, and Ottoman empires. Even in the mid-1990s, it took five hours by mountainous roads (or an hour by helicopter)[22] to cover the approximately 155 miles from Baku to Stepanakert, today Nagorno-Karabakh's capital.

A few miles south of Stepanakert, along one of the old silk routes in Nagorno-Karabakh, is Shusha/Shushi, once an important cultural centre. Perched on a tiny plateau of its own and surrounded by forested gorges that deeply frame ancient, isolated cottages on green riverside plots and copses below, the town held special allure for its architecture, places of worship, commerce, poetry, and magnificent horses (see Chapter 4). From 1874 to 1920, it saw a flourishing print culture take hold, with the publication of 21 newspapers and magazines (19 in Armenian and two in Russian).[23] Azerbaijanis attribute Shusha's importance to its being the 'cradle of Azerbaijan's music and poetry,' according to journalist and South Caucasus specialist Thomas de Waal.[24]

Prior to World War I and throughout most of the twentieth century, the town was inhabited by concentrations of Armenians and Azerbaijanis, each composed of a minority of highly educated, better-off individuals and the poor, mostly peasants. Muslims and Armenians never fully integrated, though relations were not distinctly unfriendly until 1905. When the Armeno-Azeri 'war' broke out in 1905, it quickly unfolded into the more general acts of violence set off by Bloody Sunday and the Russian Revolution. Armenian and Azeri brutality engulfed the region for the better part of the next two years, including in Karabakh and Shushi/Shusha.

The region as a whole did not see major fighting again until after the signing of the 1918 Mudros Armistice and withdrawal of the occupying Ottoman armies from the Caucasus. While the treaties were being negotiated in Paris, the Turkish War of Independence was getting underway, the Armenians and Azerbaijanis waged a new struggle for possession of Karabakh. The Karabakh Armenians aimed to unite with the nascent Armenian republic.[25] The Azerbaijanis were assisted by Ottoman officers and agents who had stayed behind after Mudros. Soon, however, the Soviets made their entry onto the scene, and, acting as the self-appointed negotiator for the Armenians, Azerbaijanis, and Georgians, drew the new borders in conjunction with Kemalist Turkey. In 1923, Moscow designated the parts of Nagorno-Karabakh heavily inhabited by Armenians as an autonomous, partly self-governing political unit, the Nagorno-Karabakh Autonomous Oblast (NKAO) within Azerbaijan.

[22] T Goltz, *Azerbaijan Diary: A Rogue Reporter's Adventures in an Oil-Rich, War-Torn, Post-Soviet Republic* (Abingdon, Routledge, 1998) 87.

[23] MA Harutyunyan, *Artsakhi parberakan mamuli patmutyunits (1874–2009 tt)* (Stepanakert, Dizak Plyus, 2010) 31–32.

[24] De Waal, *Black Garden*, 185.

[25] RG Hovannisian, *The Republic of Armenia*, vol 1: *The First Year, 1918–1919* (Berkeley, University of California Press, 1971) 1, 83, 164.

VIII. COLLECTIVE TRAUMAS TRANSMITTED TO ACTORS AND REPEATED IN NAGORNO-KARABAKH

Under the Soviets, general repression quashed simmering enmity between the Armenians and the Azerbaijanis. A few years before the breakup of the Soviet Union, however, Moscow's control loosened, leaving an opening for the expression of long-repressed anger and resentment by both, resulting not only from raw, unprocessed traumas of the past but also over possession of Karabakh going forward. Beginning in early 1988, benefiting from the more liberal political environment generated by Gorbachev's reforms, peaceful demonstrations in Nagorno-Karabakh and Armenia unsuccessfully appealed to the central leadership of the USSR for transfer of the NKAO from Azerbaijan to Armenia.

In apparent response to this appeal, Azerbaijanis carried out pogroms against Armenians in three Azerbaijani cities, starting on 26 February 1988 in Sumgait, north of Baku. Retaliations followed. Later that year 'Karabakhi Armenians destroyed the 300-year-old symbolic forest called Topkhana' near Shusha/Shushi, prompting large demonstrations by Azerbaijanis.[26] Baku blockaded Armenia, preventing 'fuel transfers and cutting other supply lines, which came from Azerbaijani territory'.[27] As a result, for some years Armenians in Armenia and Nagorno-Karabakh survived winters in freezing-cold houses.

In 1991, Soviet authority in all three Transcaucasian republics collapsed. Karabakh Armenians held a referendum and voted for independence from Azerbaijan. The government of the new Azerbaijani republic refused to allow it. Nagorno-Karabakh unilaterally proclaimed independence. Azerbaijan's response was an effort to reassert military control over Nagorno-Karabakh. Full-scale war erupted again, lasting until the 1994 ceasefire.

During the war, each party conducted a massive ethnic cleansing of the other, causing great loss of life and property damage. In all, some 350,000 Armenians and close to 750,000 Azerbaijanis were internally displaced or became refugees living in exile. An Armenian woman in Baku who survived these events has written:

> My family and I were hunted ... like animals. The image from the 12th floor of my home in Baku ... has haunted me all my child and adult life ... I watched from our balcony, as tens of thousands of Azerbaijani men gather in the boulevard, chanting to cleanse the city of Armenians. Absolute fear, my mother grabbing me away from the balcony, turning off the lights. ... After the rally, the men were given lists, addresses of Armenian neighborhoods, homes and places of employment. Immediately my family went into hiding. ... No one was spared, complete anarchy. Thousands of Armenians were brutally tortured, sodomized, burned alive ... pregnant women and babies, toddler girls, women and even grandmothers were gang raped as our brothers, fathers, husbands were forced to watch. Women were forced to dance in the streets naked, then drenched in gasoline and set on fire alive. Babies smashed against sidewalks. (Forgive me for sharing the details ... we live with these memories) ... Over 300,000 Armenians purged overnight out of their homes, grabbing what they

[26] B Özkan, 'Who Gains from the "No War No Peace" Situation? A Critical Analysis of the Nagorno-Karabakh Conflict' (2008) 13 *Geopolitics* 578, 588.

[27] Özkan, 589.

> can carry fleeing for safety. This is how my family became refugees, this is what we miraculously survived.[28]

For Azerbaijanis, the most painful single event of the war was claimed to have taken place in Khojaly in Nagorno-Karabakh, a staging point for attacks on Stepanakert. They claim that Armenian soldiers massacred possibly up to 200 innocents during their February 1992 assault to capture the town, leaving injured and orphaned children.[29] The truth may be otherwise, according to journalist David Davidian:

> [I]t has taken nearly 25 years for corroborating evidence from an Azerbaijani military journalist to surface in support of the Armenian position that Azerbaijan exaggerated massively and outright lies about the events in the aftermath of the tragedy in Khojaly. During these 25 years, Azerbaijanis have used their manufactured claims appearing to be victims of a crime against humanity.[30]

Nonetheless for many Azerbaijanis, 'Khojaly' still stands for Armenian wrongdoing, which, says De Waal, they cynically label 'genocide' to counter Armenia's narrative.[31]

Today violations along the line of contact patrolled by Armenian and Azerbaijani forces are not unusual, and who is at fault when shots are fired is often disputed. From this point on at least, according to different sources, claims and counterclaims to the borders and possession of Nagorno-Karabakh have created little common ground over the relevance of facts and, often, of facts themselves.

Both sides have participated in mediation undertaken by the Organization for Security and Cooperation in Europe, known as the Minsk Group process, to reach a permanent settlement, so far unsuccessfully. Azerbaijan's notably corrupt rulers[32] manipulate its impoverished and little-educated general population, generating rage against Armenians for aiming to detach Nagorno-Karabakh from Azerbaijan to make it part of Armenia. The conflict and negotiations have been exacerbated by the fact that Karabakh Armenians seized and have held on to Azerbaijani-populated territory outside and around the former autonomous republic during the war.

Although important constituencies on both sides work for compromise, leadership on neither side shows willingness. That both parties refuse responsibility for any part of the Nagorno-Karabakh conflict stands in the way of offering reassurances and expressing regret, assigning themselves to helpless defensiveness. In April 2016, a brief but vicious four-day war flared up along all points of the line of contact, resulting in many casualties but little change. In a third referendum, in 2017, the citizens of

[28] The quotation printed above comes from the Facebook page of Liyah Babayan, but she has written more about her experiences in *Liminal: A Refugee Memoir* (2018).

[29] Former Azerbaijani president Ayaz Mutalibov said that 'Khojaly' was 'organised' by his political opponents to force his resignation. C Cox, 'Ethnic Cleansing in Progress: War in Nagorno Karabakh', Sumgait Info© 2005 res(a)sumgait.info. S Abilov and Ismayil Isayev, 'The Consequences of the Nagorno-Karabakh War for Azerbaijan and the Undeniable Reality of Khojaly Massacre: A View from Azerbaijan' (2016) 45 *Polish Political Science Yearbook* 296.

[30] D Davidian, 'Genocides That Never Were: Jenin, West Bank, and Khojaly, Nagorno-Karabakh' (blog), *Times of Israel*, 6 March 2017.

[31] De Waal, *Black Garden*, 97, 98.

[32] ev, 'Corruption Perceptions Index 2019', Transparency International, www.transparency.org/cpi2019 (accessed 22 July 2020).

Nagorno-Karabakh approved a new constitution, including changing the Nagorno-Karabakh Republic's name to the Republic of Artsakh.

Libaridian sees major choices for Armenians regarding policies with their neighbours:

> The security is either with good policy, solid policy, or, it's Russia. If it's Russia, then you don't have independence … [W]e have to create those options. And, we need to work with Turkey and the Turkish people and the Turkish government … [We] have to work with them because we are agents in our own history.[33]

What other factors have helped to throw obstacles on the path toward Turkish-Armenian reconciliation? What role, in particular, does the assassination campaign of the 1970s and 1980s play in this regard? In an effort to reach the Azerbaijani population, as differentiated from its rulers, should apologies be issued? Many, perhaps most Armenians, might react negatively to that idea, 'Why should we apologise? This was a tiny loss for Turks compared to what they did to us!' they might say. The comparison is of course correct. But what the Ottoman Empire did, and for which the republic of Turkey today bears important and unassumed responsibility, is different from Armenians' own responses to and responsibility for campaigns waged by ASALA and the other modern Armenian terrorist organisations. Being agent in its own history means a people's actions are theirs and belong to them. They are responsible for them at some point on the continuum between voluntary and involuntary reacting. I do not know whether a segment of Armenian civil society ought or ought not to apologise, but the question could be meaningfully considered, for example, in a 'deliberative poll' or a 'national dialogue' (see Conclusion).

To be independent of greater neighbouring powers is to be relatively free of their pressure. The dependency on Russia is historically conditioned both materially and psychologically. To become independent, at least psychologically, is to have processed the trauma rather than being determined by it. This then brings with it the responsibility of making difficult choices, requiring profound consideration.

[33] G Sonmez-Poole, 'Conversations on Armenian-Turkish Relations', interview with Professor GJ Libaridian, *Armenian Mirror-Spectator* (17 January 2015) 5.

18

Meaning Making with Trauma and Relative Power among Turks

> You and I once spent an hour on this question … In the thirties and forties of the twentieth century, who was more disgusting, Russia or Germany? They were, I said. Much more disgusting. [*'You and I' are inmates in a Soviet work camp in Siberia.*] … They were much more disgusting than we were. Still, they recovered and we did not. Germany isn't withering away, as Russia is. Rigorous atonement – including, primarily, not truth commissions and state reparations, but prosecutions, imprisonments, and, yes, executions, sacramental suicides, crack-ups, self-lacerations, the tearing of hair – reduces the weight of the offense. Or what is atonement for? What does it do? In 2004, the German offense is a very slightly lighter thing than it was. The Russian offense, in 2004, is still the same offense.
>
> Yes, yes, I know, I know. Russia's busy. That's that other feature of national life: permanent desperation. We will never have the 'luxury' of confession and remorse. But what if it isn't a luxury? What if it's a necessity, a dirt-poor necessity? The conscience, I suspect, is a vital organ. And when it goes, you go.
>
> If it was up to me, I'd demand a formal apology, in writing. Say sorry, someone. Someone tell me they're sorry. Go on. Cry me the Volga, cry me the Yenisei, cry me the Moscow River.
>
> Martin Amis[1]

THE FOLLOWING ANALYSIS, critical of aspects of official Turkey and Turkish culture, neither began with the assumption nor came to the conclusion that the Turkish people are uniquely traumatised or essentially evil. It certainly does not rest on a view that my own country is close to perfect, even though the American record on civil or human rights is superior to Turkey's. The chapter's basis are the facts that the Ottoman Empire adopted unjustifiable, murderous policies towards its Christian minorities and that the Republic of Turkey has continued to damage itself by its denial of such matters. To become the *genocidiaire* spoke to prior collective trauma and, since possessed of sufficient power, to the ability to seek revenge in an attempt to redo their own historical trauma. This course, not a law of nature but a frequently followed law of history, leaves lasting marks on the collective actor.

[1] M Amis, *The House of Meetings* (New York, Knopf, 2006) 211–19.

Following the previous chapter's pattern that presented collective trauma's marks on the Armenian people, this chapter identifies current symptoms of collective trauma stemming from the past that the Turkish people as a whole manifest today. These symptoms arise, in part, out of people's memories and what they have been taught about historical events, but also their subsequent experiences related to them. Before describing the symptoms then, I recap those events and destructive actions, which remain today's Turks' psychological and moral responsibility.

I. CONTEXTUALISING THE ESTABLISHMENT OF THE REPUBLIC OF TURKEY

The Ottoman Muslim elites and ordinary citizens had grown accustomed to the state ruling over great territory and wielding power over subject peoples, often exercised violently, a collective lifestyle to which they felt entitled. By 1900 contemporaries had witnessed a great reduction of imperial territory over the previous quarter of a century, and the empire seemed only to face the prospect of further losses. The possible forfeiture of empire, Kévorkian writes, 'gradually became an obsession … with every fresh territorial loss only intensifying the dominant group's trauma and humiliation'.[2] I repeat the important observation of Göçek, namely the effects of the humiliation during the Balkan Wars: 'The visceral emotional reaction to the Balkan Wars whitewashed and annulled any serious reflection'.[3] She describes how terror can flood the rational mind and impair cognition.

As the Ottoman elite came to confront the threat of overwhelming external power, their perceptions and judgement became limited or distorted by fearful anticipation. Out of this turmoil emerged a wartime culture that was at once traumatised and traumatising. Within Ottoman society, there was no lawful process to protect those who might differ from the powerful.

Muslims throughout the empire knew grave loss when their young men went off to fight, when they failed to return or returned badly injured, and when families, neighbours, and whole communities at home, grew increasingly impoverished. The influx of Ottoman Muslims from the Balkans fleeing Christian reprisals introduced a new element of discriminatory treatment of Ottomans of different backgrounds in what was left of the Ottoman Empire. When authorities transferred former Armenian property to house the refugees during World War I, those Muslims who had once been neighbours of Armenians and resentful of their relative status would have experienced conflicting feelings, ranging from entitlement to shame. Some would have probably also felt sorrow at the loss of the Armenian neighbours, shock at how their removal was carried out, compassion at the sight of impoverished refugees, and anxiety about how this influx would affect them.

The end of the war brought fresh upheavals. Discussions about the peace terms with the Ottoman Empire began in earnest only after the conclusion of the treaties of Versailles and St Germain-en-Laye. Before their effort paid off in the signing of the Treaty of Sèvres in 1920 (two years after the Armistice of Mudros ended hostilities

[2] R Kévorkian, *The Armenian Genocide: A Complete History* (London, IB Tauris, 2011) 266.

[3] F Müge Göçek, *Denial of Violence: Ottoman Past, Turkish Present, and Collective Violence against the Armenians, 1789–2009* (New York, Oxford University Press, 2015) 234.

between the Ottoman Empire and the Allies), Mustafa Kemal, at the head of a Turkish nationalist army, challenged the treaty even as its terms were being hammered out, just as the Ottomans had done during negotiations at Brest-Litovsk. Had it been implemented, the Treaty of Sèvres would have dismembered and reduced the Ottoman Empire to a rump state in central Anatolia and apportioned the remainder to France, Great Britain, Italy, Greece, and Armenia. What happened was entirely different. By 1923 the Turkish nationalist forces had murdered or driven out the Armenians, the Greeks, the Italians, and all other non-Muslim claimants to the fast-unravelling empire and in that same year forced the Allies to return to the negotiating table.

Kemal now firmly established himself as the country's national leader. He deposed the empire's last sultan and met with the Allies to negotiate new peace terms in Lausanne, Switzerland, where he secured generous terms in the resulting Treaty of Lausanne. The Arab lands of the former Ottoman Empire were shorn off, but Anatolia and Eastern Thrace came under full Turkish sovereignty. The country proclaimed itself a republic and adopted a constitution that granted rights to Turkish citizens. Though the Allies had insisted on and then monitored courts-martial trials of the chief genocide perpetrators during the post-war Ottoman government, the convictions were not enforced. Most remaining Greeks and Armenians were massacred or expelled from Turkish soil. Kemal refused any responsibility for his countrymen's crimes against those Christians. His claim became official Turkish dogma, part of the founding myth of the Turkish Republic.[4]

According to official figures, approximately 80,000 Armenians live in Turkey today, including some 50,000 guest workers from Armenia who make a living doing menial jobs.[5] Turkey's border with the tiny landlocked state of Armenia remains closed, preventing the realisation of the economic benefits that would come to and are needed by people on both sides of the border. There is also a mostly publically unacknowledged minority of unknown size of Turkish citizens with at least one Armenian grandparent, who, in 1915, were forced to choose between death or conversion to Islam and integration into a Turkish or Kurdish household.[6]

II. OFFICIAL DENIAL OF GENOCIDE IN TODAY'S TURKEY

In 2001, according to Akçam, the Turkish government created an institution specifically to deny genocide:

> [G]enocide denial is … a state policy of primary importance. The National Security Council, Turkey's highest constitutional authority established … a Coordinating Committee for

[4] See EJ Zürcher, 'Renewal and Silence: Postwar Unionist and Kemalist Rhetoric on the Armenian Genocide' in RG Suny et al, *A Question of Genocide: Armenians and Turks at the End of the Ottoman Empire* (Oxford, Oxford University Press, 2011) 306–16; UÜ Üngör, *The Making of Modern Turkey: Nation and State in Eastern Anatolia, 1913–1950* (Oxford, Oxford University Press, 2011); F Ulgen, '"Sabiha Gökçen's 80-Year-Old Secret": Kemalist Nation Formation and the Ottoman Armenians' (PhD thesis, University of California, 2010).

[5] T de Waal, *Great Catastrophe: Armenians and Turks in the Shadow of Genocide* (Oxford, Oxford University Press, 2015) 100; L Marchand and G Perrier, *Turkey and the Armenian Ghost: On the Trail of the Genocide*, trans D Blythe (Montreal, McGill-Queen's University Press, 2015) 108–109.

[6] A Hadjian, *Secret Nation: The Hidden Armenians of Turkey* (London, IB Tauris, 2018).

> the Fight Against Baseless Claims of Genocide. All of the important ministries, including the Armed Forces, are represented on this committee, which is chaired by the vice prime minister. I repeat: Denying the genocide is one of the most important national policies of the Turkish state. You need to realize that you aren't just confronting a simple 'denial', but you're up against a 'denialist regime'.[7]

III. EXPLANATIONS FOR THE REFUSAL TO RECOGNISE GENOCIDE

Turkey's reasons for denial of the Armenian genocide have shifted over the decades. Nonetheless, even today, all these arguments can be found in circulation, creating confusion that may itself be a strategic choice. They may be enumerated as follows:

- There were no Armenians in Turkey;
- Armenians were a disloyal group who revolted for no reason;
- There was a civil war between Armenians and Turks;
- Armenians were merely relocated from the war zone and protected;
- Since the number of Armenians who lived in the Ottoman Empire is not known, then the number who died during the war cannot be known;
- Some Armenians were killed not under the sanction of the government but by rogue elements, mainly Kurds;
- Any Armenian deaths are to be regretted but do not constitute genocide.

Another reason proclaims why Muslims could, all but essentially, not commit genocide. When he was prime minister, Turkey's current president, Recep Tayyip Erdoğan, for example, stated:

> 'It is not possible for those who belong to the Muslim faith to carry out genocide'.

Accordingly, Erdoğan refuses to accept that Sudanese paramilitaries committed genocidal acts against the population of Darfur, or that Sudan's former president, Omar al-Bashir, is guilty of the crimes for which he has been indicted by the International Criminal Court.[8]

IV. MOTIVATIONS FOR TURKEY'S DENIAL

As the remainder of this chapter argues, Turks deny because they fear the emotional pain of truth as well as the material cost of admission and consequently aim to avoid both. Acknowledging commission of crimes against humanity after more than a century of denial would be immensely shaming and humiliating, and would sow confusion about their history, themselves and mistrust of the government. Insistent denial, without any actor employing powerful pressure to enforce payment of

[7] Taner Akçam, interview by Guilluame Perrier, *Le Monde*, 7 January 2012 (republished in *Armenian Weekly*, 25 January 2012).

[8] S Freedman, 'Erdogan's Blind Faith in Muslims', *Guardian*, 12 November 2009.

reparations, enables its avoidance. As stated in the Preface to this book, an important Turkish official volunteered the following in an off-the-record meeting with a colleague and me in the 2010s: 'We know it was genocide. We won't say so because we would have to pay reparations'. At today's values the cost of full reparations would indeed be staggering, and the threat of it presumably highly motivates the government to do everything possible to avoid it.[9] This chapter addresses some tactics adopted, conscious and unconscious, for avoidance of shame, humiliation, and the payment of reparations.

V. HATRED AND CONTEMPT, SILENCING AND BLAMING

From the genocide onwards, Turkish hostility, official and non-official, toward the tiny number of Armenians remaining in the country hardened. After the 2009 event at Harvard featuring Cemal, a Turkish citizen who had attended wrote to me about an apparent paradox: 'Yet even as Turks are ignorant, they are taught to hate and despise Armenians as infidels and think it is fine to show contempt'. According to a study on Turkish national identity, social scientist Hatice Çoban Keneş found that 'presented as "dirty Others" [are] mostly Kurds, Alevis, and Armenians ... In light of increasing forms of "new racism" in Turkey, it is the minorities who bear the brunt of the impact'.[10]

In his family memoir, Garin Hovannisian, a grandson of historian Richard Hovannisian, writes how his father Raffi, at the end of a month long trip to Turkey in 1982, handed his US passport to a security official at Istanbul's Yeşilköy Airport, only to be treated with contempt:

> five security officers ... were waiting ... They spoke to each other in Turkish, and Raffi made out a couple of words ... 'Armenian' and 'infidel'. In Raffi's suitcase, the officers found two socks full of soil – the soil of Bazmashen, Kharpert ... [that was] to be sprinkled on the graves [of genocide survivors in California]. The soil was confiscated ... the officers examined the tour leader's maps; eastern Turkey was identified as Western Armenia. They spat on the maps.[11]

In general today's Turks are kept ignorant, and what little they are taught is heavily laden with national myths and mistruths.[12] Social psychologists Rezarta Bilali, Linda R Tropp, and Nilanjana Dasgupta have investigated how the genocidal violence is understood, asking how Turks apportioned responsibility for it. They learned that Turks viewed all of them – themselves, the Armenians, and others – as bearing responsibility for inciting and carrying out the violence, and that Turks'

[9] A Manuk-Khaloyan et al, 'The Endless Arc of International Justice: Reparations after the Armenian Genocide' in J Bhabha et al (eds), *Time for Reparation? Addressing State Responsibility for Collective Injustice* (Philadelphia, University of Pennsylvania Press, forthcoming).

[10] AB Çelik et al, 'Patterns of "Othering" in Turkey: A Study of Ethnic, Ideological, and Sectarian Polarisation, South European Society and Politics' (2017) 22 *South European Society and Politics* 217, 221.

[11] GK Hovannisian, *Family of Shadows: A Century of Murder, Memory, and the Armenian American Dream* (New York, HarperCollins, 2010) 128.

[12] See JM Dixon, *Dark Pasts: Changing the State's Story in Turkey and Japan* (Ithaca, NY, Cornell University Press, 2018).

responsibility was greater for the results of that violence while the responsibility of Armenians and others was greater for the instigation. Their respondents concluded that '[Turkish] harm doing' was justified and thereby felt that that their blame was 'reduced'.[13] Then and today, the Turkish educational system conveys the message that Armenians' actions neçessitated massacres of hundreds of thousands.

Another way to ensure denial in the general population is to foster ignorance. Bilali examined eighth- and eleventh-grade textbooks in Turkey (all under control of the Ministry of Education) and found that only 1–3 pages covered 'the events of 1915', which in any case are also justified by the 'other side' argument described just below by Mamigonian.[14] That is, there is no mention of events constituting genocide. Ensuring ignorance is furthermore carried out by the widespread erasure of Armenian churches, graveyards, names of towns, and other evidence of Armenians' existence, brought about by neglect or deliberate destruction.[15]

As of 2013 the policy had worked as intended. '[T]he majority [in Bilali's] sample (65%) believed that both groups have harmed each other equally ... 10% of the sample ... believed that Turks were the victims while Armenians were the harm doers'.[16] Some Turks do not even know that the Armenians ever lived in Turkey and remain ignorant, therefore, of their fate. In an email received after the Cemal event, the same young man quoted earlier continued his speculation on the difference between young Armenians and Turks:

> ... To be a Turk [in this conflict] in your typical state ... is to be normal. You grow up knowing nothing. ... Then, when you grow up, you have a choice to become a denialist (and a 'patriot' I guess) ... The young [Turkish] guy asked yesterday [at the event], ok, maybe my ancestors did something wrong, what do you want from me? A normal and logical question.

VI. DENIAL'S REFUGE IN CONSTRUCTIVISM

Mamigonian has studied how, with knowledge of the genocide growing among the interested public, Turkish academics and their sympathisers in the United States now claim that it is impossible to establish whether there was a genocide, arguing that is because there are two irreconcilable sides to the story:

> The body of documentation of and critical scholarship on the Armenian Genocide that has grown over the past several decades has rendered traditional strategies of silencing and denial increasingly untenable. This has not, however, brought denial to an end. Turkey and those who support its official narrative have responded by developing a more effective

[13] R Bilali et al, 'Attributions of Responsibility and Perceived Harm in the Aftermath of Mass Violence' (2012) 18(1) *Peace and Conflict: Journal of Peace Psychology* 28.

[14] R Bilali, 'National Narrative and Social Psychological Influences in Turks' Denial of the Mass Killings of Armenians as Genocide' (2013) 69 *Journal of Social Issues* 19. See also Jennifer Dixon's work examining the construction of official narratives in Turkey and postwar Japan in *Dark Pasts*.

[15] For a study that examines the more general aspects of the intentional destruction of architectural heritage, with reference to the Armenian case, see R Bevan, *The Destruction of Memory: Architecture at War* (London, Reaktion Books, 2006).

[16] Bilali, 'National Narrative and Social Psychological Influences in Turks' Denial of the Mass Killings of Armenians as Genocide', 25.

> model that seeks to establish itself as the legitimate 'other side of the story'. Like tobacco industry lobbyists starting in the 1950s – as well as such latter-day ideological and rhetorical descendants as deniers of global warming – apologists for the 'Turkish position' labor to construct denialism as part of a legitimate intellectual debate – a scholarly controversy that will never and can never be resolved.[17]

According to Akçam, Turkey sponsors academic research and writing that either denies the genocide or aims to sow doubt about otherwise established realities. At a speech delivered at the 2012 National Association for Armenian Studies and Research Annual Assembly, Akçam stated:

> The Turkish government is following a very systematic and aggressive policy ... to make the idea that '1915 was not genocide' as accepted a ... belief as the idea that '1915 was genocide' in US universities ... The argument ... is ...: 'We want freedom of speech at American universities. We want the same freedom to say that 1915 was not a genocide, that's been given to those who say it was' ... The idea that the events of 1915 constituted genocide isn't being directly attacked. Rather what it wants to say is you have your idea about history, I have mine.[18]

Some Turkish Americans support denialist projects, including at least one private individual, Turkish-American businessman Yalçın Ayaşlı, who spent $30 million of his own funds to found a substantial organisation, the Turkish Coalition of America, which supports the Turkish Studies Project at the University of Utah. According to Mamigonian, the organisation has made the 'academic controversy' argument a major focus, funding publications that attempt to undermine the historicity of the Armenian genocide.[19]

If Armenian-American groups lobby members of Congress for genocide recognition, Turkish groups pay American lobbyists and public relations firms to carry out Turkey's denial policy to combat genocide recognition.[20] Turkish interests contribute to the campaigns of members of Congress whose constituents include American corporations that sell expensive military hardware to Turkey. In 2017 some 14 American firms paid American lobbyists to represent Turkish interests.[21] (Even so, in a historic December 2019 vote, members of both parties in the US Congress agreed unanimously to recognise the Armenian genocide.)

[17] MA Mamigonian, 'Academic Denial of the Armenian Genocide in American Scholarship: Denialism as Manufactured Controversy' (2015) 9 *Genocide Studies International* 62; and RN Proctor and L Schiebinger (eds), *Agnotology: The Making and Unmaking of Ignorance* (Stanford, CA, Stanford University Press, 2008). See also G Kenyon, 'The Man Who Studies the Spread of Ignorance', *BBC Future*, 6 January 2016, www.bbc.com/future/story/20160105-the-man-who-studies-the-spread-of-ignorance. Proctor also wrote about the 'manufactured controversy' concept in *Golden Holocaust: Origins of the Cigarette Catastrophe and the Case for Abolition* (Berkeley, California University Press, 2012).

[18] Taner Akçam, speech (National Association for Armenian Studies and Research Assembly, Belmont, MA, 19 May 2012).

[19] Mamigonian, 'Academic Denial of the Armenian Genocide in American Scholarship', 61–82.

[20] RW Smith et al, 'Professional Ethics and the Denial of Armenian Genocide' (1995) 9(1) *Holocaust and Genocide Studies* 1, https://doi.org/10.1093/hgs/9.1.1 (accessed 23 July 2020).

[21] A Shalal-Esa, 'CEOs Warn Against Armenia "Genocide" Bill', *Reuters*, 2 March 2010, www.reuters.com/article/us-usa-turkey-armenia/ceos-warn-against-armenia-genocide-bill-idUSTRE62157G20100302 (accessed 23 July 2020).

VII. THE MEANING OF TURKEY'S HONOUR CULTURE

Collective denial in Turkey means being protective of honour and reacting fiercely against anything that Turks may take as making them appear less than honourable, whether true or not, to protect the Turkish psyche. Thus, it is a crime to insult 'Turkishness' or the Turkish nation under Article 301 of the country's penal code. Should anyone speak publicly of the Armenian genocide or of something construed as insulting to Turkish national sensibilities, they would be liable to prosecution.

In *Turkey: A Modern History*, Zürcher links a rise in violence during a period of political instability in the late twentieth century in part to the culture of honour:

> The number of victims of political violence rose quickly from around 230 in 1977 … to between 1,200 and 12,500 two years later. … the political extremism in Turkey … overlay a traditional culture in which honor and shame, an extreme contrast between one's own family or clan and outsiders, played a prominent role.[22]

However, the defensiveness was present in Turkey much earlier. The restriction against 'insulting Turkishness' has existed at least since 1926, when a group of Jews protested the murder of a Jewish girl by a government official.[23]

Thus, insulting Turkishness is understood as an offence against national honour. A study of honour in contemporary Turkey, in comparison to the American south, finds that in Turkey honour means being held in respect and esteem by others, while violated honour is understood as most commonly caused by being humiliated and falsely accused, according to social psychologist Ayse Uskul. Insults constitute attacks on one's honour and are taken personally. Thus, who is honourable or dishonourable is decided by others, not by oneself. Violence is used to restore honour particularly where law enforcement is weak and the economy is fragile.[24] To regain honour, one must take 'punishment into one's own hands' and defend it.[25]

In an article published in Turkey about his 2013 memoir, Turkish journalist Ahmet Abakay revealed that his mother was Armenian, and that, as a result of learning this, his family believed themselves to have been dishonoured: '[My mother] was deposited on a doorstep and kept it a secret for 82 years, telling him a few weeks before her death and making him promise to tell no one' until her death, he said in an interview, continuing:

> Some relatives denied the story, while others claimed that his mother was too old to be aware of what she was saying. 'My uncle's children told me, "How dare you call our aunt Armenian and insult our family's honor. You will remove the Armenian part from your book, otherwise we will pull it off the shelves.ⁱ"'.[26]

As Abakay's story reveals, both honour and dishonour are transmitted generationally.

[22] EJ Zürcher, *Turkey: A Modern History*, 3rd edn (London, IB Tauris, 2004) 263.

[23] This was the Elza Niyego affair. See A Levi, *Türkiye Cumhuriyet'inde Yahudiler: Hukuki ve Siyasi Durumları* (Istanbul, Iletişim, 1996).

[24] AK Uskul at al, 'Honor Bound: The Cultural Construction of Honor in Turkey and the Northern United States' (2012) 43 *Journal of Cross-Cultural Psychology* 1131.

[25] Uskul at al.

[26] 'My Mother Was Armenian, Journalist Group Chair Reveals', *Hürriyet Daily News*, 22 December 2013.

VIII. COLLECTIVE DYSREGULATION

The Ottomans experienced the loss of the territories of empire but continued to feel entitled to its greatness and glory. If in the end the Ottoman Empire stood on shaky ground, the image created by Kemal, and hence for Turkey and the Turks, did not. He saved Turkey's pride and image by, for one thing, freeing the country of occupiers. For decades he himself was the great hero, idealised, the father of a collective rebirth, as in 'Atatürk', meaning 'father of the Turks'. A mystical cloud of glory surrounded his name. The shameful treatment of minorities was 'forgotten', a stain that, however apparently ignored, denied, or pushed under the rug, nonetheless diminished the value of his victory to his country. He left the country under the spell of the magical thinking of denial: Turkey's idealisation and glorification of Turks, and, until recently, of him, preserves the people's own self-respect: 'Glorified self-images', Bilali finds, 'position the in-group as superior to others [and] establish a positive national identity'.[27]

Even as former Ottomans became proud inheritors of their new nation, the fear created by the traumatic threat of dismemberment of their lands created by the Treaty of Sèvres, known as the 'Sèvres Syndrome', lingered in their minds. Turkish civil and military officials feared that they would be swept out of the lands that remained and constituted the new republic. The fear was of utter vulnerability, easily triggered, and was understandable – to an undefinable point – exemplifying how trauma mixes reality and imagination. After all, the Great Powers had long deliberated on how to seize and partition Ottoman territory. The Treaty of Sèvres marked the culmination of these efforts in its reducing the Ottoman Empire to a rump state. Turks could not be certain that European powers would not try to take over even this truncated shadow of the former empire. Many feared the claims of Armenians whose families' lands and property had been expropriated. While the state of Armenia has repeatedly stated that it has no irredentist claims over Turkish territory, a handful of Armenians unsuccessfully investigated possibilities for regaining property during the Cold War,[28] and some still persist in the belief that Sèvres remains a binding document. The memories of the loss of empire, the easily stimulated fears of further loss, mixed with guilt and fear about deserving to lose the land that was stolen from Armenians,[29] still trigger the Sèvres Syndrome.

The sense of humiliation and wounded honour can appear in individuals in ways that damage the functioning of the Turkish collectivity with regard to freedom of expression. When he was Istanbul's mayor, Erdoğan was jailed for four months by the then-secularist national government on a trumped-up charge in order to punish him for his Islamist tendencies and suppress his growing influence. At the time many turned against him, and he felt insulted, humiliated, and angry.[30] Even after his

[27] Bilali, 'National Narrative and Social Psychological Influences in Turks' Denial of the Mass Killings of Armenians as Genocide', 20.

[28] In the 1960s and into the 1980s, a handful of Turkish Armenians attempted to retrieve the properties that had once belonged to their families by appealing to the Turkish legal system, but in the end all efforts came to naught. See T Akçam and U Kurt, *The Spirit of the Laws: The Plunder of Wealth in the Armenian Genocide*, trans A Arkun (New York, Berghan, 2015) 172–84.

[29] Marchand and Perrier, *Turkey and the Armenian Ghost*, 104–105.

[30] D Filkins, 'The Deep State', *The New Yorker*, 12 March 2012, 38–49.

enormous electoral victory as prime minister in 2001, Erdoğan remained profoundly affected by that experience, according to Dexter Filkins in his profile in *The New Yorker*. Nuray Mert, a former journalist and one-time ally of Erdoğan's, told Filkins, 'He was traumatized, I think – by the military, by the people who tried to hold him back'.[31] When Erdoğan became prime minister, the European Union declined to advance his country's application for membership in the bloc. Erdoğan again experienced the rejection as a personal humiliation and, according to Filkins, 'mix[ed] his paeans with bitter allusions to enemies and slights'.[32] Since then, Turkey under Erdoğan has chipped away at free speech and minority rights.

In fact the Turkish psychologist Murat Paker sees that when Erdoğan's new AKP government had enhanced the country's chances of gaining entry into the European Union by allowing for greater freedom of expression, the country's ongoing hostility towards minorities barely abated. Anxiety over minority rights, writes Paker, are merged with ancient, unprocessed anxieties, namely:

> ... an annihilation/disintegration anxiety dating back to the collapse of the Ottoman Empire. An attempt to grant some minority rights is confronted with paranoid manifestations stemming from that anxiety, and traumatic memories of the collapse of the Ottoman Empire are compulsively re-experienced.[33]

In 2014, in Istanbul, protests in Gezi Park began over plans for the park's urbanisation. When the government broke up the demonstrations, the protesters demanded respect for their civil rights. The government immediately suspected the worst, unable to distinguish friends from enemies. The fears preceding the loss of the Ottoman Empire were reawakened and applied to that situation. The Turkish novelist Elif Shafak observed that Turkey was again slipping into 'a state of collective psychosis, a nation in the grip of paranoia, suspicious of everyone':

> Several government officials insinuated that dark forces were operating behind the scenes, including the Jewish diaspora, the CIA, the BBC, CNN and the interest-rate lobby, a term for a cabal of domestic and foreign banks that officials believe want to harm Turkey to further their own interests. A Turkish BBC reporter was openly accused of being a foreign spy. Protesters in Taksim Square were called terrorists. The German airline Lufthansa, it was suggested, was trying to scuttle an important new airport for Istanbul. On social media there are endless rumors about 'deep state within deep state'.[34]

In mid-2018, Sinan Ülgen, a visiting scholar at Carnegie Europe, confirmed that the Erdoğan regime's move to the right, was in step with its new 'ultranationalist' political partner, the National Movement Party. The party's agenda 'prioritizes national security concerns over personal freedoms'. It rests on 'a firm belief that Turkey has no friends at the international level ... bolstered by a siege mentality that regards Turkey's national interests as constantly under threat by foreign actors [and] ... nurtures an equal disdain for all foreigners'.[35]

[31] Filkins, 43.
[32] Filkins, 40.
[33] M Paker, 'Türk-Ermeni Meselesinin Psiko-Politik Düğümleri', *Birikim* (May–June 2005) 193–94.
[34] E Shafak, 'A Tempest of Fear in Turkey', *New York Times*, 24 February 2014.
[35] S Ülgen, 'Get Ready for a More Aggressive Turkey', *Foreign Policy*, 2 July 2018.

As stressed throughout in this book, an overgeneralised sense of danger is a common trauma symptom. Although some Turks claim that 'Turks are not affected by what the West thinks of them',[36] a siege mentality means fear of exactly that, creating hypervigilance and defensiveness. But the honour code may proscribe any admission of feeling dishonoured by outsiders' criticism, making it taboo for Turkey even to consider trying to open up about the past.

Both shame and hypervigilance are unintentionally conveyed in a proverb Turkish children are taught in school: 'The only friend of the Turk is another Turk'. According to human rights journalist Berivan Orucoglu:

> The proverb's relevance today has been confirmed by recent opinion data from the Pew Research Center. According to a survey … 86 per cent of Turks said they disliked Israel, followed by Iran with 75 per cent. The United States and Russia shared third place … scoring a 73 per cent disapproval rating … 70 per cent of Turks said they dislike NATO, 66 per cent disapprove of the European Union.
>
> In fact, it is hard to find any country or organization the Turkish people really like, except, of course, Turkey itself … According to our spring 2012 poll, 78 per cent of Turks said they had a favorable view of their country.[37]

Orucoglu's insight is both supported and not supported by Turkish journalist, Semih Idiz:

> It is almost as if there is a cultural need to believe that, with a few exceptions, the world hates us, so the best thing is to have a blanket suspicion of all … [This is] not the sign of a healthy society. As for the saying, 'The only friend a Turk has is another Turk', it is sufficiently clear today that this is not the case. Turks do not just hate others, they also hate each other, and this hatred is constantly stoked by politicians, opinion makers, and officials.[38]

The long psychological life of the Sèvres Syndrome suggests that the Turkish nation constantly feels unsafe in the world, including feeling ashamed and inadequate when facing others. Being hostile and contemptuous of others can provide defences against awareness and processing of guilt, anxiety, fear and humiliation.

IX. RESTRICTED CRITICAL THINKING

As has also been stressed, lack of processing trauma disables gaining perspective, that is, psychological space, around one's attachments and loyalties on difficult realities. Critical or independent thinking requires such perspective. Critical thinking, which includes knowing the historical record and understanding Ottoman motives and actions in their context, is as important for Turks as for Armenians. As argued in Chapter 17, it is possible that the Yeniköy Accord, if adopted, might not have worked out, and Armenians might have been able to separate from the empire.

[36] Ahmet Altan (lecture, Harvard University, Cambridge, MA, 25 January 2012).
[37] B Orucoğlu, 'The Turk Has No Friend but the Turk', *Foreign Policy*, 14 November 2014.
[38] S Idiz, 'Why Are Turks Xenophobic?' *Hürriyet Daily News*, 14 November 2014.

That was a reason for the Committee of Union and Progress's (CUP) fear of loss of part of their own homeland, but, as said, being a reason did not make it a justification for their genocidal method of solving the problem. For Turks, as for Armenians, reasons for a situation do not justify the taking of any and all kinds of actions to deal with it.

X. HIDDEN KNOWLEDGE AND A MORALLY INJURED CULTURE

The CUP heads of government knew full well that their treatment of Armenians had diminished their moral standing in the West. In late 1917, the journalist Julius Becker visited Talât in Istanbul to discuss Zionist-Ottoman relations. According to Kieser, Becker observed that the CUP rulers lacked confidence and direction:

> These imperial rulers had angst. They felt unable to manage up-and-coming, economically prospering, and self-reliant groups. In the end, they insisted only on external boundaries of the empire *without embracing a viable and vital internal project*.[39] (emphasis added)

He continued:

> Becker revealed [the] main factors of CUP rule and psychology: fear and intimidation, along with defiance and the pretense of superiority, bound to feelings of inferiority vis-à-vis non-Muslims.[40]

During the inter-war period Falih Rifki Atay, once Djemal's and Talât's deputy and finally Kemal's close companion, made the same observation:

> When the Armenians were deported, out of the same fear we have burned down all their still inhabitable quarters in the towns of Turkey … This was not by pure destructiveness, but an inferiority complex played a role. All that appeared to be European was like Christian and strange, and therefore strictly and fatefully not ours.[41]

Bullying or overaggressive behaviour often covers feelings of inferiority and shame. Although he was a bully, and the treatment of Armenians that he authorised was overaggressive, Talât himself seems mostly not to have felt inferior or ashamed. It is nonetheless entirely possible that he hid such feelings behind the personality he projected. As the end of the war became evident, he was aware that the crimes he had authorised against Armenians were morally wrong in the eyes of those he would have to negotiate with. Defeat was taking him down from the high of excitement first of pursuing victory with power and then of hoping to survive in the face of others' greater power; at which times he would not have paid heed to such matters. But now at the end, if he had been taught, as he probably was when growing up, conventional, general moral rules forbidding the killing of innocents and stealing property, he may have

[39] H-L Kieser, *Talaat Pasha: Father of Modern Turkey, Architect of Genocide* (Princeton, NJ, Princeton University Press, 2018) 301.

[40] Kieser, *Talaat Pasha*, 360.

[41] Kieser, *Talaat Pasha*, 360.

paused and, in the face of the shame of defeat, he himself, like other imperial citizens, may well have sensed himself to be morally injured and that his country was as well.[42] As many have pointed out, if the Armenian genocide does not undermine Turkey's foundational narrative as a civilised and modern nation,[43] its denial may. Bilali and social psychologist Johanna Vollhardt write that:

> [when p]erpetrator groups try to cope with moral identity threats and preserve a positive image of [their group ...,] society has lost its moral sensitivity to past genocide as well as to current and possibly future episodes of mass violence. With the disappearance of the Armenian Genocide and other mass violence from public discourse, a prevailing mindset that makes future mass crimes possible has also been granted tacit support.[44]

The Turkish Republic is a signatory to the United Nations Convention on the Prevention and Punishment of the Crime of Genocide. What does that mean to Turks today? Is their signature to the Convention part of the denial, added merely to improve their image? Is it similar to the feigned concern for the Armenians' welfare that Talât evinced as the First World War drew to an end and an Allied victory became an ever more distinct reality (Chapter 15)?[45]

XI. CHANGE IN TURKEY?

For a very long time, the Turkish public had been little exposed to the veracity of the Armenian genocide. There was a brief period between 2007 and 2014 when Turkey seemed ready to allow freer speech and the discussion of once-forbidden topics, and the collective understanding of the truth of the past in Turkey acquired some momentum. For example, in 2013, in southeastern Turkey (a Kurdish centre), a number of Kurds acknowledged the genocides of the Armenian and Assyrian peoples.[46] The occasion was the installation of a monument in which apology 'in the name of Kurds' was written in six languages. The event was hosted by Abdullah Demirbaş, the mayor of the municipality of Sur, the historic district in the large Kurdish city of Diyarbakır, where the Kurds, along with other Turkish Muslims, had perpetrated crimes against the Armenians. In recent decades it has long been a site of frequent and extremely violent conflict between the Turkish government and the Kurdistan Workers' Party (PKK) and other Kurdish nationalists.

[42] MC Lamia, 'Shame: A Concealed, Contagious, and Dangerous Emotion', *Psychology Today*, 4 April 2011, www.psychologytoday.com/us/blog/intense-emotions-and-strong-feelings/201104/shame-concealed-contagious-and-dangerous-emotion (accessed 23 July 2020).

[43] See Ulgen, 'Sabiha Gökçen's 80-Year-Old Secret'; A Zarakol, 'Ontological (In)security and State Denial of Historical Crimes: Turkey and Japan' (2010) 24 *International Relations* 3; and T Akçam, *A Shameful Act: The Armenian Genocide and the Question of Turkish Responsibility* (New York, Metropolitan Books, 2006).

[44] R Bilali and JR Vollhardt, 'Victim and Perpetrator Groups' Divergent Perspectives on Collective Violence: Implications for Intergroup Relations' (2019) 40 *Political Psychology* 75.

[45] R Lemkin, *Totally Unofficial: The Autobiography of Raphael Lemkin*, ed. Donna-Lee Frieze (New Haven, CT, Yale University Press, 2013) 200–201.

[46] The Assyrian (Christian) population of the Ottoman Empire was also targeted for destruction in 1915–16.

At the installation ceremony, Demirbaş said, 'We Kurds, in the name of our ancestors, apologise for the genocide of the Armenians and Assyrians in 1915. We will continue our struggle to secure atonement and compensation for them'.[47] Demirbaş called on Turkish authorities, too, to be held accountable, apologise, and atone for the genocide:

> We invite them to take steps in this direction. This memorial is dedicated to all peoples and religious groups who were subjected to genocide in these lands. The Monument of Common Conscience was erected to remember and demand accountability for all the massacres that took place since 1915.[48]

A few years later, in 2015, Demirbaş spoke again: 'I want for Armenians the same things as I want for Kurds'.[49]

The ending of Demirbaş's efforts is, however, tragic and speaks to the current treatment of those who deviate from the official line. Diyabakir was once an Armenian centre as well as a Kurdish and Assyrian one. Its historic Armenian church had been painstakingly restored in 2011, after being almost completely destroyed during the genocide. It was then reopened as a gesture of reconciliation between Turks and Armenians. But in 2016 the restored church was again heavily damaged during clashes between the Turkish army and Kurds demanding their rights. Demirbaş himself has been in jail for some years and known to be in very poor health. His important efforts at making Diyarbakır and its famous church a centre of tolerance have been willfully destroyed.

Changing the culture of violence and intolerance toward minorities is necessary for Turkey's people and their democracy. Many sultans' lives were cut short by others who wished to hold the title. From 1908 to 1914, several constitutional governments were replaced not through elections but through coups and violence. Kemal took power by force, becoming the uncontested ruler for life. Since he died in 1938, four changes of government have been facilitated by military intervention. Even the current AKP government, initially peacefully and optimistically elected to power, has increasingly ruled through intimidation backed by the corrupted judiciary that the regime has empowered. In 2015, Sevgi Akarçeşme, in her column in the once-pro-AKP and now-defunct popular Gülenist *Zaman* newspaper, called the AKP an 'arbitrocracy',[50] a modern term for absolutism. Thus, according to political scientist Mine Eder, a general mistrust among many Turks corresponds with a return to arbitrary government:

> [S]ociety … operates through informal networks and does not trust the state in providing basic social services equally for all … [S]uch arrangements are likely to undermine the trust in, and legitimacy of, the state institutions [and] may be on its way to change the very basis of the state-citizen relationship. As citizens … become willing and ready to accept any litmus tests or community loyalty in order to survive, the prospects for a transparent

[47] G Akkum, 'Kurdish Leaders Apologize for 1915 during Monument Inauguration in Diyarbakir', *Armenian Weekly*, 12 September 2013.

[48] Akkum, 'Kurdish Leaders Apologize for 1915 during Monument Inauguration in Diyarbakir'.

[49] A Haroian, 'Letter to the Editor', *Armenian Weekly*, 1 September 2015.

[50] S Akarçesme, 'Turkey's Vengeful President Erdoğan Is Squashing His Country's Rise', *Quartz*, 14 April 2015.

> welfare governance based on rule of law, equality and all-encompassing state institutions might diminish. What is worse, so far, neither the privatization nor the politicization … have addressed the structural poverty and/or reduced the insecurity and economic vulnerability in the country.[51]

Trauma can instil wisdom, but only after some healing. As outsiders have increasingly recognised the commission of the crime of genocide, Turkey has lost some standing as a trustworthy member of the international community. Collective processing of that loss today might first mean Turkish acceptance of having committed the genocide of Armenians (and Greeks and Assyrians), then grieving and making amends. Another loss yet to be grieved is the loss of these peoples as living parts of their society. These Ottoman losses and misdeeds could be integrated into a balanced narrative of Turkish history, rebuilding trust between Turks and others internationally.

In parts of Turkey where many Armenians once lived, denial of the Armenian genocide cannot be easy. In eastern Turkey particularly, where most Armenians once lived, memories about Armenians have been transmitted to later generations. Testimonials are all around – the decaying, empty houses in former Armenian villages and districts, crushed Armenian gravestones, and crumbling churches dotting overgrown fields. There the Armenian past is thus partially still present. The small but important minority, including some public intellectuals, who explicitly acknowledge and discuss the facts of history, includes many who have been prosecuted and jailed under Article 301.

This acknowledgement of truth has come at great personal cost. In 2007 the widely admired Turkish-Armenian journalist Hrant Dink, who promoted better Armenian–Turkish relations in Turkey, was shot and killed in Istanbul in cold blood in broad daylight. Although the teenage murderer was seized immediately, a wider conspiracy seemed afoot, but nothing yet is proved as justice has still not been served. Temelkuran notes that '100,000 Turks marched in honor of Dink after his murder'. She asks what this meant for Turkish identity and attempts to offer a hopeful answer:

> So who are these 'Turks'? Why are their shoulders slumped? Because of the bodies they bear on their backs, grieving Hrant and those before him – … tired of being killer Turks.[52]
>
> They want the 'poisoned blood' to flow forth, just as Hrant said. They want it to flow forth and flow away, so that they can live among people who don't kill and aren't killed. They wish to be not killer Turks, but Turks who are able to shed tears for the dead. They want to be themselves. They want the bloody past to end and a bloodless future to be built. They don't want history to repeat itself – they want it gone, and they want it to leave the Turks in peace. They don't want to share the Turkishness of Turks who kill their Armenians. They don't want to share a country with those who kill Kurds and who kill fellow Turks for being insufficiently Turkish.[53]

The issues raised in this chapter about Turkey and Turks are not ultimately about the Armenian genocide. The end of genocide denial could be the start to putting

[51] M Eder, 'Retreating State? The Political Economy of Welfare Reform Change in Turkey' (1999) 2 *Middle East Law and Governance* 184.

[52] E Temulkuran, *Deep Mountain*, trans K Dakan (London, Verso, 2010) 172.

[53] Temulkuran, 173.

Turkey on the road to becoming a true democracy. In Germany, the recognition of Nazi crimes, followed by the apology and reparations made to Jews and Israel, have benefited Germany greatly. Turkey's failure to exercise constructive authority in its region may be partly because of its failure to face its history and thereby gain the trust of its neighbours. Ambassador Morgenthau tried to inspire the Turks he addressed with his vision of what Turkey could become.[54] He linked it to what he saw as the melting pot of the United States. If Morgenthau were speaking in early 2020, he could not point to the same American inspiration. Burcu Gültekin Punsmann, a scholar practitioner in conflict transformation, does, however, write today, 'Turkey has the potential to support transformation and reform within the societies of the South Caucasus though soft power'.[55] As before in its history, Turkey may feel torn between so-called Eastern and Western values, but today's values of human rights are universal. It can choose to go there with soft power.

At the start of this chapter, Martin Amis laid out universal essentials for a country to begin to address the moral injury it did to itself.

[54] H Morgenthau, *All in a Lifetime* (New York, Doubleday, 1923) 201–202.

[55] BG Punsmann, 'Implications of Turkish-Azerbaijani Relations for Regional Security and Development' (working paper 13/28, Instituto Affari Internazionali, Rome, August 2013).

Conclusion: Processing Collective Trauma Collectively: Will We?

At the Paris Peace Conference the victorious Allied Powers had adopted the principle of collective – rather than individual – rights and protections for national groups and minorities. The Treaty of Lausanne had decreed protection for Turkey's minorities. However, Turkish lawmakers did not grant full protection to the country's few remaining Armenians, Greeks, and Jews. Only Turkish Muslims had full and unconditional citizenship (Kurds were nominally included because Muslim).[1]

From then on the Republic of Turkey made no visible effort to overcome the deeply established attitude that the country's Turks were collectively entitled to superior status over all other ethnic groups. The new republic's authorities did not see tolerance as a principle to be seriously embraced and never took steps to foster an inclusive climate in Turkish society. They were not interested in creating a multiethnic state anew, but rather a homogenous political entity with Muslim Turks at the top of the social hierarchy. Non-Muslim minorities as well as Alevis and Muslim Kurds were conceptualised as 'others' – as peoples who could not be trusted to assimilate willingly or shed their ethnic identity in exchange for integration within the newly emerging body politic. These minority groups were expected to act in complete accord with the state's dictates and repeatedly demonstrate their complete obedience and loyalty even as they were barred from holding military and bureaucratic office and stripped of many cultural rights. Thus, today, according to law, although Kurds as well as Armenians, Greeks, or Jews are entitled to be judges or generals, Turkey has no Christian, Jewish, or unassimilated Kurdish judges or generals. Those Muslims of Kurdish origin who do hold high positions are totally assimilated within the Sunni Muslim milieu.[2] And thus, while legally prohibited from discriminating against minorities, Turkey continues to do so against those minorities with impunity, because this is normal, 'as things should be', according to an anonymous expert.

[1] K Tsitselikis, 'The Minority Protection System in Greece and Turkey Based on the Treaty of Lausanne (1923): A Legal Overview', background information presented at the 7th International Student Conference, Borjan Tanevski Memorial Fund, ACT/Anatolia College, University of Macedonia, Thessaloniki, 14 May 2010, www.sophia.de/borjan/BTConference2010 (accessed 23 July 2020). See also M Mazower, 'Minorities and the League of Nations in Interwar Europe' (1997) 126 *Daedalus* 47; C Fink, *Defending the Rights of Others: The Great Powers, the Jews and International Minority Protection 1878–1938* (Cambridge, Cambridge University Press, 2004); and L Ekmekçioğlu, *Recovering Armenia: The Limits of Belonging in Post-genocide Turkey* (Stanford, CA, Stanford University Press, 2016) 103–108.

[2] Taner Akçam informed me of the information in these two sentences and assured me that no citation was needed because these facts are common knowledge.

Following the Soviet takeover of 1920–21, an uneasy calm settled over Transcaucasia. Once the Bolsheviks had vanquished their political rivals in the civil war, they reasserted their power and authority and moved back into the region with the assistance of native ideologues, crushing all opposition. The most enduring legacy pertaining to Armenian–Azerbaijani relations was the Bolsheviks' 1921 decision to assign Karabakh to the newly created Soviet Azerbaijan. When the three republics of the South Caucasus declared their independence in 1991, the Armenian and Azerbaijani conflict over the enclave began anew and continues to this day.

I. THE KARABAKH CONFLICT TODAY

The Karabakh conflict is widely regarded as near impossible to resolve even as violence breaks out in the region with depressing frequency. It is also seen as benefiting certain actors; according to political scientist Behlül Özkan, 'the conflicting parties … [and] the regional and global actors [do not] feel compelled to challenge the status quo and find a peaceful solution for the conflict' because in the decade before they 'developed methods and strategies to benefit from the deadlock'. He goes on to say that

> their behavior accrues them great wealth, helps them to hold on to power, and sacrifices the creation of a democratic environment and development of a civil society, making it unlikely that they will risk their status for a solution that requires compromise from both sides.

He speaks of the need to 'imagine other ways in which the nation-state is not the only parameter to establish peaceful coexistence'.[3]

In 2013, Gayane Novikova, a South Caucasus security expert, judged the conflict over Karabakh to be the most potentially explosive in that region. She listed several issues that still work against settlement:

- The negative influence of the dominant great power, Russia, which benefits from the conflict and discourages involvement of other powers whose influence would likely be far more constructive;
- The increasing militarisation of the region, and the trend within these states toward authoritarianism;
- In the lawless borderlands between the conflicting parties a robust underground economy is based on human trafficking and smuggling.[4]

Since 2005 the scholar-practitioner Philip Gamaghelyan, my colleague of some years when together we, with others, convened the Armenian–Turkish workshops, has worked in a nonofficial capacity to resolve this conflict. In 2010, he, too, like Özkan and Novikova, found that the Armenian and Azerbaijani governments were resistant to change. He observed that both governments gained power 'on radical

[3] B Özkan, 'Who Gains from the "No War No Peace" Situation? A Critical Analysis of the Nagorno-Karabakh Conflict' (2008) 13 *Geopolitics* 578, 593–95.

[4] G Novikoa, 'The South Caucasus and the European Security Strategy' in E Felberbauer and F LaPierre (eds), *Building Confidence in the South Caucasus: The European Union's and NATO's Soft Security Initiative* (Vienna, 2013) 43.

nationalistic slogans with mutually exclusive claims to deliver Nagorno-Karabakh to their respective communities'. Thus, during the years in which the three commentators cited here produced their analyses of the conflict, the government heads of Armenia, the Nagorno-Karabakh Republic and Azerbaijan succeeded in either convincing or so manipulating the public that possibilities for resolution shrank and shrank. Since then influential individuals in the region cannot demonstrate that Gamaghelyan's depressing assessment is finally outdated:

> Every politician who takes a moderate stand and tries to improve relations is inevitably stamped as a traitor ... This war of rhetoric, produced mostly for internal consumption, forces leaders on both sides to adopt an increasingly radical stance vis-à-vis the other side. It widens the gap between the two parties and leaves little room for a solution.[5]

Such views go back a long time. In 1913, Ismail Ziyatkhanov, a member of the Russian State Duma (parliament), spoke of their effect when better relations between Armenians and Azeris were what was needed:

> We, the Muslims, were told by the [tsarist] administration: You have been economically enslaved by the Armenians. They are arming themselves and plan to create their state; one day they will do away with you. The Armenians were told that the idea of Pan-Islamism had put down deep roots in all strata of the Muslim community, and one day the Muslims would massacre them. Such was the pattern of the provocation.[6]

Gamaghelyan stresses the deep roots that this propaganda takes within the cultural realm of both countries: 'The rhetoric penetrates the media and educational institutions, gradually transforming them into propaganda machines. Entire generations have been raised on this propaganda during the 20 years of conflict'. The predictable result is that it has intensified 'mutual mistrust and hatred, while elevating the mutually exclusive myths of Nagorno-Karabakh to such a level that no politician can suggest any concession without producing public outrage'.[7] While Özkan, Novikova, and Gamaghelyan surely differ on the varying aspects of the Nagorno-Karabakh entanglement, they do seem to agree that the current situation is one that keeps on wounding hundreds of thousands, and deepening bad feeling among all. Özkan remarks that:

> [T]he cost of the status quo is very high for both the societies living ... with over one million refugees and internally displaced persons. They are clearly on the losing side, and as long as they will not be able to influence the decision-making process in a free and democratic environment, it will be impossible to challenge the status quo for a peaceful solution ...[8]

I will return to the question of the possibility of improving these relations at the end of this chapter after presenting general ideas for recovery from collective trauma.

[5] P Gamaghelyan, 'Rethinking the Nagorno-Karabakh Conflict: Identity, Politics, Scholarship' (2010) 15 *International Negotiation* 33, 39.

[6] T Swietochowski, *Russian Azerbaijan, 1905–1920, The Shaping of a National Identity in a Muslim Community* (Cambridge, Cambridge University Press, 1995), from (1913) 2(12) 'Pervia musul'manskia gazeta na Kavkaze' 882–87.

[7] Gamaghelyan, 'Rethinking the Nagorno-Karabakh Conflict: Identity, Politics, Scholarship', 40.

[8] Özkan, 'Who Gains from the "No War No Peace" Situation?', 595.

II. HOW PROCESSING COLLECTIVE TRAUMA COLLECTIVELY MIGHT LOOK

Van der Kolk observes that 'We are on the verge of becoming a trauma conscious society'.[9] My question is 'Can we become a collective-trauma-conscious society and a collective-trauma-healing society? Van der Kolk further notes that 'We have the knowledge necessary to respond [to trauma] effectively'.[10] He is speaking of knowledge that has been developed and applied to individuals and family systems. The situation is different with collective trauma, about which we have some – but not all – of the knowledge needed for effective response.

The following seven ideas for working with collective trauma collectively are experimental and ambitious. They bring trauma work together with the work of intranational and international relations in joint activities at a greatly expanded scale. No one of these trauma-informed innovations on its own would do more than make a small difference, but if consolidated and enacted at the same time, such efforts have a chance of producing an exponentially greater effect.

A. Establishing and Broadly Disseminating Facts and Attitudes

Popular wisdom may claim that facts do not change minds, but political scientist Brendan Nyhan's studies demonstrate that over time they do indeed and that glimmers of doubt are important even in the face of frequent denying, exaggerating, stereotyping, or cherry-picking propaganda.[11] But if an agreed set of facts would begin to make productive dialogue and change possible, establishing such a basis is conditioned on free speaking, listening, determining, and disseminating facts. For decades in Armenian–Turkish–Azerbaijani relations, the denial and exaggeration has overwhelmed efforts to base narratives on fairly presented and established facts.

Furthermore, in Turkey freedom of speech has long been under siege in the country's limited democracy. However, around 2005 Turks and visitors to the country could reasonably expect to begin speaking their minds without fear of punishment. Discussion opened about the genocide. For example, after the 17 January 2007 assassination of the Turkish Armenian journalist and intellectual, Hrant Dink – Dink's life's work, admired by many Turks, was devoted to improving relations between Armenians and Turks – 100,000 people felt safe enough to express grief and gather publicly in Istanbul (see Chapter 18).

Dink's assassination moved his great friend Hasan Cemal to embark on his own personal journey of rediscovery of the Armenian genocide and his grandfather's role in it, leading him to offer gestures of acknowledgment – his visit to the Genocide

[9] B van der Kolk, *The Body Keeps the Score: Brain, Mind, and Body in the Healing of Trauma* (New York, Viking, 2014) 331.

[10] Van der Kolk, *The Body Keeps the Score*, 331.

[11] B Nyhan and J Reifler, 'Do People Actually Learn from Fact-Checking? Evidence from a Longitudinal Study during the 2014 Campaign', 30 November 2106, www.dartmouth.edu/~nyhan/fact-checking-effects.pdf (accessed 23 July 2020).

Memorial – and of reconciliation – he met with the grandson of those directly involved in his grandfather's assassination – in Yerevan in 2008. Soon Cemal used the word 'genocide' publicly. In 2012, his book *1915: The Armenian Genocide*[12] was published in Turkey, where it became a bestseller.

Another initiative, which had already begun in 2005, continued for the next 10 years. It was the informally led Workshop on Armenian and Turkish Scholarship (WATS), in which scholars met (outside Turkey) to discuss papers on contentious events that had occurred in the genocide period. Libaridian, one of WATS's three organisers, reported that the purpose was to see

> ... if the issue of Turkish-Armenian relations and ... events during World War I, could be taken out of the politically charged atmosphere and reworked as a problem with a historical context [with] input from other fields ... [allowing for] non-conventional opinions ... in a non-political environment [with respectful listening and discussion .... [A]rtificial 'middle' or 'balanced' positions [were not the goal; rather it was to achieve a] more complex and nuanced portrayal of the past ... [to] bridge the gap between the two histories ... without a predetermined outcome.

The organisers believed that

> ... this Workshop has been the single most successful endeavor to bring down the wall that separated scholars on this matter ... WATS has caused a shift in the 'politics' of scholarship on the subject and redefined the field. From being considered on the fringes of the spectrum, it has become the 'center'. Now it is those who oppose this approach that are considered extreme or marginal.[13]

WATS was awarded the Middle East Studies Association's Academic Freedom Prize in 2005. According to Kaligian, the WATS meetings had positive effects on the thinking of the Armenian and Turkish scholars who attended, including their agreement on the following:

> The Turkish official narrative has little to do with history and scholarship [and] the Armenian discourse often lacks the context, the rigor and the amplitude that would explain all aspects of events; that it is particularly weak in exploring the causation process ...[14]

WATS was always primarily directed to scholars. However, its work could today contribute still further by reaching and educating schoolchildren, teachers, and civil society about the history of the conflict and about how the WATS' process brought 'enemies' together. For the purpose of creating openness and building trust in both peoples to listen and learn about the other side, WATS' participants could compile short, simplified histories based on their agreed findings for different audiences and make such write-ups available online.

Another major initiative at the time of the centenary of the Armenian genocide was the 'I apologise' campaign, in which tens of thousands of Turkish intellectuals signed a statement of apology to Armenians. The apology was not for the 'genocide',

[12] H Cemal, *1915: The Armenian Genocide* (Istanbul, Hrant Dink Foundation, 2015).

[13] G Libaridian, 'A Report on the Workshop for Armenian/Turkish Scholarship' (Ann Arbor, 2006) unpublished document prepared for internal use by WATS.

[14] D Kaligian, 'The Use and Abuse of Armeno-Turkish Dialogue', *Armenian Review* (Fall–Winter 2008) 88.

but used a different phrase (below), one that often serves to circumvent the use of the forbidden 'genocide':

> My conscience does not accept the insensitivity showed to and the denial of the Great Catastrophe that the Ottoman Armenians were subjected to in 1915. I reject this injustice and for my share, I empathize with the feelings and pain of my Armenian brothers. I apologize to them.

While leading Turkish intellectuals voiced their support for this statement, Armenian and other Turkish intellectuals judged the wording of the apology to be crucially imperfect. One objection was that the statement offered no responsibility for wrongdoing.[15] Another was that, given the ongoing denial by the Turkish government, the campaign 'unleashed public expression of anti-Armenian sentiment .... [T]hese prominent denialists', in the opinion of journalist and human rights activist Ayse Gunaysu, can get away with what they say 'because they know that the overwhelming majority in their country is far from being aware of simple facts related to the fate of the Armenians of the Ottoman Empire'.[16] Although the apology and reactions to it were publicly discussed and disputed, we do not know whether the statement dented or thickened the Turkish wall of denial.

Other non-official steps were taken towards conciliation between the Armenian people and Turkey during that brief window that opened before the 2015 centenary of the genocide, probably in part because of the government's anticipated discomfort about what the world would say about it during the centenary. The window closed sometime after 2015, under the shadow of Erdoğan's growing authoritarianism.

B. Lessening the Toxic Power of Prejudice and Stereotypes

Establishing facts in Armenian–Turkish–Azerbaijani relations, or in any other frozen conflict, is one component for dealing with collective trauma collectively. Conscious use of our capacity for empathy in transforming attitudes is as essential; Babbitt et al wrote of its successful use with a small group of Israelis and Palestinians.[17] Empathy, the ability to know and feel what another is feeling, usually means feeling compassion. It is not necessarily easy to use empathy in this way. Neuroendocrinologist Robert Sapolsky finds that the human brain has a built-in barrier to experiencing empathy towards those who are different. While it is 'natural' to empathise compassionately with those we perceive to be similar to us, putting ourselves in the shoes of those we perceive to be different, 'unappealing', or 'aversive' is not. Rather it is an enormous cognitive and emotional task.[18] We resist it, he says, until we decide 'whether a particular

[15] M Mamigonian, 'Commentary on the Turkish Apology Campaign', *Armenian Weekly*, April 2009.

[16] A Gunaysu, 'About the Apology Campaign', *Armenian Weekly*, 10 January 2009.

[17] EF Babbitt et al, 'Combining Empathy with Problem-Solving in Israel: The Tamra Model of Facilitation in Yaad/Miaar' in C Zelizer and RA Rubenstein (eds), *Building Peace: Practical Reflections from the Field* (Sterling, VA, Kumairan Press, 2009) 157.

[18] RM Sapolsky, *Behave: The Biology of Humans at Our Best and Worst* (New York, Random House, 2017) 532.

misfortune is worthy of empathy'.[19] Sapolsky's discovery is discouraging. So is psychologist Paul Bloom's cautionary discourse on the understanding of empathy.[20]

Yet important, albeit somewhat indirect, evidence exists of empathy's important effect. More than 60 years ago, psychologist Gordon Allport[21] hypothesised that putting together people who were different from one another in face-to-face interactions would go part of the way towards removing or minimising prejudice, that is, in removing or minimising the 'barrier' Sapolsky identified. In 2006, social psychologists Thomas Pettigrew and Linda Tropp published a meta-analysis of some 515 studies, in each of which social scientists had tested the Allport hypothesis under many different situations and conditions.[22] Pettigrew and Tropp's study found the effect of contact to be real, that its power increased with institutional support, and that progress toward reducing prejudice was made even without such support. Through contact people come to see others as humans like themselves. We become familiar enough with the differences to see our own humanity reflected in them. The value of human contact in reducing stereotypes is indisputable.

C. Recognising Triggering as Opportunity and Pitfall

After experiencing humanly-caused collective trauma, we are primed for fight, flight, or freeze. That is, we are primed to being triggered. Thus, unsurprisingly, conflict resolution processes are triggering. As such, they provide the opportunity for human contact and attitude transformation through conscious processing both with our own people and with the other people. The illustration that follows is from a three-day conflict-resolution workshop with 14 influential Israelis and Palestinians some years ago. I was one of the student facilitators. At one point during the morning session of day two, a prominent Palestinian participant rose from the table and said he was 'feeling suicidal'. I doubt that anyone thought that this person had spoken literally. Yet all of us, participants and facilitators, evidenced shock. The lead facilitator, who had experienced collective trauma at a young age, said nothing. The Palestinian walked out. We did not find out why he left. Something he kept to himself had stopped him from speaking about it.

We lost an opportunity in that moment. When this man stood up and spoke, one of the facilitators could have responded. The Palestinian himself could have explained. Other participants could have reacted. We all could have and should have, but did not. At that moment, all of us were likely triggered to something flooding our minds that we brought into the workshop effort, perhaps rendering us unable to think well enough even to articulate even a simple, human response. Instead we may have asked ourselves such questions as 'Might speaking break a taboo?' 'What if he gets upset by what's said?' 'What if what's said falls flat?' 'What if it falls flat before

[19] Sapolsky, 532.

[20] P Bloom, *Against Empathy* (New York, Harper Collins, 2017).

[21] GW Allport, *The Nature of Prejudice* (Oxford, Addison-Wesley, 1954).

[22] TF Pettigrew and LR Tropp, 'A Meta-Analytic Test of Intergroup Contact Theory' (2006) 90(5) *Journal of Personality and Social Psychology* 754.

this company of peers and influential actors?' 'Why doesn't the authority (the lead facilitator) do something?'

Someone, facilitator or participant (though I believe it was the facilitators' job), needed to validate his anguish – even with a simple 'What!' or 'I'm sorry'. Someone absolutely needed to ask about the connection with the purpose of the workshop, to which his words surely referred – 'What does everyone here imagine that we are not doing now to help achieve the elusive possibility of progress in the Israeli–Palestinian relationship?' A facilitator might have said, 'We all have the great concerns about the situation [on the ground of the wider conflict]. We're indebted to [the Palestinian] for bringing the depth of concern into this room'. Had the man said more, or had the facilitators or participants intervened, the exchange might have led to hearing about his and others' concerns in relation to the workshop. Instead, even after the man left, no one mentioned the incident and no one asked, 'What might he have been communicating to us by leaving?' We continued as if nothing unusual or concerning had happened. We let the elephant sit in the middle of the room.

The opportunity of connecting with this participant's disappointment, fear, despair, and anger (I assume) was lost to our triggering. He had expressed some genuine, deep emotion. It was right on the surface, right in the room, but not identified and thus neither were the thoughts tied in with it. Had we connected with the emotion we would have opened into potentially transformative dialogue. The other participants would have had important feelings and thoughts about what he had said. Even after he left, the remaining participants could have explored what he might have meant as it mattered to them. Such interactions would have created space for others to speak about what is important to them and led to a discussion of what could and would be done by those in the workshop about the situation for building trust and helping healing. If such a process can happen in such a room, it can happen outside it. But when minds remain collectively frozen in a triggered state, as ours did in that instance, it is likely that relations harden while cynicism and hopelessness about change are reinforced.

Another illustration of a similar failure of this kind took place in another three-day Track 2 (that is, non-official) workshop with about a dozen Armenians and Turks in 2007, towards the end of the second day. As the lead facilitator, I had not yet learned what I needed to, either from the experience with the Palestinians and Israelis described above, or from my very own personal memories indirectly related to the discussion. Nor had I yet received clinical training for working with traumatised individuals' triggering. On this occasion, as Berktay described it (see Preface), after an Armenian said, 'What happened in 1915 was clearly genocide, and to discuss whether it happened or not is to manipulate or hijack the issue', a Turk responded, 'It wasn't a genocide', and two of the Armenians pushed back from the table, looking fed up and showing that they were about to disengage. The Turks pressed the matter, and the two parties stared angrily at each other. The conversation became accusatory and angry. All the members of the facilitation team were, like me, apparently at a loss as to how to intervene to help the conversation continue productively.

I recall fearing that the workshop would collapse and fail. Although it did not, it did not progress. The next morning, we facilitators referred to what had happened but failed to address explicitly the tense, 'make nice', atmosphere that had blanketed the end of the previous day and carried into the next. Yet I believe there was sufficient positive goodwill in the room and we could have taken advantage of that to deepen the discussion. Only long afterwards did I 'come to' an intervention that might have made a difference at that moment, the kind of moment for which the workshop had been set up: 'Something important is happening, and it belongs to us all. Let's slow down and take time to examine it together. What did you see? What did you feel? What did it mean to you? To your identities?'[23]

The proposed response would have avoided the pitfall of making any one person into the problem or the only one in the room with the problem. It is a pitfall because focusing on one person gives the others the message that it's fine to sit back, avoid discomfort, and observe someone else doing the group's heavy lifting. Recognising and working with triggering is essential to developing a capacity for processing traumatic memories and current fears. This can be difficult because most of us are used to repressing and disguising being triggered. But we humans sometimes respond to second and third chances; moreover recognising triggering afterwards is easier and can be as effective. In sum, when the opportunities of triggering are well used, the *basis* of discussion can shift, while unprocessed triggering surely contributes to unproductive conflict-resolution meetings.

Assuming that the WATS participants were implicitly invested in achieving deeper and more-informed relations among themselves, their face-to-face meetings provided the contact that allowed that. Such meetings convened for professional discussions could add deliberate, explicit processing of participants' experience of collective trauma in relation to Armenian–Turkish–Azerbaijani relations.

Becoming a collective trauma-conscious society would mean creating public awareness and acceptance of triggering as a normal biological response. It would mean developing a widespread ability to recognise triggering in ourselves and others and normalising, not shaming, it. It would mean teaching mindfulness and other techniques in a manner that is respectful of the difficulties involved, serious about the situation, and non-trivialising about the discomfort, to help identify it and thereby manage fight, flee, or freeze impulses. Why not?

D. Training Trauma-Informed Facilitators

One reason why not is the certainty of uncertain results. It is not easy to say just the right thing. It is also unnecessary, but there may be an assumption that that is what is required. What is necessary is to keep the conversation going at the level of meaning expressed that the triggering opens up. That means discomfort, which facilitators

[23] Intervention demands perception, wisdom, and empathy in the moment. Intervenors should have a rationale for themselves that relates to the meeting's purposes. To process the collective trauma, as in this case, facilitators should widen and open up discussion to normalise and validate the presence of the strong feelings linked with concerns and resist pressure from participants wishing either to fight and argue or to flee, in this case, to make everything polite again to relieve their discomfort. We should not focus on the 'combatants' in the room by asking them to explain themselves, which would make them alone carry the burden that was everyone's. The proposed intervention I finally came to would have normalised the feelings and invited others to speak about what the interchange meant to them.

must articulate as valid and normal. Otherwise, getting uncomfortable leads to disengagement. If managing triggering supports the trusting, safe, and open state of mind in which people become able to hear one another and lower the level of toxicity in their relationship in the room, intervenors trained in trauma work would be able to help make use of triggered moments.

Those engaged in conflict-resolution work as intervenors or participants may, like me, have experienced personal and/or collective traumas. If we had processed our trauma and received training about working with triggering, having been traumatised then becomes a resource because of the understanding and healing it can then produce. Education and training for such moments, along with having perspective on our own process, is as important as having empathy for and perspective on others. Having a trauma specialist experienced in group work on the facilitation team could help to normalise the emotional intensity that is triggered, to get it appropriately expressed, and to guide subsequent intervention and discussion about the issues that arise. Trained intervenors in other situations for discussing or processing troubled intergroup relations could help similarly.

E. Dealing with Triggering at the Level of the Body

Psychiatrist James Gordon specialises in working with large groups of traumatised people, from everyday individuals to decision- and policy-makers in trauma-torn societies, from handfuls to hundreds, worldwide, from Rwanda to Washington to Bosnia. He conducts his work with individuals aiming to live less trauma-ridden lives, not to resolve intercommunal conflicts.[24] Acknowledging that dealing with triggers can be difficult and not easily 'comprehensible to our conscious minds',[25] Gordon teaches simple, unobtrusive, surprisingly powerful techniques (meditation, breathing) that can be used anywhere, anytime, to increase self-awareness and reduce and integrate emotional reactivity by calming the nervous system and help modulate reactions to being triggered. These mindfulness techniques, once mastered, can be rapidly deployed on the spot. A few minutes of such exercises could be integrated into meetings at all levels about frozen conflicts involving collective trauma. Establishing such new norms might arouse prejudice against 'touchy-feely' methods, but that can be overcome.

F. Preparing Parties for Productively Meeting with the Other, Internally and Externally, while Strengthening Democracy

Chances of progress when conflicting parties meet would also improve if each party has come to some understanding and gained some perspective among themselves

[24] There are many others with great psychological knowledge and experience in working with trauma and who write about trauma processing and healing. Those whose works are used in this book include Yael Danieli, Natan Kellerman, Thomas Hübl, Bessel van der Kolk, and Vamik Volkan.

[25] J Gordon, *The Transformation: Discovering Wholeness and Healing after Trauma* (New York, HarperCollins, 2019) 187.

about their past and future relationship with the other. This would include processing the differences within their own party. Getting to common ground within one's own people in situations of protracted conflict between traumatised parties can be as difficult as doing so with the other. Two recent, impressive large-scale processes, 'deliberative democracy' and 'national dialogues', have evolved and are continuing to refine possibilities for working with and integrating knowledge and awareness of collective trauma into 'rational' single-party understandings. Neither approach currently includes the processing of collective trauma, but both could explicitly incorporate self-conscious processing in the moment. Ground rules would then include this aim as part of these processes so that participants know what to expect and agree to it. It could be added to both of these potentially significant, promising advances.

The central mechanism of 'deliberative democracy', explained in his most recent book *Democracy When the People Are Thinking*, by Stanford University political scientist James Fishkin, is what he calls 'deliberative polls'. The aim is to provide 'meaningful opportunity for public will formation', giving the 'people … real opportunity to think in depth about what they really want done'.[26] 'Meaningful opportunity' means that the deliberations have an impact:

> Deliberation … is key to a democracy of thoughtful self-rule. The idea is to equally count everyone's views under conditions where they can really think in order to give expression to a meaningful public … Such consultations can be done in contexts that are consequential so that the resulting opinions can provide a useful input to policy.[27]

Over some years, Fishkin and his team have organised large groups (numbering in the hundreds) to address important and divisive issues in non-official settings in 27 countries around the world including Brazil, China, Denmark, Mongolia, Uganda, Poland, Bulgaria, and the United States. Apart from Bulgaria and Poland, these groups have not been convened in former Soviet bloc countries, such as Armenia and Azerbaijan, nor in Turkey.

Fishkin and associates choose participants for small deliberative groups who represent a given country's range of political and ethnic constituencies, ensuring validity of results.[28] Once chosen, individuals are then educated by experts, also chosen for representativeness, on each issue to be discussed. This is followed by a number of days of deliberating together, enabling participants to dive deeply and interactively into the agenda's issues. Afterwards, their opinions are recorded privately. The results are shared publicly (but not individuals' identities) and understood as legitimately expressing the popular will of the country.

Fishkin finds that a full range of participants produces substantively informed opinions,[29] and that the process makes them feel newly empowered as citizens. This is of the greatest importance. The empowerment that comes from healing from trauma helps correct the disempowerment of the traumatic experience, *and* in this process simultaneously strengthens democratic decision-making. The traumatised previously

[26] JS Fishkin, *Democracy When the People Are Thinking* (Oxford, Oxford University Press, 2018) 1.
[27] Fishkin, 7.
[28] Fishkin, 74.
[29] Fishkin, 151.

unintegrated parts of the individual and societal psyches become integrated, bringing a whole new potential for similarly integrated concrete responses to conflicts in the society and its politics.

It might be very difficult to conduct deliberative polls in Turkey or Azerbaijan, countries whose autocratic heads of state frequently threaten and punish dissenters. But if such polls could somehow be held, and participants could acquire knowledge and exchange information and understandings while concealing their identities from the authorities, organisers, and one another, the true will of the peoples of these countries could be assessed.

The other relatively new process for national discourse, called 'national dialogues,' is designed specifically for improving the success of between-state negotiations, writes practitioner Katia Papagianni. National dialogues are 'negotiating mechanisms intended to expand participation in political transitions beyond political and military elites ... allowing diverse interests to influence ... negotiations'.[30] Less public and occurring 'out of the glare of media attention'[31] than official negotiations, they deliberately involve participants who tend to be influential outside official circles. Specifically directed to official dialogues, they are held before, during, and after official meetings take place, and are sometimes employed to help stabilise 'a peace process when formal processes have broken down'.[32] The influence of national dialogues on policies and decisions is indirect, 'exerted by their members on decision makers and through informal relationships established between institutional players'.[33]

Unsurprisingly, getting a national dialogue off the ground, according to Papagianni, is 'messy and contentious'[34] in terms of its size, composition, mandate, powers, and relationship to other government processes.[35] Judging the success of national dialogues is also contentious and difficult but, like Fishkin's deliberative polls, empowers people as they strengthen not only 'a culture of debate and free speech' but also achieve 'the breaking of taboo issues which after the dialogue may be much more openly discussed'. Pappagianni identifies additional benefits:

> ... the entrenchment of certain norms of inclusion and representation in politics of marginalized groups, including women and minorities; and, the ability to keep all the political actors inside the political process ... [thus] may ... manage to avert conflict, and to convince political actors to continue engaging with the political process ... [and] among the public.[36]

Because of the impact of collective trauma on large-group identity, national dialogues might be an ideal place for large-scale collective trauma processing in preparation for international dialogue.

[30] K Papagianni, 'National Dialogue Processes in Political Transition' (Civil Society Dialogue Network discussion paper no 3, European Peacebuilding Liaison Office, Brussels, Belgium, 2013).

[31] D Brown, *Nonformal Dialogues in National Peacemaking* (Washington, DC, United States Institute of Peace, 2017) 6.

[32] Brown, *Nonformal Dialogues in National Peacemaking*, 5.

[33] Brown, *Nonformal Dialogues in National Peacemaking*, 6.

[34] Papagianni, 'National Dialogue Processes in Political Transition', 7.

[35] Papagianni, 'National Dialogue Processes in Political Transition', 1.

[36] Papagianni, 'National Dialogue Processes in Political Transition', 11.

G. Broadening the Base to a Critical Mass and the Unique Opportunities of Scale

The learning that occurs in the workshops for Track 2 conflict resolution efforts for fewer than 20 individuals, such as the workshops with Israelis and Palestinians and with Armenians and Turks illustrated above, has always been meant to be spread throughout society.[37] But many years of these small workshops have not led to the development of a critical mass (the minimum amount of people 'required to start [and] maintain a … venture' and turn it into a sustainable voice).[38] While participants in these interventions represent their constituencies, whether formally or informally, and reach back into them after participating in intervention processes, any changes or transformations participants might experience may prove frustratingly transient upon return to their trauma- and conflict-permeated environments.

Currently, the numbers exposed to, and who became convinced of, the possibilities for change, are far too few. To develop, a critical mass needs to be exposed to processing and understanding, and more than on a single occasion, to achieve attitude change. In democracies, citizens can vote for change. I posit that the resistance of entrenched elites will only be overcome without violence through leadership emerging from large numbers of informed people who have together processed their collective trauma, gained perspective, and learned more about the other. Thus, I propose that work with large groups is essential.

If so, it is time to challenge the blanket applicability of lessons long accepted from Gustave Le Bon's *The Crowd: A Study of the Popular Mind* (1895) and Elias Canetti's *Crowds and Power* (1960). Both works stress how politicians stir up negative, scapegoating fevers in large groups, often to destroy another people, start a war, or take it out on a minority. Small groups can and do equally reproduce the dynamics of the more powerful party. They may implicitly repress open discussion, at all levels of decision-making, as understood and compellingly illustrated, for example, in the now classic 'groupthink' study.[39] While these are common realities about group dynamics, both large and small, it is equally true that great leaders such as Lincoln, Gandhi, Mandela and King mobilised groups, large as well as small, well enough to jump-start significant positive change.

When carefully planned, large groups offer crucial opportunity for bringing such positive change. I learned this in organising and putting together the Hasan Cemal event (see Preface). That event was attended by 150 to 200 people, obviously far more than in usual conflict-resolution workshops and meetings for between eight and 20. At the start, we conveners, both of us facilitators, stated the objective: dialogue between speakers and audience to open hearts and minds, providing a forum for asking, listening, and learning, not arguing, convincing, or debating. We stated ground rules for achieving this. Those were the meeting's soft necessities. There was also a hard necessity: we arranged for a police presence, which silently conveyed our serious intention about the nature and conduct of the intended dialogue. Although people carried placards outside the hall protesting the meeting, and there may have been a brief shout

[37] P Jones. *Track Two Diplomacy in Theory and Practice* (Stanford, CA, Stanford University Press, 2015) 24.
[38] As defined at www.vocabulary.com (accessed 23 July 2020).
[39] IL Janis, *Groupthink: Psychological Studies of Policy Decisions and Fiascoes*, 2nd edn (Boston, Houghton Mifflin, 1982).

of complaint against the meeting from the floor at the start, the discussion flowed as hoped.

Whether small or large, a meeting's purpose and agenda framework, choice of speaker(s), ground rules, setting, publicity, and facilitation make the difference. If in such a meeting keynote speakers are featured, it is important to strike a balance between the speakers and participants. Facilitators should plan the event as much for participant engagement as for speaker promotion so that the interaction becomes an active learning process rather than the one-sided delivery experience that would result if the focus were exclusively on, or essentially emphasising, the speakers' charisma.

If large meetings are needed, so is a broad participation base. The efforts of elite participants in conflict-resolution processes have not led to effective attitude change in leaderships or in realities on the ground in certain conflicts. For decades, Herbert Kelman held that attitude change trickles down from elite discussions,[40] but even he finally became discouraged by the incapacity 'of leadership on either side ... to make concessions required'.[41] He acknowledged that leaders instead would raise 'obstacles to a peaceful resolution ... whenever there seems to be a sign of progress'.[42]

In order for a people to heal to achieve societal-level change, it is necessary to have engaged a critical mass. Working with collectively traumatised peoples needs to go wide as well as deep. The experience of collective trauma is a partial leveller of elite and non-elite populations in the sense that an entire population has experienced the same collective trauma. This means they all share the need to work through that trauma. But a people cannot heal collectively from collective trauma if the healing process is siphoned off into individual therapy work. One reason is that collective healing and recovery require much of what is entailed by individual healing *and* much more. The entire spectrum of things that need to be healed collectively is different from that of an individual. Even if everyone in a populace were engaged in individual trauma work, they would not heal their collective trauma. Finally, even if large numbers of individuals have healed from collective trauma, this cannot work without the needed supporting structural changes at the collective level. To be sustained, the supporting structural changes require many healed individuals.

*

In sum, to address collective trauma, facilitated encounters of large numbers of different subgroups in a given population need to work together. Such groups should identify and work with trauma symptoms such as triggering and what is triggered, such as invasive thoughts and projection. Such groups must address the group's dynamics in relation to the larger conflict environment on the ground, which will be reflected in the relationships between the peoples whose members are interacting in the room. Ongoing group discussion should move among and connect all these factors. If many

[40] Eg, Jones, *Track Two Diplomacy in Theory and Practice*, 24.

[41] HC Kelman, 'A One-Country/Two State Solution to the Israeli-Palestinian Conflict' (2011) XVIII(1) *Middle East Policy* 29.

[42] Kelman, 'A One-Country/Two State Solution to the Israeli-Palestinian Conflict', 29.

large, carefully-designed meetings covering all details were conducted in the societies involved in a protracted, entrenched conflict and took place for a few consecutive days and weeks, they would have a chance of producing a significant ripple effect.

III. OTHER FIELDS THAT CAN ADDRESS COLLECTIVE TRAUMA

Understanding and trying to heal collective trauma are multi-disciplinary and interdisciplinary challenges involving the academic fields of history, social sciences, political science, psychology, neuroscience, religion, ethics and international affairs. In addition, the fields of law, human rights, public health, and government/diplomacy also address situations of collective trauma and are inclusive of practices that provide, by different names and in different ways, opportunities for working with it.

The field of education is the most important, but not singled out below because this book is all about education: education about trauma, education about peoples' histories' of collective traumas, and education about possible processes for collective healing.

A. Negotiation: Track 1 and Track 2 Diplomacy

Track 1 (official) and Track 2 (non-official) negotiations are linked areas of practice. When a country's diplomats pressure another country, or pressure conflicting parties to halt the imposition of traumatising conditions on others, Track 1, or official diplomatic negotiations, have been the primary non-violent vehicle to accomplish this. When Track 1 negotiations do not deliver, non-official practitioners sometimes initiate Track 2 efforts – Track 2 being a large field of practice with many variations that often addresses more fundamental matters than does Track 1. In particular, for decades many Track 2 efforts, such as Kelman's and those he inspired, including those my team and I convened for Armenians and Turks, were directed to enabling participants to identify their fundamental collective needs – which boil down to security and respect for their peoples – and how each party could meet its own *and the others' such needs*. The idea was that the information taken in would be communicated not just to non-governmental organisations and people generally but also to governments, which would then negotiate officially to see that both sets of needs were met, making the resolution of protracted conflicts possible.

Because, as stated, that approach has not brought the hoped-for results, this book proposes that conflict-resolution practitioners and any intervenors in such conflicts should become 'trauma informed'. Working with collective trauma should at a minimum be considered as a factor in Track 1 work and an integral part of Track 2 efforts. I emphatically do not suggest that this would resolve these conflicts, but that it is a necessary tool in a peace-building process.

Another variation for Track II diplomacy is being developed and worked on by my colleague, Jeffrey Seul. He and his colleagues put parties' 'worldviews' at the centre.[43]

[43] The Seul-led Track 2 efforts, which are being carried out in the context of the Israeli–Palestinian conflict, start with exploring stakeholders' divergent worldviews. Seul has worked for years in Jerusalem

Seul, a lawyer, is also a negotiator and a conflict resolution practitioner, and understands well that official diplomacy works with the terms of negotiation, that is, 'packages of mostly material trade-offs thought to address the stakeholders' respective interests – interests conceived of mostly in mundane ... terms'.[44] The 'worldviews' idea is meant to enhance, not replace, the scope and effectiveness of Track 1, as a variation of Kelman's basic needs approach. Seul looks to the basic failure of Track 1 in terms of negotiation theory and practice, into which context he brings the idea of worldviews and recommends that Track 2 can help fill in this fundamental gap in Track 1. He believes that both tracks should address what matters most deeply to parties, which he sees as their 'symbolic and normative foundations'.[45] Seul's idea is to enable stakeholders to identify options for resolving the most contentious value-laden issues in the conflict, such as the treatment of religious structures.

In this book a people's core is understood to value their homelands and cultures around them – homes, communities, businesses, farming, hospitals, wilderness and recreation areas, other natural resources, religious structures and practices, schools, libraries, history, and music and art,[46] as well as the symbols of these things. But the connection between collective trauma and the sacred, non-negotiable heart of cultural identities is critical. Seul's model does not deal with collective trauma per se. But if each party's most consequential values, understood as composed of its 'worldview', are brought together under the frame of its 'worldview', and violating those values contributes to collectively traumatising a given people, the worldview and collective trauma approaches could possibly strengthen each other.

B. Human Rights

The peace settlements and decolonisations that ensued in the wake of World War I gave birth to new nation states in central Europe and the Middle East. At that historical moment the nation state was widely thought of as an ideal. But once established, many nation states became harshly discriminatory, ie collectively traumatising, toward their minorities. After the devastating human costs of Nazism and World War II, the ideal of nation states lost its luster and a new ideal, that of human rights, entered the international lexicon as a counter to the excesses of nationalism. In 1948 it led to the United Nations' adoption of the Universal Declaration of Human Rights,[47] stressing individual rights as the standard for all. After that, many countries integrated into their legal systems many of the rights spelled out in the declaration.

The values inspiring human rights rest on understanding that the humanity common to all individuals means that all are equally entitled to these human rights

with Christian, Jewish, Muslim, and secular 'stakeholders' (in this book 'stakeholders' are called 'peoples' and have 'ethno-religious identities'; groups with self-described 'secular' identities have not been covered) in the belief that if they agree on how to move forward with one another, this will help transform attitudes in their constituencies.

[44] J Seul, 'Mediating across Worldviews' in C Turner and M Waehlish (eds), *Rethinking Peace Mediation: Challenges of Contemporary Peacemaking Practice* (Bristol, Bristol University Press, forthcoming).

[45] Seul, 'Mediating across Worldviews'.

[46] See A Ryan, 'Whose Nationalism?' *New York Review of Books*, 26 March 2020, 56.

[47] See www.ohchr.org/EN/UDHR/Documents/UDHR_Translations/eng.pdf (accessed 23 July 2020).

and that none of the myriad differences among individuals entitles one category of humans to be more or less deserving of those rights than another. Common humanity eclipses differences. Today, many states have agreed to honour and enforce human rights, including in principle the right for all others to live by and express their own distinctive ethno-religious, cultural, or secular identities, as long as they do not violate others' human rights.

The body of human rights was not specifically conceived to prevent 'collective trauma'. But although understandings of some of the specific rights have evolved since 1948, and violations within and among states have been profound even to the point of genocide, the body of rights still constitutes the primary global framework that would, if adhered to, prevent humanly-imposed collective trauma and punish the perpetrators of its abuses. Thus, countries with laws that enshrine human rights can be understood to intend to prevent it, or if justice is later delivered, at least to alleviate collective traumatisation, and to some extent also heal it. Thus, incorporating human rights law into a political entity's existing body of laws can help secure needed structural and attitudinal change.

As I write, few governments are responding effectively to direct and indirect threats or violations of rights as found, for examples, in extreme economic inequality, climate change and mass migrations. Such failures create a vast psychological space in which humans' fears and anxieties flourish alongside ignorant, fear-based, and corrupt decision-makers, coinciding with the reappearance of extreme ethnic nationalism. As in Europe between the First and Second World Wars, today peoples are contracting into their identity groups, responding to being whipped into becoming more fearful, angry, and threatening toward those who are different. Given these stresses, will human rights continue to be valued as a universal standard, even theoretically? Can conflict resolution combine with trauma healing and human rights to protect those under threat and help improve world order?

C. Public Health

Healing communal-wide psychological trauma in peoples engaged in oppressive relations or violent conflict is proposed here as necessary to building sustainable, fair, nonviolent relations. By definition, violent conflict and collective traumatisation degrade public health and the capacity of a health care system to deliver care. Healing large numbers of people and preventing their further traumatisation is already understood as part of public health's mission – to prevent and treat 'anything that affects the health of the community on a mass basis',[48] while scholar-practitioners in the field of public health have broken new ground in different situations of collective trauma,[49] sometimes in partnership with governments and the media.[50]

[48] Institute of Medicine, Committee for the Study of the Future of Public Health, *The Future of Public Health* (Washington, DC, National Academies Press, 1988) 830.

[49] See, eg, TS Betancourt, 'Developmental Perspectives on Moral Agency in Former Child Soldiers' (2011) 54 *Human* 307.

[50] See, eg, J Shaw, 'The Resurrection of the Marlboro Man', *Harvard Magazine*, September–October 2019.

'Public health is the area of health outside the capability of the individual private practitioner'.[51] Given that, categorically, collective traumatisation cannot be healed in private settings working with one or a few individuals at a time, the condition of collective traumatisation should be centrally recognised and addressed as such in the public health field. In fact, the heart of the public health field – the prevention of widespread, especially predictable, conditions that harm the public's health[52] – is close to being synonymous with the purpose of healing collective trauma in order to improve relations among peoples. If 'the core of public health is the capacity to identify problems, and having found them, measure them and attempt to intervene',[53] South Africa's Truth and Reconciliation Commission was one such grand pilot program for healing collective trauma and preventing future violence. With all its limitations, the process surely had a net positive impact on public health.

IV. FRATERNAL RELATIONS AND THE WAY FORWARD

Turkey and the South Caucasus Today

Source: https://images.app.goo.gl/yD1N57wVUYL1G7JR7.

Today the Armenians of both the Armenian republic and of Nagorno-Karabakh (Azerbaijanis and Kurds form a minuscule fraction of Karabakh's total population) remain allied in the long-unsettled conflict with Azerbaijan. This alliance depends on Armenia's own formal defence agreement with Russia. Pashinyan congratulated Putin on his recent achievement of the constitutional change awarding him two more

[51] Institute of Medicine *The Future of Public Health*, 844.

[52] See, for example, the mission statement of the Harvard TH Chan School of Public Health, www.hsph.harvard.edu/ (accessed 23 July 2020).

[53] Institute of Medicine *The Future of Public Health*, 1016.

years in office, wishing 'peace, welfare and prosperity to you and the fraternal people of Russia'.[54]

Azerbaijan strives to maintain a similar relationship with Turkey. The late president of Azerbaijan, Heydar Aliyev, once described the two Turkic peoples, Turks and Azerbaijanis, as 'one nation with two states'.[55] As this book neared completion, a news report stated, 'The Turkish Parliament recently approved a bill that would allow [Azerbaijan] to accept money from Turkey that would then be used for buying defense equipment from Turkey, including Turkish drones'. It noted, moreover, that Turkey has already used drones against 'Kurdish groups in Turkey and across Turkey's border in Iraq and Syria', and are likely to 'bolster their position in their conflict with Armenia over the Nagorno-Karabakh region'.[56] As discussed earlier, these close relations go back to the March Days in 1918, begun in partial reaction against the Armenians and Karabakh Armenians.

Today the conflict over Karabakh takes the form of diplomacy as well as violence along borders. Each side accuses the other of deliberately breaking the cease-fire that has been in place since 1994. Citizens of both countries continue to be maimed or killed by landmines planted during the war that the truce was supposed to have ended. But feelings are strong and raw and on edge; expectedly, collective trauma and collective transmitted trauma remain embedded in these two fraternal sets of relationships. Its presence is palpable when those involved talk about it, and it is evident in much of the writing about their relations.

The trauma of decades of massacres imposed by the Turks on Armenians since the 1890s leaves the Armenian people in the region feeling imperiled because Turkey has not acknowledged what it did, much less apologised, made reparations, or unequivocally assured Armenians of peaceful intentions. Therefore, Armenians, including the Karabakh Armenians, remain wary of Turkey's policy agenda in the region. To the extent that Armenians identify Azerbaijanis with Turks, compromise over Nagorno-Karabakh may appear to be a compromise over whether there was genocide as well as over their national security.

Although Azerbaijanis generally do not acknowledge the Armenian genocide, and perhaps do not understand what the issue has to do with them, some nonetheless understand Armenians' occupation of Karabakh as revenge against the Turks for the massacres displaced onto them. Thus, Armenians' fear of Turkey, and partly by extension, of Azerbaijan, and Azerbaijan's fear and anger of being on the receiving end, as they see it, of misplaced revenge, need to be made explicit as part of the efforts to improve their relations. Another factor that also keeps the conflict alive, according to many observers, is the Azerbaijani leadership's use of Karabakh as a diversion from the country's widespread poverty and extremely wealthy, corrupt autocracy that excludes most citizens from participating in governance.[57]

[54] 'Pashinyan Congratulates Putin on Passage of Russian Constitutional Reform', *USA Armenian Life* #1736, 4 July 2020.

[55] For a recent collection of essays on modern Azerbaijani-Turkish relations, see M Ismayilov and NA Graham (eds), *Turkish-Azerbaijani Relations: One Nation – Two States?* (London, Routledge, 2016).

[56] C Larson, 'Attack! Turkey and Azerbaijan are Teaming Up on Drones', *The National Interest*, 26 June 2020.

[57] See A Ohanyan, *Networked Regionalism as Conflict Management* (Stanford, CA, Stanford University Press, 2015); A Ohanyan (ed), *Russia Abroad: Driving Regional Fracture in Post-Communist Eurasia and*

This concern, too, needs to be adopted in the public discourse by both those parties to and outside of the conflict.

*

I posit that to help improve relations, Karabakh Armenians and Azerbaijanis process their common history. As I researched and wrote Part III's chapters on the history of these relationships, I became hopeful as I learned about Azerbaijani aspirations from early on in the last century and the fleeting moments when an independent federative Transcaucasia seemed possible. I propose that much wider knowledge of their joint history – awareness of the repetitive hurts each has inflicted on the other and of the commonality of many basic values, such as love of homelands, shared Caucasian culture, and each people's desire to live as a people live together in a federated state – would add greater understanding to the Azerbaijani and Armenian relationship and possibly provide a basis for working to live by common values.

Suppose *for a start* that Armenians in non-official capacities, acknowledged the Armenians' role in the massacres of Azeris in the March Days of 1918, apologised for it, and articulated a pledge of never allowing such scenes to play out again: Armenians would have taken responsibility for one great wrong. Suppose *for a start* that Azerbaijanis in a non-official capacity acknowledged their ready participation in the massacres of Armenians in the September Days of 1918 and articulated an intention of never repeating. Then they, too, would have taken responsibility for one past great wrong. Such mutuality might inaugurate a positive process. Thereafter, both parties might be less inclined to shift blame to each other when it doesn't belong as fully. They could begin their overdue process of healing.

James Gordon writes about the start of a non-official group process for dealing with trauma. Although designed for individuals, this process could also be used to start a larger process for a single people or for two parties to begin work both on their collective trauma and on improving their relations:

> And so it goes around the circle, each of us revealing, beginning to peel away the legacy of generations of being oppressed, or indeed, oppressing others, of fear and pain and constraint. Speaking, listening to one another, we become more aware of how trauma in the lives of previous generations has been limiting us, distorting how we see the world, constraining what we are allowed to feel and whether and how we can speak about it.[58]

Today perhaps the main obstacles to improved relations between the two peoples are the nature of their governments and occupants of the highest offices, stressed by both Özkan and Gamaghelyan, as set out at the start of this chapter. Given that participants in conflict-resolution processes need to feel safe enough to speak freely and to have a potential impact on improving relations, the election of the current

Beyond (Washington, DC, Georgetown University Press, 2018), especially the chapter by L Broers, 'The South Caucasus: Fracture without End?' and 'Competitive Authoritarianism: Hybrid Regimes after the Cold War'; L Broers, *Armenia and Azerbaijan: Anatomy of a Rivalry* (Edinburgh, Edinburgh University Press, 2019); and S Levitsky and L Way, *Competitive Authoritarianism: Hybrid Regimes after the Cold War* (Cambridge, Cambridge University Press, 2010).

[58] Gordon, *The Transformation*, 234.

Armenian prime minister in 2018, Nikol Pashinyan, has made that a possibility for his country. Pashinyan has shown himself to be serious about eliminating corruption and eschewing its perks.[59] His aim may be to establish a solidly corruption-free, democratic government before going out on a limb in his own country to try to resolve the over-charged Karabakh situation. He is surely well aware that speaking of compromise would entail facing accusations of being a traitor. He would have to resist adopting, as Gamaghelyan said, 'an increasingly radical stance vis-à-vis the other side'.

If Pashinyan's popularity in Armenia holds and grows, along with his genuine appeal to more democratically-minded and hopeful Azerbaijanis, he may be able to turn the problem into an opportunity for change in the region. Of course, unlikely though it is, Erdoğan and Azerbaijan's patrimonial president, Ilham Aliyev, have the power and freedom to embark on a process for change themselves. Addressing collective trauma would lay a foundation for any such efforts or support such an initiative once undertaken. In spite of the obstacles, an ongoing civil society Track 2 effort aiming for a better future has continued for years. It takes place alongside a long-term official process by the Minsk Group, co-chaired by France, Russia, and the United States. However, the discouraging course of recent events has retriggered these peoples, adding to the further hardening of attitudes.

Certainly not uniquely, yet nonetheless sadly, to the best of my knowledge the Armenians – including the Karabakh Armenians – Turks, and Azerbaijanis, have not considered engaging in the processes proposed here. Thus, my unsurprising answer to the question raised in the preface, 'How can we liberate the present from being captive to the past and learn from it?', would begin with each of these peoples' unofficially processing their own collective traumas in a series of one or another kind of large meetings discussed in this chapter.

However, exercising free speech and association would be necessary for effective participation in groups convened for such a purpose. Although they are democracies on paper, Freedom House ranks Armenia and Nagorno-Karabakh as 'partly free' and Azerbaijan and Turkey as 'not free'.[60] Armenians do enjoy freedom of speech and association but it is rather precarious, since the authoritarian tendencies of their former heads of government, the strong pressures not to consider any compromise with Azerbaijan over Karabakh, and the uncertainty of the current government's survival, discourage taking bold steps in diplomacy. Both these rights are by and large denied in Turkey and Azerbaijan.

Tensions between Armenians and Azerbaijanis would probably be helped by discussions about the impact of the past imposed by Russian and Soviet policies and the unlikely possibility that Russia itself will acknowledge, repair, and reassure going forward. The same can be said about the role Turkey has played and continues to play today. Joint, explicit recognition by Armenians and Azerbaijanis might enable them to see that a drawing down of the revenge they take out on each other is an outlet for an inability to have any impact on Russia in this way or, for Armenians, on Turkey.

[59] A Ohanyan and L Broers, *Armenia's Velvet Revolution: Authoritarian Decline and Civil Resistance in a Multipolar World* (London, IB Tauris, forthcoming).

[60] Report, 2020, at Freedomhouse.org.

*

First, we humans, collectively, create many of the widespread, destructive conditions that then traumatise us collectively. Traumatisation then affects our nervous systems, shapes our collective meaning-making, and imperils our institutions, cultures, and societies. Isn't it past time for Armenians, Turks, and Azerbaijanis – and the rest of us – to face ourselves and our collective traumas and attend to some fundamental truths?

As a 'good enough' starting goal, I adopt the following from psychologist Steven Pinker: 'Frankly, I don't love my neighbors, to say nothing of my enemies. Better, then, is the following idea: Don't kill your neighbors or enemies, even if you don't love them'.[61] Nowhere does this book advocate that people should collectively forgive or love one another. Those goals are not, if they ever were, the starting points or midpoints of processes for achieving better, non-violent relations after histories of massacre, discrimination, and, between Armenians and Turks, genocide. But knowing and understanding the Other is a starting point. Then trusting, but verifying.

Over and over again Armenians, Turks, and Azerbaijanis have shared their humanity and the same soil for hundreds of years. They are attached to their distinct ethno-religious cultures, and each is due respect for them, as long as those attachments do not entail harming each other.

At times I feel enraged that there has been so much destruction of homelands and peoples and so much denial of justice; so much lying and indecency. I have tried to find the strength to face it and not look away, and in the process found the best of human resilience, faith, and efforts. If you have made it this far, so have you. Together we can find the strength to grieve, and the awareness and will to change course.

[61] S Pinker, *The Better Angels of Our Nature* (New York, Viking, 2011) 591.

Bibliography

Archives

National Archives and Records Administration (NARA), College Park, MD.

Official Publications and Collections of Documents

Bunyan, James, and HH Fisher (eds), *The Bolshevik Revolution, 1917–1918: Documents and Materials* (Stanford, CA, Stanford University Press, 1934).

Gooch, GP and Harold Temperley (eds), *British Documents on the Origin of the War, 1898–1914*, 11 vols (London, HMSO, 1926–38).

Lenin, VI, *Selected Works*, 2 vols (Moscow, Foreign Languages Publication House, 1946–47).

Lepsius, Johannes, *Armenia and Europe: An Indictment* (London, Hodder and Stoughton, 1897).

Nersisian, MG and RG Sahakian (eds), *Hayots tseghaspanutyune Osmanyan kaysrutyunum: Pastatghteri yev nyuteri zhoghovatsu* (Yerevan, Hayastan, 1991).

Pambukian, Y (ed), *Niwter HH Dashnaktsutean patmutean hamar*, 12 vols to date (Beirut, Hamazkayin, 1984–).

Sarafian, Ara (ed), *The Treatment of Armenians in the Ottoman Empire, 1915–1916: Documents Presented to Viscount Grey of Falloden by Viscount Bryce*, uncensored edn (Princeton, NJ, Gomidas Institute, 2000).

Troinitskogo, NA (ed), *Pervaia vseobshchaia perepis naseleniia Rossiskoi Imperii, 1897 g*, 89 vols (St Petersburg, Tsentralnyi Staticheskii Komitet, 1904).

US Department of State, 'Patterns of Global Terrorism Report – 1996'.

USSR (Union of Soviet Socialist Republics), *Dokumenty vneshnei politiki SSSR*, 21 vols (Moscow, Politizdat, 1957).

Yeghiayan, Vartkes (ed), *Armenians and the Okhrana, 1907–1915* (Los Angeles, Center for Armenian Remembrance, 2016).

Memoirs and First-hand Accounts

Balakian, Grigoris, *Armenian Golgotha*, trans Peter Balakian with Aris G Sevag (New York, Alfred A Knopf, 2009).

Banian, Karnig, *Goodbye, Antoura: A Memoir of the Armenian Genocide* (Stanford, CA, Stanford University Press, 2015).

Cemal, Hasan, *1915: The Armenian Genocide* (Istanbul, Hrant Dink Foundation, 2015).

Djemal Pasha, *Memories of a Turkish Statesman, 1913–1919* (New York, George H Doran Company, 1922).

Dunsterville, LC, *The Adventures of Dunsterforce* (London, Edward Arnold, 1920).

Goltz, Thomas, *Azerbaijan Diary: A Rogue Reporter's Adventures in an Oil-Rich, War-Torn, Post-Soviet Republic* (Abingdon, Routledge, 1998).

Giulkhandanian, Abraham, *Hay-tatarakan undharumnere*, 2 vols (Paris, Haratch, 1933).

His Holiness the Dalai Lama, Archbishop Desmond Tutu, with Douglas Abrams, *The Book of Joy: Lasting Happiness in a Changing World* (New York, Random House, 2016).

Hovannisian, Garin K, *Family of Shadows: A Century of Murder, Memory, and the Armenian American Dream* (New York, HarperCollins, 2010).

Khatisian, Aleksandr, *Hayastani Hanrapetutean tsagumn u zargatsume* (Beirut, Hamazkayin, 1968).

Morgenthau, Henry, *Ambassador Morgenthau's Story* (Garden City, NY, Doubleday, Page & Company, 1919).

—— *All in a Lifetime* (New York, Doubleday, 1923).
Oz, Amos, *A Tale of Love and Darkness* (London, Vintage, 2004).
Papazian, Vahan, *Im hushere*, 3 vols (Beirut, Hamazkayin Unkerutiwn, 1950–57).
Paraquin, Ernst, 'Politik im Orient', *The Berliner Tageblatt*, 24 January 1920, translated into English and republished as 'Turkish Dreams and German Blunders' (1920) *The Living Age* 304.
Price, M Philips, *War and Revolution in Asiatic Russia* (London, G Allen and Unwin, 1918).
Solzhenitsyn, Aleksandr, *The Gulag Archipelago 1918–56* (Boulder, CO, Westview Press, 2002).
Temelkuran, Ece, *Deep Mountain*, trans Kenneth Dakan (London, Verso, 2010).
Toumani, Meline, *There Was and There Was Not: A Journey through Hate and Possibility in Turkey, Armenia, and Beyond* (New York, Henry Holt, Metropolitan Books, 2014).
Ussher, Clarence D, *An American Physician in Turkey: A Narrative of Adventures in Peace and in War* (Boston, Houghton Mifflin, 1917).
Villari, Luigi, *The Fire and Sword in the Caucasus* (London, T Fisher Unwin, 1906).
Vratsian, Simon, *Hayastani hanrapetutiwn* (Beirut, Mshag, 1958).
Yessayan, Zabel, *In the Ruins: The 1909 Massacres of Armenians in Adana, Turkey*, trans GM Goshgarian (Boston, Armenian International Women's Association, 2016).

Secondary Sources

Adams-Silvan, Abby, and Mark Silvan, '"A Dream Is the Fulfillment of a Wish": Traumatic Dream, Repetition Compulsion, and the Pleasure Principle' (1990) 71(3) *International Journal of Psychoanalysis*.
Ahmad, Feroz, *The Young Turks: The Committee of Union and Progress in Turkish Politics, 1908–1914* (Oxford, Clarendon Press, 1969).
Ahrens, Courtney E, 'Being Silenced: The Impact of Negative Social Reactions on the Disclosure of Rape' (2006) 38(3–4) *American Journal of Community Psychology*.
Akarçesme, Sevgi, 'Turkey's Vengeful President Erdoğan is Squashing His Country's Rise' *Quartz*, 14 April 2015.
Akçam, Taner, *From Empire to Republic: Turkish Nationalism and the Armenian Genocide* (London, Zed Books, 2004).
—— Interview by Guilluame Perrier, *Le Monde*, 7 January 2012.
—— *A Shameful Act: The Armenian Genocide and the Question of Turkish Responsibility* (New York, Metropolitan Books, 2006).
—— Speech presented at the National Association for Armenian Studies and Research Assembly, Belmont, MA, 19 May 2012.
—— 'When Was the Decision to Annihilate the Armenians Taken?' (2019) 21 *Journal of Genocide Research*.
—— *Young Turks' Crime against Humanity: The Armenian Genocide and Ethnic Cleansing in the Ottoman Empire* (Princeton, NJ, Princeton University Press, 2012).
Akhavan, Payam, *Reducing Genocide to Law: Definition, Meaning, and the Ultimate Crime* (Cambridge, Cambridge University Press, 2012).
Akkum, Gulisor, 'Kurdish Leaders Apologize for 1915 during Monument Inauguration in Diyarbakir' *Armenian Weekly*, 12 September 2013, www.armenianweekly.com.
Akmeşe, Handan Nazir, *The Birth of Modern Turkey: The Ottoman Military and the March to World War I* (London, IB Tauris, 2005).
Aksakal, Mustafa, 'The Ottoman Empire' in Jay Winter (ed), *The Cambridge History of the First World War*, vol 1: *Global War* (Cambridge, Cambridge University Press, 2014).
—— *The Ottoman Road to War in 1914: Ottoman Empire and the First World War* (Cambridge, Cambridge University Press, 2008).
Alexander, Jeffrey C et al, *Cultural Trauma and Collective Identity* (Berkeley, University of California, 2004).
Allen, WED and Paul Muratoff, *Caucasian Battlefields: A History of the Wars on the Turco-Caucasian Border, 1828–1921* (Cambridge, Cambridge University Press, 1953).
Allport, GW, *The Nature of Prejudice* (Oxford, Addison-Wesley, 1954).
Altstadt, Audrey, Foreword to *The Azerbaijani Turks* (Stanford, CA, Hoover Institution Press, 1992).
—— *The Politics of Culture in Soviet Azerbaijan, 1920–40* (London, Routledge, 2016).
Altstadt-Mirhadi, Audrey [Audrey Altstadt], 'Baku: Transformation of a Muslim Town' in Michael F Hamm (ed), *The City in Late Imperial Russia* (Bloomington, Indiana University Press, 1986).

American Psychiatric Association, *Diagnostic and Statistical Manual of Mental Disorders*, 5th edn (Arlington, VA, American Psychiatric Publishing, 2013).

Amis, Martin, *The House of Meetings* (New York, Knopf, 2006).

Anderson, MS, *The Eastern Question, 1774–1923: A Study in International Relations* (London, Macmillan, 1966).

Antaramian, Richard E, *Brokers of Faith, Brokers of Empire: Armenians and the Politics of Reform in the Ottoman Empire* (Stanford, CA, Stanford University Press, 2020).

Arslanbenzer, Hakan, 'Kazim Karabekir: Primary Opponent of Ataturk' *Daily Sabah*, 31 March 2018.

Assman, Jan, and John Czalpicka, 'Collective Memory and Cultural Identity' (1995) 65 *New German Critique*.

Astourian, Stephan, and Raymond Kévorkian, 'Conclusion: Continuities in Violence and Some Explanations' in Stephan Astourian and Raymond Kévorkian (eds), forthcoming book.

Aydemir, Şevket Süreyya, *Enver Paşa Makedonya'dan Ortaasya'ya, 1860–1908*, 3 vols (Istanbul, Remzi Kitabevi, 1970).

Babbitt, Eileen F et al, 'Combining Empathy with Problem-Solving in Israel: The Tamra Model of Facilitation in Yaad/Miaar' in Craig Zelizer and Robert A Rubenstein (eds), *Building Peace: Practical Reflections from the Field* (Sterling, VA, Kumairan Press, 2009).

Badem, Candan, '"Forty Years of Black Days?": The Russian Administration of Kars, Ardahan, and Batum, 1878–1918' in Lucien J Frary and Maria Kozelsky (eds), *Russian-Ottoman Borderlands: The Eastern Question Reconsidered* (Madison, University of Wisconsin Press, 2014).

Baer, Marc David, *The Dönme: Jewish Converts, Muslim Revolutionaries, and Secular Turks* (Stanford, CA, Stanford University Press, 2009).

Bairamian, William, 'Book Review: There Was and There Was Not', *The Armenite*, 26 December 2014.

Baker, Mark R, 'The Armenian Genocide and Its Denial: A Review of Recent Scholarship' (2015) 53 *New Perspectives in Turkey*.

Balakian, Peter, *The Burning Tigris: The Armenian Genocide and America's Response* (New York, HarperCollins, 2003).

Bardakci, Murat, 'Askerin siyasete yerleşmesi 31 Mart isyanıyla başladı', *Sabah*, 16 April 2007.

Barron, James, 'Nation Reels after Gunman Massacres 20 Children at School in Connecticut', *New York Times*, 14 December 2012.

Bazyler, Michael J, 'From Lamentation and Liturgy to Litigation: The Holocaust-Era Restitution Movement as a Model for Bringing Armenian Genocide-Era Restitution Suits in American Courts' (2011) 95 *Marquette Law Review*.

Berda, Yael, *Living Emergency: Israel's Permit Regime in the Occupied West Bank* (Stanford, CA, Stanford University Press, 2018).

Berktay, Halil, Interview by Khatchig Mouradian. Aztag Daily, 12 November 2005, available at https://hyetert.org/2005/11/15/the-specter-of-the-armenian-genocide-an-interview-with-halil-berktay/.

Beşikçi, Mehmet, *The Ottoman Mobilization of Manpower in the First World War: Between Voluntarism and Resistance* (Leiden, Brill, 2012).

Betancourt, Theresa S, 'Developmental Perspectives on Moral Agency in Former Child Soldiers' (2011) 54 *Human*.

Bevan, Robert, *The Destruction of Memory: Architecture at War* (London, Reaktion Books, 2006).

Bilali, Rezarta, 'National Narrative and Social Psychological Influences in Turks' Denial of the Mass Killings of Armenians as Genocide' (2013) 69 *Journal of Social Issues*.

Bilali, Rezarta et al, 'Attributions of Responsibility and Perceived Harm in the Aftermath of Mass Violence' (2012) 18(1) *Peace and Conflict: Journal of Peace Psychology*.

Bilali, Rezarta, and Johanna Ray Vollhardt, 'Victim and Perpetrator Groups' Divergent Perspectives on Collective Violence: Implications for Intergroup Relations' (2019) 40. *Political Psychology*.

Bjørnlund, Matthias, '"A Fate Worse than Dying": Sexual Violence during the Armenian Genocide' in Dagmar Herzog (ed), *Brutality and Desire: War and Sexuality in Europe's Twentieth Century* (New York, Palgrave Macmillan, 2009).

Bloom, Paul, *Against Empathy* (New York, HarperCollins, 2017).

Bloxham, Donald, *The Great Game of Genocide* (New York, Oxford University Press, 2005).

Bogosian, Eric, *Operation Nemesis: The Assassination Plot that Avenged the Armenian Genocide* (New York, Little, Brown, 2015).

—— 'An Evening with Eric Bogosian', Interview by Alex Dinelaris, Live Talks LA, Alex Theatre, Los Angeles, 5 May 2015.

Boyadjian, Sarine, 'The Psychological Impact of the Armenian Genocide', Armenian National Committee of America, https://anca.org/haytoug-preview-the-psychological-impact-of-the-armenian-genocide/.

Bozarslan, Hamit, 'L'extermination des Arméniens et des Juifs; quelques élements de comparaison' in Hans-Lukas Kieser and Dominik J Schaller (eds), *Der Völkermord an den Armeniern und die Shoah/ The Armenian Genocide and the Shoah* (Zürich, Chronos, 2002).

Bozkurt, Gülnihal, 'Review of the Ottoman Legal System' (1992) 3 *Journal of the Center for Ottoman Studies Ankara University*.

Briere, John N, and Catherine Scott, *Principles of Trauma Therapy: A Guide to Symptoms, Evaluation, and Treatment* (Thousand Oaks, CA, Sage Publications, 2005).

Brown, Derek, *Nonformal Dialogues in National Peacemaking* (Washington, DC, United States Institute of Peace, 2017).

Brubaker, Rogers, *Ethnicity without Groups* (Cambridge, MA, Harvard University Press, 2004).

Brunner, Markus, 'A Plea for a Fundamental Social Psychological Reflection of Traumatization Processes' in Catherine Barrette et al (eds) *Traumatic Imprints: Performance, Art, Literature and Theoretical Practice* (Oxford, Inter-Disciplinary Press, 2012).

Burg, Avraham, *The Holocaust Is Over: We Must Rise from Its Ashes* (New York, Palgrave Macmillan, 2008).

Buruma, Ian, 'The Violent Mysteries of Indonesia', *New York Review of Books*, 22 October 2015, www.nybooks.com/articles/2015/10/22/violent-mysteries-indonesia/.

Çelik, Ayşe Betül et al, 'Patterns of "Othering" in Turkey: A Study of Ethnic, Ideological, and Sectarian Polarisation, South European Society and Politics' (2017) 22 *South European Society and Politics*.

Charuvastra, Anthony, and Marylene Cloitre, 'Social Bonds and Posttraumatic Stress Disorder' (2008) 59 *Annual Review of Psychology*, www.ncbi.nlm.nih.gov/pmc/articles/PMC2722782/.

Cloître, Marylene et al, 'A Developmental Approach to Complex PTSD: Childhood and Adult Cumulative Trauma as Predictors of Symptom Complexity' (2009) 22(5) *Journal of Traumatic Stress*.

Cuskun, Bekirt, 'My Mother Was Armenian, Journalist Group Chair Reveals', *Hürriyet Daily News*, 22 December 2013.

Çiçek, Talha M, *War and State Formation in Syria: Cemal Pasha's Governate during World War I, 1914–1917* (New York, Routledge, 2014).

Dadrian, Vahakn, *The History of the Armenian Genocide: Ethnic Conflict from the Balkans to Anatolia to the Caucasus*, rev edn (New York, Berghahn Books, 2003).

—— *Warrant for Genocide: Key Elements of Turko-Armenian Conflict* (New Brunswick, NJ, Transaction, 1999).

Danieli, Yael, 'Assessing Trauma across Cultures from a Multigenerational Perspective' in John P Wilson and Catherine S Tang (eds), *Cross-Cultural Assessment of Psychological Trauma and PTSD.* International and Cultural Psychology Series (Boston, Springer, 2007).

—— 'It Was Always There' in Charles Figley (ed), *Mapping Trauma and Its Wake: Autobiographic Essays by Pioneer Trauma Scholars*, Brunner-Rutledge Psychosocial Stress Book Series (New York, Routledge, 2006).

Danieli, Yael et al, 'Multigenerational Legacies of Trauma: Modeling the What and How of Transmission' (2016) 86(6) *American Journal of Orthopsychiatry*.

Davidian, David, 'Genocides That Never Were: Jenin, West Bank, and Khojaly, Nagorno-Karabakh' *Times of Israel* (blog), 6 March 2017.

Davison, Roderic H, *Reform in the Ottoman Empire, 1856–1876* (Princeton, NJ, Princeton University Press, 1963).

—— 'Turkish Attitudes Concerning Christian-Muslim Equality in the Nineteenth Century' (1954) 59 *American Historical Review*.

Deringil, Selim, '"The Armenian Question Is Finally Closed": Mass Conversions of Armenians in Anatolia during the Hamidian Massacres of 1895–1897' (2009) 51 *Comparative Studies in Society and History*.

—— *The Well-Protected Domains: Ideology and Legitimation of Power in the Ottoman Empire, 1876–1909* (New York, IB Tauris, 1998).

Der Matossian, Bedross, 'From Bloodless Revolution to Bloody Counterrevolution: The Adana Massacres of 1909' (2011) 6 *Genocide Studies and Prevention*.

—— *Shattered Dreams of Revolution: From Liberty to Violence in the Late Ottoman Empire* (Stanford, CA, Stanford University Press, 2014).
De Waal, Thomas, *Black Garden: Armenia and Azerbaijan through Peace and War* (New York, New York University Press, 2003).
—— *Great Catastrophe: Armenians and Turks in the Shadow of Genocide* (Oxford, Oxford University Press, 2015).
—— *The Caucasus: An Introduction*, 2nd edn (Oxford, Oxford University Press, 2019).
Dixon, Jennifer M, *Dark Pasts: Changing the State's Story in Turkey and Japan* (Ithaca, NY, Cornell University Press, 2018).
Dolbee, Samuel, 'The Desert at the End of Empire: An Environmental History of the Armenian Genocide' (May 2020) 247 *Past and Present.*
Eagle, Gillian, and Deborah Kaminer, 'Continuous Traumatic Stress: Expanding the Lexicon of Traumatic Stress' (2013) 19(2) *Peace and Conflict Journal of Peace Psychology.*
Eder, Mine, 'Retreating State? The Political Economy of Welfare Reform Change in Turkey' (2009) 2 *Middle East Law and Governance.*
Ehrenreich, John H, 'Understanding PTSD, Forgetting "Trauma"' (2003) 3(1) *Journal of Social Issues.*
Ekmekçioğlu, Lerna, *Recovering Armenia: The Limits of Belonging in Post-genocide Turkey* (Stanford, CA, Stanford University Press, 2016).
Elias, Norbert, *The Germans: Power Struggles and the Development of Habitus in the Nineteenth and Twentieth Centuries* (New York, Columbia University Press, 1996).
Elsayed, Danah et al, 'Anger and Sadness Regulation in Refugee Children: The Roles of Pre- and Post-Migratory Factors' (2019) 50(2) *Child Psychiatry and Human Development.*
Engelstein, Laura, *Russia in Flames: War, Revolution, Civil War, 1914–1921* (Oxford, Oxford University Press, 2017).
Erikson, Erik, *Childhood and Society* (New York, WW Norton, 1950).
Erikson, Kai, *Destruction of Community in the Buffalo Creek Flood* (New York, Simon and Schuster, 1976).
Figes, Orlando, *A People's Tragedy: The Russian Revolution, 1891-1924* (New York, Penguin Books, 1998).
—— *The Crimean War: A History* (New York, Metropolitan Books, 2010).
Findley, Carter Vaughn, 'The Tanzimat' in Kasaba, *The Cambridge History of Turkey.*
Fink, Carole, *Defending the Rights of Others: The Great Powers, the Jews and International Minority Protection 1878–1938* (Cambridge, Cambridge University Press, 2004).
Finkel, Caroline, *Osman's Dream: The History of the Ottoman Empire* (New York, Basic Books, 2006).
Fischer, Fritz, *Germany's Aims in the First World War* (New York, WW Norton and Co, 1967).
Fishkin, James S, *Democracy When the People Are Thinking* (Oxford, Oxford University Press, 2018).
Forestier-Peyrat, Etienne, 'The Ottoman Occupation of Batumi, 1918: A View from Below' (2016) 4 *Caucasus Survey.*
Fortna, Benjamin C, *Imperial Classroom: Islam, the State, and Education in the Late Ottoman Empire* (Oxford, Oxford University Press, 2002).
—— 'The Reign of Abdülhamid II' in Kasaba, *The Cambridge History of Turkey.*
Freedman, S, 'Erdogan's Blind Faith in Muslims'. *Guardian*, 12 November 2009.
Friedman, Matthew J, 'PTSD History and Overview', National Center for PTSD, US Department of Veterans Affairs, www.ptsd.va.gov/professional/treat/essentials/history_ptsd.asp.
Fromkin, David, *A Peace to End All Peace: The Fall of the Ottoman Empire and the Creation of the Modern Middle East* (New York, Henry Holt, 1989).
Fromm, Gerald, 'Treatment Resistance and the Transmission of Trauma' in GM Fromm (ed), *Lost in Transmission: Studies of Trauma across the Generations* (London, Karnac Books, 2012).
Gamaghelyan, Philip, 'Rethinking the Nagorno-Karabakh Conflict: Identity, Politics, Scholarship' (2010) 15 *International Negotiation.*
Gawrych, George W, 'The Culture and Politics of Violence in Turkish Society, 1903–14' (1986) 22 *Middle Eastern Studies.*
Gelvin, James L, *The Modern Middle East: A History*, 4th edn (Oxford, Oxford University Press, 2016).
Göçek, Fatma Müge, *Denial of Violence: Ottoman Past, Turkish Present, and Collective Violence against the Armenians, 1789–2009* (New York, Oxford University Press, 2015).
Gökalp, Ziya, *The Principles of Turkism*, trans Robert Devereux (Leiden, EJ Brill, 1968).

Gordon, James, *The Transformation: Discovering Wholeness and Healing After Trauma* (New York, HarperCollins, 2019).
Grinage, Bradley D, 'Diagnosis and Management of Post-traumatic Stress Disorder' (2003) 68(12) *American Family Physician*.
Gross, Jan T, *Neighbors: The Destruction of the Jewish Community in Jedwabne, Poland* (London, Penguin Books, 2002).
Guliyev, Farid, 'Armenia's Velvet Revolution in the Discourse of the Azerbaijani Elite' (2018) 104 *Caucasus Analytical Digest*.
Gunaysu, Ayse, 'About the Apology Campaign', *Armenian Weekly*, 10 January 2009.
Gutman, David, *The Politics of Armenian Migration to North America, 1885–1915: Sojourners, Smugglers and Dubious Citizens* (Edinburgh, Edinburgh University Press, 2019).
Hadjian, Avedis. *Secret Nation: The Hidden Armenians of Turkey* (London, IB Tauris, 2018).
Hagenaars, Muriel A, 'Tonic Immobility and PTSD in a Large Community Sample' (2006) 7(2) *Journal of Experimental Psychopathology*, doi.org/10.5127/jep.051915.
Haidt, Jonathan, 'The Emotional Dog and Its Rational Tail: A Social Intuitionist Approach to Moral Judgment' (2001) 108 *Psychological Review*.
Halperin, Eran, *Emotions in Conflict: Inhibitors and Facilitators of Peace Making* (New York, Routledge, 2015).
Hanioğlu, M Şükrü, *A Brief History of the Late Ottoman Empire* (Princeton, NJ, Princeton University Press, 2008).
—— *Preparation for a Revolution: The Young Turks: 1902–1908* (Oxford, Oxford University Press, 2001).
—— *Türkiye Diyanet Vakfı Islâm ansiklopedisi*, sv 'Talat Paşa' (Istanbul, Türkiye Diyanet Vakfı, Islâm Ansiklopedisi Genel Müdürlüğü, 2010).
—— *The Young Turks in Opposition* (New York, Oxford University Press, 1995).
Haroian, Ani, 'Letter to the Editor' *Armenian Weekly*, 1 September 2015.
Harvard Health Publishing, 'Understanding the Stress Response', March 2011, www.health.harvard.edu/staying-healthy/understanding-the-stress-response.
Hawkins, Michael, 'Social Darwinism and Race' in Stefan Berger (ed), *A Companion to Nineteenth-Century Europe: 1789–1914* (Chichester, Wiley-Blackwell, 2009).
Herman, Judith, *Trauma and Recovery: The Aftermath of Violence – From Domestic Abuse to Political Terror* (New York, Basic Books, 1992).
Hewsen, Robert H, '"Van in This World; Paradise in the Next": The Historical Geography of Van/Vaspurakan' in Richard G Hovannisian (ed), *Armenian Van/Vaspurakan* (Costa Mesa, CA, Mazda, 2000).
Hirschberger, Gilad, 'Collective Trauma and the Social Construction of Meaning' (2018) 9 *Frontiers in Psychology*, doi:10.3389/fpsyg.2018.01441.
Hobsbawm, Eric J, *Nations and Nationalism since 1780*, 2nd edn (Cambridge, Cambridge University Press, 1992).
Hofmann, Tessa, 'New Aspects of the Talât Pasha Court Case: Unknown Archival Documents on the Background and Procedure of an Unintended Political Trial' (1989) 42 *Armenian Review*.
Holquist, Peter, 'The Politics and Practice of the Russian Occupation of Armenia, 1915–February 1917' in Suny et al, *A Question of Genocide: Armenians and Turks at the End of the Ottoman Empire* (Oxford, Oxford University Press, 2011).
Hovannisian, Richard G, *Armenia on the Road to Independence, 1918* (Berkeley, University of California Press, 1967).
—— *The Republic of Armenia*, vol 1: *The First Year, 1918–1919* (Berkeley, University of California Press, 1971).
—— *The Republic of Armenia*, vol 2: *From Versailles to London, 1919–1920* (Berkeley, University of California Press, 1982).
—— 'The Armenian Question in the Ottoman Empire, 1876–1914' in Richard G Hovannisian (ed), *The Armenian People from Ancient to Modern Times*, vol 2: *Foreign Domination to Statehood: The Fifteenth Century to the Twentieth Century* (New York, St Martin's Press, 2004).
—— 'Armenia's Road to Independence' in *The Armenian People from Ancient to Modern Times*.
—— *The Armenian People from Ancient to Modern Times*, vol 2: *Foreign Domination to Statehood: The Fifteenth Century to the Twentieth Century* (New York, St Martin's Press, 1997).

—— 'Introduction: Confronting the Armenian Genocide' in Richard G Hovannisian (ed), *Looking Backward, Moving Forward: Confronting the Armenian Genocide* (New Brunswick, NJ, Transaction Publishers, 2003).
—— (ed), *The Armenian Communities of Asia Minor* (Costa Mesa, CA, Mazda Publishers, 2014).
Hovannisian, Richard G and Armen Manuk-Khaloyan, 'The Armenian Communities of Asia Minor: A Pictoral Essay' in Richard G Hovannisian (ed), *The Armenian Communities of Asia Minor* (Costa Mesa, CA, Mazda Publishers, 2014).
Hurd, Michael, 'The Psychology of Anger and Revenge' *Capitalism Magazine*, 15 August 2002, www.capitalismmagazine.com/2002/08/the-psychology-of-anger-and-revenge/.
Idiz, Semih, 'Why Are Turks Xenophobic?' *Hürriyet Daily News*, 14 November 2014.
Institute of Medicine, Committee for the Study of the Future of Public Health, *The Future of Public Health* (Washington, DC, National Academies Press, 1988).
Ismayilov, Murad and Norman A Graham (eds), *Turkish-Azerbaijani Relations: One Nation – Two States?* (London, Routledge, 2016).
Janis, Irving L, *Groupthink: Psychological Studies of Policy Decisions and Fiascoes*, 2nd edn (Boston, Houghton Mifflin, 1982).
Jones, Peter, *Track Two Diplomacy in Theory and Practice* (Stanford, CA, Stanford University Press, 2015).
Jørgenson, Bent D, 'Ethnic Boundaries and the Margins of the Margin in a Post-colonial and Conflict Resolution Perspective' (1997) 4 *Peace and Conflict Studies* 4.
Junger, Sebastian, *War* (New York, Twelve, 2010).
Kalayjian, Anie, and Mariam Weisberg, 'Generational Impact of Mass Trauma: The Post-Ottoman Turkish Genocide of the Armenians' in Jerry S Piven et al (eds), *Jihad and Sacred Vengeance: Psychological Undercurrents of History*, vol 3 (Lincoln, NE, Writers Club Press, 2002).
Kalayjian, Anie S et al, 'Coping with Ottoman Turkish Genocide: An Exploration of the Experience of Armenian Survivors' (1996) 9(1) *Journal of Traumatic Stress*.
Kaligian, Dikran Mesrob, *Armenian Organization and Ideology under Ottoman Rule: 1908–1914* (Piscataway, NJ, Transaction Publishers, 2011).
—— 'The Use and Abuse of Armeno-Turkish Dialogue' *Armenian Review* (Fall–Winter 2008).
Kansu, Aykut, *Politics in Post-revolutionary Turkey, 1908–1913* (Leiden, Brill, 2000).
Karagueuzian, Hrayr S, and Yair Auron, *A Perfect Injustice: Genocide and Theft of Armenian Wealth* (New Brunswick, NJ, Transaction Publishers, 2009).
Karapetyan, Murad, *Haykakan kamavorakan khmbere ev azgayin gumartaknere Kovkasyan razmachakatum (1914–1917 tt)* (Yerevan, HH GAA Gitutyun Hratarakchutyun, 1999).
Karenian, Hatsantour et al, 'Collective Trauma Transmission and Traumatic Reactions among Descendants of Armenian Refugees' (2010) 57(4) *International Journal of Social Psychiatry*, doi:10.1177/0020764009354840.
Karpat, Kemal H, *Ottoman Population, 1830–1914: Demographic and Social Characteristics* (Madison, University of Wisconsin Press, 1985).
—— *The Politicization of Islam: Reconstructing Identity, State, Faith, and Community in the Late Ottoman State* (Oxford, Oxford University Press, 2001).
Kasaba, Reşat (ed), *The Cambridge History of Turkey*, vol 4: *Turkey in the Modern World* (Cambridge, Cambridge University Press, 2008).
Kayaloff, Jacques, *The Battle of Sardarabad* (The Hague, Mouton, 1973).
Kazemzadeh, Firuz, *The Struggle for Transcaucasia, 1917–1921* (New York, Philosophical Library, 1951).
Kegan, Robert, *The Evolving Self* (Cambridge, MA, Harvard University Press, 1982).
—— *In Over Our Heads: The Mental Demands of Modern Life* (Cambridge, MA, Harvard University Press, 1994).
Kegan, Robert, and Lisa Lahey, *How the Way We Talk Can Change the Way We Work: Seven Languages for Transformation* (San Francisco, Jossey-Bass/Wiley, 2001).
Kelechian, Maurice Missak, 'My Journey of Love, Turkification of Armenian Children in Antoura Lebanon – Inauguration of Khachkar and Bronze Statue', *MassisPort*, 29 September 2010.
Kellerman, Natan PF, 'Transmission of Holocaust Trauma – An Integrative View' (2001) 64(3) *Psychiatry*.
Kelman, Herbert C, 'Social Psychological Dimensions of International Conflict' in I William Zartman (ed), *Peacemaking in International Conflict: Methods and Techniques*, rev edn (Washington, DC, US Institute of Peace, 2007).

—— 'A One-Country/Two State Solution to the Israeli-Palestinian Conflict' (2011) 18(1) *Middle East Policy* 18.

Ketsemanian, Varak, 'Straddling Two Empires: Cross-Revolutionary Fertilization and the Armenian Revolutionary Federation's Military Academy in 1906–1907' (2017) 4 *Journal of the Ottoman and Turkish Studies Association.*

Kévorkian, Raymond, *The Armenian Genocide: A Complete History* (London, IB Tauris, 2011).

—— 'The Cilician Massacres, April 1909' in Richard G Hovannisian and Simon Payaslian (eds), *Armenian Cilicia* (Costa Mesa, CA, Mazda, 2008).

—— 'Zohrab and Vartkes: Ottoman Deputies and Armenian Reforms' in Hans-Lukas Kieser et al (eds), *The End of the Ottomans: The Genocide of 1915 and the Politics of Turkish Nationalism* (London, IB Tauris, 2019).

Khachatourian, Ara, 'Inappropriate Academic Discourse', *Armenian Weekly*, 19 February 2009, www.armenianweekly.com/2009/02/19/inappropriate-academic-discourse/.

Kieser, Hans-Lukas, *Talaat Pasha: Father of Modern Turkey, Architect of Genocide* (Princeton, NJ, Princeton University Press, 2018).

—— 'From 'Patriotism' to Mass Murder: Dr Mehmed Reşid (1873–1919)' in Suny et al, *A Question of Genocide: Armenians and Turks at the End of the Ottoman Empire* (Oxford, Oxford University Press, 2011).

Kieser, Hans-Lukas, and Donald Bloxham, 'Genocide' in Winter, *The Cambridge History of the First World War.*

Kieser, Hans-Lukas et al, 'Reform or Cataclysm? The Agreement of 8 February 1914 Regarding the Ottoman Eastern Provinces' (2015) 17 *Journal of Genocide Research.*

Klein, Janet, *The Margins of Empire: Kurdish Militias in the Ottoman Tribal Zone* (Stanford, CA, Stanford University Press, 2011).

Kogan, Ilany, 'The Second Generation in the Shadow of the Terror' in M Gerard Fromm, *Lost in Transmission: Studies of Trauma across the Generations* (London, Karnac Books, 2012).

Kübler-Ross, Elizabeth, *On Death and Dying: What the Dying Have to Teach Doctors, Nurses, Clergy and Their Own Families* (New York, Simon and Schuster, 1969).

Kurat, Akdes Nimet, *Türkiye ve Rusya XVIII: yüzyıl sonundan Kurtuluş Savaşına kadar Türk-Rus ilişkileri (1798–1919)* (Ankara, Türk Tarih Kurumu Basımevi, 2011).

Kurt, Ümit, 'Legal and Official Plunder of Armenian and Jewish Properties in Comparative Perspective: The Armenian Genocide and the Holocaust' (2015) 17(3) *Journal of Genocide Research.*

—— 'Reform and Violence in the Hamidian Era: The Political Context of the 1895 Armenian Massacres in Aintab' (2018) 32(3) *Holocaust and Genocide Studies.*

Kurz, Anat and Ariel Merari, *ASALA: Irrational Terror or Political Tool* (Boulder, CO, Westview Press, 1985).

Kuyumjian, Rita Soulahian, *Archeology of Madness: Komitas, Portrait of an Armenian Icon*, 2nd edn (Princeton, NJ, Gomidas Institute, 2001).

Lahey, Lisa Laskow et al, *A Guide to the Subject-Object Interview: Its Administration and Interpretation* (Cambridge, MA, Subject-Object Research Group, Harvard Graduate School of Education, 1988).

Lamia, Mary C, 'Shame: A Concealed, Contagious, and Dangerous Emotion'. *Psychology Today*, 4 April 2011, www.psychologytoday.com/us/blog/intense-emotions-and-strong-feelings/201104/shame-concealed-contagious-and-dangerous-emotion.

Landau, Jacob M, *Tekinalp, Turkish Patriot 1883–1961* (Leiden, Uitgaven van het Nederlands Historisch-Archaeologisch Instituut te Istanbul, 1984).

Lazic, Radmila, 'Psalm of Despair', *New York Review of Books*, trans Charles Simic, 19 December 2013.

Ledoux, Joseph E, and Daniel S Pine, 'Using Neuroscience to Help Understand Fear and Anxiety: A Two-System Framework' (2016) 173(11) *American Journal of Psychiatry.*

Lemkin, Raphael, and Donna-Lee Frieze (ed), *Totally Unofficial: The Autobiography of Raphael Lemkin* (New Haven, CT, Yale University Press, 2013).

Levitsky, Steven, and Daniel Ziblatt, *How Democracies Die* (New York, Crown, 2018).

Libaridian, Gerard J, *Modern Armenia: People, Nation, State* (New Brunswick, NJ, Transaction Publishers, 2004).

—— Dedication to *The Karabakh File* (Cambridge, MA, Zoryan Institute, 1988).

Lih, Lars T, *Bread and Authority in Russia, 1914–1921* (Berkeley, University of California Press, 1990).

Lindgren, Carolyn L et al, 'Chronic Sorrow: A Lifespan Concept' (1992) 6(1) *Scholarly Inquiry for Nursing Practice.*

Litz, Brett T et al, 'Moral Injury and Moral Repair in War Veterans: A Preliminary Model and Intervention Strategy' (2009) 29(8) *Clinical Psychology Review*, doi.org/10.1016/j.cpr.2009.07.003.

Loewenberg, Peter, 'Clinical and Intergenerational Perspectives on the Intergenerational Transmission of Trauma' in Gerard Fromm (ed), *Lost in Transmission: Studies of Trauma across Generations* (London, Karnac Books, 2012).

Lohr, Eric, 'Politics, Economics and Minorities: Core Nationalism in the Russian Empire at War' in J Leonhard and U von Hirschhausen (eds), *Comparing Empires: Encounters and Transfers in the Long Nineteenth Century* (Göttingen, Vandenhoeck & Ruprecht, 2012).

MacCurdy, Marian Mesrobian, 'Resistance and Resilience', *Armenian Weekly*, 22 June 2015, https://armenianweekly.com/2015/06/22/resistance-and-resilience/.

MacMillan, Margaret, *Paris 1919: Six Months that Changed the World* (New York, Random House, 2002).

Maguen, Shira, and Brett Litz, 'Moral Injury in Veterans of War' (2012) 23(1) *PTSD Research Quarterly*, https://pdfs.semanticscholar.org/38c5/d697a34d8e7da3dd82be5d919c45a12e63d8.pdf.

Makdisi, Ussam, *Age of Coexistence: The Ecumenical Frame and the Making of the Modern Arab World* (Berkeley, University of California Press, 2019).

Maksudyan, Nazan, *Orphans and Destitute Children in the Late Ottoman Empire* (Syracuse, NY, Syracuse University Press, 2014).

Mamdani, Mahmood, *When Victims Become Killers: Colonialism, Nativism, and the Genocide in Rwanda* (Princeton, NJ, Princeton University Press, 2001).

Mamigonian, Marc A, 'Academic Denial of the Armenian Genocide in American Scholarship: Denialism as Manufactured Controversy' (2015) 9 *Genocide Studies International.*

—— 'Commentary on the Turkish Apology Campaign', *Armenian Weekly*, April 2009.

Manuk-Khaloyan, Armen, Ümit Kurt and Pamela Steiner, 'The Endless Arc of International Justice: Reparations after the Armenian Genocide' in J Bhabha et al (eds), *Time for Reparation? Addressing State Responsibility for Collective Injustice* (Philadelphia, University of Pennsylvania Press, forthcoming).

Marchand, Laure, and Guillaume Perrier, *Turkey and the Armenian Ghost: On the Trail of the Genocide* trans Debbie Blythe (Montreal, McGill-Queen's University Press, 2015).

Markarov, Alexander, 'Armenia's Foreign Policy Priorities: Are There Any Major Changes Following the Spring 2018 Political Transformation?' (2018) 104 *Caucasus Analytical Digest.*

Marsden, Philip, *Rising Ground* (London, Granta Books, 2014).

Maslovskii, EV, *Mirovaia voina na Kavkakzskom fronte, 1914–1917 g: strategicheskii ocherk* (Paris, Vozrozhdenie-La Renaissance, 1933).

Mazower, Mark, 'Minorities and the League of Nations in Interwar Europe' (1997) 126. *Daedalus.*

—— *Salonica, City of Ghosts: Christians, Muslims, and Jews, 1430–1950* (New York, Vintage, 2006).

McCann, Lisa, and Laurie Anne Pearlman, *Psychological Trauma and the Adult Survivor: Theory, Therapy, and Transformation*, Brunner/Mazel Psychosocial Stress Series no 21 (Abingdon, Routledge, 1990).

McCarthy, Justin, *Death and Exile: The Ethnic Cleansing of Ottoman Muslims, 1821–1922* (Princeton, NJ, Darwin Press, 1995).

McMeekin, Sean, *The Berlin-Baghdad Express: The Ottoman Empire and Germany's Bid for World Power* (Cambridge, MA, Belknap Press of the Harvard University Press, 2010).

—— *The Russian Origins of the First World War* (Cambridge, MA, Harvard University Press, 2011).

Melikian, GS, *Oktiabrskaia revoliutsiia i Kavkazskaia Armiia* (Yerevan, Aiastan, 1989).

Melkonyan, Ashot A, 'The Kars Oblast, 1878–1918' in Richard G Hovannisian, *Armenian Kars and Ani* (Costa Mesa, CA, Mazda, 2011).

Meyer, James H, *Turks across Empires: Marketing Muslim Identity in the Russian-Ottoman Borderlands, 1856–1914* (Oxford, Oxford University Press, 2014).

Middleton, Warwick, Adah Sachs, and Martin J Dorahy, 'The Abused and the Abuser: Victim–Perpetrator Dynamics' (2017) 18(3) *Journal of Trauma and Dissociation*, https://doi.org/10.1080/15299732.2017.1295373.

Miller Donald E and Lorna Touryan Miller, *Survivors: An Oral History of the Armenian Genocide* (Berkeley, University of California Press, 1993).

Miller, Owen Robert, '"Back to the Homeland" (*Tebi Yergir*): Or, How Peasants Became Revolutionaries in Muş' (2017) 4 *Journal of Ottoman and Turkish Studies.*

Minassian, Gaïdz F, 'Les relations entre le Comité Union et Progrès et la Fédération Révolutionnaire Arménienne à la veille de la Premiere Guerre mondiale d'après les sources arméniennes' (1995) 1 *Revue d'histoire arménienne contemporaine*.

Mkrtchian, Shahen, and Schors Davtian, *Shushi: The City of Tragic Fate* (Yerevan, Amaras, 1999).

Montefiore, Simon Sebag, *Young Stalin* (New York, Alfred A Knopf, 2007).

Morris, Benny and Dror Ze'evi, *The Thirty-Year Genocide: Turkey's Destruction of its Christian Minorities, 1894–1924* (Cambridge, MA, Harvard University Press, 2019).

Moumdjian, Garabet K, 'Rebels with a Cause: Armenian-Macedonian Relations and their Bulgarian Connection, 1895–1913' in Hakan M Yavuz and Isa Blumi, *War and Nationalism: The Balkan Wars, 1912–1913, and the Sociopolitical Implications* (Salt Lake City: University of Utah Press, 2013).

Mutz, Diana C, 'Status Threat, Not Economic Hardship, Explains the 2016 Presidential Vote' *Proceedings of the National Academy of Sciences* 155, no 19 (8 May 2018), www.pnas.org/content/115/19/E4330.short?rss=1.

Nalbandian, Louise, *The Armenian Revolutionary Movement: The Development of Armenian Political Parties through the Nineteenth Century* (Berkeley, University of California Press, 1963).

Nercessian, Nora N, *The City of Orphans: Relief Workers, Commissars and the 'Builders of the New Armenia', Alexandropol/Leninakan, 1919–1931* (Hollis, NH, Hollis Publishing, 2016).

Nichanian, Marc, *The Historiographic Perversion* (New York, Columbia University Press, 2009).

Nichanian, Marc, and David Kazanjian, 'Between Genocide and Catastrophe' in David L Eng and David Kazanjian (eds), *Loss: The Politics of Mourning* (Berkeley, University of California Press, 2003).

Noam, Gil G, 'Normative Vulnerabilities of the Self and Their Transformations in Moral Actions' in Gil G Noam and Thomas EW Wren (eds), *The Moral Self: Building a Better Paradigm* (Cambridge, MA, MIT Press, 1993).

—— 'The Self, Adult Development, and the Theory of Biography and Transformation' in Daniel K Lapsley and F Clark Power (eds), *Self, Ego and Identity* (New York, Springer, 1988).

Novikoa, Gayane, 'The South Caucasus and the European Security Strategy' in Ernst Felberbauer and Frederic LaPierre (eds), *Building Confidence in the South Caucasus: The European Union's and NATO's Soft Security Initiative* (Vienna, 2013).

Nyhan, Brendan, and Jason Reifler, 'Do People Actually Learn from Fact-Checking? Evidence from a Longitudinal Study during the 2014 Campaign', 30 November 2016, www.dartmouth.edu/~nyhan/fact-checking-effects.pdf.

Ohanyan, Anna, and Laurence Broers, *Armenia's Velvet Revolution: Authoritarian Decline and Civil Resistance in a Multipolar World* (London, IB Tauris, forthcoming).

Oppenheimer, Joshua, '*The Act of Killing* Has Helped Indonesia Reassess Its Past and Present', *Guardian*, 25 February 2014, www.theguardian.com/commentisfree/2014/feb/25/the-act-of-killing-indonesia-past-present-1965-genocide.

Ornstein, Anna, 'Survival and Recovery: Psychoanalytic Reflections' (2001) 9(1) *Harvard Review of Psychiatry*.

Ornstein, Anna et al, 'Survival, Recovery, Mourning, and Intergenerational Transmission of Experience: A Discussion of Gomolin's Paper' (2019) 88(3) *Psychoanalytic Quarterly*.

Orucoğlu, Berivan, 'The Turk Has No Friend but the Turk', *Foreign Policy*, 14 November 2014.

Özkan, Behlül, 'Who Gains from the "No War No Peace" Situation? A Critical Analysis of the Nagorno-Karabakh Conflict' (2008) 13 *Geopolitics*.

Paker, Murat, 'Türk-Ermeni Meselesinin Psiko-Politik Düğümleri' (May–June 2005) *Birikim*.

Panossian, Razmik, *The Armenians: From Kings and Priests to Merchants and Commissars* (New York, Columbia University Press, 2006).

Papagianni, Katia, 'National Dialogue Processes in Political Transition', Civil Society Dialogue Network discussion paper no 3, European Peacebuilding Liaison Office (Brussels, Belgium, 2013).

Payaslian, Simon, 'The End of the Armenian Communities of Asia Minor' in Richard G Hovannisian (ed), *The Armenian Communities of Asia Minor* (Costa Mesa, CA, Mazda Publishers, 2014).

Pekesen, Berna, 'Expulsion and Emigration of the Muslims from the Balkans', *European History Online*, 7 March 2012, www.ieg-ego.eu/pekesenb-2011-en.

—— 'Demographic and Ethnographic Changes in Transcaucasia, 1897–1956' (1959) 13 *Middle East Journal*.

Pettigrew, Thomas F, and Linda R Tropp, 'A Meta-Analytic Test of Intergroup Contact Theory' (2006) 90(5) *Journal of Personality and Social Psychology*.

Pinker, Steven, *The Better Angels of Our Nature* (New York, Viking, 2011).
Proctor, Robert N, and Londa Schiebinger (eds), *Agnotology: The Making and Unmaking of Ignorance* (Stanford, CA, Stanford University Press, 2008).
Pugsley, Sophia, and Fredrik Wesslau (eds), 'Russia in the Grey Zone', European Council on Foreign Affairs, 9 January 2016, www.ecfr.eu/wider/specials/russia_in_the_grey_zones?utm_content=buffer689e4&utm_medium=social&utm_source=twitter.com&utm_campaign=buffer.
Punsmann, Burcu Gültekin, 'Implications of Turkish-Azerbaijani Relations for Regional Security and Development', Working paper 13/28 (Rome, Instituto Affari Internazionali, August 2013).
Pye, Lucian, 'Traumatized Political Cultures: The After Effects of Totalitarianism in China and Russia' (2000) 1(1) *Japanese Journal of Political Science.*
Quataert, Donald, *Social Disintegration and Popular Resistance in the Ottoman Empire, 1881–1908: Reactions to European Economic Penetration* (New York, New York University Press, 1983).
Rabinowitch, Alexander, *The Bolsheviks in Power: The First Year of Soviet Rule in Petrograd* (Bloomington, Indiana University Press, 2007).
Reiss, Tom, *The Orientalist: Solving the Mystery of a Strange and Depressing Life* (New York, Random House, 2005).
Reyes, Gilbert et al, *Encyclopedia of Psychological Trauma* (Hoboken, NJ, Wiley, 2008).
—— (eds) 'History of Psychological Trauma' in *The Encyclopedia of Psychological Trauma* (New York, John Wiley & Sons, 2008).
Reynolds, Michael A, *Shattering Empires: The Clash and Collapse of the Ottoman and Russian Empires 1908–1918* (Cambridge, Cambridge University Press, 2011).
Riga, Liliana, *The Bolsheviks and the Russian Empire* (Cambridge, Cambridge University Press, 2012).
Rioch, Margaret, 'The Work of Wilfred Bion on Groups' in Arthur D Colman and W Harold Bexton (eds), *Group Relations Reader* (Washington, DC, AK Rice Institute, 1975).
Ritchie, Elspeth Cameron, 'Moral Injury: "A Profound Sense of Alienation and Abject Shame"', *Time*, 17 April 2013, https://nation.time.com/2013/04/17/moral-injury-a-profound-sense-of-alienation-and-abject-shame/.
Rogan, Eugene, *The Fall of the Ottomans: The Great War in the Middle East* (New York, Basic Books, 2015).
—— 'Sectarianism and Social Conflict in Damascus: The 1860 Events Reconsidered' (2004) 51 *Arabica.*
Royal Swedish Academy of Sciences 'The Prize in Economic Sciences 2017', Press release, 9 October 2017.
Ryan, Alan, 'Whose Nationalism?', *New York Review of Books*, 26 March 2020.
Sanborn, Joshua A, *Imperial Apocalypse: The Great War and the Destruction of the Russian Empire* (Oxford, Oxford University Press, 2014).
Saparov, Arsène, *From Conflict to Autonomy in the Caucasus: The Soviet Union and the Making of Abkhazia, South Ossetia and Nagorno Karabakh* (Abingdon, Routledge, 2015).
Sapolsky, Robert M, *Behave: The Biology of Humans at Our Best and Worst* (New York, Random House, 2017).
Sarafian, Ara, 'What Happened on 24 April 1915? The Ayash Prisoners', *Submissions*, Gomidas Institute, 22 April 2013, www.gomidas.org/submissions/show/5.
Sargsian, YG, 'Hayeri masnaktsutyune paterazmin yev kamavorakan sharzhume' in TsP Aghayan et al (eds), *Hay zhoghorvrdi patmutyun*, vol 6: *Hayastane 1870–1917 tvakannerin* (Yerevan: Haykakan SSH Gitutyunneri Akademiayi Hratarkachutyun, 1981).
Sarkissian, AO, *History of the Armenian Question to 1885* (Urbana, University of Illinois Press, 1938).
Sarkissian, KM Greg, 'The Centennial Commemoration is about Truth, Memory and Justice, not Hatred', Zoryan Institute, 1 January 2015, https://zoryaninstitute.org/1481-2/.
Saroyan, William, *Inhale and Exhale* (New York, Random House, 1936).
Scholz, Regine, 'Collective Trauma, Memories, and Identity', paper presented at the International Association for Group Psychotherapy Trauma and Identity Workshop, Sarajevo, 10 May 2014.
Sebag-Montefiore, Simon, *Jerusalem: The Biography* (New York, Random House, 2012).
Şeker, Nesim, 'Demographic Engineering in the Late Ottoman Empire and the Armenians' (2007) 43 *Middle Eastern Studies.*
Somel, Selçuk Akşin, *The Modernization of Public Education in the Ottoman Empire, 1839–1908: Islamization, Autocracy, and Discipline* (Leiden, Brill, 2001).
Seligman, Martin EP, 'Learned Helplessness' (1972) 23(1) *Annual Review of Medicine.*

Seltzer, Leon F, 'Don't Confuse Revenge with Justice: Five Biggest Problems with Revenge and Their Best Remedies', *Psychology Today*, 22 January 2014, www.psychologytoday.com/intl/blog/evolution-the-self/201401/five-biggest-problems-revenge-and-its-best-remedies.

Sen, Amartya, Foreword to Paul Farmer, *Pathologies of Power: Health, Human Rights, and the New War on the Poor*, California Series in Public Anthropology (Berkeley, University of California Press, 2003).

Seul, Jeffrey R, 'How Transformative Is Transformative Mediation? A Constructive-Developmental Assessment' (1999) 15(1) *Ohio State Journal on Dispute Resolution*.

—— 'Mediating Across Worldviews', in C Turner and M Waehlish (eds), *Rethinking Peace Mediation: Challenges of Contemporary Peacemaking Practice* (Bristol, Bristol University Press, forthcoming).

Shafak, Elif, 'A Tempest of Fear in Turkey', *New York Times*, 24 February 2014.

Shalal-Esa, Andrea, 'CEOs Warn Against Armenia "Genocide" Bill', 2 March 2010, www.reuters.com/article/us-usa-turkey-armenia/ceos-warn-against-armenia-genocide-bill-idUSTRE62157G20100302.

Shay, Jonathan, 'Casualties' (2011) 140(3) *Daedalus*.

Shephard, Ben, *A War of Nerves: Soldiers and Psychologists in the Twentieth Century* (Cambridge, MA, Harvard University Press, 2001).

Smith, Michael G, 'Anatomy of a Rumour: Murder Scandal, the Musavat Party and Narratives of the Russian Revolution in Baku, 1917–20' (2001) 36(2) *Journal of Contemporary History*.

—— 'The Russian Revolution as a National Revolution: Tragic Deaths and Rituals of Remembrance in Muslim Azerbaijan' (2001) 49 *Jahrbücher für Geschichte Osteuropas*.

—— 'Traumatic Loss and Azerbaijani National Memory' in Dmitrii Furman (ed), *Azerbaidzhan i Rossia: obshchestva i gosudarstva* (Moscow, Sakharov Institute, 2001).

Smith, Roger W et al, 'Professional Ethics and the Denial of Armenian Genocide' (1995) 9(1) *Holocaust and Genocide Studies*, https://doi.org/10.1093/hgs/9.1.1.

Snyder, Timothy, *Black Earth: The Holocaust as History and Warning* (London, Tim Duggan Books, 2015).

Sohrabi, Nader, *Revolution and Constitutionalism in the Ottoman Empire and Iran* (Cambridge, Cambridge University Press, 2011).

Soloman, Burt, 'The Tragic Futility of World War I', *Atlantic*, 27 July 2014.

Sotero, Michelle M, 'A Conceptual Model of Historical Trauma: Implications for Public Health Practice and Research' (2006) 1(1) *Journal of Health Disparities Research and Practice*.

St Clair, William, *That Greece Might Still Be Free: The Philhellenes in the War of Independence*, 2nd edn (Cambridge, Open Book Publishers, 2008).

Suárez-Orozco, Marcelo, and Antonius CGM Robben, 'Interdisciplinary Perspectives on Violence and Trauma' in Antonius CGM Robben and Marcelo M Suárez-Orozco (eds), *Cultures under Siege: Collective Violence and Trauma* (Cambridge, Cambridge University Press, 2000).

Substance Abuse and Mental Health Services Administration, *Trauma-Informed Care in Behavioral Health Services*, Treatment Improvement Protocol (TIP) Series 57, HHS Publication No (SMA) 13–4801 (Rockville, MD, 2014).

Suleymanov, Manaf, 'Dni Minuvshie' (1989) 9 *Literaturnyi Azerbaidzhan*.

Suny, Ronald Grigor, *The Baku Commune, 1917–1918* (Princeton, NJ, Princeton University Press, 1972).

—— 'Eastern Armenians under Tsarist Rule' in Richard G Hovannisian (ed), *The Armenian People from Ancient to Modern Times*, vol 2: *Foreign Domination to Statehood: The Fifteenth Century to the Twentieth Century* (New York, St Martin's Press, 2004).

—— *The Making of the Georgian Nation*, 2nd edn (Bloomington, Indiana University Press, 1994).

—— *'They Can Live in the Desert but Nowhere Else': A History of the Armenian Genocide* (Princeton, NJ, Princeton University Press, 2015).

Suny, Ronald Grigor, Fatma Müge Göçek, and Norman M Naimark, *A Question of Genocide: Armenians and Turks at the End of the Ottoman Empire* (Oxford, Oxford University Press, 2011).

Swietochowski, Tadeusz, *Russian Azerbaijan, 1905–1920: The Shaping of a National Identity in a Muslim Community* (Cambridge, Cambridge University Press, 1985).

Tanielian, Melanie S, *The Charity of War: Famine, Humanitarian Aid, and World War I in the Middle East* (Stanford, CA, Stanford University Press, 2018).

Thompson, Elizabeth, *Colonial Citizens: Republican Rights, Paternal Privilege, and Gender in French Syria and Lebanon* (New York, Columbia University Press, 2000).

Tokluoglu, Ceylan, 'Definitions of National Identity, Nationalism and Ethnicity in Post-Soviet Azerbaijan in the 1990s' (2005) 28(4) *Ethnic and Racial Studies*.

Toprak, Zafer, *Türkiye'de 'Millî iktisat' 1908–1918* (Ankara, Yurt Yayınları, 1982).

Totten, Samuel, and Paul Robert Bartrop, *Dictionary of Genocide*, sv 'Nazim, Dr Mehemed' (Westport, CT, Greenwood Press, 2008).

Toynbee, Arnold, *The Western Question in Greece and Turkey: A Study in the Contact of Civilisations* (London, Constable, 1922; repr New York, H Fertig, 1970).

Trumpener, Ulrich, *Germany and the Ottoman Empire, 1914–1918* (Princeton, NJ, Princeton University Press, 1968).

Tsitselikis, Konstantinos, 'The Minority Protection System in Greece and Turkey Based on the Treaty of Lausanne (1923): A Legal Overview', background information presented at the 7th International Student Conference, Borjan Tanevski Memorial Fund, ACT/Anatolia College, University of Macedonia, Thessaloniki, 14 May 2010, www.sophia.de/borjan/BTConference2010.

Tuchman, Barbara, *Practicing History: Selected Essays* (New York, Knopf, 1981).

Tucker, Phebe, and Elizabeth A Foote, 'Trauma and the Mind-Body Connection', *Psychiatric Times*, 1 June 2007, www.psychiatrictimes.com/somatoform-disorder/trauma-and-mind-body-connection.

Tucker, Spencer C, *The Great War, 1914–18* (Bloomington, Indiana University Press, 1998).

Ülgen, Sinan, 'Get Ready for a More Aggressive Turkey', *Foreign Policy*, 2 July 2018.

Ülker, Erol, 'Contextualising "Turkification": Nation-Building in the Late Ottoman Empire, 1908–18' (2005) 11 *Nations and Nationalism*.

Üngör, Uğur Ümit, 'The Armenian Genocide in the Context of 20th-Century Paramilitarism' in Alexis Demirdjian (ed), *The Armenian Genocide Legacy* (New York, Palgrave MacMillan, 2016).

—— *The Making of Modern Turkey: Nation and State in Eastern Anatolia, 1913–1950* (Oxford, Oxford University Press, 2011).

Uskul, Ayse K et al, 'Cultural Emphasis on Honor, Modesty, or Self-Enhancement: Implications for the Survey-Response Process' in Janet A Harness et al (eds), *Survey Methods in Multinational, Multiregional, and Multicultural Contexts* (Hoboken, NJ, John Wiley, 2010).

Uskul, Ayse K et al, 'Honor Bound: The Cultural Construction of Honor in Turkey and the Northern United States' (2012) 43 *Journal of Cross-Cultural Psychology*.

Van der Hart, Onno et al, 'Pierre Janet's Treatment of Post-traumatic Stress' in Jeffrey M Lating and George S Everly Jr (eds), *Psychotraumatology: Key Papers and Core Concepts in Post-traumatic Stress* (New York, Spring, 1995).

Van der Kolk, Bessel, *The Body Keeps the Score: Brain, Mind, and Body in the Healing of Trauma* (New York, Viking, 2014).

—— 'The Complexity of Adaptation to Trauma' in Bessel van de Kolk et al (eds), *Traumatic Stress* (New York, Guilford Press, 1996).

—— 'The Compulsion to Repeat the Trauma: Re-enactment, Revictimization, and Masochism' (1989) 12(2) *Psychiatric Clinics of North America*.

Van der Kolk, Bessel A et al, *Traumatic Stress: The Effects of Overwhelming Experience on Mind, Body, and Society* (New York, Guilford Press, 1996).

Venkov, Andrei V and Khamitbi B Mamsirov, 'Kavkazskaia Konnaia Tuzemnaia Diviziia i ee komandir Velikii Kniaz Mikhail Aleksandrovich v Period Pervoi Mirovoi Voine' (2014) 183 *Izvestiya VUZov Severo-Kavkazskii region*.

Volkan, Vamik, 'Bosnia-Herzegovina: Ancient Fuel of a Modern Inferno' (1996) 7 *Mind and Human Interaction*.

—— 'Transgenerational Transmissions and Chosen Traumas: An Aspect of Large-Group Identity' (2001) 34(79) *Group Analysis*.

Volkan, Vamik and Norman Itzkowitz, *The Immortal Ataturk: A Psychobiography* (Chicago, University of Chicago Press, 1984).

Walker, Christopher, *Armenia: The Survival of a Nation*, rev 2nd edn (New York, St Martin's Press, 1990).

Weisz, George M, 'Secondary Guilt Syndrome May Have Led Nazi-Persecuted Jewish Writers to Suicide' (2015) 6(4) *Rambam Maimonides Medical Journal*.

Weitz, Eric D, 'Germany and the Young Turks: Revolutionaries into Statesmen' in Suny et al, *A Question of Genocide: Armenians and Turks at the End of the Ottoman Empire* (Oxford, Oxford University Press, 2011).

Wheeler-Bennett, JW, *The Forgotten Peace: Brest-Litovsk, March 1918* (New York, William Morrow, 1939).

Winnicott, Donald W, *The Child, the Family, and the Outside World* (Harmondsworth, Penguin, 1973).

Winter, Jay (ed), *The Cambridge History of the First World War*, vol 1: *Global War* (Cambridge, Cambridge University Press, 2014).

Worringer, Renée, *Ottomans Imagining Japan: East, Middle East, and Non-Western Modernity at the Turn of the Twentieth Century* (New York, Palgrave Macmillan, 2014).
Yael, Danieli et al, 'Multigenerational Legacies of Trauma: Modeling the What and How of Transmission' (2016) 86(6) *American Journal of Orthopsychiatry*.
Yamskov, AN, 'Ethnic Conflict in the Transcaucasus: The Case of Nagorno-Karabakh' (October 1991) 20 *Theory and Society*.
Ybert, Edith, 'Islam, Nationalism and Socialism in the Parties and Political Organisations of Azerbaijani Muslims in the Early Twentieth Century' (2013) 1 *Caucasus Survey*.
Yılmaz, Şuhnaz, 'An Ottoman Warrior Abroad: Enver Paşa as an Expatriate' in Sylvia Kedourie (ed), *Seventy-Five Years of the Turkish Republic* (London, Frank Cass, 2000).
Zürcher, Erik Jan, 'Greek and Turkish Refugees and Deportees, 1912–1914', *Turkology Update Leiden* Project, January 2003, www.transanatolie.com/english/turkey/turks/ottomans/ejz18.pdf.
—— 'Ottoman Labour Battalions in World War I' in Hans-Lukas Kieser and Dominik J Schaller (eds), *Der Völkermord an den Armeniern und die Shoah = The Armenian Genocide and the Shoah* (Zurich, Chronos, 2002).
—— *Turkey: A Modern History*, 3rd edn (London, IB Tauris, 2004).
—— *The Young Turk Legacy and National Building: From the Ottoman Empire to Atatürk's Turkey* (London, IB Tauris, 2010).
—— 'Renewal and Silence: Postwar Unionist and Kemalist Rhetoric on the Armenian Genocide', in Suny et al, *A Question of Genocide: Armenians and Turks at the End of the Ottoman Empire* (Oxford, Oxford University Press, 2011).

Theses and unpublished works

Altan, Ahmet, Lecture presented at Harvard University, Cambridge, MA, 25 January 2012.
Gölbaşı, Edip, 'The Anti-Armenian Riots of 1895–1896: The "Climate of Violence" and Intercommunal Strife in the Ottoman Eastern Province', paper presented on a panel titled 'Reform, Violence and Revolutionary Organizations in the Late Nineteenth-Century Ottoman East' at the Middle East Scholars' Association annual meeting, Boston, 19 November 2016.
Kurt, Ümit, 'The Breakdown of Previously Peaceful Coexistence: The Aintab Armenian Massacres of 1895', paper presented on a panel titled 'Reform, Violence and Revolutionary Organizations in the Late Nineteenth-Century Ottoman East' at the Middle East Scholars' Association annual meeting, Boston, 19 November 2016.
Hagopian, J Michael, 'Hyphenated Nationalism: The Spirit of the Revolutionary Movement in Asia Minor and the Caucasus, 1896–1910', PhD thesis, Harvard University, 1942.
Libaridian, Gerard J, 'Conversations on Armenian-Turkish Relations', interview by Gonca Sonmez-Poole, *Armenian Mirror-Spectator*, 17 January 2015.
—— The Clash of Empires: World War I and the Middle East', keynote speech presented at University of Cambridge, Cambridge, 14 June 2014.
—— 'The History of Imperial Politics and the Politics of Imperial History', keynote speech presented at the Centre for the Study of the International Relations of the Middle East and North Africa, University of Cambridge, Cambridge, 13 June 2014.
—— 'A Report on the Workshop for Armenian/Turkish Scholarship', Ann Arbor, 2006. Unpublished document prepared for internal use by WATS.
Murgul, Yalçin, 'Baku Expedition of 1917–1918: A Study of the Ottoman Policy Towards the Caucasus', thesis, Bilkent University, 2007.
Pipes, Daniel, 'Distinguishing between Islam and Islamism', paper presented at the Middle East Forum, Center for Strategic and International Studies, Washington, DC, 30 June 1998.
Riegg, Stephen B, 'Claiming the Caucasus: Russia's Imperial Encounter with Armenians, 1801–1894', PhD thesis, University of North Carolina, 2016.
Sicotte, Jonathan H, 'Baku: Violence, Identity, and Oil, 1905–1927', PhD thesis, Georgetown University, 2017.
Turkyilmaz, Yektan, 'Rethinking Genocide: Violence and Victimhood in Eastern Anatolia, 1913–1915', PhD thesis, Duke University, 2011.
Young, Pamela J, 'Knowledge, Nation, and the Curriculum: Ottoman Armenian Education (1853–1915)', PhD thesis, University of Michigan, 2001.

Index